IMAGINE THERE'S NO HEAVEN

IMAGINE THERE'S NO HEAVEN

HOW ATHEISM HELPED CREATE THE MODERN WORLD

MITCHELL STEPHENS

palgrave
macmillan

IMAGINE THERE'S NO HEAVEN
Copyright © Mitchell Stephens, 2014.
All rights reserved.

First published in 2014 by PALGRAVE MACMILLAN® in the United States—
a division of St. Martin's Press LLC, 175 Fifth Avenue, New York, NY 10010.

Where this book is distributed in the UK, Europe and the rest of the world, this
is by Palgrave Macmillan, a division of Macmillan Publishers Limited, registered
in England, company number 785998, of Houndmills, Basingstoke, Hampshire
RG21 6XS.

Palgrave Macmillan is the global academic imprint of the above companies and
has companies and representatives throughout the world.

Palgrave® and Macmillan® are registered trademarks in the United States, the
United Kingdom, Europe and other countries.

ISBN 978-1-137-00260-0

Library of Congress Cataloging-in-Publication Data
Stephens, Mitchell.
    Imagine there's no heaven : how atheism helped create the modern world /
Mitchell Stephens.
        pages   cm
    Includes bibliographical references and index.
    ISBN 978-1-137-00260-0 (alk. paper)
    1. Atheism—History. 2. Atheism—Influence. I. Title.
BL2747.3.S748   2014
211'.809—dc23

                                                                    2013035039

A catalogue record of the book is available from the British Library.

Design by Letra Libre, Inc.

First edition: February 2014

10 9 8 7 6 5 4 3 2 1

Printed in the United States of America.

To Esther, Bernie, Lil, Beth, Walter, Anne,

Artie, Lauren, Seth and Noah

Come no chimeras! Let us go abroad; let us mix in affairs; let us learn and get and have and climb. . . . Let us have to do with real men and women, and not with skipping ghosts.

—Ralph Waldo Emerson[1]

CONTENTS

EVERYTHING MUST BE EXAMINED

A revolution is always accomplished against the gods.

—Albert Camus[1]

D ENIS DIDEROT FIRST CAME TO PARIS AS A TEENAGER IN 1728 to continue the education he had begun with the Jesuits. He was an enthusiastic student, even deciding at one point to become a Jesuit. But Diderot soon learned that another kind of education was available in Paris in the eighteenth century. Evenings spent in conversation with the city's impoverished bohemians and budding intellectuals eventually cost the young man his faith in the church, the Jesuits and then in Christ. His father ordered him to leave Paris. Diderot stayed. He had a new aspiration: to become a philosopher.

Diderot married a woman who desired fidelity. He found a mistress who desired money—in shorter supply among his crowd even than fidelity. This, along with the birth of two children, encouraged Diderot's transition from mere café *habitué* to published author.

His early efforts included a translation of a history of Greece, an erotic novel and a project that would prove noteworthy: Diderot signed on to help with the translation into French of an Englishman's *Cyclopoedia,* or *Universal Dictionary of the Arts and Science.*[2] He was also writing philosophy—increasingly controversial, clandestinely published philosophy. For, after some more years of impassioned discussion, reading and writing, Denis Diderot no longer believed in any sort of god.

In recounting the history of atheism, this book will have many such tales to tell. Yes, it is true that in just about all human societies at just about all times most believed that the universe is governed by a supernatural Being (or beings). However, many individuals in many societies at many times surrendered, as did Diderot, that belief. The names of some of them are familiar: Percy Bysshe Shelley, Charles Darwin, Karl Marx, Sigmund Freud, Virginia Woolf, Albert Camus, Simone de Beauvoir, Salman Rushdie and even the Marquis de Sade. Others who chose to live without religion—Ernestine Rose and Charles Bradlaugh are examples—should be better known, given their historical import and former notoriety.

Most societies at most times scorned those who denied their God (or gods), so atheists sometimes suffered persecution, displayed courage, led lives of struggle. The book in which Diderot worked out his argument against the existence of God, *Letter on the Blind,* was published under a pseudonym, but the authorities connected it to him. Diderot's punishment was three months in the Vincennes prison—one of them in its dungeon.[3]

However, despite the fact that they often had to hide their ideas or publish clandestinely, despite the fact that they sometimes were thrown in prison, nonbelievers such as Diderot helped lead the way to the modern world. Indeed, the struggles of those who challenged the supernatural and insisted that we concern ourselves instead with the natural contributed, I will argue, to what may be humankind's greatest accomplishments: the advancement of knowledge and the expansion of human rights. Subtracting overbearing gods from the heavens encouraged the growth of learning and liberty on earth.

This book focuses mostly, but not entirely, on the West. It ends in the twenty-first century with religion showing signs of weakening even in that hotbed of belief, the United States. It starts in Greece in Thucydides' time, when myths receded and history, science and philosophy began racing ahead.

Enlightenment Paris was another place where the value for new thinking of turning away from old gods was particularly apparent. The attacks on religion that energized cafés, salons and underground bookstalls inspired challenges to church-supported prejudices and tyrannies. Atheism in eighteenth-century France promoted egalitarianism. Discouraging reliance upon church authority also encouraged the era's voracious pursuit of secular knowledge—exhibited in the Enlightenment's great work: the thirty-five-volume *Encyclopédie.*

Indeed, rarely have the contributions of atheism to the creation of the modern world been as apparent as in the person of Denis Diderot. His parish priest dubbed this unflinching, if mostly clandestine, critic of religion a "monster of impiety."[4] He was also a "monster" of liberty: an unflinching, if mostly clandestine, critic of the old, despotic political system, an opponent of colonialism as well as slavery. And Diderot, sometimes known in Paris as "The Philosopher" (an honorific previously reserved for Aristotle),[5] was the main editor of the *Encyclopédie*.

He had substituted for the small *Cyclopoedia*, which he was supposed to be translating, an original work: a huge compendium—71,818 articles in total—of current human (or at least European) knowledge, in alphabetical order. The authors of those articles included many of the major thinkers of the day. Diderot and other nonbelievers made the editorial decisions. Faith had its testaments. The *Encyclopédie* stood, with Isaac Newton's *Principia Mathematica*, as probably the greatest testament to reason and secular understandings since Aristotle.

"Everything must be examined," is how Diderot explained the guiding principle of the *Encyclopédie*, "everything must be shaken up, without exception and without circumspection."[6] "Everything" in eighteenth-century Europe usually meant two things: the church and the monarchy.[7] Religion as well as government, the point was, could not be immune to honest, searching examination if social, political and intellectual progress was to continue. The critique of religion in the *Encyclopédie* was in fact circumspect, but it was apparent to those familiar with the arguments.

"Religion retreats to the extent that philosophy advances," Diderot had concluded as he was losing his belief in even the wispiest of gods.[8] But this book will argue that the retreat of religion is not just a result of intellectual progress; it is a crucial cause of that and other kinds of progress. When ancient ways and ancient texts are no longer held sacrosanct, some comfort or confidence may be lost, but when "everything" is "examined," much can be improved. The escape from fairy stories and dogma has opened minds.

The contributions of religion have been manifold and important—in individual lives but also to art and, at times, to morality. However, our world was born, too, of this struggle against religion—long before and well after, not just during, the Enlightenment.

Tens of thousands of histories have been written of various beliefs in various gods. This book is something different: an account of the development and power of the idea that we live without gods (or God)—a history of atheism and all that it has accomplished.

1

HOW CAN THAT BE?

WHY DISBELIEF

Lost in an immense forest during the night I only have a small light to guide me. An unknown man appears and says to me: "My friend, blow out your candle so you can better find your way." This unknown man is a theologian.

—Denis Diderot[1]

WHO IS HISTORY'S FIRST KNOWN ATHEIST?
In 415 BCE a bronze tablet was placed on the Acropolis in Athens offering a sum of money to anyone who brought Diagoras of Melos back alive for trial and half as much money to anyone who killed him. The evidence is strong that Diagoras had been accused of impiety: scoffing at and exposing the mysteries of a local religious rite. It is less clear that this was the same Diagoras who had achieved renown as a poet and was said to have abandoned belief in the gods after someone stole and had a success with one of his poems.[2]

Atheists appeared early in Greece. The word is of Greek origin. (*Atheos* meant, originally, "ungodly," though it came to mean "without gods" or "denier of gods."[3]) But India offers at least one name that might compete with that of Diagoras for the title first-known atheist—depending on how we read hazy accounts and interpret hazy dates.[4]

Ajita Kesakambali is one of the participants in a Buddhist dialogue, the *Sāmaññphala Sutta* in which a king interrogates leaders of major sects about the value of the religious life of renunciation.[5] The Buddha, not surprisingly, goes last and wins over the king. Ajita's earlier response is, however, more surprising: he tells the king that there is, in fact, no value whatsoever in the religious life. "It is an empty lie, mere idle talk, when men say there is profit therein," he insists. Ajita sees no merit in alms, sacrifices or offerings. In his view "there is neither fruit nor result of good or evil deeds." He rejects, too, the notion that there are "beings springing into life without" mother or father. Ajita denies that some enlightened beings have somehow "understood . . . both this world and the next." He denies the existence of a world that might be called "the next." "Fools and wise alike," Ajita concludes, "on the dissolution of the body, are cut off, annihilated, and after death they are not."

That is a forceful dismissal of religion by the standards of just about any era, even Diderot's. This dialogue was written down long after the time of the Buddha, if there was a Buddha. It might have taken place, if it did take place, in the fifth or fourth century BCE—possibly before, probably after Diagoras. (Dates in India are hard to establish before Alexander's invasion in 327 BCE.[6]) And we hear no other tales about Ajita—if he was a real, not mythical, character. However, it is clear that such ideas were in the air in India. For the country did have a long-lived sect of nonbelievers, the Cārvāka, and there is evidence that they date back to about this time.

The texts in which the Cārvāka's views are said to have been recorded have not survived.[7] That is a common problem in the history of atheism. Important writings questioning religion were always vulnerable to elision or destruction during periods of intolerance. To learn what the Cārvāka thought, it is necessary to rely—not for the last time in this book—upon generally hostile sources and, for fuller accounts of the philosophy of the Cārvāka, upon much later sources. (Jennifer Michael Hecht's work acquainted me with writings on the Cārvāka—and much else.)

Nevertheless, it is possible to establish that the Cārvāka entirely rejected the supernatural. "Only the perceived exists," they insist, according to an explanation of their philosophy from the ninth century of the Common Era.[8] High on the list of entities in which the Cārvāka did not believe, because such beings could not be perceived, were gods.

This literal atheism was not that unusual or shocking in ancient India. Various forms of Buddhism or Jainism underplay or ignore gods. But the Cārvāka also reject rebirth, enlightenment, *nirvana* and *karma* (that satisfying, you-get-what-you-deserve link between behavior and destiny). "Uncivilized ignorant fools," they proclaim, according to one much later account, " . . . imagine that spirit is something different from body and reaps the reward of actions in a future state; we might as well expect to find excellent fruit drip from trees growing in the air."[9]

A good summary of the credo of this Indian sect survives from the ninth century[10]:

- A person is happy or miserable through [the laws] of nature; there is no other cause.
- Who paints the peacocks, or who makes the cuckoos sing? There exists here no cause excepting nature.
- The soul is but the body characterized by the attributes signified in the expressions, "I am stout," "I am youthful," "I am grown up," "I am old," etc. It is not something other than that. . . .
- There is no world other than this; there is no heaven and no hell.

The Cārvāka are not the only answer to the argument that atheism is a phenomenon limited to the West, or that other, earlier societies did not have the requisite understanding of the natural to dismiss the supernatural or that their societies were insufficiently liberal or pluralistic to tolerate atheism. They are not the only answer to the argument that atheism is a product of modernity, the Enlightenment or the Scientific Revolution.[11] But the Cārvāka, whose views seem compatible with those of twenty-first-century atheists like Christopher Hitchens or Richard Dawkins, may be the best answer to these arguments.

And they also demonstrate that a view of the world based on disbelief in the supernatural can have staying power, as they appear to have been around in India in one form or another for a couple of millennia.

One of this chapter's purposes is to demonstrate that disbelief in gods has not been that uncommon. Another of its purposes is to explain why.

Atheism in one person or culture is not identical to atheism in another. Just as we have varieties of religions, we have varieties of disbelief (though they tend not to be so mutually intolerant). With the help of philosophy and science, atheism has strengthened and deepened in recent centuries. But atheism did not originate in recent centuries. The Cārvāka were remarkable, but they were not alone. Where it is possible to look, outspoken nonbelievers* frequently turn up.

---

*A note on terminology: Diderot was an *atheist* and the Cārvāka, too, qualify, but some of those I discuss in this book were less steadfast in their rejection of religion. I sometimes use broader terms such as *nonbeliever* or *disbelief* so as not to exclude their contributions.

Indeed, a kind of unbelief also appears even where it is *not* possible to look directly: in societies that left no written record, in preliterate societies. Here, in trying to understand preliterate disbelief, we are dependent on the anthropological record: on Westerners who encountered these cultures in the last few centuries.

An account survives, for example, of a native of the Tonga Islands in the South Pacific, early in the nineteenth century, whose unbelief had gone pretty far. That account comes from a British teenager, William Mariner, who was stranded on the islands when the natives captured his ship, and whose adventures and observations were later recounted in a book.[12] The preliterate native of those islands with that skeptical perspective on religion was their king, Finow. "Finow had often stated to Mr. Mariner," the book reports, "his doubts that there were such beings as the gods. He thought that men were fools to believe what the priests told them."[13]

Finow lived more than 2,000 years after that Greek nonbeliever, Diagoras. But his story—available to us only because he was visited by some Europeans—is a clue that in the tens of thousands of years before recorded history there likely were plenty of others who doubted "there were such beings as the gods."

And Finow is far from the only preliterate nonbeliever in the anthropological literature. Among the !Kung Bushmen in southern Africa in the 1920s, some men believed that lions harbor the spirits of powerful dead Bushmen. But, according to the anthropologist Viktor Lebzelter, other members of the same tribe chuckled at the idea. That's "just a tale," they said.[14] Another anthropologist, A. B. Ellis, describes the various reactions in a crowd at an initiation ceremony for some new Ashanti priests in West Africa in the nineteenth century. "The old people, particularly the old women," he explains, demonstrated "the most implicit faith." But many of the younger people "appeared skeptical, and some openly laughed."[15]

These were less carefully worked out and probably less sweeping forms of disbelief than that of the Cārvāka: in a preliterate society, less energy may be devoted to coming up with coherent and consistent philosophies.[16] But even individuals in preliterate societies can marshal a pervasive and compelling doubt.

Anti-religious sentiments are difficult to measure in a society. They are often halting, inchoate or confused. And such sentiments are frequently submerged, since their expression can prove embarrassing or even dangerous. Preliterate religions, like postliterate religions, can make life unpleasant for those who question their practices—and therefore their power. King Finow on the Tonga Islands was not unwise enough to express his doubts in public, but word that Finow was "disrespectful to the gods" got around. He died suddenly—probably poisoned by a priest.[17]

No animals demonstrate evidence of religion. All human societies that have been studied by anthropologists do. Preliterate societies may have their Finows, their doubters, but there is no evidence that there has ever been a whole tribe of doubters or nonbelievers.[18] (Despite the best efforts of the Soviets, the modern world, too, has yet to achieve such a society, though some *arrondissements* in Paris may come close.)

Why? If religion is defined as a shared belief in supernatural beings (or a supernatural Being),[19] why do all human societies, beginning with preliterate societies, feature such beliefs, especially since hard and fast evidence of the existence of such beings has been conspicuous in its absence?

The answer is probably not primarily because religion provided comfort to our ancestors. When your existence is painful, it might be cheering to imagine the possibility of another, less painful existence. No doubt it is reassuring to think that you and those you hold dear don't really, finally, absolutely cease existing. It must be a comfort for those !Kung Bushmen who did believe to imagine some of their heroes carrying on as lions. It must be a comfort to think that they themselves might stick around that way, too. The role of religion in taking some of the sting out of death should not be underestimated.

But it shouldn't be overestimated either. Many preliterate societies are not just looking for some way to comfort the bereaved; they are concerned with making sure all those potentially cranky dead people—and they do add up—don't hang around and cause trouble.[20] "The presence of the recently dead is far more likely to be dangerous than reassuring," explains the anthropologist Pascal Boyer.[21]

Gods, too, can be troublemakers in preliterate societies. They are sometimes called upon, sometimes fended off. Indeed, it is not clear that the manipulative, demanding, jealous, deceptive and often amoral spirits and gods most preliterate societies have attempted to engage offer much comfort.[22]

Nor, according to Boyer, do societies have religion primarily because of some deep human need to explain where we come from, why we die or why there is suffering in the world. For one thing, most religions among preliterate peoples do not much concern themselves with such sweeping, unwieldy questions. They may have something to say about why this particular person died at this particular time. But even on such smaller questions the answers can be unhelpfully baroque—some complex tale about the behavior of quirky, headstrong supernaturals.[23] Contemporary religions may do better with consolation, metaphysics and ethics, but most of them, too, trace their ancestry, if you go back far enough, not to a philosophical mission but to the cult of a stubborn, praise-loving supernatural.

Religions can, no doubt, encourage and preserve some useful behaviors—burying the dead, avoiding potentially diseased pork, resting one day a week, refraining from killing your neighbor. But religions also support many behaviors that not only do not contribute to the survival of their members and their genes, but are potentially harmful—fasting, staying celibate or picking fights with infidels, for example. Usefulness is only a small part of the answer.

Instead, to understand religion it is worth considering a study of one of the species of nonbelievers with which we share the planet: pigeons. In 1948, the experimental psychologist B. F. Skinner put hungry pigeons in a cage into which food appeared every fifteen seconds. The behavior of the pigeons had absolutely no effect on whether or when the food arrived, but in most cases the birds convinced themselves that it did. Soon most of the pigeons began repeating dances—dances that, Skinner believed, had become associated in their minds with the coming of the food.[24]

Skinner titled his article on the subject, "'Superstition' in the Pigeon" (though the pigeons presumably had no sense of the supernatural). The behavior of these birds in their attempts to spur the arrival of food—turning counterclockwise a few times, for example—seems awfully foolish; just as some may find it foolish for a basketball player to cross himself before taking a foul shot. But, the point is, pigeons disposed to finding connections between their behaviors and eating are, as a rule, more likely to survive than more reserved and less easily convinced (less "superstitious"?) birds.[25]

Similarly, humans disposed to find a connection between a prayer to a god and success in war are more likely to spot a connection between watering holes and the presence of animals, between certain bushes and sweet berries or between surrounding and capturing.[26] Evolutionarily successful animals with and without feathers, in other words, possess an excess of this itch to make connections, and the same mental muscle that works out natural connections also fashions supernatural connections.[27] We are prepared to consider both planting a seed and making a sacrifice as *causes* in these incessant efforts to gain some control over *effects*. Whole societies might, like those pigeons, end up believing the most unreasonable sounding things, they may cling to these beliefs in the face of a surfeit of contradictory evidence, but somewhere back in the prehistory of a belief is usually a pragmatic impulse to operate effectively in the world.

Those who have been pondering this subject have suggested that other useful mental muscles are also involved in the production of belief. (I am depending here on the work of Scott Atran, Pascal Boyer and Daniel C. Dennett.[28]) Our nervous systems are, they note, hypersensitive to the presence of hidden threats. Those humans who ran because they thought they saw a hostile face in that bush—even if nine out of ten times they were wrong—were more likely to survive and pass on their genes than their more sanguine or oblivious neighbors. And a byproduct of a hypersensitivity to faces in bushes is a tendency to see gods in clouds.

Add to that exaggerated alertness to threats an exaggerated alertness to the presence of other minds. It is important for our survival that we realize that behind that face is a conscious being *just like us*—with needs, irritations and purposes; capable of loving but also of plotting and deceiving.[29] It is so important that we tend to overdo it and see conscious beings, *just like us,* in the stars, in the dead or determining our fate. Thus the moon demands its share of the food. Thus our ancestors protect us. Thus everything happens for a reason.

Our minds were also selected for their ability to focus on the extraordinary, the counterintuitive: the fact that the sky has suddenly darkened, the fact that the baby has suddenly stopped crying, the fact that our mate did not return before bedtime. And nothing is as extraordinary and counterintuitive as super-powerful, immortal beings. Such characters grab attention. Such characters stick in the mind. We have a weakness for the fabulous.

Religion, as those who study its causes like to point out, has high costs: gods must be propitiated, animals sacrificed, temple fees paid, religious wars fought. Yet, early hominids with a propensity toward belief in the supernatural probably had certain advantages—because such beliefs occasionally enforce valuable behaviors but, more important, because such beliefs are *unintended consequences* of ways of thinking that are eminently valuable. An analogy—an unsympathetic one—could be made to an interest in pornography as an unintended consequence of our impulse to procreate. According to this compelling recent research, belief is, to employ Boyer's term, a "side effect" of extremely useful, genetically programmed habits of mind.[30]

But our genes also encourage questioning.

Compelling as it may be, the world of spirits has not really been humankind's home. "The majority of men live in it only at moments," explains the distinguished anthropologist Clifford Geertz. Farmers may check the omens before planting but will likely devote much more energy to weeding and watering after planting. Basketball players may spend a few seconds crossing themselves before a foul shot, but they likely will have spent many hours in the gym practicing foul shots. "The everyday world of common-sense objects and practical acts . . . is the paramount reality in human experience," Geertz states.[31]

To live successfully in the "common-sense," "practical," "everyday world" we have to *test* the connections we spot and sharpen the theories we formulate. "This is the third time I've come to this watering hole, and I've yet to see any animals." We have to be alert to inconvenient facts. We have to be concerned with what is true. We are, consequently, disposed to probe, even to doubt: "Does this bush really produce good berries?" To survive it helps to question.

Disbelief tends to come upon us for three reasons and appear to us in three corresponding varieties. They are all very old, so discussing them— in this chapter and the next—also provides an opportunity to complete a quick sketch of the early history of atheism. They are all seductive and help, consequently, to explain why disbelief has proven, as this book will demonstrate, so resilient, even common. And they are all potent. They encourage certain views of the world—rather modern views. So there is support here for my argument that atheism has helped form *our* view of the world. The first of these explanations for disbelief is this basic human compulsion to question.

Did the shaman succeed in curing that sick woman? Did the rainmaker manage to make it rain? Wasn't that witch doctor, who had seemed to draw a red substance out of a patient's body, recently spotted in a garden where flowers of exactly that color grew?[32] Questioning—doubt—is where atheism begins. Why have I never encountered any of those spirits? How can they survive without bodies? Where are those other worlds? How can a being exist, as the Cārvāka asked, that is capable of painting peacocks and teaching cuckoos to sing? How can there be gods, as Diagoras may have asked, who would allow someone to get away with stealing someone else's poem?

If the urge to make connections can push us toward the supernatural, the urge to question those connections can pull us back. And humans—with the benefit of language—are in a better position to formulate such questions than, say, pigeons: "Are dead Bushmen really somehow inside of lions?"

In a culture permeated by belief, such stimulants to disbelief, however, work slowly. B. F. Skinner succeeded in "extinguishing" the "superstitious" response to the regular arrival of food he had been able to produce in one hungry pigeon. He simply stopped supplying the food. Eventually the pigeon stopped doing the dance it associated with the food. The absence of food became, in other words, the inconvenient fact that undercut the pigeon's *sense* (if we can use such a word) of the efficacy of its dance. However, before this behavior faded the hungry pigeon repeated it—futilely—another 10,000 (!) times.[33]

One question is particularly important to the slow process of surrendering belief—a skeptical, often rhetorical question: *how can that be?* This question was enunciated—for instance, my favorite instance—during a debate on the validity of religion in Africa in the 1860s.[34] Arguing the affirmative was an upper-class, religious Englishman, Samuel White Baker, who was on his way to discovering one of the sources of the Nile. Arguing against religion, or at least Baker's version of religion, was a man he encountered along the way—a man Baker describes as a "wild, naked savage." His name was Commoro, and he was a chief of the Latooka tribe in East Africa. They communicated through interpreters:

> BAKER: Have you no belief in a future existence after death? . . .
> COMMORO: Existence after death! How can that be? Can a dead man get out
>   of his grave, unless we dig him out?
> BAKER: Do you think man is like a beast that dies and is ended?
> COMMORO: Certainly. . . .

When mulling over this debate between Baker and Commoro—or the millions of similar debates engaged in by believers and nonbelievers in other times or places—it is probably wise to keep in mind this observation about our species: humans are odd mixtures of credulity and incredulity. There are limits to what we are willing to swallow. Some of us—like Commoro—aren't prepared to accept all that much on faith.

The question we consequently ask, often just to ourselves—*how can that be?*—makes a negative but important contribution to learning. For it is impossible to figure out what does make sense without determining what doesn't. Commoro's question would prove crucial, therefore, to the development of such fields of knowledge as logic and science. If all living creatures die and humans are living creatures, then how can it be that we live forever? Or, if the sun gives off heat, how can it be that it traverses the sky on a god's chariot?

The Greeks, who made great contributions in logic and science, had a name for this kind of thinking: skepticism. Their skepticism, which they took far, wasn't always aimed at religion. Indeed, skeptics have also been known to criticize what they consider to be the smugness of atheists. But skepticism often leads to a variety of disbelief in the supernatural—a logic-based, take-nothing-for-granted critique of religion. How can it be, asked the great Greek Skeptic Carneades, that perfect beings can possess virtues? Could an invulnerable god, for example, display courage? Don't our virtues depend upon our very human flaws?[35]

Skepticism, as a school of philosophy (deserving of a capital *S*), flourished for a time in Greece and Rome.[36] It was rediscovered in Europe in the sixteenth century and, in less formal versions, has continued to undercut certainties and hone understandings to this day. But it was not beyond the capabilities of many, many other humans living in many, many different times and places—including a preliterate, Latooka chief.

The dialogue between Samuel White Baker and Commoro, as reported by Baker, continued:

> BAKER: "Then you believe in nothing; neither in a good nor evil spirit! And you believe that when you die it will be the end of body and spirit; that you are like other animals; and that there is no distinction between man and beast; both disappear, and end at death?"
> COMMORO: "Of course they do."

Baker, struggling to fend off this redoubtable doubt, hazarded an analogy: "Some corn had been taken out of a sack for the horses," Baker writes, "and a few grains lying scattered on the ground, I tried the beautiful metaphor of St. Paul as an example of a future state. Making a small hole with my finger in the ground, I placed a grain within it: 'That,' I said, 'represents you when you die.' Covering it with earth, I continued, 'That grain will decay, but from it will rise the plant that will produce a reappearance of the original form.'"

> COMMORO: "Exactly so; that I understand. But the *original* grain does *not* rise again; it rots like the dead man, and is ended; the fruit produced is not the same grain that we buried, but the *production* of that grain: so it is with man—I die, and decay, and am ended; but my children grow up like the fruit of the grain."

Baker's response? Having judged "the religious argument . . . a failure," he writes, "I was obliged to change the subject of conversation."[37]

Writing was invented in Sumeria around 3500 BCE. By the end of that millennium it had been adopted in Egypt. But many centuries passed before this new invention was employed in recording tales or spells. The "Pyramid Texts"—a collection of hieroglyphic spells found on the walls of ten Egyptian pyramids in Saqqara—qualify, therefore, as among the oldest surviving religious texts. They likely date from between about 2350 and 2100 BCE.[38]

And then—in the early centuries of descriptive writing and, therefore, of recorded history—what may stand as the oldest surviving evidence of disbelief arrives. For these ancient Egyptian writings on religion are followed remarkably quickly (given these timescales) by an ancient Egyptian text that, despite occasional references to gods, is suspicious of religion. It is a papyrus copy of a song said to have been inscribed on the tomb of a pharaoh, Intef, who died in 2118 BCE.

Both the Pyramid Texts and that Egyptian song are haunted by death. In the case of those religious spells etched on pyramid walls, the focus is on what awaits the pharaoh *after* his death. We learn that his "face" will be "as that of falcons," that his "wings" will be "as those of birds." (Amalgams of humans and animals are *de rigueur* in early belief systems.) We learn that the pharaoh will, thus, be "flown . . . to the sky." The Pyramid Texts note that certain behaviors have been or will be required of the pharaoh to ensure the journey's success, including making offerings to the various deities and purifying himself "in the Marsh of Reeds." But the pharaoh's reward, the texts make clear, will be substantial: "Your bones will not perish; your flesh will not pass away . . . for you are one of the gods." And this reward will endure, these texts proclaim, for "eternity."[39]

That Egyptian song, on the other hand, is devoid of speculation about an afterlife. The dead are gone for good: "One generation passes, another stays behind." That's all we know:

> There is no return for them
> To explain their present state of being.[40]

So what is the song's suggested response to the inevitability of death? It has to do with life:

> So spend your days joyfully
> And do not be weary with living!
> No man takes his things with him,
> And none who go can come back again.

After the urge to question and ask *how can that be?*, this sense that we ought to find what joys we can in this world—not in some sort of magical afterlife—is the second major spur to atheism. And it leads to a second ancient variety of disbelief: a commitment to our mortal lives—freely and exuberantly lived. Over the millennia the dream of gods and their eternal kingdoms of the sky has often dissipated as we commit ourselves to the pleasures, however ephemeral, of the earth.

The Epic of Gilgamesh, humankind's oldest surviving epic, is also much concerned with death.[41] In fact, Gilgamesh is overwhelmed by an encounter with it. After his best friend succumbs to the curse of a goddess, the hero moans "like a woman mourning"; he rages "like a . . . lioness robbed of her whelps" (becoming, in his grief, female); he tears out his hair; he cries for seven days and nights—refusing to let his friend be buried until the body begins to rot.[42] And losing someone you love is only half the problem. Gilgamesh soon confronts the other half: "What my brother is now," he realizes, "that shall I be when I am dead." This awareness of his own mortality overwhelms the hero. "How can I rest, how can I be at peace?" he asks. "Despair is in my heart." Gilgamesh is badly in need of the comfort of an afterlife. He will not find it.

The poems that make up *The Epic of Gilgamesh* (most of the poems originally written in Sumerian) were etched, in cuneiform, on clay tablets in the first centuries of the second millennium BCE, a few centuries after the Egyptian song (though the Gilgamesh poems, like many of these early writings, likely were transcriptions of older oral works).[43] Gilgamesh ends up spending the rest of the epic searching for the sort of pathway to immortality outlined in the Pyramid Texts—in vain. The poems do not hold out the hope that there is life for humans beyond death. Instead, this epic seems to settle on a response to death close to that of the Egyptian song.

That message is imparted by, among others, a young woman—a maker of wine named Siduri: "Gilgamesh, where are you hurrying to?" she asks.[44] "You will never find that life for which you are looking. When the gods created man they allotted to him death, but life they retained in their own keeping." Then Siduri presents her own, quite appealing version of that "spend-your-days-joyfully" exhortation—a second ancient version:

> As for you, Gilgamesh, fill your belly with good things; day and night, night and day, dance and be merry, feast and rejoice. Let your clothes be fresh, bathe yourself in water, cherish the little child that holds your hand, and make your wife happy in your embrace; for this, too, is the lot of man.

With writing we can listen in for the first time on the religious and philosophical speculations of our ancestors. On the always-insistent subject of death we hear, of course, much testimony, beginning with the Pyramid Texts, about far-away heavens and blissful eternities. But other voices are audible, saying, as Siduri did, that since death is coming, we had best "be merry"—here, now!

A poem quoted in some ninth century CE writings in support of the Cārvāka position makes a similar suggestion:

> While life is yours, live joyously;
> None can escape Death's searching eye.[45]

This philosophy—this simple and often anti-religious philosophy—has gained a name: "anacreontic."

Anacreon was a Greek poet, born around 570 BCE and known for the enthusiasm with which he tried to "live joyously." Many of his poems, sung to the accompaniment of the lyre, recount his efforts (often unsuccessful) to seduce much younger lovers (male and female) and his concomitant efforts (often successful) to achieve a pleasant level of intoxication.[46]

On honey-cake I first did dine,
Broke off a little piece,
And then I drank a jar of wine,
And then my harp did seize.
Now with its strains I serenade
My lovely friend, the pretty maid.[47]

Anacreon's name became associated with ardent efforts to enjoy life—so indelibly associated with them that, for example, an eighteenth-century London gentlemen's club would be named the Anacreontic Society and the theme song its members composed would be called the "Anacreontic Song." (Francis Scott Key borrowed its tune for the "Star Spangled Banner.") It was a drinking song—a paean to the partnership of wine and love.

Atheism is often viewed as barren and negative, but with this anacreontic "spend your days joyfully" philosophy arrives a positive view of what life might be free of the supernatural—positive because it is joyful, positive because it extols the pleasures of life here on earth, positive because it sees the inevitability of death making those pleasures still more precious.

This variety of disbelief—disbelief in the afterlife, at least—is well summed up in two (Latin) words: *carpe diem,* usually translated as "pluck [or "seize"] the day." They are from an ode by the Roman poet Horace, who lived from the time of Julius Caesar to that of Jesus. Horace's poem is haunted by the notion that "life is brief": "Even while we speak, envious time has passed: *Carpe diem,* putting as little trust as possible in tomorrow!"[48] James Thrower, whose work on early manifestations of disbelief has helped orient my own, suggests that *carpe diem* is the first and most "subversive" challenge to religion.[49] Perhaps not the first, I must note, but ancient, pervasive and as subversive as any.

The anacreontic philosophy appears in one additional and unexpected place in the ancient world: the Hebrew Bible. No movement rejected as many gods as Jewish monotheism—a product mostly, scholars now believe, of the seventh and sixth centuries BCE in Judea, particularly during the reign of King Josiah.[50] The one God who survived was stern, praise-loving, upright and, since all the other gods were gone, unmarried. That is why it is surprising to find in their Bible the suggestion that we ought to have some fun.

Ecclesiastes was probably written around 250 BCE—three centuries after Anacreon, two centuries before Horace. Koheleth, the sage who holds forth in this book, maintains that "there is no action, no reasoning, no learning, no wisdom in the grave, where you are going." He concludes, therefore, that "the only good a man can have under the sun is to eat and drink and enjoy himself."[51] Might this have been a sign of Greek influence, which was strong in Israel after Alexander?[52]

At times the editors of Ecclesiastes or the compilers of the Bible seem to have interjected pious injunctions to rein in Koheleth's anacreontic exhortations. Note, for example, the admonition that sits uncomfortably in the middle of this piece of advice to "youth": "Follow the desires of your heart and the glances of your eyes—but know well that God will call you to account for all such things—and banish care from your mind, and pluck sorrow out of your flesh!"[53]

An overly intense commitment to enjoyment can, of course, be morally suspect: too much pleasure seeking, not enough concern for the future consequences of one's current behavior, not enough concern for the effect of that behavior upon others.[54] So this anacreontic form of disbelief can seem morally suspect—as if, without a God to call youth to account, they might indeed be led to dissipation or cruelty. Anacreon, after all, presents himself as something of a drunk, a lech, a dirty old man.

This is a real issue for this variety of disbelief and for atheism in general. Indeed, one of this book's purposes is to search for an ethic of atheism. It is not—there being no commandments—a simple undertaking.

We can begin, however, by looking to the Cārvāka, that long-lived Indian sect of nonbelievers, for a demonstration that the license to "live joyously" does not necessitate living immorally, amorally or apolitically. In one of their later incarnations, they attacked India's rigid caste system, which was upheld by religion.[55] And the Cārvāka were alert to unjust restrictions upon women: "Fie on those who . . . hold women in check out of jealousy," a Cārvāka character proclaims in an eleventh- or twelfth-century poem; "but do not likewise restrain men, though the blindness of passion is common to both."[56] Not that the Cārvākas had any problem with passion—in men or women—or any illusions about passion: "It is our wisdom," they state, "to enjoy the pure pleasure as far as we can and to avoid the pain which inevitably accompanies it."[57]

We can also find some reassurance in the fact that some of the exponents of eating, drinking and enjoying yourself quoted here seem not at all dissolute or lecherous. Siduri emphasizes parental and marital love. The cynical, painfully wise Koheleth does acknowledge—and this sounds like him, not his redactors—the value of being "with a woman you love."[58]

It is possible, the point is, to "enjoy . . . pleasure," "avoid . . . pain," "follow the desires of your heart" and "pluck," when you can manage the operation, "sorrow out of your flesh," without being insensitive to the pleasures, pains, desires and sorrows of others—without being a lech. Joys can be shared. Joys are best when shared.

Near the end of Ecclesiastes, Koheleth is allowed to restate his theme poignantly and to emphasize a gentle pleasure: "What a delight for the eyes to behold the sun! Even if a man lives many years, let him enjoy himself in all of them, remembering how many the days of darkness are going to be. The only future is nothingness!"

Do all atheists have within them a little of the first variety of disbelief—a *how-can-that-be* skepticism? That seems likely. The first step toward disbelief is usually finding one or another recourse to the supernatural unpersuasive—suspecting, in other words, that a particular pigeon dance doesn't have much to do with our well-being after all.

Greece's candidate for history's first known atheist, Diagoras of Melos, was, based on what little we know, a lower-case-*s* skeptic: he scoffed at a religious rite; he saw injustice where religion would seem to have promised justice. India's possible candidate for that title, Ajita Kesakambali, argued that claiming the religious life has value is "an empty lie, mere idle talk." That's pretty skeptical. And Koheleth's seemingly anti-religious suggestions in Ecclesiastes do not just extend to eating, drinking and enjoying; this sage is also deeply, even bitterly skeptical of the chance of finding any meaning in life: "All is futile!" he writes.[59]

Whether inspired by the fact that the rainmaker failed to bring the promised rain or by a deep-seated appreciation for life's meaninglessness, such skepticism seems the most elemental form and probably the most pervasive form of disbelief. Questioning and doubt are so elemental and probably so pervasive that it is hard to imagine a society or perhaps even an individual mind without at least a hint of them. The rhetorical question *how can that be?* is there, if not expressed aloud, more than most believers would like to admit. Or maybe they do admit it, since there is plenty of skepticism quoted, and dismissed, in the Bible—Old and New Testaments.[60]

Not all atheists, however, are anacreontics. Many, of course, never get a fair shot at life's pleasures. And not everyone is looking for them. It seems unlikely, for example, that Ajita in India was out for enjoyment, since the second name by which he is known, Kesakambali, means "one who wears a robe of human hair," and hair shirts, or hair robes, are, as one scholar puts it, "the most miserable of all garments."[61] But the suspicion that we should, if we are fortunate enough to have a chance, do our best to wear comfortable attire and enjoy our too-short lives is hardly rare. It may not qualify as omnipresent, but it is elemental—available to just about anyone with access to food, drink and some time in the sun.

You don't have to have read Ecclesiastes or even know how to read to wonder how someone can rise from the dead or why you should wait to find joy until after you are dead. You don't have to know mathematics or know your way around the night sky. You don't have to go to school or have been born in the West to doubt or try to savor your time under the sun. A skeptic, an anacreontic, can pop up anywhere in the world at any time. It helps if there is another skeptic or anacreontic around to pass on some lore, some ideas, but it is not necessary. You don't have to know who Diderot was, or Darwin.

There are, consequently, more nonbelievers scattered about human history than most versions of that history acknowledge. This book will uncover quite a few, but most, of course, never had the opportunity to have their thoughts recorded. Disbelief of these two varieties can be generated spontaneously. It can come and go. It has come and gone over and over again—often so quietly that it has had little effect upon culture or society. But sometimes the world trembles when a little boy cries, "The heavens are bearing no emperor," or a little girl sighs, "But what about our happiness right here, right now?"

And disbelief also arrives in a third variety—one that has shaken the world more consistently, more thoroughly and more profoundly. This variety of disbelief is largely dependent upon learning, but it also is a great stimulant to learning. In fact, this variety of disbelief strengthens and develops over the millennia, over the centuries, in tandem with science, history and philosophy. It is the subject of the next chapter, which focuses on one of the great periods of learning in human history.

A CLEAR UNDERSTANDING OF WHAT HAPPENED

DISBELIEF AND LEARNING ARRIVE TOGETHER IN GREECE

The lightning is his slave; heaven's utmost deep
Gives up her stars, and like a flock of sheep
They pass before his eye, are numbered, and roll on!
The tempest is his steed, he strides the air;
And the abyss shouts from her depth laid bare,
Heaven, hast thou secrets? Man unveils me; I have none.

—Percy Bysshe Shelley, *Prometheus Unbound*[1]

N ATURAL EXPLANATIONS ARE ANOTHER CAUSE OF REDUCED BE-
lief in supernatural explanations. The Greeks, of course, were remarkably skilled at coming up with natural explanations—for heavenly
phenomena, for human illness, for historical events, even for religion itself.

Indeed, the pursuit of knowledge was so much a part of the Greek
identity that their myths include stories of outsmarting the gods. Consider
Sisyphus, the legendary king of Corinth. When Death, Thanatos, came to
get him—a bit on the early side, as sometimes happens—Sisyphus somehow managed to turn the tables and chain Thanatos up. This meant for a
time, with Death out of commission, that nobody could die—a circumstance particularly vexing for Ares, the god of war. In order for armies to be
able to resume killing each other, Ares had to intervene, freeing Thanatos
and making sure Sisyphus was hustled off to Hades.[2]

But Sisyphus, whom Homer describes as "the craftiest of all mankind," was still unready to go gently.[3] He instructed his wife not to bury him, and then, demonstrating audacity as well as craftiness, moaned to various gods in Hades that he was unburied. They allowed him to return to the world of the living to rectify the situation.[4] The French writer Albert Camus, in his essay on the Sisyphus myth, gives an account of what happened next: "When he had seen again the face of this world, enjoyed water and sun, warm stones and the sea, he no longer wanted to go back to the infernal darkness." So Sisyphus stuck around. Having once again tricked the gods out of death, Sisyphus lived "many years more" experiencing, in Camus' phrase, "the smiles of the earth."[5]

Of course, in the end the gods, as also happens, had the last smile. Odysseus, according to Homer, comes upon Sisyphus on his tour of Hades. That is the main source of the image of Sisyphus trying, endlessly, to roll that stone up to the top of a hill only to have "the ruthless boulder . . . bound and tumble down to the plain again."[6]

Homer never explains what earned Sisyphus this classic punishment, but the Greeks did have their theories. The broad charge would have to be "impiety"; putting Death in chains and wheedling your way out of Hades would certainly qualify as that.[7] Indeed, in what Camus calls "his scorn of the gods, his hatred of death, and his passion for life," Sisyphus might be seen as an archetypal anacreontic rebel against the pious.[8]

However, some Greek accounts charge Sisyphus with an additional form of disrespect toward the gods—one that may also be a manifestation of his extraordinary craftiness: he is accused of stealing, divining or revealing the gods' secrets. In some versions the secret is relatively small: Sisyphus tattled on Zeus to the father of a nymph whom the lusty chief god had carried off. But elsewhere the implication is that the secrets in which Sisyphus trafficked are profound and powerful.[9] The secret that Prometheus, another rebel against the gods, was punished for revealing certainly was: the secret of fire.

Greece was the first society on earth with widespread literacy—among free-born males, that is. Stealing, divining or revealing the secrets of the gods may have been a theme in Greek mythology because investigating the secrets of the earth and sky was beginning to be an element of Greek culture.

Thales, who lived in the seventh and sixth centuries BCE, is the first Western philosopher of whom we have record, and he had a go at solving one of the more perplexing mysteries of the heavens: why the moon and the sun, on rare occasions, go dark. Herodotus reports that Thales succeeded in predicting an eclipse.[10] Some Greek sources suggest that Sisyphus' greatest crime was that he managed to get hold of and reveal to humankind perhaps the most closely held of divine secrets: knowledge of "everything that was to happen."[11] Had Thales not accomplished some of that?

Aristotle distinguishes between those who rely on myth and the supernatural to explain the world, *theologi,* and those who rely on natural forces. Thales was the first of these *physiologi,* Aristotle says.[12] In Greece the *physiologi* were on the rise.*

New knowledge is rarely worn easily, and theologians do not surrender without a fight. Unraveling heavenly mysteries was punished in the case of Prometheus by an eagle perpetually picking at his liver, or in the case of Sisyphus by that timeless nightmare of frustration and futility. It was a fraught activity for the Greeks. Powerful new learning discomfited the Hebrews, too, as evidenced by the consequences of Adam and Eve's transgression at the Tree of Knowledge.[13] For as humans grow smarter their dependence upon the gods, or those who presume to interpret the gods, diminishes.

The danger science held for religion seemed particularly apparent in the fifth-century-BCE work of Anaxagoras of Klazomenae. He questioned one of the cornerstones of the Greek religion—its god-driven cosmology—but not just because he couldn't see how that could be. Instead, Anaxagoras actually examined a meteorite and, based on his observations, came up with a more reasonable alternative. For Anaxagoras the sun is a red-hot mass of metal which "puts brightness into the moon."[14] There are reports that Anaxagoras was prosecuted for impiety in Athens.

The natural understandings did not always come from science. Some maintain that the historian Thucydides studied with Anaxagoras in Athens.[15] Thucydides certainly managed to demonstrate a similar commitment to evidence and reason. He also demonstrates an impatience with myth and the supernatural.

---

* I realize that it seems odd to be employing the Sisyphus myth in a chapter and book about the overcoming of myths, but this myth, as a piece of cultural evidence, helps demonstrate a concern, if not an obsession, in Greek culture with the ascendance of the *physiologi.*

Near the start of his account of the Peloponnesian War, Thucydides reports on a terrible plague (which he himself caught but survived) that struck Athens in 430 and 429 BCE, just after that war began. He notes that the people responded with "supplications at temples and consultations of oracles and the like." He even reports that "old men" in Athens recalled an ancient prophecy: "A Dorian war will come, and bring a pestilence with it."[16]

However, Thucydides concludes that, during the plague, those visits to temples, "consultations" with oracles and other recourses to religion or superstition "were of no avail"; they proved, to switch to another translation, "utterly useless."[17] And the historian goes out of his way to mock that supposed prophesy predicting a "Dorian war," bringing "a pestilence": the Peloponnesian War was not exactly a Dorian war and, he notes, another version of the prophesy had the word "famine" instead of "pestilence."[18]

Indeed, Thucydides is not shy about criticizing the behavior of one Athenian general for being "too much under the influence of divination and omens."[19] And he coldly notes how at least one group of people who put their "trust" in "the gods" (the Melians) wind up with all their grown men put to death and their women and children sold as slaves.[20]

Compare this treatment of the supernatural to that of the world's first major historian, Herodotus, who was only about a generation older than Thucydides. At one point in his *Histories,* for example, Herodotus recounts the circumstances surrounding the demise of Cambyses, a Persian king who apparently suffered an accidental sword wound to his thigh while in the city of Ecbatana. Cambyses' wound, Herodotus insists portentously, was "just in the spot where he had previously struck Apis the sacred Egyptian bull." Then the historian adds that "there had been a prophecy from the oracle at Buto that he would die at Ecbatana."[21]

Herodotus is also not above telling the tale of a rich singer, Arion, who, to escape being murdered for his money by the crew of a ship, rides over the sea on the back of a dolphin.[22] He reports the prophecy that a woman's child "will be a millstone which will fall upon the rulers" in Corinth and then tells how the child—Moses-like—survives efforts to kill him and, of course, goes on to fulfill the prophecy.[23]

Thucydides refuses to indulge in such tales. "It may be that the lack of a romantic element in my history," he writes, "will make it less of a pleasure to the ear: but I shall be content if it is judged useful by those who want to have a clear understanding of what happened."[24] Thucydides continually looks for natural, not supernatural, explanations. "He explains events entirely in human terms," writes the historian R. J. Rhodes in an introduction to the book, "without any suggestion of intervention by the gods or fulfillment of divine plans."[25] Thucydides admits that—"chance"—plays a major role in human affairs; he does not admit that gods do. Those who search most rigorously for "a clear understanding of what happened" often fail to find a role for gods. There is no evidence Thucydides believed gods existed.[26]

Indeed, to accomplish what this historian accomplished impiety is almost required. Thucydides debunked myths. Indeed, he debunked the very process of relying upon myths. But his impiety extended well beyond that. Sisyphus usurped a power of the gods in trying to gain knowledge of "everything that was to happen." Thucydides too was a usurper. He presumed to recount everything that *had* happened during the years of the Peloponnesian War. He presumed to observe humankind from a precise, knowing, almost Olympian perspective. He demonstrated, in other words, not only that the myths were wrong but that they were unnecessary—that humans could do what gods had done: they could offer explanations of their own.

An inclination toward *natural explanations*—whether of human events or astronomical phenomena—is the third major and ancient spur to disbelief. (Two more, which are not ancient, will be introduced many chapters hence.) And the search for natural explanations also leads to a particular kind of disbelief—characteristically, though hardly exclusively, Western. Here supernatural understandings are not just undercut by skepticism or overwhelmed by an affirmation of mortal life. They are, instead, displaced by rational understandings—by human efforts to obtain "a clear understanding of what happened." This is another positive variety of disbelief—it proposes more plausible alternatives to religious explanations. Darwin will follow Anaxagoras and Thucydides in this tradition.

Religions are often enchanting. They exude mystery and power. They can ease concerns. They can preserve ancient wisdom—moralities, philosophies. But religions—particularly as their precepts and strictures ossify over the centuries—tend to divert us from efforts to further understandings of how the world works and how we might improve our lot in it. We risk becoming like those pigeons: doing the same unproductive dances over and over again.

The growth of learning and all it can bring requires that some of those myths be challenged. That begins with skepticism, *how can it be* that a man rode across the sea on a dolphin? It is possible to argue that humankind produces new knowledge only by overcoming superstition, by debunking myths. The anacreontic focus on *this* world is also crucial. But it is the search for *natural explanations*—Thucydides' search, Anaxagoras' search—that has done the most to change the world. That was certainly true in Greece. It has proven true again in the last half millennium in the West. This is the most intellectually ambitious and potent of these three varieties of disbelief in gods (or God) for it does not just debunk old superstitions; it replaces them by coming up with new, rational understandings.

This third variety of disbelief arrives through reasoning, through investigation, through study—based, in most cases, upon reading, conversation and education. Thucydides, of course, had easy access to all of the above as he was raised in Athens. This variety of disbelief is less likely to pop up in some isolated village somewhere. Here preliterate societies or illiterate individuals do have a distinct disadvantage. This variety of disbelief is the product of considerable thought not just by individuals but by societies. It is preserved in writings. It builds over the generations. It builds over the centuries. The search for "a clear understanding of what happened," for natural explanations, creates knowledge. Thucydides created knowledge.

He had been a participant in the war with Sparta—the history of which he would later so impressively recount. Thucydides was in command of a fleet of seven Athenian warships near Amphipolis when Spartan troops, aided by rebels inside the city, attacked Amphipolis. Thucydides' fleet arrived too late to help. "The enemy possession of Amphipolis caused major alarm at Athens," Thucydides reports in his history.[27] The Athenians voted to punish their general for his failure. "The fact that I was in exile from my own country for 20 years after my command against Amphipolis gave me opportunity to observe affairs on both sides . . . and to reflect on them in relative calm." That may have proved a blessing. Living mostly in Thrace, Thucydides devoted himself, as he explains, "to the intellectual pursuit of an accurate understanding of events."[28]

Thucydides presented his readers with a great treasure trove of efforts at "a clear understanding." His contemporaries learned from him. We continue to learn from him. The modern world was built in large part by men and women who, like Thucydides, not only rejected myths but worked to come up with alternative explanations. The modern world was built in part by men and women who, like Thucydides, not only found the gods unbelievable but made them unnecessary by demonstrating how the world worked without them. Athens had, not coincidentally, more than its share of such individuals.

There is evidence that in the fifth and then the fourth centuries before the Common Era Athens sheltered a gaggle of nonbelievers. Diagoras and Anaxagoras were in Athens for some years while Thucydides was there—or while Thucydides was in exile from there. And Plato, a generation younger than Thucydides, complains of having "known many" who hold that "the gods do not exist."[29] The development of atheism in the West may not have begun in Athens at that time, but it certainly accelerated there then.

Socrates, Thucydides' contemporary and Plato's teacher, was not an atheist. He listened to dreams, oracles and his own inner voice, which he identified as "the voice of God."[30] However, his relentless, ironic questioning tended to turn traditional understandings, including traditional religious understandings, on their heads. One of the crimes for which Socrates was executed in Athens in 399 BCE was impiety.

The Sophists—often targets of Plato and Socrates—were itinerant wise-men-for-hire who had begun instructing Greek youth on such practical subjects as political rhetoric. They had some of Socrates' subversive habit of calling into question. According to the classicist A. B. Drachmann, Sophists may have done more to weaken religious belief in Greece than even philosophers, with a scientific bent, such as Thales and Anaxagoras.[31]

The best known statement of probably the best known Sophist, Protagoras of Abdera, is: "Man is the measure of all things."[32] This was an early and important contribution to the idea of disbelief—because of its implied relativism, because of its undisguised humanism and because it so clearly excludes Olympian measuring devices. Protagoras also was in Athens during this period.

"Concerning the gods," Protagoras writes, "I am unable to discover whether they exist or not, or what they are like in form; for there are many hindrances to knowledge: the obscurity of the subject and the brevity of human life."[33] This was the first sentence of a book, *On the Gods*. We don't have the rest of that book, but it is difficult to see how a work with such a beginning could be particularly pious. And Protagoras is, indeed, another Greek philosopher said to have been charged with impiety in Athens.* Some of the ideas in Thucydides' history have been traced to Protagoras.[34]

---

* Reports of impiety trials in Athens besides those of Socrates and Diagoras appear impossible to verify given the fragmentary and contradictory accounts upon which they are based—usually second- or third-hand and written centuries after the fact. The absence of contemporary accounts of such prosecutions against Protagoras or Anaxagoras—in the writings of Plato or Thucydides, for instance—is probably the best

The Sophists may have done the most damage to belief through their philosophical inclination to divide the world into two categories: "law" and "nature." This distinction was a product of the sort of theoretical analysis becoming common in Athens at the time, and it proved subversive: shouldn't religious practice, since it was carefully prescribed in each city and changed from city to city, be listed as part of "law" (or culture), not "nature" (or the world itself)?[35] Religion, relegated to this category, appeared to be merely a human invention.

In his dialogue *The Laws*, Plato disparages those who assert that "the gods are human contrivances," that "they do not exist in nature but only by custom and law."[36] He had Sophists in mind. However, with few exceptions (Protagoras possibly among them) these professional teachers avoided pushing their ideas to what might have been their logical conclusion. Questioning the existence of gods remained dangerous and certainly wasn't a good way to win work educating upper-class youth. Nevertheless, upper-class, male youths, like Thucydides, had been imbibing these ideas.

Plato himself was not an atheist. In *The Laws*, sounding old and jaded, he has his spokesman, the Athenian, "address" an "impious" young man who denied "the existence of the gods":

> You and your friends are not the first or the only persons who have had these notions about the Gods. There are always a considerable number who are infected by them. [37]

This is when Plato adds, "I've known many myself." He then goes on to insist that the "opinion" these atheists hold is inevitably outgrown with age; still Plato suggests that laws should be passed "commanding the impious to renounce their evil ways."[38] The fact that he deemed it necessary to legislate against atheism is another indication that the number of those "infected" by these "notions" in Athens in the fifth century BCE was high. Some historians label this period the "Athenian Enlightenment."[39]

W hat was it about classical Greece—with its path-breaking playwrights, poets, mathematicians, historians, politicians and philosophers?

---

evidence *against* their having taken place; the fact that Socrates and Diagoras were convicted of impiety in Athens is the best indication that other such trials may indeed have occurred.

What was it in particular about Athens where, in the late fifth and early fourth centuries BCE, so many of them congregated? Why did human understanding seem to grow at such a rapid pace there—or in India at the time of the Buddha or in Paris during the Enlightenment? What can we make of the fact that atheists have a way of turning up in such places during such periods?

Probably we know of an unusually large number of nonbelievers in classical Athens—or in India at the time of the Buddha or in Paris during the Enlightenment—in part because these societies at these times were more open than most or, at least, more thoroughly chronicled. And certainly such periods of learning tend to encourage all sorts of questioning—even questioning of religion.

However, the questioning of religion also encourages periods of learning. My point is that some of the intellectual breakthroughs in Athens at that time—of which the world is still in awe—would not have been possible had disbelief in the supernatural not been spreading. Atheism proved fertile. Atheism often does.

Cults and superstitions, it must be acknowledged, were rampant in Athens in these decades.[40] After all, what looks in retrospect like a golden age was probably experienced as a turbulent and frightening time: a plague raged, a war and an empire were lost, a democracy was overthrown. Cults and superstitions are common enough in human history; they may be particularly common in turbulent and frightening times.

But Athens in these decades was also experiencing a period of contagious "rationalism," as the historian E. R. Dodds explains, if only "for the few."[41] Such periods were relatively rare before modern times. The argument here is that Thucydides, for example, could not have written his superstition-free history had that rationalism not been infecting an influential portion of the population of Athens—his teachers, his friends. For Thucydides was no radical.[42] It is difficult to imagine him producing a history subtracting heavenly interference from human events—probably the world's first such history—without the ideas and comfort of the promulgators of the Athenian Enlightenment.

And Thucydides was indebted to the rationalism developing in Athens at the time for more than just his freedom from superstition. For a mind in the habit of questioning myths is better equipped to weed out even nonmystical distortions and exaggerations—to get the facts right. After dismissing the role of oracles, prophecies and healers in the plague that devastated

Athens, Thucydides spends many pages, for example, detailing the actual nature of the disease and the failure of various efforts to treat it.[43]

An unwillingness to settle for supernatural explanations, the point is, encourages the process of coming up with careful, rigorous natural explanations. That which can no longer be credited to gods now not only *can* be credited to men, women or nature but *must* be credited to men, women or nature. There's no choice but to study human behavior, nature's behavior, more closely. It is possible, needless to say, to do fine history and believe in God (or gods): Herodotus, despite his enthrallment with prophecies and fate, certainly managed to provide some information on numerous crucial historical events. But the explanations offered by Herodotus too often end with prophecies and fate.[44] That's where the inquiry ceases. Reliable and thorough history—history that goes further—is in some sense a consequence of a mindset that can be traced back to the arrival of "rationalism": a compulsion to seek non-mystical answers.

And history, of course, was not the only beneficiary of the shucking off of superstitions and myths—the rejection of gods—among "the few" in Athens in the fourth and fifth centuries BCE. It did wonders for science. The point is not just that Anaxagoras, if he still believed that Apollo drove the sun around the sky, could not have formulated his theory that a burning hot sun "puts brightness into the moon." The point is that Anaxagoras, if he took seriously some version of that mythology, probably would not even have bothered examining a meteorite. Science progressed in Athens and elsewhere in Greece in part *because* individuals like Anaxagoras abandoned the notion that gods drove heavenly bodies around.

Something similar can be said about medicine, though that field was perhaps progressing less rapidly. The physicians at the school founded by Hippocrates on the island of Kos were unaware of the role of pathogens and were instead excessively concerned, by modern standards, with the "balance" of elements in a patient's body. Nonetheless, they had no patience, as one of them writes, with viewing diseases as having a "divine origin"; they had no patience with temple healers, who "cured" through snakebites and magic. Humankind still had a lot to learn about disease, but free of such obvious superstitions, Hippocrates' followers could at least set us on a path toward learning it. They observed; they examined; they noted.[45] Medicine took a small step forward.

Philosophy, too, benefited from this contagious rationalism among "the few"—whether or not the philosophers themselves were atheists. It is doubtful that a society more in the grip of a traditional religion could have produced the Sophists or exemplary and original questioners like Socrates and Plato, not to mention that great champion of the rational, Plato's student Aristotle.

Might diminished allegiance to gods also have left space for democracy? Pericles, Athens' most celebrated democratic leader, is reported to have been, like Thucydides, a student of Anaxagoras.[46] By Anaxagoras' "instructions," writes Plutarch (more than half a millennia later, alas), Pericles "seems . . . to have become . . . superior to that superstition" that "possesses the minds of people unacquainted with . . . causes."[47]

Is it not reasonable to suppose that democracy itself in Athens might have gained not only from Pericles' levelheaded leadership but from such a superiority to superstition—particularly the traditional partnership of gods and monarchs? Does this not hint at what will become one of the major themes of this book: that atheism can further liberty?

Gods, after all, originally mimicked kings—with their commands, their retinues, their whims and idiosyncrasies, plus their seemingly insatiable need for praise. With the gods established, kings claimed special access to them, claimed to be favored by them and, yes, mimicked them (or, better yet, Him)—insisting on their own divine right, on their own infallibility. Elected leaders on the other hand, with their circumscribed powers, didn't have any obvious analogy in the heavens. Who there serves limited terms and must depend upon the consent of the governed?

But while kings need the gods—to explain why they are entitled to rule, to explain their exalted status—democratic leaders have an alternate, reasonable, natural justification for their power: the will of the voters. Monarchs need myths. Democracy is hardly always rational. Plenty of elected leaders have called upon the gods. Nations, authoritarian and democratic, deify their founders and proclaim themselves, in one way or another, chosen. They hold onto their illusions. But don't non-hierarchical, fallible, mutable, reasonable, undivine democracies benefit, in the end, from the rejection of at least some myths?

Belief in gods was itself, not surprisingly, also among the subjects for which the Greeks had begun looking for natural explanations. Xenophanes of Colophon lived, as did Anacreon, in the sixth century BCE. He had seen, as anyone who traveled a bit in the ancient world could have seen, that different peoples each worshipped different gods. And Xenophanes had a pretty good idea why. "Ethiopians say that their gods are snub-nosed and black," he observed, "Thracians that theirs are blue-eyed and red-haired." Xenophanes took the thought further: "If horses or oxen . . . could draw with their hands . . . , horses would draw the figures of the gods as similar to horses, and the oxen as similar to oxen."[48] That's a start toward an explanation for belief in gods.

In the next century the Greeks took that natural explanation further. The following fragment from a satiric play, which was written in Athens, also credits gods to the inclinations of humans, but it does so with such cynicism and force that it appears to leave no room for the possibility that gods of any sort actually exist. It credits "lying speech" with having "established the Deity" in an effort to better police behavior:

> Some shrewd man, wise in judgment first,
> Invented for mortals the fear of gods,
> To serve as terror for the bad, even though
> Their actions, words or thoughts be secret.[49]

This passage is probably spoken by the title character of that play, the rest of which has not survived. The play's name was: *Sisyphus*. Therefore, what is probably the oldest surviving undisguised expression of atheism in the West—arguing that gods were "invented" through lies—was likely attributed to that crafty, impious, unhumble rebel himself. We don't know what position is taken on these matters, or this character, in the rest of the play. But there is some evidence that *Sisyphus'* likely author, Critias, shared the fragment's cynicism about belief in the gods.[50]

Critias was an aristocrat, a student of Socrates, a second cousin of Plato, an athlete, a playwright, a philosopher, a poet. Unfortunately, Critias was also a brutal tyrant—a leader of "the Thirty," the bloody regime that replaced the Athenian democracy in 404 BCE, after the city's defeat in the Peloponnesian War. The evidence that Critias himself was not a believer comes from an incident in which he risked the gods' wrath by ordering that a political opponent, who had taken refuge atop a sacred altar, be dragged away and killed.[51]

This initial statement of Western disbelief could, alas, have been penned by a more worthy hand. Critias' politics weaken the case for a connection between atheists, if he was indeed one, and liberty. Critias' crimes make the problem of locating an ethic in atheism, again if that was his position, more difficult. And his explanation for belief in the gods is not the one settled upon earlier in this book. Still, despite its source and although it may not be correct, this qualifies as another of the efforts being made in Greece, in Athens, to find natural causes—in this case political or anthropological—for the apparently supernatural.

The fading of the supernatural among some in Thucydides' time helped make possible the extraordinary burst of cold-eyed, natural-explanation-oriented thinking in Greece at that time. And that search for "a clear understanding of what happened" also contributed to the fading of the supernatural. In other words, something of a virtuous cycle operates here and elsewhere in this history of atheism: disbelief in the gods encourages and facilitates vigorous investigations of the natural, but such investigations also further disbelief in gods.

However, the cycle can also turn the other way.

3

THEY FORBID RATIONAL SPECULATION

DISBELIEF AND LEARNING DECLINE TOGETHER IN CHRISTIAN EUROPE

"Faith is believing what you know ain't so."

—Mark Twain[1]

IT IS NOT DIFFICULT TO TRACE A LINE OF WELL-KNOWN NONBE-
lievers from Greece in 415 BCE, when Diagoras was convicted of impiety, through the Roman Empire in the second century of the Common Era.

Despite all the city gods, all the cults and a vogue for a god-infused
philosophy, Stoicism, these were not entirely religious societies. "The various modes of worship which prevailed in the Roman world," the notable
eighteenth-century historian Edward Gibbon concludes, with some over-
statement, "were all considered by the people as equally true; by the philosopher as equally false; and by the magistrate as equally useful."[2] And,
as Gibbon's quip about "the magistrate" indicates, these were not entirely
tolerant societies. Greek and then Roman authorities remained, as a rule,
suspicious of, if not infuriated by, those who did not at least go through
the motions of honoring their gods. We know about one of the members
of this line of Greek and Roman nonbelievers through a trial for impiety.

However, the gods these societies worshipped, or pretended to worship, didn't care if you went through the motions of honoring some other
city's gods, too—even that God with the big temple in Jerusalem. Paganism
was not exclusive. It didn't presume to judge religious sincerity. And, for

the most part, these societies encouraged questioning and were respectful of learning.

So, the fact that it remained possible to have "met a great many" non-believers in this part of the world in these centuries should not be surprising. What is surprising is the abruptness and completeness with which this line of nonbelievers ends—when a religion that was exclusive, that was obsessed by religious sincerity and that did not put much stock in questioning and nonreligious learning began gaining power in the West.

We can jump, in this line of well-known nonbelievers, from Anaxagoras, Thucydides and all the (presumably young) individuals in Athens who, according to Plato, were convinced that "gods do not exist," to Epicurus—born into an Athenian family living outside of Athens shortly before Plato died. Epicurus' name would become and has remained synonymous with a variety of disbelief. For Epicurus was an anacreontic, although less a proponent of bodily pleasures (i.e., good food) than contemporary use of the term *epicurean* would suggest. And Epicurus insisted that we should stop bothering ourselves about gods. He did, however, have one weakness as a link in a chain of nonbelievers: Epicurus said he believed gods existed. But he thought those gods have absolutely no interest in or effect upon human life. So they might as well have not existed.

Still, if we want a more orthodox nonbeliever for our line, we have Epicurus' contemporary, Theodorus, who was probably—once again the reports are sketchy—prosecuted for impiety in Athens.[3] Theodorus was associated with the Cyrenaics, a staunchly anacreontic school of philosophy. The Cyrenaics, founded by one of Socrates' less sanctimonious disciples, *were* proponents of bodily pleasures.[4] The best evidence that Theodorus himself was a nonbeliever—and therefore that disbelief remained a factor in Athens—was the name by which he became known: Theodorus the Atheist.

Carneades, next in this line, was born a few dozen years after Theodorus died. By the second century BCE we find this Skeptic, perhaps history's greatest Skeptic, heading the Academy that Plato had founded in Athens. Carneades, an "Academic" Skeptic, was eager to challenge claims about the nature of things—dogmatic claims, idealistic claims, more or less all claims, his own often included. Although Carneades never proclaimed himself an atheist (he wasn't in the habit of proclaiming himself anything), religion was among his primary targets.

The assault Carneades mounted on claims about the gods begins with what is known as the *consensus gentium* (or "agreement of the people") argument: how could all of humankind be wrong in thinking there are gods? Carneades answers in three ways, as outlined by Cicero: First, he challenges the existence of such a consensus by pointing to apparent nonbelievers, among them Diagoras. Second, Carneades observes that the fact that so many humans believe does not prove that their belief has "reasons," only that it has "causes" (which Xenophanes and Critias had begun investigating). Finally, Carneades notes, according to Cicero's account, that people, including masses of people, can be wrong.[5]

Many statements about Carneades' views come attached to the phrase "according to Cicero." Cicero, born a couple of decades after Carneades died, was a consequential and controversial politician in Rome at the time of Julius Caesar. He was also a consequential, if not always original, thinker—who had studied under Philo, a pupil of Clitomachus, who had been in turn a pupil of Carneades. Cicero considered himself an "Academic Skeptic"—a follower, in other words, of Carneades.

Cicero is hard to pin down as an atheist. That may have been intentional: he had a political career to worry about. Indeed, Cicero occupied, as did many Roman politicians, a ceremonial position in the Roman religion, the cult of Jupiter: Cicero was an augur. If he had any religious feelings, however, they seem to have been quite shallow.[6] In one despondent letter to his wife, Cicero writes, "Neither the gods, whom you have worshipped with such pure devotion, nor men, whom I have ever served, have made us any return."[7]

And Cicero was the author of a dialogue, *The Nature of the Gods*, in which the arguments for the existence of gods are debated and demolished, one by one, mostly by a character, Cotta, representing Academic Skepticism. One of the proponents of the existence of gods in the dialogue notes as evidence, for example, the world's, or at least Rome's, "abundant blessings." But Cotta later responds that "many objects are found which are inimical, hostile and baneful to us. . . . What benefit," he asks, "can be observed in mice or cockroaches or snakes?" Cotta then, as befits an Academic Skeptic, asks, in essence, *how* a God who allows such "baneful" things to exist, *can be*? He then expresses one of the major arguments against the existence of God—or at least against the existence of a benevolent and all-powerful God—the problem of evil:

Either God wishes to remove evils and cannot, or he can do so and is unwilling. . . . If he has the will but not the power, he is a weakling, and this is not characteristic of God. If he has the power but not the will, he is grudging, and this is a trait equally foreign to God.[8]

At the end of this book Cicero denies that his Academic Skeptic has won the debate, but that conclusion—which is hard for most readers of his book to accept—may also have been a way to avoid controversy.

If Cicero won't do as a first-century-BCE atheist, we might substitute Lucretius—a follower, a few centuries later, of Epicurus. We have only one work by Lucretius: a long and remarkable poem. In it he insists that the universe "was certainly not created for us by divine power." How could gods manage the universe even if they wanted to, Lucretius asks, in a prose translation of his poem:

Who can rule the sum total of the measureless? Who can hold in coercive hand the strong reins of the unfathomable? Who can spin all the firmaments alike and foment with the fires of ether all the fruitful earths? Who can be in all places at all times?

Instead, Lucretius' poem states, "nature runs the universe by herself without the aid of gods."[9]

Lucretius' lengthy poem—divided into five books—is mostly occupied with explaining how the universe gallops along without such a "coercive hand" holding its "reins." And—leaning on Epicurus' scientific ideas, which leaned, in turn, on the atomic theory of an earlier Greek, Democritus—Lucretius probably presented as sophisticated an account of the universe as any that would be produced until the scientific revolution in Europe more than a millennium and a half later. For Lucretius not only portrayed, as Democritus did, a universe filled with atoms and empty space, but one with no center and no boundary, which would not last forever, and which operated physically and biologically through a kind of survival of the fittest. Indeed, this first-century-BCE Roman provides particularly compelling evidence that the less we assume mysterious gods do, the more we will understand of what intelligible nature does.

So my line of well-known nonbelievers in Greek and Roman society includes, in some combination, Epicurus, Theodorus, Carneades, Cicero and Lucretius. There were more, but these are among the most interesting—all, except Theodorus, important figures in the history of western thought. My purpose has been to demonstrate that anti-religious beliefs remained, if not common, both possible to express and important in the centuries after Thucydides. This line ends, more or less, with Lucian, a second-century Greek satirist.

Lucian made belief in the gods seem foolish in part by portraying them as bumblers: Zeus, in one of Lucian's satires, hurls his thunderbolt at his enemy, Anaxagoras, but hits a temple instead.[10] And Lucian also demonstrated the silliness of religion simply by imagining the day-to-day reality of these beings—Zeus, for example, attempting to answer the multitude of selfish, contradictory prayers he receives each day: "Of those at sea, one prayed for a north, another for a south wind."[11] Lucian was, in other words, among those asking, *How can that be?*

"Anything to do with the supernatural is anathema to him," one of his translators, Lionel Casson, writes. "There are no gods; there is no providence; all oracles are *ipso facto* fakes."[12] In one of his satires Lucian even took a swipe—a gentle one by his standards—at a relatively new religion in the Roman Empire: Christianity. In so doing he produced one of the small number of surviving references to Jesus at this time from a non-Christian writer: "that crucified Sophist," Lucian dubbed him.[13]

Despite his atheism, Lucian's satires were widely read and enjoyed, and surprisingly well tolerated by Roman authorities. They not only allowed him his success but rewarded him with a lucrative government job near the end of his life. However, the Roman Empire in which Lucian lived and thrived was about to experience what may have been the most far-reaching setback the world has ever seen to such challenges to religion—satirical or otherwise.

The timing gets a little rough here: Lucian dies almost a century before Constantine, who would convert the Roman Empire to Christianity, was born. But public professions of atheism would be extinguished in the Roman Empire at some point after Lucian, who may therefore qualify as the last undisguised atheist we know of in Europe for more than a thousand years. It is no coincidence that those were also bad years for learning in Europe.

The new religion of Jesus and Paul was intolerant in some new ways. Christians, like Jews, refused to pay others the common courtesy of honoring their gods—sometimes even on pain of death. They denounced the worship of any god other than their own. And Christianity distinguished itself from Judaism, from whence it sprang, in part by raising the standards for acceptable worship: it was not enough merely to act as if you believed in what Christians believed; you had to *truly* believe—in your "heart."

Christianity demanded *faith*—in the Resurrection, in Jesus' divinity, in the coming, though oft-postponed, Kingdom of Heaven. "All things are possible," Jesus is quoted as proclaiming, "for one who believes."[14] As Christianity gained power, life became much more difficult for those who did not believe.

The faith-denying question *how can that be?*—Commoro's question—was, to begin with, becoming intolerable. Tertullian was the first significant Christian thinker to write in Latin. Early in the third century he produced the statement that may best indicate what seemed so bothersome about Christian ways of thinking not just for philosophically inclined Greeks and Romans but for all proponents of common sense and logic. It is a statement of faith, stunning in its directness: "The Son of God died; it must needs be believed because it is absurd," Tertullian asserts. "He was buried and rose again; it is certain because it is impossible."[15]

An appreciation for earthly joys was also being decried as sinful. The ascetic and the anacreontic are, of course, enemies. Plenty of other systems of belief in the supernatural had encouraged renunciation of pleasures—fasts, chastity, even the welcoming of physical pain. But Christianity, with its emphasis on the imminent arrival of the "kingdom of heaven," was often particularly enthusiastic in disparaging life before death and its pleasures—including sexual intercourse (said not even to have been involved in the Son of God's conception).[16] With Christianity, the struggle against the desires of the body sometimes became ferocious.

In the fourth century, Jerome, later Saint Jerome, attempted to remove temptation by exiling himself to the Syrian desert: "this prison house," he calls it, "where my only companions were scorpions and wild beasts." Yet, even there, Jerome admits, "the fires of lust kept bubbling up before me." In this barren desert, Jerome couldn't stop imagining "bands of dancing girls."[17]

Jesus had appeared to offer one gruesome solution to the "fires of lust" problem, noting, according to Matthew, "There are eunuchs who have made themselves eunuchs for the Kingdom of Heaven."[18] The theologian Origen, whose work Jerome translated, was known for his allegorical readings of scripture, but this statement by Jesus he apparently took literally. Early in the third century, Origen is said to have castrated himself, presumably to prevent lust from interfering with his quest "for the Kingdom of Heaven."[19] "Those who obey the teachings of the Savior," Origen writes, "are martyrs in every act whereby they crucify the flesh; with its passions and desires."[20]

Most, of course, did not go nearly this far. And there were many Christians in succeeding centuries—including priests and popes—who still managed to indulge a variety of "passions and desires." But they mostly did so in secret or as winking hypocrites. The anacreontic had been submerged. Arguments for the importance of enjoying life were muffled and would remain muffled in Europe for perhaps a millennium.

However, perhaps the greatest loss—in these centuries of blind faith—was the reasoned search for natural explanations. Christian thinkers were upfront about it: "Let us Christians prefer the simplicity of our faith to the demonstrations of human reason," the man now known to Catholics as Saint Basil the Great wrote in the fourth century. "For to spend much time on research about the essence of things would not serve the edification of the church."[21]

In the fourth century of the Common Era, Emperor Constantine lifted Christianity from a persecuted sect to the state religion of the Roman Empire, and the unprecedented power of that empire fell in behind this devaluation of "human reason." Science, one of the disciplines that had moved forward together with disbelief in Greece, retreated with it. Consider, for one example, what happened to study of the heavens in Christian Europe: Detailed astronomical observations had been made in Athens until the year 475. These were the last significant contributions to astronomy in Europe for perhaps a thousand years.[22] The nature of the heavens would now mostly be accepted on faith.

Eight hundred years after Aristotle's death, the *theologi* had more than reversed the gains of the *physiologi*. They had defeated the *physiologi* so completely that there was no more room in Christian Europe for *physiologi* and would not be for about a millennium. The Academy in Athens—founded by Plato, once led by Carneades—had survived for 900 years. It was closed by Emperor Justinian, a great defender of Christianity, in 529.[23]

Many books disappeared in these centuries. Except for some texts on logic, which had been translated into Latin, Europe lost contact with

Aristotle's great treatises—those unsurpassed demonstrations of the power of human reason.[24] Christians in these centuries apparently were not interested in these books: "Unhappy Aristotle!" sneers Tertullian, "who invented . . . the art of building up and pulling down, an art so far-fetched in its conjectures, so harsh in its arguments, so productive of contentions—embarrassing even to itself."[25]

However, since these treatises were preserved elsewhere in the world, that was not the worst of it. Aristotle also wrote dialogues.[26] They are much praised by Cicero. But Aristotle's dialogues seem to have disappeared entirely sometime after the third century CE, perhaps also victims of Christian indifference or distaste. Tertullian adds, "After Christ Jesus we desire no subtle theories, no acute inquires. . . ."[27]

The theories and inquires in a number of the Greek works that have been mentioned in this book must also have been undesirable: a book Anaxagoras wrote, Critias' play *Sisyphus,* Protagoras' *On the Gods.* Except for occasional fragments or references to them in other books, they, too, disappeared. Everything written by the anacreontic Cyrenaics is also gone. Carneades had not put his skeptical ideas in writing, but his student Clitomachus had. Those books, which Cicero had relied upon, also were lost.[28]

Most probably were not burned. Flames were reserved in these centuries primarily for the work of Christian heretics, not pagan nonbelievers.[29] Instead, classical texts underwent a kind of winnowing. In order for a papyrus roll written before the Common Era to make it onto a printing press more than a millennium and a half later it had to be repeatedly recopied. Copying a book by hand was a laborious task. There had to be good reason to undertake it. And most of that copying was eventually done in monasteries.

Irreligious books—by scientists, Skeptics or other philosophers—undoubtedly were not much in demand by Christians. Origen had been one Christian scholar known for encouraging his students to read the Greek philosophers. He allowed those students access to everything—almost. "Only those authors who denied the existence of a deity or a divine providence," explain L. D. Reynolds and N. G. Wilson, in their book *Scribes and Scholars,* "were to be avoided."[30] Most of the authors discussed here would, therefore, have been "avoided." These books had no chance of making it into the curriculum being used in most of the empire's schools. Nine plays by Euripides were part of that curriculum. In his play *Bellerophontes*

Euripides has a character state, in what context we don't know, that the gods "do not exist." *Bellerophontes* was not included in the curriculum and has not survived.[31]

A few anti-religious books did make it. Cicero's own remarkable dialogue, *The Nature of the Gods,* obviously was recopied—perhaps because his character was debunking pagan, not Christian, beliefs; perhaps because at the end Cicero insists one of the believers has won the debate.[32] However, even this widely known book has a section missing—perhaps the most important section, where his Academic Skeptic refutes two crucial arguments: first that the universe was "built" (designed) and second that the universe is governed by a divine intelligence.[33] Surely it was not mere chance that this section in particular happened to disappear.

The survival of Lucretius' poem, *On the Nature of the Universe,* may have been a matter of luck as much as anything else. Manuscripts were scarce, and worms, mold, a flood or a fire in the wrong library at the wrong time might have broken the thin chain of copies that kept it alive until the poem was rediscovered in the Renaissance.[34]

Many books that were not great works of reason or challenges to prevailing religious beliefs also, it is true, have been lost. Still, the disappearance of such a large proportion of this particular selection of books appears more than just a coincidence. Christian Europe in these early centuries wanted no part of celebrations of reason or criticisms of religion. And it succeeded, if only by neglect, in expunging many of them.

We saw in Athens the intellectual benefits of the struggle against belief in the supernatural. Christian Europe in these centuries experienced the renewed, even intensified hegemony of the supernatural: a heavenly Father, a virgin birth, the Son of a god, a resurrection from death, a Holy Ghost, a realm populated by the dead, along with various subtle yet insisted-upon conclusions about the nature and relationship of these miraculous entities and occurrences. The price paid for that re-immersion in the supernatural was the end, for the most part, of science, the smothering of non-Christian philosophy, the loss of many important books. The price paid for the increased strength of religion—to state the point without nuance or qualification—was a significant decline in learning and the ability to learn.

Now to some qualifications: Not everything, of course, was in decline. Christianity did bring consolation, charity, humility, a sense of community, kinds of morality and some increased concern for the downtrodden. And there were exceptions to this decline in learning: some did still think deeply—Augustine, in the fourth and fifth centuries is an example; so is Thomas Aquinas, more than eight centuries later. However, if that thought was to be made public, it had to be compatible with Catholic mythology. Free thought—that is thought that stepped beyond the boundaries of the currently accepted interpretation of Christianity—was, to the extent that such a thing is possible, banned. Even Thomas Aquinas, trying to find a logic that might buttress aspects of Christian belief, had initially run afoul of the church. Some of his efforts were condemned by the bishop of Paris in 1277.[35]

And this suggestion that religion was responsible for intellectual decline in medieval Europe requires another qualification: the acknowledgment that there were other causes of a decline in learning in these centuries. They included the series of invasions the tottering Roman Empire had undergone and the drying up of trade and communication once that empire split and, in the West, disintegrated. Some have also seen signs of moral and philosophical exhaustion in late pagan culture. However, the rise of an unavoidable, mostly unbending, intolerant, unabashedly anti-rational religion certainly was a proximate cause of Christian Europe's centuries-long loss of old knowledge and the ability to create new knowledge.

So here, then, is this book's prime example of a vicious cycle—the opposite of the virtuous cycle, in Athens for example, of increasing disbelief in the supernatural feeding increasing understanding of the natural, which, in turn, fed increasing disbelief in the supernatural. In Europe after Christianity's triumph, it went the other way: as faith in one particular mix of the supernatural stifled intellectual life, the sort of thinking that might challenge that faith was silenced.

Disbelief in religion never entirely disappears: the next chapter will present evidence of that. But the public expression of disbelief in religion was silenced to an extraordinary extent in the late Roman Empire and then in medieval Europe.

In about the year 378, then Bishop Epiphanius, later Saint Epiphanius, had published his great contribution to the science of "heresiology": an account and refutation of eighty different heresies. Why did it include precisely eighty heresies or "poisonous snakes"? Because Solomon is listed in the Bible as having had eighty concubines.[36] In this world of faith, conclusions often preceded investigations.

Twenty of Epiphanius' heretical sects are not Christian. They go back to the creation and include "Barbarism" ("which lasted for ten generations, from Adam's time till Noah"), Judaism, Stoicism and Epicureanism (which "held that pleasure is the goal of well-being, and that neither God nor providence directs affairs").[37] The other sixty of Epiphanius' heresies are Christian. "Heretic" derives from the Greek word for choice.[38] Epiphanius believed in one, true, narrowly defined faith, not choice.

Epiphanius' book is significant for the clue it provides to what, in the fourth century, was no longer even being considered a possible choice. He wrote only two centuries after the irreverent religious satires of Lucian. Yet, in none of Epiphanius' eighty heresies (Epicureanism included) is the existence of God mocked or denied. Skepticism is not mentioned; nor is anything that might qualify as rationalism.

By the end of the fourth century, disbelief in God had become so feeble a public force in the now Christian Roman Empire that it couldn't even earn a place on a list of eighty heresies. The teaming of the power and authority of the empire with the deep faith of Christianity, begun under Constantine, had made challenges to a powerful set of beliefs in the supernatural essentially impossible. Investigations of the natural in the West more or less ceased.

Early in the ninth century, a renowned, well-connected poet, known for homoerotic verses, is said to have responded to the reading of a selection from a holy book that began, "Oh! You unbelievers . . . ," by yelling out: "Here I am!"[39]

The poet's name was Abū Nuwās. The holy book was the Qur'ān. This incident is said to have taken place in a mosque. And Abū Nuwās, whose hair curled down to his shoulders, was an Arab who spent most of his life in Basra and Baghdad—at the heart of the Arab empire. It is unlikely he could have said such a thing in public and lived safely in Europe.

In other parts of the world, after Christianity had spread over most of Europe, "human reason" was still receiving its due and disbelief in God (or gods) was still sometimes surfacing. The Cārvāka remained active in one incarnation or another in India. And Baghdad, then capital of the Arab empire, had some important flowerings, if not of atheism then of something close in and around the ninth century.

I have been suggesting that disbelief and learning tend to come and go together. This period, under the rule in Baghdad of the Abbāsid caliphs, is known as "the golden age of Islam." It was a time of great accomplishment in fields ranging from literature to science. A variety or religious ideas— Sunni, Shi'a, Christian, Jewish, Manichean, Buddhist, Hindu and others— were being promulgated in Baghdad in these years. And so were critiques of religious ideas. Writings were available attacking Judaism, Christianity and also, we're told, Islam.[40] It was a time when disbelief could—once in a while—appear in public.

Baghdad will be the destination for this book's final excursion beyond the West until the twentieth century. It provides not only a demonstration that other parts of the world escaped that vicious cycle in Europe but that they managed to see, for a time, a virtuous cycle of growth in learning feeding disbelief in the supernatural, which in turn stimulated further growth in learning.

No, freedom of thought was hardly complete under the Abbāsid caliphs: heretics were upon occasion persecuted. But freedom of thought was, at moments, possible. Abū Nuwās, that self-proclaimed unbeliever, was a poet of the first order (though appreciating his technical skill is difficult in translation). That helped him get away with some remarkably irreligious statements. And he served as *nadīm* or, to borrow an archaic English translation, "boon companion" to the caliph—one of the talented fellows the ruler kept around because, in essence, they were great good fun.[41] That definitely helped protect him.

If tales about him recorded in *One Thousand and One Nights* and his own poems are to be believed, Abū Nuwās' status as *nadīm* was well earned: he was also a carouser of the first order. Here is how he characterizes himself:

> The vanguard of depravity,
> The spearhead of debauchery,
> Arch-enemy of chastity
> And all that smacks of sanctity.[42]

However, that caliph, Amīn, was not above tossing Abū Nuwās in jail for a while, when he needed support from the clerics during a war with his brother. This may have been accompanied by a plea for a bit more propriety: "The caliph has commanded me . . . Refrain from further revelry." But this poet appears to have been difficult, if not impossible, to tame:

Where is the man who's never sinned and never shown dissent?
Well, critic, tear your hair out now, for I shall not repent.

Amīn lost that war with his brother. The caliph was beheaded in 813. Without his patron, Abū Nuwās may finally have been defeated himself. Amīn's *nadīm* died two years later—perhaps poisoned. But for most of his life at the center of the Arab empire, the poet's outrageous behavior seems to have been accepted. This seems particularly significant since, although God gets some mentions in his poems, Abū Nuwās was anything but a religious man: "Always I have and will," he writes, "scatter God and gold to the four winds. . . . I delight in what the Book forbids. And flee what is allowed."[43]

Abū Nuwās was exceptionally talented and exceptionally daring—being some sort of unholy fool was undoubtedly part of his charm. But he could not have flourished as he did unless there was some tolerance for and even some interest in his ideas in early-ninth-century Baghdad. Abū Nuwās likely was not the only one to hold such views—in the wine rooms he frequented, certainly, but also, perhaps, in the palace and elsewhere in Baghdad. Most others must have lacked the boldness and the talent for their voices to remain audible. But two later "unbelievers" in Baghdad were also brave enough to proclaim, "Here I Am!"

Curious individuals in the Middle East at this time were fortunate to have access to books by Greek thinkers like Ptolemy, Archimedes and Euclid (on astronomy, mechanics and geometry, respectively)—books that had disappeared in the West. They also could peruse—in Arabic beginning in the ninth century—eight books by Aristotle, then also lost to Christian Europe, on metaphysics, politics, ethics, science and the soul.[44]

Abū Bakr al-Rāzī, who would have been able to read most of these books, is a good example of the intellectual accomplishment of Islam's "golden age" and of its tolerance for challenges to religion. He practiced medicine and chemistry in Baghdad in the ninth and tenth centuries with, by all accounts, remarkable skill and a definite scientific, empirical orientation.[45] Al-Rāzī is reported to have selected the best location for a new hospital in Baghdad by leaving meat out in various sections of the city and then determining where it rotted slowest. A few of al-Rāzī's medical treatises and textbooks were translated into Latin and were still being consulted in Europe eight centuries after his death. "The uncontested physician of the Arabs," one source dubs al-Rāzī.[46] This may help explain why he could get away with writing what he did on religion.

Al-Rāzī's anti-religious writings have, typically, not survived. Probably they were destroyed during less tolerant periods in Islamic culture. The attacks upon those writings survived quite well, however. Even al-Rāzī's critics do not accuse him of outright atheism—which will make him an exception in this book. But he seems to have had no use for religion.

According to his critics, al-Rāzī asserts in a book that people are "deluded" by the "lies" and "senseless myths" of a religion—any religion, though it is clear he had the local faith in mind: "If the people of this religion are asked about the proof for the soundness of their religion," al-Rāzī is quoted as having written, "they flare up, get angry and spill the blood of whoever confronts them with this question. They forbid rational speculation." The result? "Truth" becomes "thoroughly silenced and concealed."[47] Al-Rāzī certainly has something of the skeptic in him, but he is mostly a partisan of the Thucydides-like effort to come up with natural explanations.

Al-Rāzī rejected revelation—quite a rejection for a Muslim to make. His own attempt at a more rational philosophic system was built upon matter, but it did include the soul and the Creator among its eternal principles.[48] His attack on belief had its limits. However, according to Sarah Stroumsa's impressively researched study of free thought in this place and period, there was at least one other major thinker in the Islamic world whose thinking on religion may have been freer still.

Ibn al-Rāwandī was born to a Jewish, or formerly Jewish, father half a century before al-Rāzī, in about the year 815. His life too—as with Arab intellectual life in general at the time—centered around Baghdad. Again his own work does not survive, but, according to his critics, al-Rāwandī discounted "the miracles of Abraham, Moses, Jesus and Muhammad."[49] That would take him as far as al-Rāzī.

But al-Rāwandī went further. According to one source, he attacked God: "Thou didst apportion the means of livelihood to Thy Creatures like a drunkard who shows himself churlish."[50] One of al-Rāwandī's books, a reader maintains, includes "such blasphemous sayings as to make one's hair stand on end."[51] Comparing Allah to a "churlish" "drunkard" might indeed qualify as blasphemous. But here, for a religious person, may be the ultimate blasphemy—an attack not just on God but on His existence: "The world and everything in it . . . is pre-eternal," al-Rāwandī is said to have asserted, according to one of his critics; "it has neither a maker nor a governor, neither an initiator nor a creator."[52]

These were incendiary theories, incendiary words—certainly in contrast to what has, or has not, been publicly expressed in most of the Islamic world in the early twenty-first century; incendiary even for Baghdad in the ninth century. "No sensible person has ever held the view that totally denies the existence of a creator to the world," a later author writes. "then Ibn al-Rāwandī took this thesis and defended it in his book."[53] And al-Rāwandī, though not as renowned as the physician al-Rāzī or the poet Abū Nuwās, does not seem to have been merely a fringe character. By one account, he was the author of 114 books.[54]

So we have disbelief in Baghdad in these years. We also have a period of great intellectual progress—a "golden age." "The sciences of the Greek curriculum—mathematics, philosophy, astrology, astronomy and medicine—were translated, interrogated and improved upon by Arabic-speaking Christians and Muslims," explains the historian Amira K. Bennison. " . . . Engineering, hydraulics and agricultural science all flourished."[55] New styles of literature arrived and thrived.[56] We have, then, the elements of an Athens-like virtuous cycle of overt expressions of disbelief and intellectual progress.

Disbelief and intellectual progress do have that common progenitor: openness. An openness to other cultures—Greek and Persian in particular—certainly contributed to this "golden age" in Baghdad. But the disbelief did help nudge aside some of the superstitions (astrology excepted in this case) that can retard intellectual progress. Al-Rāzī could, for instance, locate his hospital by testing how meat rotted; he didn't have to consult a religious leader or see if anything from the Qur'ān might somehow be brought to bear on the question. And that growth in learning—increased understanding of what encourages putrefaction, for instance—in turn helped push aside superstition, religion.

Proving cause and effect at any place along such cycles is probably impossible; history does not often limit variables. And this "freethinking," to use Sarah Stroumsa's term, existed in its strongest form only during the ninth and tenth centuries.[57] But perhaps we shouldn't use the word "only" for centuries. And the affinity such expressions of disbelief and intellectual progress seem historically to have shown for each other is certainly impressive. Especially since in the West at this time intellectual progress seemed to have slowed almost to a halt. And overtly anti-religious arguments—like those of al-Rāwandī, al-Rāzī and Abū Nuwās—were excluded from acceptable discourse.

Nonetheless, that did not mean—that never means—that no one in Christian Europe was thinking anti-religious thoughts. Indeed, the disbelief in religion that would begin to flower in the West in the seventeenth and eighteenth centuries grew from seeds planted much earlier. The argument here is that the intellectual progress that also flowered in those centuries grew with it—from some of the same seeds.

4

NOTHING BUT THIS VISIBLE WORLD

EUROPE'S RETURN TO REASON

The deepest, the only theme of human history, compared to which all others are of subordinate importance, is the conflict of skepticism with faith.

—Johann Wolfgang von Goethe[1]

D ARK AGES, ENTERPRISING HISTORIANS HAVE TAUGHT US, ARE hardly without their sparks and flares. A whole continent, a whole culture, does not entirely stop reasoning. Adventurous minds—even when there is little space for intellectual life outside of the church—find subjects and thoughts with which to interest themselves. Certainly, that was true in Christian Europe.

Peter Abelard was born in Brittany in about the year 1079. With the support of his father, a soldier who had some acquaintance with the world of learning himself, Abelard set off to be educated. That required, at the time, travel—to track down various elusive manuscripts and to study under various scattered scholars. The best teachers were connected with cathedrals. In fact, the grip of the church upon learning was so firm that being a scholar also necessitated being a churchman. Abelard took the minor orders of the church.[2]

With the threat from invasions having eased, France and other parts of Christian Europe were beginning to devote more attention to education. And the subjects upon which it was possible to be educated in the West were changing, too. The new rage among the most bookish: logic, as illuminated by the few works of Aristotle that had not been lost to the West. That was Abelard's specialty.

Christian Europe at the time, it seems fair to say, had need of a little work in logic. We have, for an example, the story of a bishop's interrogation in Orléans in 1022 of two heretics who had denied the virgin birth.[3] "Do you believe that you yourselves had human parents, or not?" the bishop asks. The two heretics acknowledge having such a belief. "If you believe that you were procreated by your parents when you did not exist before," the bishop says, "why do you refuse to believe that God was born of God without a mother before time and born of the Virgin by the shadow of the Holy Spirit within the limits of time?" The two heretics fail, somehow, to succumb to the force of this logic and are burned at the stake.

And then there is the example of Anselm, who became archbishop of Canterbury in Norman-ruled England in 1093. Anselm, a very religious man, became enamored with some of the tools of logic. "I do not attempt, O Lord, to penetrate Thy profundity, for I deem my intellect in no way sufficient thereunto," Anselm wrote. "But I desire to understand in some degree Thy truth."[4] In his search for that understanding, Anselm was prepared to apply logic to nothing less than the question of God's existence.

Anselm was not trying to *disprove* anything—far from it. In fact, his treatise examining whether God exists was, in a rather dramatic example of begging the question, addressed to God. Anselm just thought it ought to be possible to use the power of logic to prove what everybody knew was true anyway.

"We believe," he begins, "that Thou art a being than which nothing greater can be conceived." But this concept, Anselm ingeniously argues, "cannot exist in the understanding alone"; for a being that also exists "in reality" would be "greater" than one that exists only in the understanding. So in order to be "a being than which nothing greater can be conceived," such a being can't just be imagined; it would have to be real. Now we arrive at the logician's favorite word, "hence": "Hence, there is no doubt that there exists a being, than which nothing greater can be conceived, and it exists both in the understanding and in reality."

Ontology is the study of being. This is Anselm of Canterbury's famous "ontological proof" of the existence of God.[5] Anselm's rickety logic was attacked soon after it appeared. A monk named Gaunilo suggested that the same reasoning might be applied to our dream of an island more perfect than any other than can be conceived—without having "established the

existence of that island with any degree of certainty."[6] The church, however, was so impressed with his logic that Anselm is now Saint Anselm.

So, yes, there was room for a re-examination of the subject as Peter
Abelard began studying logic in Europe at the beginning of the twelfth
century. Abelard was, we are told, a charismatic character—handsome, a
skilled musician and poet, a jokester, extraordinarily sharp.[7] But he had
his own sense of right and wrong, and he took his logic seriously. Abelard
wasn't sufficiently foolhardy to challenge the virgin birth or Anselm's ontological proof, but this star teacher and logician—perhaps a best-of-the-
century intellect—was arrogant and not particularly prudent. Consider
what had happened in his personal life: Abelard had seduced a teenaged
student of his, named Heloise. The result was catastrophic: her uncle dis-
patched men to castrate him.

Abelard's scholarship was also incautious. He came to Paris specifically
to attend the lectures on logic of William of Champeaux, "who at the time
was," Abelard writes, "the supreme master of the subject."[8] Abelard quickly
stood out in the classroom, and student and teacher proceeded to establish
a lifelong relationship—a relationship similar to that Abelard would establish with other teachers. It was founded upon deep and abiding enmity.[9]

The issue upon which they fought, a fight that had many of the students
in and around Paris choosing sides, was the question of "universals"—the
categories in which we place things: men, goats, beautiful, good.[10] As Abelard explains in an autobiographical essay, William insisted that each of
the items in these universal categories (men, for example) is "essentially
the same," and that "variety" among them is only "due to multiplicity of
accidents." That provided Abelard with a fine target for his logical skills.[11]
He tells us little about his critique, but clearly it wasn't deferential. And it
likely was based on the difficulty of saying, for instance, that Socrates and
Caligula are "the same" because they both belong to the category men.

This philosophical dispute was not as esoteric at it may sound. William
was making a safe and very Catholic argument.[12] The idea that we—all
men and women—are "the same" is inherent, after all, in the concept of
original sin. The effort to fit behavior into the "universal" category good—
as defined presumably by God—also had quite a bit of importance for
Christians. In challenging universals, Abelard was making a not-so-safe,
not-so-obviously-Catholic, Aristotelian argument.

Abelard's best-known book, *Sic et Non* (*Yes and No*) was no *tour de
force* of logic—just an application of the law of contradiction. Abelard

simply lays out propositions upon which church fathers differ—157 of them. On the question of whether marriage is good, for example, he quotes Saint Augustine allowing that it might be and Saint Jerome arguing the negative.[13] He presents these arguments fairly. And the result is a compendium of places where Catholic doctrine contradicts itself—in the words not of heretics but of the most orthodox. Abelard never says that these contradictions cannot be reconciled, but he never reconciles them. This was obviously dangerous.

Abelard's career demonstrates that it was occasionally possible to stretch the bounds a little in medieval Europe. He managed to engage in some heated and important intellectual battles. He managed to publish some work that was, for the time, controversial and forward looking. Still, the atmosphere in which Abelard studied, wrote and taught remained enormously repressive. He must have been continually aware that a significant divergence from church doctrine could end his career, if not his life. And eventually, some combination of Abelard's arrogance, his fascination with Aristotle and his affection for reason did bring him into conflict with the church—in the person of Bernard of Clairvaux, a tremendously influential abbé, the future Saint Bernard.

Bernard made clear that he did not have much use for those who "called themselves philosophers"; in his view, he said, they "should rather be called slaves of curiosity and pride."[14] Bernard's conclusions about Abelard's teachings were harsh: "The faith of the simple is being ridiculed," he writes; "God's secrets are being torn out by the guts; questions about the highest things are being recklessly aired."[15]

At Bernard's instigation, Abelard was condemned by the pope as a heretic in 1140 and ordered to remain perpetually silent. After some sort of reconciliation with Bernard, this sentence was lifted, but Abelard never again appeared in public. He died in 1142 or 1144.

The word "modern" derives from a medieval Latin term whose implications were beginning to be debated in Abelard's day.[16] Over the centuries in Christian Europe a small, ragtag group of thinkers exploited, at great risk, what openings a monolithic, even totalitarian, but often clumsy and self-contradictory church provided. They began—slowly, almost imperceptibly—to break through the hegemony of the supernatural and nudge medieval Europe in the direction of the Renaissance, the Scientific Revolution and then the Enlightenment. It probably required arrogance. It certainly required an obsession with uncovering "a clear understanding." But these thinkers—Abelard among them—helped set Europe on a path that would eventually lead to what we think of as modern.

We have been speaking here, as historians usually speak, of publicly expressed ideas. Those are the ideas—presented in lectures, published in books—that can grow and develop, and engender even better ideas. Those are the ideas that, together with their descendants, occasionally end up overturning regimes, systems, even cultures. But there are times—times of great repression—when private thoughts remain ahead of these public ideas. Abelard's was one such time.

It's easier to stretch the bounds in private. You can't get burned at the stake for ideas you keep to yourself. You're unlikely to get punished for conclusions shared only with loved ones or trusted friends. In fact, around the hearth, under the covers, in the fields, over beers, free thought had probably never entirely left medieval Europe. The trick, for a historian, is finding ways to listen in.

The text has, fortuitously, survived of some private letters composed in twelfth-century France. They were written by a nun—in fact by the respected abbess at a convent near Paris[17]; they are addressed to her former lover; and they are shocking: "If Augustus, emperor of the whole world, thought fit to honor me with marriage, and conferred all the earth on me to possess forever, it would be dearer and more honorable to me to be called not his empress but your whore." This nun is declaring, to be clear, that she would be the "whore" not of Christ nor any other religious or allegorical figure but of a mortal man—a man, now himself a monk, with whom she had once had a torrid affair: "The sole possessor of my body and my will," she calls him. And this nun's thoughts about their affair are oddly devoid of repentance: "The pleasures of lovers which we shared have been too sweet," she writes "—they cannot displease me."

These letters were written in Abelard's day. In fact, they were written to Abelard by the woman—now grown—he had seduced, Heloise. They demonstrate, for our purposes, that an anacreontic rebellion against the strictures of religion was still possible—even in twelfth-century France, even for an abbess. They demonstrate the frailty of religion when confronted by love and sex at their mightiest.

Others in Christian Europe in the Middle Ages acknowledged the power of sex and the threat it might pose to religion. Here is Saint Anselm on the subject:

> This is one evil, an evil above all others, that I am aware is always with me, that grievously and piteously lacerates and afflicts my soul. It was with me from the cradle, it grew with me in childhood, in adolescence, in my youth and it always stuck to me, and it does not desert me even now that my limbs are failing because of my old age. This evil is sexual desire, carnal delight, the storm of lust that has smashed and battered my unhappy soul, drained it of all strength and left it weak and empty.[18]

Heloise, however, can't help remembering this inescapable "sexual desire" as having left her strong and full. She refuses to regret it. "How can it be called repentance for sins, however great the mortification of the flesh," Heloise asks (with Abelard's castration serving, presumably, as that "mortification of the flesh"), "if the mind still retains the will to sin and is on fire with its old desires?"

There is something particularly profound in this nun's, this abbess' insistence that feeling for another person—in the flesh—can be more compelling than feeling for an ethereal, incorporeal God. "I would have had no hesitation, God knows, in following you or going ahead at your bidding to the flames of Hell," Heloise writes to Abelard.

Heloise was not writing for public consumption. She was not a polemicist. I am not claiming that Heloise, who is comfortable with words such as "God" and "Hell," considered herself an atheist. But her letters demonstrate that some starkly anti-Christian notions could exist in a medieval mind, even in a convent, even in an abbess.

And implicit in Heloise's letters are two arguments of great significance for atheism—new versions of the anacreontic argument and new components of the positive case for life without God. The first argument is that love—an earthly, human, sexual love of the sort many of us have the privilege to feel—is more important than religion. The second argument is that *individuals*—"I" and "you"—are more important than some "universal" view of men and women, aiming for a "universal" goodness. Heloise had, after all, been Abelard's student as well as his lover.

In southwestern France two centuries after Heloise, we get to overhear the anti-religious thoughts not of an educated person but of a peasant. His name was Raymond de l'Aire. It is surprising to begin with that we know anything this man said. Raymond was almost undoubtedly illiterate; he worked the meadows and fields in a tiny town in the Pyrénées in the fourteenth century.[19] If it were not for a confluence of unusual circumstances, we would know as much of Raymond de l'Aire's opinions on religion as we know of the opinions on religion of almost all of the rest of Europe's peasants during the Middle Ages; we would know nothing. However, Raymond got caught up in the Inquisition as it was attempting to expunge an unrelated heresy. And that effort was run by a particularly diligent bishop who kept particularly meticulous records.[20] The French historian Emmanuel Le Roy Ladurie has studied those records.

But what is most surprising is what Raymond is reported to have said. At least one distinguished twentieth-century historian, Lucien Febvre, insists that "it is absurd and puerile" to imagine that individuals in sixteenth-century Europe achieved an "unbelief . . . in any way comparable to our own."[21] Yet Raymond de l'Aire, this peasant two centuries before the sixteenth century, managed to dismiss God as "nothing but this visible world around us." He insisted that, in Le Roy Ladurie's paraphrase, "heaven was when you were happy in this world, hell was when you were miserable, and that was all." As for the soul? It was, according to Raymond, just blood and, therefore, did not continue after death. In the village square one day, according to testimony against him, Raymond announced that Christ was created "through . . . rocking back and forth and fucking, in other words through the coitus of a man and a woman, just like all the rest of us."

Some of Raymond's whispered rejection of religion was based on a Commoro-like, how-can-this-be skepticism. Some was based on a while-life-is-yours, anacreontic rebellion against Christianity's devaluation of earthly life and its pleasures—a rebellion that Heloise might have understood. Was this "unbelief . . . in any way comparable to our own"? It may not have been as consistent or carefully reasoned. But the answer certainly seems to be, yes.

Was Raymond de l'Aire some sort of prodigy—an Enlightenment man somehow deposited four centuries early in the Pyrénées? Le Roy Ladurie, after pouring through all these records, is impressed with Raymond: "a peasant larger than life." And he does situate him "at the margin of local mentalities."[22] But the historian does not find Raymond's intelligence or his views that extraordinary.

Indeed, Le Roy Ladurie uncovers in the records of this Inquisition a catalog of irreligious as well as heretical views:[23] Some "rural freethinkers," as this historian puts it, "occasionally maintained that the whole Mass . . . was rubbish." One man standing near a bridge reassures another, who has heard that "the end of the world is near," by saying, "The world has neither beginning nor end," to which he adds, it presumably being late, "Let's go to bed." A man joking with a woman shows her his thumbs and says, "Shall we come to life again with this flesh and these bones? What an idea! I don't believe it." In front of a priest, an impoverished local nobleman insists that, in Le Roy Ladurie's paraphrase, "it was not God who watched over the harvest but nature alone."

Raymond's conclusion that "the soul is nothing but blood," according to testimony before the Inquisition, was borrowed from a local woman. And Raymond himself admits that a man with whom he was cutting a meadow first acquainted him with the idea that "God" is "nothing but what we see and hear." Interesting, indeed, the sorts of conversations an investigation can uncover among individuals cutting a meadow in fourteenth-century Christian Europe!

Was this area of southwestern France exceptionally irreligious?[24] It was the sort of place, Le Roy Ladurie tells us, where Mass was the main community event. But—with that odd inconsistency that seems to turn up in the Middle Ages, as in many ages—bounds were stretched even here: for Catholics were joined in church on Sunday by heretics and probably even by nonbelievers.

And in this church-going area in the Pyrénées, according to Le Roy Ladurie, "high amorous passions, or sometimes even ordinary ones, could break forth and have free reign."[25] By his calculations, a minimum of 10 percent of the population lived in sin, often openly, and many others took lovers.[26] Perhaps Raymond de l'Aire was therefore the product of an area where religion was worn more loosely. A more likely explanation would seem to be that peasants in Europe at the time—though it was supposed to be an intensely religious time—were simply more anacreontic and less consistently respectful of Christian morality than one might have thought.

The hold of religion in the villages Raymond knew may have been weakened by the fact that there were remnants of a heresy in the area: Catharism (which emphasized the battle of good and evil and espoused, as Puritans would, a strict moral purity). That offered the local peasants a good view of the "contestation," to use Le Roy Ladurie's word, between religions—and when religions contest, when they challenge each other's practices and mythologies, doubts can grow.[27]

The realization may also arrive, in such a circumstance, that others treat a different variety of religion with all the reverence and devotion with which you treat yours. That's the pathogen of relativism; it can begin to sap the strength of a religion, maybe even of religion; it can lead to skepticism. That realization was certainly available in Raymond de l'Aire's part of the Pyrénées. However, heresies—whether calling for renewed moral purity or fiddling with the relationship between Father, Son and Holy Ghost—were not uncommon in medieval Europe, and the contestation between different versions of Christianity became inescapable after the fifteenth century.

Raymond and his neighbors also had a good vantage point from which to observe clerical hypocrisy—another perennial stimulant to disbelief, another possible route to skepticism. They may not have known of popes with children, but Raymond would have known that a supposedly celibate Catholic priest in the area—Pierre Clergue—was the biggest rake in town. The transcript of this Inquisition connects this priest with about a dozen (mostly uncomplaining) women. The list of Pierre Clergue's mistresses, which is undoubtedly incomplete, includes a girl of fourteen or fifteen, whose mother approved of their relationship and, after the priest later found her a husband, whose husband approved. It includes the wife of one of his brothers and the local noblewoman, whom he wooed in confession and first made love to in his church. "You priests desire women more than other men do," she is quoted as concluding, in some awe.[28]

Le Roy Ladurie describes Raymond de l'Aire as an "uncompromising anti-cleric."[29] However, given the misbehavior and hypocrisy of so many Catholic clerics with regard to money and power as well as sex, anti-clericalism was not uncommon in the Middle Ages.

It is hard not to conclude that Raymond's area was unusual primarily in the fact that a bishop was interrogating peasants on their religious views and meticulously recording what they said. In fact, in other places where the views of common people were given such attention—usually for similarly repressive purposes—similar views turn up.

In England in 1448, for example, a man is reported to have held such extreme anti-religious views that a historian writing about him in 1965 cannot resist calling him "a lunatic." According to testimony before the Inquisition in Worchester, Thomas Semer, who probably had some education but was working as a tailor, denied the Trinity, Christ's divinity and the immortality of the soul, as well as the existence of heaven and hell.[30]

"It is problematic," writes another historian, Keith Thomas, about England in the sixteenth and seventeenth centuries, "whether certain sections of the population at this time had any religion at all." In 1573, Robert

Master of Kent was accused of heresy "for that he denieth that God made the sun, the moon, the earth, the water, and he denieth the resurrection of the dead." In 1600, the bishop of Exeter complained that "a matter very common to dispute" in his diocese was "whether there be a God or Not."[31]

So Raymond de l'Aire was not an exotic creature—a man out of place in his time. To the contrary: there likely were numerous Raymonds in these centuries in Christian Europe—concluding that life after death and virgin births did not make sense, while sewing clothes or working the fields. Again, it does not take book learning to deduce that Christ was created "through the coitus of a man and a woman, just like all the rest of us." You listen to the priests. You look around some on your own. You ask, *How can that be?*[32]

There also likely were numerous Heloises of all genders and sexual orientations—surrendering at least some of their attachment to religion as they experienced the power of romantic love. For, again, you don't have to be a philosopher to notice that sketchy tales of heavenly kingdoms cannot easily match the profundity of such a love.

Lucien Febvre cautions, in the strongest terms, against anachronisms, against placing modern ideas in premodern minds. He sees that as akin to arming the Roman god Mars with "a machine gun." Enlightenment-style disbelief, in Febvre's view, was simply impossible at a time when—"in what we call Europe and what was then Christendom"—"Christianity was the very air one breathed."[33] This is the time about which even so wise a critic of religion as John Stuart Mill states: "There was in those days an absolute and unquestioning completeness of belief."[34] However, both Febvre and Mill have underestimated the capacity of men and women—at any time and place, even such an intellectually stifling time and place—to scoff at religion.

They are certainly not always allowed to express it. And many generations of historians have overlooked it. But the puzzlement, the doubt, the skepticism, the incredulity, the disavowals, seem always to have been there—"at the margin of local mentalities," at the margin, perhaps, of many individual mentalities. Anacreontic rebellions also seem inevitable and inextinguishable. And a conclusion begins to force itself upon us: there has probably never been a human society that has sustained "an absolute and unquestioning completeness of belief." There likely has always been a certain level of what we might call *folk disbelief*.[35]

It didn't lead far, of course, in medieval Europe. These isolated men and women may have concluded that there was "nothing but this visible world," but they were not in a position to investigate the nature of that visible world further. Even a scholar like Abelard had to contend with, and was ultimately silenced by, a severe suspicion of scientific and philosophical thought. Advances in these areas would require the rediscovery in Christian Europe of an older, Greek and Roman tradition of appreciation for "the demonstrations of human reason." Although Raymond de l'Aire, working the meadows and fields in the Pyrénées, was not in a position to benefit from it, that rediscovery was already underway—slowly and only for the few with access to education.

The flow of ideas that would lead to the Renaissance began to swell after the year 1085, when Abelard was six. That's when Christians conquered the Islamic city of Toledo in what is now Spain. It was not, of course, anything the Christians, in the form of the kingdom of Castile, brought to that city; it was what they took away.

Christians, Muslims and Jews lived together peaceably in Toledo for a time. And, as the newly arrived Christians began nosing about the libraries of their neighbors, they discovered a series of Greek works (in Arabic translations) that from their perspective had not only been lost but were in some cases unknown. Among them were those books by Ptolemy, Archimedes and Euclid that Baghdad's scholars had access to and, perhaps of most value, those eight unfamiliar books by Aristotle.

It took a while for these books to be translated into Latin. The industrious translating enterprise run by the archbishop in Toledo beginning in 1130 produced uncensored Latin copies of many of them. Abelard, as a major Aristotle buff, probably knew that additional writings by Aristotle were being discovered and translated on the other side of the Pyrénées. However, Abelard died not that long after the translations in Toledo had begun, and he did not know Greek, let alone Arabic. There is no evidence that he ever read versions of any of these newly discovered works by Aristotle. We do know that a Latin version of previously unavailable writings by Aristotle, probably from Toledo, was seen by a former student of Abelard's in Paris. Meanwhile, new Greek manuscripts of Aristotle's work began turning up—some taken from Constantinople after it was conquered by the Crusaders in 1204. They were being translated elsewhere in Europe.[36]

After Europe's masters and students began organizing—unifying— themselves into "universities," obtaining an education required less travel than it had for Abelard. The curriculum at the University of

Paris—chartered in 1200, about a century after Abelard first arrived in Paris—was very much based on the newly translated classical works that were seeping into Christian Europe. Before going on to specialize in theology, medicine or law, students completed a Bachelor of Arts degree. To study the arts meant, increasingly, to study natural philosophy; and to study natural philosophy meant, almost exclusively, to read and ponder Aristotle—"The Philosopher," as he was now called—and his interpreters.

So it came as a shock when in 1210 a council of bishops ordered that "neither Aristotle's books of natural philosophy nor commentaries [on them] are to be read publicly or privately in Paris, and this under penalty of excommunication."[37] The bishops had decided—not without reason—that Aristotle and Christianity did not mix.

Aristotle was not quite an atheist. At the beginning of his cosmology he did see a need for a "First Cause" or "Unmoved Mover," responsible for getting everything going. However, his work posed a deep threat to religion in Christian Europe. "Beneath the learned conversational style lies a bedrock assumption," writes Richard E. Rubenstein in *Aristotle's Children*, an engaging account of Aristotle's return to Europe: "the notion that humans are, above all, thinking creatures, rational beings who, having discovered the truth, will accept it, and, having accepted it, will act upon it."[38] Most Catholics in these centuries, of course, saw humans as fallen and truth coming primarily from revelation and faith.

And there were specific points of conflict: the question of the age of the universe prominent among them. Aristotle argued that the universe was, save for that initial First Cause, eternal. That didn't leave much room for Genesis or Judgment Day. The historian Edward Grant suggests that this idea was as controversial in the thirteenth century as Copernicus' system was in the sixteenth and seventeenth centuries and Darwin's theory of evolution was in the nineteenth and twentieth centuries.[39] However, the larger problem may have been the old Greek's tireless insistence on the supremacy of reason—a direct challenge to the supremacy of faith. No wonder the bishops were concerned by his effect on schools in Paris.

But Aristotle's breathtakingly brilliant thought was not easy to ban. After his books were forbidden in 1210, the church had to condemn teachings loosely connected to The Philosopher again in Paris in 1215, 1270 and 1277.[40] Some of the ideas it was forbidden to hold—on pain of excommunication—had to do, not surprisingly, with the eternity of the universe.[41] Many of these forbidden notions are radical indeed.

The last of the twelve propositions condemned by the bishop of Paris in 1270 was: "That human actions are not ruled by divine Providence." And here are some others of the 219 beliefs that were prohibited in Paris by the bishop's 1277 list:

37. That nothing should be believed unless it is self-evident or could be asserted from things that are self-evident.

40. That there is no higher life than philosophical life.

133. That the soul is inseparable from the body. . . .

138. That there was no first man, nor will there be a last. . . .

153. That nothing is known better because of knowing theology.

172. That happiness is had in this life and not in another.[42]

Together these propositions undercut much of what was connected to belief in God at the time.

Was this sort of thing being formally taught at the University of Paris in 1277? The consensus is that no one would have dared. Then why bother to condemn these propositions? Probably because ideas like these were being expressed in private.[43] And the likelihood that such ideas were in circulation, even if only among students and faculty in a university town, is significant—in 1277, in the center of Catholic Europe, before the Renaissance had even begun to stir in Italy.

Thomas Aquinas, who spent time at the University of Paris when these matters were being contested, tried to reconcile Aristotle and Christianity. Thomas insisted that reason—mastery of which, typically, he attributed mostly to Aristotle—can help illuminate most matters of faith: Not that "God is Three and One"—"certain things that are true about God," Thomas states, "wholly surpass the capability of human reason." But the existence of God is an idea, he insists, "attainable by human reason."[44]

Thomas, a Dominican friar, outdid Anselm by reasoning out five logical proofs for the existence of God.[45] The first four are mostly variations on Aristotle's argument that there must have been an "Unmoved Mover" or "First Cause" to kick-start the universe.[46] This is known as the "cosmological argument" for the existence of God. Thomas' fifth proof is a version of the third traditional logical argument for the existence of God (with Anselm's "ontological argument"): the "teleological argument."[47] *Teleology* is a term for being directed toward a goal. Thomas' argument is based on the premise that all "things which lack intelligence, such as natural bodies, act for an end . . . as the arrow is shot to its mark by the archer. Therefore some intelligent being exists by whom all natural things are directed to their end; and this being we call God."

Such arguments, of course, lend themselves to rebuttal: What caused the "First Cause"? Why can't causes go back infinitely if time does? What is the evidence that things "act for an end"? But it wasn't flaws in his logic that got Thomas in trouble in his time. Like many theologians he faced a conundrum: Failing to provide reasoned arguments for religion risks making religion seem unreasonable. On the other hand, it is difficult to provide reasoned arguments for religion—of whatever merit—without making it seem as if religion requires reasoned arguments. Thomas' eagerness to buttress Christianity with Aristotelian logic was initially seen as implying that church authority is not enough. Some of Thomas' assertions, consequently, showed up among the 219 that were condemned in Paris in 1277—three years after he died at the age of 49.[48]

Nonetheless, if the Catholic Church were to retain any relationship with scholarship, it needed some sort of accommodation with Aristotle. Thomas' carefully wrought ideas on the subject wore well, and 49 years after his early death, Thomas Aquinas was canonized.

Saint Thomas' accommodations and Aristotle's thought both would harden into new dogmas—religions being prone to dogma formation. Still, reason had gained a beachhead in Christian Europe. Despite church control of medieval scholarship and medieval society, faith was beginning to lose its grip on some medieval minds.[49]

And then the Renaissance did begin to stir in Italy.

Perhaps no common person in these centuries has had his anti-religious speculations recorded with as much thoroughness as Domenico Scandella—an Italian miller, with a large family—known as Menocchio. The record was kept, once again, by the Inquisition and then examined by the Italian historian Carlo Ginzburg.[50]

Menocchio was born in 1532—a couple of centuries after Raymond de l'Aire. He spent his life in Montereale, a small hill town near the Friuli mountains, north of Venice. One reason we know so much about this miller's views is that, when it came to matters religious, Menocchio just couldn't shut up. All his neighbors understood that. He was popular enough—even serving a term as mayor—but meeting Menocchio meant getting an earful on Jesus, Mary, God and the origins of the universe.

"Everybody has his calling," one witness before the Inquisition recalls him saying, "some to plow, some to hoe, and I have mine, which is to blaspheme." Villagers heard Menocchio dismissing, on common-sense grounds, the virgin birth. They heard him denying that Christ was crucified. They reported his having described God, variously, as "the air," as (echoing Raymond) "everything that we see," as "nothing but a little breath, and whatever else man imagines him to be." They reported hearing him say, "We are gods."

After 30 years of this talk, a local priest, with whom he had been feuding, finally reported Menocchio to the Inquisition. And those assigned to interrogate him got an earful, too: in the end Menocchio was too excited by this chance to hold forth before an educated audience to watch his words.

Menocchio's judges were predictably shocked, not least by what they heard as atheism: "That on which all agree, and which no one has ever dared to deny," they wrote in their decision, "you dared when you foolishly said, 'God does not exist.'" Once again, however, this was not a consistent atheist: Menocchio's unique cosmology was not entirely devoid of supernatural elements.[51] Still this thoughtful but rambling miller probably was no less consistent as an atheist than his neighbors were as Catholics.

The Inquisition sentenced Menocchio to life in prison. After a few miserable years there, he managed to sound sufficiently penitent to be freed. However in 1599, when he was 67 years old and had been out of prison for thirteen years, Menocchio was arrested again. He had resumed regaling neighbors with conclusions such as: God "is nothing but air." Menocchio was tried and convicted again. "That recidivist . . . has revealed himself to be an atheist in his examinations," wrote a cardinal, who had been following the case. Menocchio was tortured in an unsuccessful attempt to force him to implicate others. He was then burned at the stake.

Menocchio was certainly a character: like Raymond de l'Aire he probably existed "at the margin of local mentalities." And local mentalities in the Friuli region were perhaps relatively conducive to challenges to authority: decades before Menocchio was born peasants in the area had rebelled, with considerable bloodshed, against the nobility. But small towns did have their characters. And rebellious areas in Europe were not that uncommon. At the margins of plenty of other local mentalities there must have been Menocchios whose thoughts, in the absence of an intervention by the Inquisition, were not recorded.

Indeed, in Italy in the sixteenth century it was becoming easier to be a critic of religion. Menocchio had, in this regard, some significant advantages over Raymond de l'Aire. His was not just folk disbelief. He probably possessed the equivalent of an elementary school education and could, therefore, manage to read and write in the vernacular. Moreover, in the interim between Raymond and Menocchio the letterpress had been invented. It was no longer necessary to travel to various monasteries to search out manuscripts. Even a miller like Menocchio could buy books—in Venice, a couple of day's walk from his town.[52] Menocchio didn't own many books, but they were precious to him. He and his friends exchanged copies. In testimony before the Inquisition Menocchio alludes to eleven books and probably was hiding his familiarity with others.

Proximity to the university town of Padua and to Venice, one the most sophisticated cities in Europe in the sixteenth century, also meant that there weren't that many degrees of separation between Menocchio and some of the most challenging ideas of his day—Italy being at the forefront of the recovery of classical learning during the Renaissance. "Something happened in the Renaissance," writes the cultural historian Stephen Greenblatt, "something that surged up against the constraints that centuries had constructed around curiosity, desire, individuality, sustained attention to the material world, the claims of the body."[53] That something was happening in Italy.

"Most of my friends are so well educated they can scarcely believe God exists," one exile from Italy reports having heard someone say.[54] That education could now include in Italy in the sixteenth century, in addition to Aristotle, numerous other decidedly un-Christian classical works: Cicero's shockingly personal and human letters; Lucretius' naturalistic poem, featuring Epicurus' anacreontic philosophy; and, to switch media, the proud, human-scale handsomeness of Greek sculpture. Humanism, stirring to life in Italy in the fourteenth century, did not abandon God, but, following the Greeks and Romans, it restored faith in humans—in their capacity to reason, in their beauty, in their dignity. This, too, did not square easily with Catholicism and its emphasis on humankind's fallen state.

In Florence in the first decades of the sixteenth century, a man who had copied by hand all of Lucretius' poem produced a guide to political scheming.[55] Niccolo Machiavelli's book, *The Prince*, also fit uncomfortably with true belief. For it included two radical and interlocking assumptions:

the first was that religion could be *used*. Machiavelli mentions some attributes that might be ascribed to a ruler: "merciful, faithful, humane, honest, and religious"; then he writes, "It is not necessary for a prince to have all the above-mentioned qualities, but it is very necessary to appear to have them." And the last of those qualities—"religious"—was, in Machiavelli's view, the most important for the prince to, if necessary, feign.[56] Implicit in that piece of advice is the second radical assumption: something possesses more value than sincere religion. Among the words Machiavelli uses for that higher virtue are: "esteem," "admiration," "fame" and "glory."[57] Heloise had placed her love for Abelard—an individual's love for another individual—above religion. Now Machiavelli had—shockingly, openly, in print—raised individual worldly glory to that level.

A learning less encumbered by religion—even uninterested in religion—was beginning to accumulate and accelerate. And this learning was not just restricted to classically minded humanists or would-be advisors to princes. It could be found—if only between the lines—in books.

The historian Nicholas Davidson has come up with many others who subscribed, according to various written records, to irreligious notions in Italy in the sixteenth century.[58] Some examples:

- Francesco Calcagno, a Franciscan friar, who was accused by the Inquisition in 1550 of having said "that God does not exist, nor the soul." Calcagno is said to have added, before he was sentenced to death, "that he would rather worship a pretty little boy in the flesh than God."
- Pietro Strozzi, a soldier and a mathematician from Florence, who picked, in 1558, both the easiest occasion (because he was finally safe from the Inquisition) and the most difficult (because the most seemed at stake) to reject both God and immortality: his death bed.
- Commodo Canuove of Vicenza, who was denounced in 1574 for arguing: "We have never seen any dead man who has returned from the other world to tell us that paradise exists—or purgatory or hell; all these things are the fantasies of friars and priests."
- Matteo de Vincenti, a turner in Venice, who proclaimed after a sermon on the Eucharist in 1576: "It's nonsense having to believe these things—they're stories. I would rather believe I had money in my pocket."

- Alvise Capuano, born in Lesina, who was imprisoned by the Inquisition in 1580 for insisting "that the world was created by chance" and "that when the body dies the soul dies also."
- Pomponio Rustico, executed in Rome in 1587, for stating: "The stories described in the Bible . . . are worthy only of derision."

We can *assume* there were many others whose love, like that of Heloise, was stronger than their religion in twelfth-century Europe. We can *hypothesize* that there were many other freethinking peasants like Raymond de l'Aire scattered across Europe in the fourteenth century. We *know* there were many like Menocchio in Italy in the sixteenth century. We would know of more such Renaissance nonbelievers, of course, but in Europe at this time a public deviation from orthodoxy—large or slight—could still result in a prosecution, as it did for Menocchio and most of the individuals on the above list.

In Spain at the end of the fifteenth century and into the sixteenth—to pick one of history's most outrageous examples—crowds would fill the streets for an *auto-da-fé*, or "act of faith," after which convicted heretics would be set on fire. (Many were former Jews who had converted after Spain's Jews had been expelled in 1492 but whose conversions had proven unconvincing.) The number of persons burned at the stake by the Spanish Inquisition at its height was in the thousands, perhaps the tens of thousands.[59] And in Europe in these centuries the heresy could hinge on the placement of a few words. And Catholics were not the only ones setting the fires.

Michael Servetus, a physician who had contributed to the understanding of pulmonary circulation, believed that Christ, as the Son of God, arrived after God. This was a decidedly unorthodox position in an old and charged debate. Servetus escaped the Catholic Inquisition but was tried by the Calvinists. On the way to the stake in Geneva on October 27, 1553, Servetus is said to have repeatedly cried, "O Jesus, Son of the Eternal God, have mercy on me!" Had he instead addressed the Savior as, "Jesus, the Eternal Son of God," he might have been pardoned.[60] Green wood was used to prolong Michael Servetus' agony.

So, yes, most irreligious thoughts undoubtedly, and wisely, continued to remain unexpressed, even during the Renaissance. Few were as reckless as Menocchio or others on the above list of Italian nonbelievers. Nonetheless, the rediscovery of classical Greek and Roman books and art was supporting, encouraging and even creating atheism. Indeed, at some point in the sixteenth century word had begun to spread of "a little book," entitled *The Three Impostors*, that dared assert that "Lord Jesus, Moses and Mohammed" were all fakes.[61]

The anonymous author of this Latin treatise was, naturally, reviled: "that villain and secretary of Hell," an English doctor labeled him in the next century.[62] Nonetheless, a selection of individuals seemed particularly intent on obtaining a copy, in order to refute the vile work or, possibly, for other purposes.[63]

The book proved difficult to locate—probably because it did not exist.[64] Still, the fact that someone could be imagined to have written a tract arguing against religion, however phantasmal, is in itself evidence that atheism was beginning to be taken seriously.

Among the most influential of the classical authors being rediscovered in Renaissance Europe was a Skeptic, a generation younger than Lucian: Sextus Empiricus. His books, written in Greek, first reappeared in Latin translations in Paris in 1562. The historian of ideas, Richard Popkin, has traced the impact of the Skepticism reintroduced by the rediscovery of Sextus Empiricus upon a succession of European thinkers in the sixteenth and seventeenth centuries. It hit Montaigne, for example, hard: this French essayist carved quotes from Sextus Empiricus into the rafters of his study.[65]

The main philosophic presence in this Roman Skeptic's books was the Greek Skeptic Pyrrho, whose saying was, "No more this than that"—one thing, in other words, is no more true or even important than another.[66] Pyrrho believed, consequently, that "we should be . . . without judgments, inclining neither this way nor that."[67] This sweeping Skepticism wasn't necessarily a threat to Christianity—in fact, because it seemed to point to the limits of judgments, of reason, it could be seen as throwing humankind back on faith.

Pyrrhonism "shows us," Montaigne writes, "man stripped of all human learning and so all the more able to lodge the divine within him, annihilating his intellect to make room for faith."[68] This justification for religion is called, "fideism"—the belief in faith as compensation for the failure of human reason, a belief that the failure of human reason is even necessary for the full experience of faith. "Weakness of judgment helps us more than strength; blindness, more than clarity of vision," Montaigne writes. "We become learned in God's wisdom more by ignorance than by knowledge."[69]

But Sextus Empiricus' books also reintroduced Europe to the Academic Skeptic, Carneades—a philosopher whose impact upon the movement of thought celebrated in this book is as great as anyone's. Carneades agreed that nothing could be proven absolutely true, but, unlike Pyrrho, he found some conclusions to be more "plausible" than others.[70] So, for Academic Skepticism some forms of "judgment" *were* possible. Figuring out plausibility *required* reason. It required, in particular, an understanding of the natural world.

A distant cousin of Montaigne's, Francisco Sanches, was another sixteenth-century thinker whose thought was transformed by Sextus Empiricus. Sanches was born to two Catholics from Spain or Portugal— forcibly converted Jews probably—who had moved to France when he was 11. In 1576, Sanches, a physician and philosopher, composed a classic work of Skepticism of his own, under a classically skeptical title: *That Nothing Is Known.* It begins with a bit of cleverness in regards to its title: "If I come to *know* how to establish this, I shall be justified in drawing the conclusion that nothing is known; whereas if I *do not know* how to establish it, then all the more so—for that is what I claimed."[71]

Sanches, however, was not a "no-more-this-than-that" Pyrrhonian. He inclined toward Carneades' Academic Skepticism. That is evident in the *nom de plume* Sanches adopted for a letter spelling out some of his philosophic views: *Carneades Philosophus.*[72] So, while he thought the search for "perfect" knowledge was hopeless, Sanches did think some sorts of tentative understandings or judgments were still possible and might be good enough. "Tell me if you have seen anything in Nature that is *perfect*?" Sanches asks in his book.[73] Sanches, like Carneades, thought we might content ourselves with the "plausible."

This kind of skepticism, unlike Montaigne's, has practical implications. And this kind of skepticism tends to target superstition. Sanches wrote a 40-page, Lucretius-like poem devoted to the much-discussed comet of 1577.[74] His purpose: to mock the host of dire, astrologically based predictions—of wars, floods, famines, plagues, fires, droughts—that greeted the comet's appearance. He was playing, in other words, a role not unlike that of Thucydides, as he debunked superstitious responses to that plague in Athens. When nonbelievers ally themselves with skepticism today, this sort of critique is usually what they mean: a questioning of too easy, implausible inferences, particularly of the supernatural variety. As a standard of evaluation, plausibility is not at all kind to religion.

But how do we determine which of our inferences—about the behavior of comets and stars, about the nature of earth and its inhabitants—are "plausible"? Carneades suggested a process whereby necessarily imperfect understandings are tested and then either "controverted" or left "uncontroverted." Here is one of his examples, according to Sextus Empiricus, of that process at work: You walk into a dark shed and vaguely make out something coiled in the corner. It is *plausible* to jump back because you think that might be a snake.[75] But wait, it didn't move when you entered or jumped. It doesn't move when you conduct a test: when you poke it with a stick. Your original conclusion has been "controverted." It still could be a snake—perhaps a sick one. You can't yet be absolutely sure, but you can make a judgment. It is now *implausible* that it is a snake. It is probably just a rope.

Sanches had some ideas of his own to contribute to this process. In a book written in 1576 he previewed a "*method of knowing*" he was working on. This method, he promised, would be outlined in a future work to be called *Methodus sciendi*. If that book was written, it has not survived.[76] Still, in discussing this proposed volume, Francisco Sanches—under the influence of Academic Skepticism—was the first person to use the term "scientific method."[77]

Sanches probably did not specifically introduce the hypothesis-experiment two-step that is currently taught in high school under this name.[78] But isn't that implicit in Carneades' testing and retesting of imperfect understandings? It is probably a snake; wait, it didn't move, even when I touched it with a stick, so it is probably not a snake. Heavy bodies fall faster than lighter bodies; no, it seems they do not.

And in attempting to understand the natural world, Sanches did champion a method that included observation, experience, evidence, experimentation, reason and the search for facts.[79] That these techniques would be involved in any effort to understand the world may now seem obvious. It wasn't then, when the word of revered authorities was so often assumed by Sanches' contemporaries to provide the surest guide. "They deliver judgment against X or Y," Sanches explains in his book *That Nothing Is Known*, "not by showing that the *facts* are thus or thus, but that 'such is the opinion of Aristotle.'"[80]

The "opinion" of the Bible and other divinely inspired authorities was, of course, even more likely to override the facts in sixteenth-century

Europe, but had Sanches criticized them, his writings would have been not only controversial but foolhardy. As it was his name ended up on a couple of seventeenth-century lists of dangerous enemies of Christianity.

Still, Sanches' method would eventually triumph. Observation, experience, evidence, experimentation, reason and the search for facts had often guided the Greeks in their efforts to understand the natural world. Now they were back. And they would be, of course, at the heart of the effort Galileo, Newton and others would make in the next century to revitalize understanding of the natural world. These scientists were very much in the business of testing, of determining what could or could not be "controverted," of determining what was "plausible."

The folk disbelief of Heloise and Raymond de l'Aire may not have contributed much, but forms of disbelief were arriving that did. They emphasized natural explanations and would lead to science, enlightenment and revolution. Together these sparks and flares in an otherwise dark age would help set off, in succeeding centuries, magnificent explosions of knowledge.

5

HOW HEAVEN GOES

DISBELIEF AND SCIENCE IN THE
SEVENTEENTH CENTURY

The scientific spirit brings about a particular attitude towards worldly matters; before religious matters it pauses for a little, hesitates and finally there too crosses the threshold. In this process there is no stopping.

—Sigmund Freud[1]

WAS GALILEO GALILEI AWARE OF FRANCISCO SANCHES, WHO coined the term "scientific method" while Galileo was a student? I've found no proof that he was. But Galileo did share Sanches' awareness of the need to test and retest theories about the earth and the heavens. He shared Sanches' view of the importance of observation, experience, evidence, experimentation, reason and the search for facts. And Galileo definitely shared Sanches' conviction that the authority of ancient texts, even the authority of Aristotle, was no substitute for such efforts. Indeed, it was Galileo's use of such methods to raise questions about a view of the heavens supported by biblical authority—as well as by Aristotle—that caused all his troubles.

Galileo certainly was aware of another revolutionary sixteenth-century thinker with an inclination toward science and astronomy.[2] Among Galileo's greatest contributions, of course, was his deployment of observation, evidence, experimentation and reason to test and confirm Copernicus' conclusion that when the sun moves across the sky it is because the earth is moving.

The prosecutions Galileo would then endure will not be the only examples in this chapter of how difficult it was for science to overcome religious strictures in Europe, but they are the classic example. Those strictures began to ease and science began to progress in the seventeenth century. That is one subject of this chapter; but the chapter's main concern is the complex but productive partnership science and disbelief thereby established in seventeenth-century Europe.

Nicolaus Copernicus had worked out his heliocentric theory by 1514. Copernicus—a physician, financier, astronomer and churchman who spent most of his life in Poland—had probably studied astronomy and Greek in Italy. His theory had some Greek antecedents but, as European science in general was getting ready to do, that theory moved well beyond them.[3] And it sounded, no doubt, ridiculous.[4] For Copernicus' theory implied that our senses are not sharp enough to notice that the ground upon which we stand is spinning and sailing. It implied, again contrary to the look of things, that bodies in the twinkly bright heavens are composed of more or less the same stuff as the stolid, dusky earth. It implied, less obviously, that the planet Venus should have phases similar to those of the moon, although no one had ever seen evidence of such phases. It even contradicted Aristotle, who was a sun-circles-the-earth guy.

Moreover—and Copernicus certainly understood the significance of this—his conception of the universe challenged such biblical pronouncements as, "The world is established, so that it cannot be moved"; not to mention that report in the book of Joshua that "the sun stood still," which wouldn't make much sense if it had not been moving across the sky in the first place.[5] Worse, in displacing the earth from the center of all existence, Copernicus' idea threatened to displace men and women from the center of God's plan. It was undeniably inconvenient for religion.

"This fool wishes to reverse the entire science of astronomy," Martin Luther sneered, after hearing an early report on Copernicus' theory.[6] The reception would prove no more enthusiastic on the other side of the Reformation. The cautious Copernicus, a Catholic, agreed to publish what he had come up with only after he was nearing death. *On the Revolutions of the Celestial Orbits* is said to have been handed to him shortly before he died in 1543.[7] To make sure that "this opinion may not creep any further to the prejudice of Catholic truth," publication of Copernicus' book was eventually "suspended" by the Catholic Church so that the book could be "corrected."[8] Publication of the book was not suspended, however, until three-quarters of a century after it first had appeared. It took that long for Copernicus' ideas to begin to have a significant impact. That impact owed a lot to Galileo.[9]

Galileo had some initial hesitations about Copernicus' theory.[10] But when he began testing, the results of his experiments on the motion of bodies turned out to fit Copernicus' scheme quite nicely. Then, after hearing that a Dutch spectacles maker had used lenses to make far objects appear closer, Galileo fashioned a telescope of his own and started observing the heavens—as no human had observed them before.[11]

A number of facts—supporting Copernicus' theory, controverting prevailing views of the heavens—quickly revealed themselves: The moon turned out to look as if it might very well be made of the same stuff as the earth. Venus did indeed display phases like those of the moon. After Galileo's telescope revealed that Jupiter had its own little family of satellites and that the sun (which, he observed, sometimes wears spots) itself rotated,[12] the matter was more or less settled, and Galileo was presented with one large inconvenient fact: Copernicus was right; church doctrine was wrong. All Galileo had to do—for the rest of his life—was pretend this wasn't true.

Meek acquiescence was not prominent among Galileo's many and considerable talents. When, in 1613, his sympathy with Copernicus' view began to be bruited about, he wrote a private letter explaining himself in which he maintained "that the Holy Scripture can never lie or err."[13] This was prudent. But Galileo then suggested that "some of its interpreters and expositors can sometimes err in various ways." This was not so prudent. Galileo next presented a complex and perhaps too clever argument designed to show that the stopping of the sun in response to Joshua's prayer would make more sense in a Copernican system (though then it would really be the stopping of the rotation of the earth). This proved anything but prudent.

Galileo's private letter soon became public. The Inquisition in Rome began an investigation. A committee organized by the church concluded that the "proposition" that the earth, not the sun, did the moving "is foolish and absurd in philosophy, and formally heretical since it explicitly contradicts in many places the sense of Holy Scripture." Galileo, who had powerful patrons, escaped with a warning: stop defending this "heretical" notion.[14]

And he did hold his tongue, for a long while.

Religion clearly could still manage to get in the way of progress in Europe in the seventeenth century. In defending himself, Galileo had quoted an impressive line from a cardinal, Cesare Baronio: "that the intention of the Holy Spirit is to teach us how one goes to heaven and not how heaven goes."[15] However, there were problems—at least from a twenty-first-century perspective—even when religion stuck to moral instruction.

Europeans, for example, were shipping 10,000 African slaves across the Atlantic every year by 1650; by 1714 that number had reached 40,000.[16] Christianity had accepted the humanity of slaves—a step forward; but it also accepted slavery. Indeed, in the New Testament Paul writes: "Let all who are under a yoke as slaves regard their own masters as worthy of all honor."[17]

Women had little power and few rights in Europe and its colonies—an injustice older than any particular religion, to be sure. But Paul's decree in the New Testament that the proper attitude for a woman is "subjection" did not help, nor did Martin Luther's statement that "women are created for no other purpose than to serve men."[18] Divorce was illegal in Catholic countries but also nearly impossible where Protestantism dominated. Here the authority, according to the Gospels, was Jesus Himself: "The man who marries a divorced woman commits adultery."[19] Homosexuality was prohibited. The Massachusetts Bay colony simply transferred a line from the Hebrew Bible into its laws: "If any man lieth with mankind as he lieth with a woman, both of them have committed abomination, they both shall surely be put to death."[20]

Judging behaviors in other times by the standards of our time can be unfair, but there is an argument to be made here. The argument is that religions—whatever good they may have done—often keep ancient, narrow-minded convictions, precepts and prejudices alive well past their time. And religions can get awfully touchy about challenges to their beliefs.

A conflicting interpretation of Christianity—or even the rumor of such a heresy—could still lead to the stake in the seventeenth century, as it had for Michael Servetus in the sixteenth. A conflicting interpretation of Christianity, widely enough held, could lead to war; indeed, in Europe in the seventeenth century it led to one particularly devastating and long (thirty years) war, in which Catholics and Protestants had it out. And since the doctrines of these denominations were detailed and far-reaching, it was frighteningly easy to come into conflict with an interpretation of Christianity—as Galileo found out.

Ancient, narrow-minded convictions, precepts and prejudices, kept alive past their time, can certainly cause conflicts with science. For, despite that statement from Cardinal Baronio, the Christian religion in Europe in the seventeenth century was not in fact particularly reticent on the subject of "how heaven goes." Christianity insisted that we imagine in the heavens an omnipotent, omniscient, omnipresent Being, who created everything, without Himself having been created, who managed everything and who could, should He so desire, suspend all the rules of nature and change anything—including the progress across the sky of the sun. Indeed, it is hard to come up with a version of this religion, or any other, that does not assert that something miraculous has happened somewhere in the heavens or here on earth. Science, therefore, has often threatened religion—and vice versa.

In 1632, about sixteen years after he was warned not to defend his "heretical" notion, Galileo published a book, *Dialogue on the Two Chief World Systems,* in which he was bold enough to discuss the Copernican system— only as a theory, to be sure, with its pluses and minuses, and those of the traditional view, noted. The problem was that figuring out which side the author thought had more pluses and fewer minuses wasn't all that difficult. The problem, in other words, was that Galileo's presentation of the idea that the earth moves struck some suspicious readers as not so hypothetical.

Galileo had been engaging in something that would be common in these centuries: a complex dance of veils designed to hint at but not conclusively reveal the extent to which he was convinced by the heretical theory. But the veils had slipped. Too much had been revealed. The Florentine scientist had been careful to secure written permission to publish this book from church officials in Florence and Rome.[21] That proved not to be protection enough.

Galileo, by then 68 years old, was ordered to come to Rome to stand trial.[22] "I do not hold this opinion of Copernicus," he proclaimed, under threat of torture.[23] But just to make sure, this great scientist was forced to "abjure, curse, and detest the above-mentioned" error and heresy. And, since it looked as if he had at the very least wandered awfully close to this error and heresy, Galileo was sentenced to live under a (loose) form of house arrest for the rest of his life. His book, of course, was banned.

In his "Abjuration," Galileo also had to "swear that I have always believed, I believe now, and with God's help I will believe in the future, all that the Holy Catholic and Apostolic Church holds, preaches and teaches."[24]

Galileo had been forced to accept a means of determining truth that may qualify as the exact opposite of the scientific method: the pronouncements of authority.

Nonetheless, the slight, barely perceptible questioning of religion that had begun in Europe was becoming more perceptible in the seventeenth century. Atheism was certainly not tolerated, but atheistic ideas were beginning to be expressed. If you succumbed to the urge to say them out loud—in a play for example—the trick was to make sure those atheistic ideas were quickly and loudly rebutted or overwhelmed by pious sentiments. Shakespeare, born the same year as Galileo, was among those light-footed enough to pull that off. Hamlet goes so far as to question the immortality of the soul while trying to get his mind around that befuddling state "not to be": is it simply "to sleep; no more"? However, before the end of this soliloquy "the dread of something after death" has been, as it had to have been, restored.[25]

More consistent nonbelievers did appear on stage, such as Edmund in *King Lear* who declares that "Nature, art my goddess; to thy law my services are bound"[26]—thus announcing his disdain for more traditional deities. Such characters had to be—as Edmund certainly is—evil; they had to be vanquished; and, before dying, they had to admit they were wrong. Edmund dies at the hand of the brother he cheated, after accepting that brother's conclusion that "the Gods are just."[27]

Not everyone succeeded in getting the mix of transgression, retribution and contrition right. In his *Don Juan,* first performed in 1665, Molière has his protagonist respond to the question of whether he believes in God, with (in his interlocutor's paraphrase) a short, shocking word: "No."[28] Molière's Don Juan—the most caddish of anacreontics—does get his due at the end: he is pummeled by bolts of lightning then swallowed by the underworld. But perhaps the punishment was a little too cartoonish, the heresy a little too brash. Certainly, the mea culpa was hard to locate. "Is there a school of atheism more undisguised?" a prince fumed after seeing Molière's play.[29] Molière had to withdraw *Don Juan* after only fifteen performances. There is no evidence his version was performed again in that century or the next.[30]

Thinkers interested in airing irreligious ideas faced the same challenge and undertook at least as great a risk. Giulio Cesare Vanini's brashness was apparent in his given names, which he had borrowed from an accomplished

Roman and given himself. Vanini was a scholar who had taught all across Europe. But the two books he wrote seemed surprisingly enthusiastic in their presentation of a critique of religion, surprisingly tepid, even ironic, in the de rigueur rebuttal of that critique. Vanini, too, had allowed the veils to slip. Indeed, he was among the many writers suspected of having authored that unveiled but phantom attack on religion, *The Three Impostors.*

Vanini was arrested by the Inquisition in 1618 in Toulouse, where he had been living under an assumed name. A six-month investigation followed, after which the Parlement of Toulouse found him guilty of "atheism, blasphemies, impieties and other crimes."[31] According to an account written close to the event, Vanini is reported to have greeted the day of his execution by commenting, "Come along, let's die cheerfully as a philosopher."[32] That contemporary account has him responding to the question of whether he would beg God for mercy by stating:

> There is neither God nor devil. For if there were a God, I would pray him to launch a thunderbolt on the wholly unjust and iniquitous Parlement here; and if there were a devil, I would pray him to swallow it up in the realm below. But because neither one nor the other exists, I will do nothing.

On February 9, 1619, Giulio Cesare Vanini, then 34, was outfitted with a placard reading, "Atheist and blasphemer of the name of God." His tongue was cut out. He was strangled. His body was burnt. His ashes were thrown to the winds.

Other more cautious thinkers were able to push forward the argument against religion in the seventeenth century and still die a natural death. Thomas Hobbes was born in England a few years after Vanini. To get some idea of what many of his contemporaries thought of Hobbes, it is best to meet him where they thought he would end up: in hell.

Hell, as might be expected, provides Hobbes with much opportunity for regret, as he informs us in a book someone published a few decades after his death in 1679. "I am," moans Hobbes' shade, "one of the most wretched persons in all these sooty territories."[33] Life in hell turns out to resemble being perpetually burned at the stake—but worse. "The fire that we endure ten times exceeds all culinary fire in fierceness," the deceased Hobbes reports. According to that book, he has figured out—"though . . . too late to do me any good"—that his conclusion on religion was wrong. "Now I know there is a God; but O! I wish there were not!—for I am sure

He will have no mercy on me, nor is there any reason that He should. I do confess that I was His foe on earth, and now He is mine in hell."

What Hobbes actually concluded about religion is a matter of some dispute. In his writing he dutifully acknowledged God and the Resurrection but still managed to introduce a strict materialism—a materialism that did not seem to allow much room for immaterial beings or supernatural doings.[34] And in his major work, *Leviathan*, published in 1651, Hobbes characterized the state, not the church, as the "leviathan"—which struck many of Hobbes' contemporaries as an outrageous demotion of religion.

In that book, Hobbes' readings of the Bible are mostly respectful, and he ends up concluding—as a man of faith would—that there is no "reason to doubt but that the Old and New Testament, as we have them now, are the true registers of those things which were done and said by the prophets and apostles."[35] But he does examine accounts of some of the miracles discussed therein with an intensity that might well have discomfited less finicky readers of the Bible.[36] Hobbes is, for example, among the first to question in print whether the "five Books of Moses" could have been written by Moses, since, among other problems, they report that the location of the tomb of Moses has been forgotten.[37]

Was Thomas Hobbes a religious man with some modern ideas or was he a nonbeliever who tossed in the occasional "our blessed Savior Jesus Christ" so as not to end up like Vanini?[38] Many of his contemporaries were convinced it was the latter.

In fact, Hobbes was so often reviled as an atheist in his time that God's anger toward this one Englishman was suspected of being the cause of the plague in London in 1665 and of the Great Fire, which destroyed four-fifths of that city, the next year. In 1666, in its efforts to defend the public against more such catastrophes, an ever-vigilant Parliament considered a bill against "Atheism and Profanity" and undertook an investigation, for "atheism, blaspheme or profaneness," of "the book of Mr. Hobbs [sic] called *The Leviathan*."[39]

Nonetheless, Hobbes not only kept himself out of court and his neck out of the noose but continued to move in the best society. He even socialized with King Charles II, who found his conversation stimulating and granted him a pension.[40] His connections undoubtedly helped, but Hobbes also showed some talent at this dance of veils. If he was an antagonist of religion, he never quite revealed it. Despite his many critics, including critics in Parliament, Hobbes died a free man—at the age of 91.

We don't know whether Hobbes had an afterlife. We do know that his ideas did. Hobbes was helping create a vocabulary for criticism of religion, and Hobbes was read and still is. However, despite his materialism, his demotion of the church and his textual critique of the Bible, Hobbes was probably not the seventeenth-century philosopher who did the most to weaken religion.

On July 27, 1656, a proclamation was read in a synagogue in Amsterdam[41]: "By decree of the angels and by the command of the holy men, we excommunicate, expel, curse and damn Baruch de Espinoza," it stated. " . . . Cursed be he by day and cursed be he by night . . . and the Lord shall blot out his name from under heaven." The subject of this decree—a 23-year-old man from a good Jewish family—was accused of "evil opinions and acts," of "abominable heresies" and "monstrous deeds," which, although not specified, were said to have been "long known."

No evidence has survived explaining exactly what those "evil opinions" and "monstrous deeds" were, but we can guess that they had something to do with the philosophic ideas that would later appear in books by this man, better known as Spinoza. Others were expelled from the Jewish community in Amsterdam in those years (40 over a period of 61 years, by one count) but no one, according to one of Spinoza's biographers, with such "vehemence and fury."[42]

There would be enough in Spinoza's ideas, once he began writing them down, to offend at the time not only most of his fellow Jews but most Christians. Indeed, Europeans of all persuasions refrained from publicly admitting to being partisans of Spinoza for at least a century after Spinoza. (Even Denis Diderot, though pretty clearly influenced by Spinoza, rarely mentions him in his books.[43]) Labeling individuals "Spinozists" was, for all those years, a sure way of dismissing them as radically and dangerously impious.[44] How impious—whether a Spinozist should be distinguished from an atheist, whether Spinoza himself might qualify as an atheist—was, and remains, a matter of dispute.

In the years after Spinoza's expulsion from Amsterdam's Jewish community, he began working on some books—treatises—that laid out his ideas on the relationship between, as he put it, religion and philosophy. They were rife with anti-religious statements. Here is one of the boldest of them: "That nature cannot be contravened but that she preserves a fixed and immutable order."[45]

So when the Bible reports that "the sun stood still" in response to Joshua's prayer, as the Israelites are conquering the promised land,[46] nature, asserts Spinoza, has not been "contravened"; rather Joshua—not being "a competent astronomer"—has simply missed a natural explanation for the fact that the day seemed longer.[47] In case the implication of this tenet for the various other miracles claimed by the Jewish and Christian religions is not sufficiently clear, Spinoza spells it out: "Hence we cannot doubt that many things are narrated in Scripture as miracles of which the causes could easily be explained by reference to ascertained workings of nature."[48]

Many things including Moses' alleged parting of the Red Sea? Yes, Spinoza suggests that this might have had much to do with "a strong east wind, which blew all night."[49] Many things even including that most significant of miracles for Europeans at the time: the resurrection of Christ? Spinoza does not dare tackle that one in a book, but in a letter he makes clear that in his view "nature" avoided being "contravened" by such a reversal of death because it simply did not happen. "I accept Christ's passion, death and burial literally . . . ," Spinoza writes, "but his resurrection allegorically."[50] Do all recourses to the supernatural by religion fall among the many things that can be explained by "workings of nature"? That seems a fair conclusion to draw from the argument in Spinoza's book, *Tractatus Theologico-politicus*.

Along with rejecting the possibility of miracles, Spinoza undertakes a long—and equally skeptical—investigation of the value of prophecy: "We infer," he concludes, "that we are never to look to the prophets for information either on natural or spiritual subjects."[51] The historian of ideas Richard Popkin gives a sense of the significance of Spinoza's analysis. "The result . . . ," Popkin writes, "is a devastating critique of revealed knowledge claims, that has had an amazing effect over the last three centuries in secularizing modern man."[52]

After reading Spinoza's book, Thomas Hobbes made a comment, according to his first biographer, that would appear to settle some questions about Hobbes' own views as well as Spinoza's. Hobbes remarked that he, himself, "durst not speak so boldly."[53]

Still, Spinoza's boldness, like that of Hobbes, had its limits. When his *Tractatus* was published in 1670, it was published anonymously with the name of a fictitious publisher. (Holland, for all its tolerance, formally banned the book in 1674.) Spinoza's other major work, his *Ethics,* he "durst not" publish in his lifetime. And both books, like Hobbes'

Leviathan, are full of respectful references to God—veils perhaps. In fact, Spinoza includes, near the beginning of the *Ethics,* a few proofs for the existence of God.[54]

And the God whose existence Spinoza says he supports in his *Ethics* is a very, very impressive God, indeed: He is "infinite" and "eternal." He is "indivisible." He is all powerful: "Nothing can be or be conceived without God." And "whatever is, is in God." Moreover, "there can be, or be conceived, no other substance but God."[55] But even here, when he is trying to sound religious, Spinoza is subversive.

For this makes Spinoza's God as large as all of nature, as large as the entire universe. A God this large—though Spinoza failed to spell it out—would be indistinguishable from Nature, from the universe. Like Raymond de l'Aire, like Shakespeare's Edmund, like many of the freethinkers who would follow him, Spinoza appears to have deified Nature.[56]

Even taking as sincere many of Spinoza's pronouncements on God leads, therefore, to a kind of atheism. Spinoza gave atheism one of its biggest boosts.

Religion was beginning to surrender some of its control of the conversation in seventeenth-century Europe. If you listened hard enough you could hear Christianity itself being interrogated: Did Moses really write the five books of Moses? Can't miracles really be explained by natural causes? Is "to die: to sleep; no more"? The range of acceptable discourse was expanding. And what was being said—even if it couldn't openly be praised—made it possible to say more.

Direct, acknowledged statements of atheism remained, of course, *verboten.* In the eighteenth century, that conversation would go public. But even before that became possible quite a bit was actually said—often anonymously, always carefully, usually indirectly or between the lines, with feints and jabs, using kinds of codes. This was happening in philosophy and the arts, but that was not where it was proving most important in the seventeenth century.

After Galileo, the situation began to improve in Europe for scientists—or "natural philosophers," as they were then mostly called.[57] Fewer ideas had to be abjured. This became, of course, the century of the Scientific Revolution. Disbelief in religion both benefited and helped.

Science's contributions to the spread of disbelief is the least controversial segment of the virtuous cycle for which I am arguing in seventeenth-century Europe. For science's methods are clearly troublesome for religion. The devout, to begin with, are not wont to view their precepts merely as propositions to be controverted or confirmed. The orthodox, as a rule, are used to arguments being settled by authority, not experiment. The hope belief offers does not always stand up well to observation and experience: life sometimes works out okay; sometimes it doesn't. Faith, particularly of the "certain-because-impossible" variety, and reason have long been tussling. Miracles are notoriously miserly with evidence. Revelation does not lend itself to experimental verification. And the mystical, by its nature, fails to produce facts.

When it is employed, the scientific method, consequently, has a way of uncovering information that is inconvenient for religion. Conflicts are inevitable with ancient holy books—most of which do end up proclaiming something or other on "how" the earth works or "heaven goes." Scientists in these centuries diverged from Scripture at their peril. Galileo learned that. But in the end the greater cost would be borne by the holy books. Catholic leaders did indeed have reason to fear that, in taking Copernicus' theory seriously, Galileo might encourage people to take the Bible less seriously.

Consider, for another example, the questions reason and experience were, cautiously, raising in Europe at this time about the account of Noah's flood in Genesis:[58] From whence did all that water—enough to cover "all the highest mountains everywhere"—come? Where did it go after those "forty days and forty nights" ended? How could one ark (Genesis specifies its dimensions) hold so many pairs of creatures? Were fish or birds on board? Observations led to more questions: what about all those new animals being encountered in America?

The discovery of fossils of sea animals far from the sea seemed to some scientists to provide a needed boost to the credibility of the flood story. "From all this," one scientist told the Royal Society at the start of the eighteenth century, "it sufficiently appears, that there was a time when the water overflowed all our earth, which could be none but the Noachian deluge." One of the seventeenth century's great fossil collectors and naturalists, John Ray, thought the matter out a little more deeply, however, and noted that a quick flood should have deposed sea animals evenly over the earth, which was not how fossils were distributed. Ray also observed that some of those fossilized sea animals no longer exist. Shouldn't they have been saved with Noah on the ark?[59]

And with science continuing to pick up speed, new observations kept arriving. The British scientist Edmond Halley undertook some calculations in 1694:

> The Rain of forty Days and Nights will be found to be a very small Part of the Cause of such a Deluge, for supposing it to rain all over the Globe as much in each Day, as it is now found to do in one of the rainiest Counties of *England* in the whole Year, *viz.* about forty Inches of Water *per Diem,* forty such Days could cover the whole Earth with but about twenty two Fathom Water, which would only drown the low Lands next the Sea.[60]

Halley did have to abjure. Acting on the advice of "a person whose judgment I have great cause to respect," he hastily retreated from his incautious analysis. However, the doubts being raised about holy writ by scientifically inclined minds were difficult to dispel.[61] John Keill, a scientist with a strong religious bent, saw the danger: "These contrivers of Deluges have furnished the Atheist with an argument which . . . is not so easily answer'd as their theories are made," Keill concedes.[62]

Religion is resilient, no doubt about that. When discussions in sacred texts become difficult to defend as historical they are defended as metaphorical. Still, seventeenth-century science was increasingly placing religion on the defensive. When biblical tales such as that of Noah are shown to have been unlikely, that makes it a little harder to subscribe to the truth of the Bible and a little easier to dismiss it.

In 1623, Marin Mersenne, a monk who was at the center of a lively and productive intellectual correspondence, insisted that Paris alone harbored 50,000 atheists.[63] In 1652, the English physician and scientist Walter Charleton wrote that his country "has of late produced . . . more swarms of atheistical monsters . . . than any age, than any nation has been infested withal."[64] Both likely were exaggerating or mislabeling attenuated Christianity as atheism. Europe's infestation of true, there-is-no-God "atheistical monsters" was probably still rather small.

But disbelief was, indeed, growing. And the science in which both Mersenne, an important correspondent of Galileo's, and Charleton were participating was taking the lead in that questioning: Did the sun really stop in the sky for Joshua? Was the entire earth actually flooded? If the mathematics of gravity can explain movements of the planets, what need is there for an omnipotent Being?

Scientists can, of course, be religious.[65] With rare exceptions (Galileo and Halley possibly among them), the men who made the Scientific Revolution appear to have sensed God behind what they were learning of the natural world. Their increasingly diligent observations, their telescopes and their microscopes enabled them to see what humans had never before seen. Their first reaction was awe, and they understood awe as a religious emotion: "'Tis the contemplation of the wonderful order, law and power of that we call nature," writes Robert Hooke, inventor of the microscope, "that does most magnify the beauty and excellency of the divine providence, which has so disposed, ordered, adapted and empowered each part so to operate as to produce the wonderful effects which we see."[66]

The logic of these awe-struck early scientists sometimes appears to have flagged, as the historian Richard S. Westfall has noted: The "beauty and excellency" of the universe are used to prove that there is a God, and He is good. And if we see things that are ugly and unpleasant—such as "mice, cockroaches or snakes"? Well, they simply "serve," as Walter Charleton put it, "as a foil to set off beauty."[67] How do we know that? Because, in essence, there is a God and He is good.

A similarly circular path leads to the conclusion that, in the words of that proponent of experimentation Francis Bacon, "the world was made for man." This happy fact is demonstrated by the world's multitudes of helpful touches, including, according to one of these scientists, the horse's ear, which conveniently turns backward to better hear commands. Thus we comprehend God's plan. And if we happen to see some things that don't appear to be doing a lot for humankind—distant heavenly bodies, for example, or the aforementioned snakes—well, that's just a sign that we can never fully comprehend God's plan.[68]

Isaac Newton, the greatest of these "natural philosophers," shared the awe felt by his contemporaries and drew similar conclusions from it. (There appears to have been a fair amount of feigning religious belief in the seventeenth century, but it seems unlikely that Newton's expressions of faith could be explained that way since they appear in numerous private as well as public writings.) Indeed, he added the following line to the second edition of his monumental *Philosophiæ Naturalis Principia Mathematica*: "This most elegant system of the sun, planets, and comets could not have arisen without the design and dominion of an intelligent and powerful being."[69] Some scientists at the time found evidence of this "design" in the complexity of the universe; Newton, having worked out his astoundingly powerful means for understanding the universe, marveled, instead, at "the simplicity in all the works of the Creator."[70]

Yet Newton and these other seventeenth-century scientists generally managed to keep their awe from interfering with their investigations. The first edition of Newton's *Principia,* published in 1687, did not contain any discussion of "an intelligent and powerful being." It does not contain any discussion of theology whatsoever.[71] It was only after his book was criticized by Gottfried Leibniz and others for impiety—for presenting space, gravity and the universe in a way that appeared not to support an orthodox conception of God—that Newton added a section discussing God's role.[72] Newton believed, but he had initially managed to produce a mathematical understanding of motion, which merely made intelligible the workings of the entire cosmos, without any overt reference to that belief.

The first edition of Newton's book, with God conspicuously absent, helps form, then, another segment of the virtuous cycle created by science and disbelief ("atheism" would be too strong a word here) in seventeenth-century Europe. The argument is that if Newton had dwelt in his book on God's role, he might not have done such a magnificent job of working out gravity's role. If he were more fearful of challenging understandings of God, if he were more content with ceding responsibility to the whims of God, if he thought human reason could never comprehend God's Creation, Newton might not have been able to outline so persuasively a physics and mathematics that manage to function so impressively on their own.

Isaac Newton was not above dabbling in the occult.[73] He spent decades experimenting with alchemy—making use of mystical sources and hoping to come upon long-lost mystical secrets.[74] The man who devised calculus, understood inertia and quantified gravity also seemed obsessed (a word that often comes to mind with Newton) with uncovering hidden secrets in the Bible, which included, he suspected, a chronology of the past *and* the future.[75]

Newton was, in other words, ready to use religion in his immense and unceasing efforts to figure things out. But he was less ready to allow religion to interfere with those efforts. "It is the temper of the hot and superstitious part of mankind in matters of religion ever to be fond of mysteries," Newton writes, "and for that reason to like best what they understand least."[76]

"The progress of religion is defined," writes the early-twentieth-century philosopher Alfred North Whitehead, "by the denunciation of gods."[77] Gods become fewer in number until there is only one—or a Father,

Son and Holy Ghost adding up to one. And the qualities of the lonely God that is left are also denounced. He loses His home: God is no longer to be found inside a temple or even, after airplanes, enthroned atop a cloud. He loses His physical form: His beard, His voice, perhaps His body or even His gender. He is neither seen nor heard in public. He grows wispier, more abstract.

Newton, the scientist, probably was responsible for subtracting—denouncing—among the most important of God's qualities: his daily responsibility for the workings of the heavens. And in his private scribblings on religion, Newton engaged in a fair number of additional denunciations, too.

This mathematician, who taught at Cambridge's Trinity College, was, for example, offended by the odd arithmetic of the Trinity—insisted upon by Anglicans as well as Catholics. He inclined, in his private writings, toward a view of Jesus as human rather than as one of three parts of one God.[78] In addition, this physicist was suspicious, as was Spinoza, of the idea that miracles "are the works of God" rather than just rare and poorly understood phenomena. Like Spinoza, Newton, when writing for himself, also had no use for a corporeal view of God.[79] Indeed, Newton—when not looking for hidden predictions, at least—was partial to Spinoza's reading of the Bible as a human document.[80]

In the historian Richard S. Westfall's view, Newton was a "religious rationalist."[81] He was looking for a stripped-down version of religion: one compatible with his physics. He was also looking for the principle that all religions have in common: "the law of righteousness and charity," he called it.[82] A religious rationalist, however, is not an easy thing to be.

To maintain a rational view of "the Author of the system" it would be necessary, for example, to resolve the contradictions that seem inherent in most conceptions of God. There is, for example, that old conundrum about omnipotence—given a twenty-first-century formulation on *The Simpsons:* "Could Jesus microwave a burrito so hot that He Himself could not eat it?"[83] There is also Carneades' argument, presented in chapter 2, that a being without flaws or weaknesses couldn't exhibit virtues. One question Newton and his contemporaries certainly struggled with was what role a Perfect Being would have after a presumably perfect Creation. Wouldn't He be redundant post-Genesis—after functioning as the First Cause? Wouldn't Jehovah end up resembling one of the Epicurean gods— left with no responsibility but to enjoy Himself?

A "religious rationalist" would also somehow have to get right the relationship between the natural and the supernatural: what status would natural laws have if a Being exists who is outside of them and violates them at least for the Creation? It would be necessary, too, to square science's methods with any sort of reliance upon religious authority, including that Bible whose secrets Newton was so interested in revealing. In addition, to be a "religious rationalist," in Newton's sense, would require precipitating "righteousness and charity" out of holy texts that do not always seem to embody them and out of a universe that does not always seem to display them.

These tasks may have been beyond the abilities of even this most able of men. Newton wrote out his private treatises on religion—and then rewrote them and rewrote them again. One appeared in at least five versions. As an old man, the Isaac Newton who had gotten the physics of the heavens right was still trying to get this rational view of Christianity right.[84]

But by then Newton had denounced enough to leave a rather hazy, unobtrusive God. In Newton's understanding, and that of many of his scientifically inclined contemporaries, God was losing not only eyes, a nose, bluster and his two other manifestations, but the inclination to fiddle with natural laws.[85]

So although he was a believer, Newton and his contemporaries help demonstrate what disbelief—or, in his case, limited belief—can contribute to science. His rejection of some of the more mystical and intrusive conceptions of God was probably necessary in order to give the sun and the planets leave to abide by equations. Newton's physics, the point is, benefited from the rejection of some religious belief.

Science usually does. Its progress, we might say, is "defined" by the diminution of God. Science requires some separation from church. This was, after Galileo, becoming available in Europe in the seventeenth century. Hobbes and Spinoza—however wary they may have been about speaking too "boldly"—helped. And the tendency of scientists—Newton among them—to push aside assumptions they considered irrational or unhelpful certainly helped. Newton's ability to leave God entirely out of the first edition of *Principia Mathematica* greatly helped.

A distinguished nineteenth-century atheist, Charles Bradlaugh, deserves the honor of making this point: "It is certainly a clear gain to astronomical science," Bradlaugh writes in an essay, "that the church which tried to compel Galileo to unsay the truth has been overborne by the growing unbelief of the age, even though our little children are yet taught that Joshua made the sun . . . stand still."[86]

Reason has been a hero of this book for many chapters now: reason versus superstition, reason versus faith. And there is no doubt that a respect for reason proved crucial to the slow rise of philosophy in Europe as well as the fast rise of science. "Authority bids us *believe,* whereas Reason *demonstrates,*" writes Francisco Sanches. His "scientific method" was very much about that which can be demonstrated.[87] Spinoza certainly had no interest in surrendering this tool. "Who but a desperate madman," he asks, "would be so rash as to turn his back on reason?"[88] But too worshipful an attitude toward what passes for reason—or "Reason"—can be another threat to science.

Reason had been associated in Europe in these centuries with the Greeks (with one Greek in particular, in fact). And the point can be made that the Greeks (including Aristotle) in their enthusiasm for reason tended upon occasion to conclude first and check later—to put the idea before the fact. They were, some of them, "conceptualists" more than "empiricists," to borrow the formulation of Ernan McMullin, a philosopher and historian of science.[89]

Aristotle reasoned—based on such grand ideas as "virtue" and "change," along with some staring at the night sky—that the heavenly bodies circling around the earth were attached to 55 different spheres, "neither more nor less."[90] Such "concepts" then tended to take on an authority, an almost religious authority, of their own. Maybe that's why Greek and Arab science went far, but only so far. Certainly, that is what happened when Aristotle's ideas met Catholicism in Europe. For science to move forward in Europe, it needed to break free of this kind of weakly grounded, too-confident, too-dogmatic Reason.

Of course, scientists do have to worry about what is reasonable—or at least most plausible. But Europe's "natural philosophers" needed to realize that theories are made to be overturned. They needed to remember that, as Montaigne wrote about Copernicus' theory, "in a thousand years' time another opinion will," perhaps, "overthrow" that which seems reasonable today.[91] A scientist must learn to trust an idea—even believe in an idea—but not too much, not so much that the idea becomes more important than the evidence, not so much that the idea interferes with the production of needed new ideas.

Skepticism could teach this. Through it Europe learned that the best reason can do is produce—and this term was starting to be used in the seventeenth century—"hypotheses," which then must be tested by experimenting with nature.[92] Through its cousin skepticism, disbelief, in other words, had found another crucial role for itself in science. It would help guard against new forms of dogma.*[93]

Isaac Newton did have a healthy suspicion of the power of pure reason. He was not a fan of attempting to puzzle out the universe by, as he put it, "inferring 'tis thus because not otherwise" or "deducing it from a refutation of contrary suppositions." Instead, Newton arrived at a new understanding, he once explained, "by deriving it from experiments." Of course, it is a mistake to dismiss the role of conceptualization in scientific thought, particularly scientific thought as innovative as Newton's, but his instincts were productively empirical. "Arguing from experiments and observations," Newton wrote shortly before he died, " . . . is the best way of arguing which the nature of things admits."[94]

Science moves forward by testing and examining more, believing less.

The virtuous cycle of disbelief and science in seventeenth-century Europe took one more half turn and made one more significant ascent. Here it was once again science contributing to disbelief. But to introduce it I am going to employ a quote that seems to make the opposite point: "Atheism is so senseless and odious to mankind," Isaac Newton once proclaimed, "that it never had many professors."

Among the reasons Newton himself did not profess disbelief in God was that he occasionally had need for God. Although he mostly excluded Him from the workings of his system, Newton did still employ Him as "the very first Cause" and as the Designer not only of "this most elegant system of the sun, planets, and comets" but of life: "Can it be by accident," he asks, "that all birds, beasts and men have their right side and left side alike shaped (except in their bowels) and just two eyes, and no more, on either side of the face . . . ? Whence arises this uniformity in all their outward shapes but from the counsel and contrivance of an Author?"[95]

---

* This book has noted how Catholicism's emphasis on the limitations of human intellect has interfered with scientific and other forms of learning. But, to be fair, this humility had—in small, weakened doses—helped skepticism inoculate European science against too high a view of its own theories and their durability.

Newton, in other words, is among those who use God as the Final Answer. If you can't figure out how everything first started rushing about, look to the Deity. If you're dumbstruck by what Newton calls "all that order and beauty . . . in the world," credit the Deity. If, as Newton writes, you can't come up with a good reason "why there is one body in our system qualified to give light and heat to all the rest," acknowledge, as Newton does, that "I know no reason," and then conclude that the reason must belong to "the Author of the system."[96]

The common assumption that God answers all has two great benefits: First, all difficult questions, thereby, gain an answer (albeit the same answer). And, second, God always has a role—because there are always going to be otherwise unanswerable questions out on the raggedy edges of human understanding.

However—and here's a drawback for the religious—after Western science began to accelerate in the seventeenth century, it became increasingly hard to ignore the fact that many such nagging questions about the natural world eventually do elicit natural answers.[97] Science demystifies. For example, thanks in part to the work on the formation of the solar system of the French scientist Pierre Simon Laplace, who lived a century after Newton, we can now explain with some confidence how "one body in our system" came "to give light and heat to all the rest."[98] After Charles Darwin did for life, roughly speaking, what Newton had done for the heavens, the bilateral symmetry found in most organisms would come to seem understandable, too—as a sexually selected sign of health.[99] Recourse to the caprice or the magic of "the Author of the system" was no longer required.

Finding God in the inexplicable, as Newton and so many other believers end up doing, means watching God be diminished ("denounced") every time some previously inexplicable phenomenon gets explained—a process that dates back at least to the Greeks. One generation's divine mysteries become the next generation's theories and equations.

Maybe the supply of questions about the nature of the universe is inexhaustible. Still, the science born in Europe in the seventeenth century changed attitudes toward such questions. The new pace of observation and experimentation tended to reduce the half-life of mysteries. And a problem likely to be resolved one of these centuries or decades weighs on us in a different way than an age-old imponderable. Awe, wonder, humility and even some bewilderment before the vast universe, will, one hopes, never be eradicated. But, through the methodical, inexorable process of question answering, the Scientific Revolution was creating a world that was increasingly ponderable.

And, if you thought about it, it was not at all clear how much God, as Final Answer, really had to contribute even to the large, keep-budding-philosophers-up-at-night questions: Could all that is have had a beginning? Can it have an ending? Why is there something rather than nothing? In a universe increasingly lending itself to scientific explanation, is the situation clarified or confused by the interposition of a profoundly unscientific Being (however obscure or powerful) between what is and the putative beginning, end or possibility of nothing?

Isaac Newton's own religious beliefs are themselves evidence of the tenacity of religion in the face of science. Still, Newton presented the most mechanical, mathematical, intelligible universe humankind had yet seen. In his system, even occurrences as mysterious as comets could be understood and predicted mathematically.[100] This believer, consequently, did as much to reduce the realm of the inexplicable, the realm of God the Explainer, as anyone who ever lived.

Alexander Pope composed this epitaph upon the death of Isaac Newton in 1727:

Nature and Nature's Laws lay hid in Night:
GOD said, "Let Newton be," and all was Light.[101]

Religion explains. Science explains. After Newton, it became hard to deny that—on many subjects at least—science explains better.

Isaac Newton's work arguably qualifies, with that of Darwin, as history's greatest example of the third spur to disbelief: the search for "a clear understanding of what happened"—the substitution of natural for supernatural explanations. From the seventeenth century to today, countless inquisitive, informed individuals have looked up at the moon, the planets, the sun; have watched the tide ebb or an apple fall; and have thought not of the mysterious and wondrous workings of God but of gravity and Newton's mechanics. Friedrich Schiller, the German poet, would name this process: the "disgodding" of nature.[102]

"Following the birth of modern science the age of unshaken faith was lost to western man," writes historian of science Richard S. Westfall."[103] It is not necessary to believe humankind has ever enjoyed a time of "unshaken faith" to accept that the Scientific Revolution and the work of Isaac Newton in particular represented a major blow to religious faith—to a view of the world as suffused with God.

In fact, by the early eighteenth century, copies of *The Three Impostors* actually, reliably began turning up in Europe![104] One edition asserted, for example, that men "subjected themselves by vain ceremonies and superstitious worship to frivolous phantoms of the imagination, whence arose this word *Religion,* which makes so much noise in the world."[105] These editions claimed to be copies of centuries old Latin texts, but in fact they borrowed heavily from Vanini, Hobbes and in particular, Spinoza. Nonetheless, the fact that this phantom book had become real was further evidence that in an age of growing scientific understanding belief in "phantoms" was weakening.

The damage that had been done to religion became clearer after Newton's death. Three-quarters of a century later, Napoleon was talking with that French scientist Pierre Simon Laplace, author of a five-volume, mechanistic account of the universe. Laplace is said to have told Napoleon "that a chain of natural causes would account for the construction and preservation of the wonderful system [of the world]."[106] That did not leave any role for "the Creator." Napoleon felt called upon to bring the omission to Laplace's attention.

The scientist's famous response: "I have no need of that hypothesis."[107]

6

OPEN YOUR EYES

THE BEGINNINGS OF THE ENLIGHTENMENT

Doubt is not a pleasant condition but certainty is an absurd one.

—Voltaire[1]

I N THE FALL OF 1735, FRANÇOIS-MARIE AROUET WAS IN EXILE IN Cirey, near the border between France and Lorraine, when he received a shocking letter from Nicolas-Claude Thiériot. Arouet wrote his plays, poems, novels, histories and philosophy under the name Voltaire, and Thiériot was one of the friends charged with keeping Voltaire up to date on the latest ideas in Paris. Thiériot's letter announced the discovery of a philosopher as important as John Locke. "What!" Voltaire exclaims in his reply.[2] As he reminds Thiériot, Locke is "in metaphysics what Newton is in the understanding of nature."

Voltaire qualifies as among history's best-connected rebels, but his aggressive assaults upon the absurdities of France's Old Regime had already landed him in the Bastille twice. His book comparing French government and society unfavorably to that of the English had just been published, without his approval, in Paris.[3] It had quickly been condemned by the authorities and publicly burned. After consulting well-placed friends, Voltaire had avoided a third prison stay by vacating Paris. Hence, Cirey: Lorraine at the time having the virtue of not being part of France.[4]

Cirey had an additional attraction: the woman Voltaire loved— Emilie, the Marquise du Châtelet—resided in the chateau there.[5] Prominent among Madame du Châtelet's charms was her skill at philosophy and mathematics at a time when possessing such skills was an "astonishing," to use Voltaire's word, achievement for a woman.[6] Emilie helped Voltaire understand Newton, whom she was translating, and encouraged his interest in the English. "I confess that she is tyrannical," Voltaire said of his companion; "one must talk about metaphysics, when the temptation is to talk of love. Ovid was formerly my master; it is now the turn of Locke."[7]

One of the sections of Voltaire's provocative new book was indeed devoted to the English political philosopher John Locke.[8] Locke, a friend of Newton's, was committed to excising from religion what he calls "strange opinions and extravagant practices."[9] Like Newton, like many English scientists at the time, like Voltaire and Madame du Châtelet, Locke was after a more "rational," more "natural" faith—one tolerant of others faiths.

Thinking had traditionally been seen as an attribute of our spiritual not our material selves: we think, the assumption is, only because we have an immaterial "soul."[10] Locke, while careful not to let go of the notion of a Creator, is (very cautiously) surrendering that hypothesis in favor of a more natural view of cognition, and Voltaire, exercising similar care (but less caution), concurs. Indeed, Voltaire goes so far as to rate Locke's thinking on the subject of souls, or their likely absence, superior not only to that of Christian thinkers but to that of the Greeks.

That was why Thiériot's letter was so shocking. And, what was more, the new philosopher whose discovery it announced wasn't even English and wasn't really a philosopher; he was a French priest. "A *curé* and a Frenchman as much the philosopher as Locke?" Voltaire asks in amazement. He pleads for a copy of this priest's writings.

The priest in question, Jean Meslier, had been dead for six years when Voltaire first learned of him. Nothing that had been known about this man while he was alive would explain why he was now becoming a sensation in Paris and would become a hero to Voltaire. There were no signs during his life that this village priest would go well beyond Locke, Voltaire and even Spinoza and become one of the staunchest proponents of the Enlightenment's most radical idea: its rejection of religion.

Jean Meslier was born in 1664 into a merchant's family in the village of Mazerny in the Ardennes region in northeastern France.[11] He was educated by the local priest and finished his studies at the seminary in Reims. In 1689, a year after he was ordained as a Catholic priest, Meslier was appointed *curé* in two villages, Etrépigny and Balaives-et-Butz, less than fifteen kilometers from where he was born. We don't know that he ever visited Paris.

This priest's life, based on what few records exist, seems to have been mostly uneventful. At some point he got into a dispute with the local nobleman—apparently because of that nobleman's attitude toward the poor. The nobleman responded by pointing out that this priest was living with a young female "servant"—a relative, the priest claimed. When Meslier was finally forced by his archbishop to say a prayer for that local lord, he is said to have asked the congregation to pray that the nobleman "be granted the grace to no longer mistreat the poor and despoil orphans."[12] However, neither spats with local lords nor cohabitation with "servants" was unheard of among French clergy at the time, and Meslier remained a reasonably well thought of priest in those two small French towns until his death in 1729.[13]

Then the bombshell exploded.[14] For Meslier had left behind four copies of a rambling manuscript: *Memoir of the Thoughts and Feelings of J. . . . M., Prie . . . , Cu . . . , of Etrép . . . and Bal. . . .* This manuscript was, according to its very long title, *To Be Addressed to His Parishioners After His Death, and to Serve as Testimony to the Truth for Them and All Like Them.*[15] Meslier's book presents what he calls, also in his title, *Clear and Evident Demonstrations of the Vanity and the Falsity of All the Divinities and of All the Religions of the World.*

In the Europe in which this book was written the educated were aware of the work of thinkers like Hobbes and Spinoza; they were aware of the Scientific Revolution. At the time, a French diplomat grumbled, with the exaggeration typical of such grumbling, that in his country "it was no longer good taste to believe in the gospel."[16] Nonetheless, this was a Europe still very much in the grip of one or another variety of Christianity. And probably no author in Europe—certainly not whomever drafted those fake *Three Imposters* books—had placed a real name atop an outright, undisguised, unabashed attack on all religion.[17]

That was what Jean Meslier had done. (Despite the use of initials, Meslier's identity could easily be divined from the title.) "I did not dare say it during my life," he writes. "But I will say it at least in dying."[18] He says that what has been preached about "miracles," about "the magnificence of the rewards of heaven," about "the dreadful castigations of hell" is "nothing but delusions, errors, lies, fictions and impostures."[19]

Jean Meslier had a message for his parishioners: "Open your eyes, my dear friends, open your eyes. . . . Your religion is not less vain or superstitious than any other; it is not less fake in its principles, nor less ridiculous and absurd in its dogmas and maxims."[20]

Where did an early eighteenth-century village priest get such ideas? From many places, no doubt, beginning with the writers mentioned in previous chapters. This particular village priest was very well read. And the implausibility of various Christian doctrines was not hard to see. It had undoubtedly weighed—over the decades, over the centuries—on the minds of other priests and ministers: A perfect Being? A virgin birth? Resurrection? One God who was also three? *How can that be?* An acceptance of misery and injustice in this life because of a supposed other life after death? *Why should that be?* Rejecting these tenuous suppositions—at the beginning of the eighteenth century—wasn't all that difficult, even for a village priest.

What was difficult was expressing out loud that perhaps-not-surprising but still hugely dangerous conclusion. After a lifetime of pretending, Meslier in this posthumous manuscript feigned no piety of any sort. He did not hide behind veils, except, of course, the veil of death. His staunchly anti-religious *Memoir* was almost, therefore, unprecedented in Christian Europe. That it came from a priest made the explosion even louder.

"Paradise on earth is where I am," an ebullient Voltaire writes while staying at the Chateau de Cirey—where he first learned of Jean Meslier.[21] That chateau belonged to the Marquis du Châtelet, who, showing classic French sophistication, was content to have Voltaire reside there, as long as his liaison with the Marquis' wife was kept reasonably (by French standards) discreet. It helped that Voltaire—wealthy from his plays, writings and investments—had taken it upon himself to fix up the place and help with his jewelry-and-gambling-loving lover's formidable bills.

Voltaire's rooms were opulent, filled, a guest reports, with "rich" and "rare" things. Madame du Châtelet's apartment (connected to Voltaire's by a not-so-hidden staircase) was all in yellow and blue and featured paintings by the best artists of the day. Dinner, supper, regular poetry and philosophy readings and theatricals (mostly performances of Voltaire's plays with Emilie taking lead roles) were, according to some reports, precisely scheduled and announced by bells.[22]

And that paradise also included lengthy and equally rigorously scheduled periods of work. This is when Voltaire was thinking out his attack on Christianity. According to one account, he and Madame du Châtelet, who was eleven years his junior, read and discussed a chapter of the Bible each day. Her book on the subject—a detailed critique, from Genesis to Revelations—was completed before his, though never published: "Each discovery . . . in physics and astronomy," Emilie writes, "revealed to us a new absurdity in this history of the Creation."[23]

In a poem to Madame du Châtelet, written shortly before he learned of Meslier, Voltaire had suggested that she read Pierre Bayle.[24] That was hardly an unusual suggestion at the time—particularly for those who were pouncing on absurdities in religion. Bayle's *Historical and Critical Dictionary*, with which Voltaire was well acquainted, was by then well on its way to becoming one of the best-selling books in Europe in the eighteenth century—the "Arsenal of the Enlightenment," it would be called.[25] It served as one of Voltaire's main sources as he worked out his thoughts on religion.[26] "The greatest master of the art of reasoning that ever wrote," Voltaire calls Bayle.[27]

Pierre Bayle had the misfortune of being born a Protestant in Catholic France at a time, 1647, when patience with these "Huguenots" was rapidly evaporating. As a young man, he converted to Catholicism; then, a few months later, he converted back—thus becoming not only a heretic but an apostate. Bayle fled France but then snuck back. In 1681, the Calvinist school at which Bayle had begun teaching was closed by authorities, and Bayle fled again, ending up where many victims of religious persecution were ending up: in Holland. That put him beyond the reach of French authorities, but Bayle's family was hounded. His father, a Calvinist minister, died in 1685, the year in which the Edict of Nantes, which had provided France's Protestants with some rights, was revoked by Louis XIV. Bayle's brother then died in prison after having been tortured.

Bayle became a writer and scholar in Rotterdam and an influential proponent of an unusual way for people of different beliefs to relate to each other: tolerance—something not much championed in Europe after Rome's adoption of Christianity, although John Locke had made some progress with the idea in England. Bayle's argument begins with the assumption that it is impossible to distinguish true beliefs from false beliefs. This is, in its quiet way, an earth-shattering assumption. It presumes that we cannot actually know for sure whether Calvin, Luther, the pope or maybe even Paul, Jesus and Moses were right. It challenges that sense of certainty that infuses religions.

And if we can't know for sure what is right we can't know for sure what is wrong. This leads to what philosophers call "a reciprocity argument":

"Everything which would be permitted to truth against error," Bayle asserts, "becomes likewise permitted to error against truth."[28]

Most French Catholics believed they had every right to inveigh against and suppress Huguenots because the Catholic religion, based on the teachings of centuries of church fathers, was correct and that of those local Protestants was foolish, dangerous and manifestly wrong. Moreover, it had long been believed in Europe that no country could survive if some of its members disagreed with the government on a matter as important as religion. The error had to be combated! But, according to Bayle's reciprocity argument, Protestants—just as convinced they were right—would have an equal right to inveigh against and suppress Catholics where they had power.

Bayle's solution: stop persecuting! "Toleration," Bayle writes, " . . . is the very source of peace and intolerance the source of confusion and conflict."[29]

This may sound obvious to most of us today, now that this kind of relativistic, open-minded, "whatever," view of religion has become accepted in many circles. It was not obvious then, at the end of the seventeenth century.[30] It was revolutionary. Religious beliefs ran deep: "Here I stand, I can do no other," Martin Luther had announced. Christian beliefs were supposed to run as deep as it is possible to run: all the way to the "heart." And if your heart is filled with a particular view of a religion how can you accept the "what if," "on the other hand," "likewise" and "possibly" upon which tolerance, as Bayle made clear, is based.

Voltaire was much taken with Bayle's writing on this subject.[31] If "tolerance" now seems an obvious, innocuous good to most of us, it is because Bayle and Voltaire and many others since have struggled to make us acknowledge something that is hugely difficult to acknowledge: that even that which we believe most strongly could be wrong. Tolerance, in some unavoidable way, implies that religious beliefs should run a little less deep. It contributes to the spread of disbelief not just the safety of nonbelievers. The eventual return of tolerance to the West, which Bayle helped set in motion, is a significant contribution to the development of atheism in the West.

In his *Historical and Critical Dictionary,* which first appeared in 1697, Bayle also began making another odd and controversial point: that atheists can be at least as moral as the religious. He was quick to acknowledge that this goes against "the usual mode of reasoning." Indeed, this was one subject upon which Voltaire was not persuaded by Bayle. This may be what he is getting at when Voltaire harrumphs that Bayle "has only taught to doubt."[32]

Nonetheless, in the "Atheism—Atheists" entry in his dictionary, Bayle sets about proving "the usual mode of reasoning" wrong:

- He maintains that history's most vicious personages were religious. His examples include: Nero, Caligula and a French tyrant, Louis XI.
- He reminds his readers that, despite Christians' professed belief "that vice ought to be renounced in order to be eternally happy and to avoid being eternally miserable," they still "often" manage to live "the slaves of vice and the constant victims of their passions." This, in late-seventeenth-century Europe, apparently required no examples.
- He names disbelievers who were "honest men," "men of regular habits," who lived virtuous, even "exemplary" lives. Most of those examples—Diagoras among them—are from classical times, but Bayle also mentions one "Vanini," who, he says, "was extremely correct in his manners."[33]

Bayle's conclusion: "Now if Atheists exist who, morally speaking, are well-disposed, it follows that Atheism is not a necessary cause of immorality."[34]

While acknowledging that not every atheist is going to be "moral and austere," Bayle scoffs at the concept of the dissolute atheist, of the sort exemplified by Shakespeare's Edmund or Molière's less successfully drawn Don Juan. "People who pass all their days amidst bottles and glasses; . . . who lay snares for the chastity of women; who seek only to kill time in debauchery"—true Don Juan types—do not, Bayle insists, "trouble themselves with arguments on the existence of God." They are more likely, he points out, to attempt to lessen the weight of their crimes by professing faith.

In these centuries, it was common to distinguish between two kinds of atheists: "theoretical," who merely promulgated these absurd and dangerous ideas, and "practical," who actually lived the reprehensible lives these ideas made possible. The evidence indicates that Bayle was not himself an atheist of any sort. Still, he was arguing that their theories are not really dangerous and that "practical atheists" are much more common in literature and religious tracts than in life.

Besides, Bayle explains, reasonably thoughtful people have plenty of other motivations for behaving morally besides a belief that the alternative leads to frying in hell. Those motivations, as spelled out by Bayle, include: "punishments and rewards in the magistrates' hands," and, even when the magistrates are not looking, "the love of praise, the fear of disgrace." These are all consequences of significance for most of us. And Bayle also includes another factor that counters, for most of us, thoughts of doing evil: our "natural temper" or "constitution"—our sense of guilt and obligation.[35]

Perhaps the most memorable formulation of the supposition that atheists must be immoral was contributed by Fyodor Dostoevsky in his nineteenth-century novel, *The Brothers Karamazov*: without God, one of his characters says, "everything is lawful" or (depending on the translation) "everything is permitted."[36] Bayle had presented the counterargument— about a century and a half earlier.

Once you entertain the possibility that Bayle had a point, religion begins to seem less necessary and atheism begins to seem less terrifying. Voltaire was among the many in his century and the next who did not entertain that possibility—even though, in his work with Madame du Châtelet he was turning into a vehement critic of Christianity,[37] even though he became perhaps Europe's leading fighter for religious tolerance, even though Voltaire had become fascinated by the writings of a nonbelieving priest.

Voltaire notes that among the flood of clandestine works on sale in Paris in the 1740s there were more than a hundred handwritten copies of Meslier's text or excerpts from it. They fetched, Voltaire reports, a good price, but handling such illicit writings could be risky. A record survives of one man (likely not well connected) having been seized by police in 1743 for having sold "the work of the *curé* of Trépigny."[38]

Then, in 1762, a small volume containing a short biography of Meslier and excerpts from his *Memoir* appeared in print. It may have been based on an existing handwritten bio and abridgement. The name of the editor of this first printed version is, of course, not given, but an analysis of Voltaire's letters at the time makes clear that this edition had been secretly, illicitly prepared for the press by Voltaire.[39]

Some of his acquaintances were reluctant to help promote the Meslier book, which was condemned and ordered burned in Paris. "You blame us for being lukewarm," Voltaire's friend the mathematician and philosopher Jean Le Rond d'Alembert writes him, "but, as I believe I have already told you, fear of the stake has a very cooling effect."[40] Voltaire, however—at a safe remove from Paris—remained ardent. "I believe that nothing will ever make more of an impression than the pamphlet of Meslier," writes this grandest of all the Enlightenment philosophers in a letter in 1762. In another, to D'Alembert, he exclaims, "All who read it are convinced: here is a man who proves and discusses. He speaks at the moment of death, when even liars tell the truth—it is the strongest of all arguments. Jean Meslier ought to convert the entire world."[41]

The excerpt from Meslier's *Memoir* Voltaire has secretly published opens with an anguished foreword, addressed by the *curé* directly to his parishioners[42]:

> As a priest I had no choice but to fulfill my ministry, but how I suffered when I was forced to preach to you those pious falsehoods that I detested with all my heart. What contempt I felt for my ministry, and particularly for the superstitious mass and the ridiculous administration of the sacraments, especially when they had to be carried out with a solemnity that attracted your piety and excited your credulity? A thousand times I was on the point of publicly exploding. I wanted to open your eyes, but a fear stronger than my strength suddenly held me back, and forced me to remain silent until my death.

Such fear was, of course, more than mere paranoia.[43] But what, one might ask, was a fellow with ideas like those of Jean Meslier doing in the church in the first place? "If I embraced a profession so directly opposed to my sentiments it was not through cupidity," Meslier answers in the forward to his *Memoir:* "I obeyed my parents." And, once he entered the profession, Meslier appears to have felt a responsibility for the welfare of his parishioners.[44] In his *Memoir,* their priest assures those parishioners, "I spoke to you as rarely as possible of our pitiful dogmas."[45]

Respect for one's parents, a desire to help and such "a fear" may seem a bit weak as excuses for a life of hypocrisy and lies—even if those lies were repeated "as rarely as possible." Diderot, after all, broke with his father. And men like Diagoras, Menocchio and Vanini had taken great risks and paid great prices for a cause that, unlike religious martydom, promised no rewards.

Perhaps Jean Meslier was insufficiently brave. Perhaps he was too much the anacreontic—unwilling to ruin the only life he had by taking on the scorn and retribution he knew an attack on religion, while he was still alive, would bring. However, the composition of his posthumous manifesto undoubtedly did exhibit a kind of courage and earned its deceased author considerable renown.

After the personal foreword, Meslier's attempt "to open . . . eyes," if not "convert the entire world," commences. It begins, in Voltaire's version of the priest's *Memoir,* with the insistence that, since "there is no one religious denomination that does not pretend to be truly founded upon the authority of God," the burden of proof must be on each particular religion to show that it is really the one that is "of Divine origin."[46] Since such proof, by Meslier's reckoning, "is lacking, we must conclude" that any religion, including the religion he practiced, "is but of human invention and full of errors and deceptions."

In fact, the theme to which Meslier, in this excerpt, devotes the most energy is the inadequacy of the evidence for religion—particularly the absence of "clear and convincing proofs" for the religion to which he had to pretend to subscribe: that of the "Christ-worshippers."[47] Holy books don't make much of an impression on him:

> For it would be necessary to know: Firstly, if those who are said to be the first authors of these narrations truly are such. Secondly, if they were honest men, worthy of confidence, wise and enlightened; and to know if they were not prejudiced in favor of those of whom they speak so favorably. Thirdly, if they have examined all the circumstances of the facts which they relate; if they know them well; and if they make a faithful report of them. Fourthly, if the books or the ancient histories which relate all these great miracles have not been falsified and changed in the course of time, as many others have been.

Meslier does not see our collected Hebrew and Christian texts meeting any of the standards he has outlined. And, unlike others who had begun questioning the authorship and validity of biblical tales, Meslier does not mince words: "All these narrations appear to be fables," he concludes. Indeed, he detects some circular reasoning in the standard defense of them: "How can faith, that is to say a blind belief, render the books reliable which are themselves the foundation of this blind belief?"

In Meslier's view, revelation holds up no better as evidence for religion:

> The most false and the most ridiculous prophecy ever made is that of Jesus, in Luke, where it is pretended that there will be signs in the sun and in the moon, and that the Son of Man will appear in a cloud to judge men; and this is predicted for the generation living at that time. Has it come to pass? Did the Son of Man appear in a cloud?

Meslier dismisses the doctrine of the "Christ-worshippers" as "the height of absurdity."

Then his argument gets more profound: if there were a God, He might have been expected to have provided, say, "all that is necessary for the well-being of His creatures." Meslier is particularly offended that the Deity is reported in the Bible to have "had the kindness to send an angel to console and to assist a simple maid, while He left, and still leaves every day, a countless number of innocents to languish and starve to death."

There was, no doubt, a kind of fury behind this effort to open eyes, to expose all these "pious falsehoods." It was the fury of a man who not only felt victimized by a deception but found himself co-opted into that deception. Nonetheless, there was also logic and scholarship there. Meslier knows his way around Christian and pagan religious texts and is well versed in European philosophy, especially Montaigne.[48] Indeed, in Meslier's *Memoir,* for one of the first times we know of in the West, a form of rational inquiry is employed in an open, unhesitating, all-out attack upon religion.

However, the excerpt Voltaire published from the book by this angry opponent of religion does include, oddly, a couple of respectful references to, of all beings, God—God as, for example, "the Author of nature." And it concludes with this paragraph:

> I will finish by begging God . . . that he deign to recall us to natural religion, of which Christianity is the declared enemy. To that simple religion that God placed in the hearts of all men, which teaches us that we only do unto others what we want to have done unto us. Then the universe will be composed of good citizens, of just fathers, of submissive children, of tender friends. God gave us this religion in giving us reason. May fanaticism no longer pervert it! I die more filled with these wishes than with hopes.[49]

The answer to the question of how Jean Meslier could have written about God as if he existed is that he did not write that. These respectful references to God and calls for a natural religion are not in his original manuscript (copies of which, remarkably, survive in France's Bibliothèque Nationale). They were added to this early excerpt by someone else. Voltaire published a distorted version of Meslier—one that conveniently coincided with (and helped sharpen) his own views.[50] For while Voltaire is, like Meslier, anti-Christian, he is not, like Meslier, an atheist.

The relationship between Voltaire and Madame du Châtelet settled over the years into an intense friendship and partnership. Emilie died in 1749, shortly after giving birth to a new lover's child. Voltaire, devastated by the loss and still mostly unwelcome in Paris, ended up settling in Ferney, near Geneva. It was there that he marshaled his thoughts on religion into a furious assault upon Christianity, of which his publication of that excerpt from Meslier's *Memoir* was just one barrage.[51] In one of his own writings from this period, Voltaire explains that he is often asked what might replace Christianity, and then replies, "What! A ferocious animal has sucked the blood of my family. I tell you to get rid of that beast, and you ask me, What shall we put in its place!" Voltaire's slogan becomes, "*Écrasez l'infâme!*"—"Crush the infamous!" "Every sensible man, every honorable man, must hold the Christian sect in horror," he insists.[52]

Giulio Cesare Vanini had been executed for saying much less in Europe a century and a half earlier. Voltaire wrote (wink, wink) clandestinely; he lived in exile. Still, this exile was the frequent guest of two kings: Stanislas of Poland and Lorraine, and Frederick of Prussia. And Voltaire's wide circle of intellectual, aristocratic and royal friends—probably the most sophisticated crowd in Europe—understood what books were his and knew of his scorn for Christianity, accepted it and, in many cases, shared it. King Frederick was himself a freethinker.

In 1764 Voltaire published his *Philosophical Dictionary* anonymously in Geneva. Its alphabetical arrangement, some of its categories and some of its ideas were similar to those in Pierre Bayle's hugely controversial but hugely successful *Historical and Critical Dictionary*. Voltaire's version displayed many of his anti-religious notions. Copies of this book were soon—inevitably and dutifully—being publicly burned in Paris and other European capitals. Voltaire—inevitably, dutifully and drolly—was soon vigorously denying authorship of what he labeled "this abominable little dictionary, a work of Satan." He was also arranging, over the next twelve years, for at least eleven new editions or reprintings.[53]

There remained for Voltaire, however, a non-bloodsucking, non-beastly religion—that "natural religion," with roots in the theological efforts of Locke and the English scientists. Voltaire was a "deist"—perhaps history's most influential deist. He believed in the Deity but rejected any organized, rigid or exclusive way of approaching Him; he acknowledged only an abstract, mostly unknowable God: "We feel that we are under the hand of an invisible Being; this is all," Voltaire writes under the heading "God—Gods" in his *Philosophical Dictionary*.[54]

Well, actually this is not quite all: Voltaire believes in a "Supreme Artificer"—both First Cause and Designer (or "necessary Being," as he and Madame du Châtelet put it)[55]: "Here is a certain truth upon which the mind reposes," he states: "Every work which shows us means and an end, announces a workman. Then," Voltaire concludes, "this universe, composed of . . . means, each of which has its end, discovers a most mighty, a most intelligent Workman."[56] The mighty Voltaire has settled upon a combination of the cosmological and teleological arguments for the existence of God, along with the argument for design.

Jean Meslier, despite those comments inserted into Voltaire's "excerpt" from his *Memoir*, would have had none of this. In his manuscript, Meslier never implores, invokes or otherwise takes seriously a deity of any sort. Meslier's name for Voltaire's "Supreme Artificer," "most mighty, most intelligent Workman," "necessary Being," "invisible Being," is unambiguous. This priest calls Him: "the imaginary God."[57]

Most of those who believe in an "invisible Being" *want* to believe in an "invisible Being"—because the existence of some sort of God would provide consolation or meaning or, and this was Voltaire's reason, because His existence would keep people behaving decently.[58]

Voltaire, of course, was hardly a rigid moralist: here, for example, is some of what he had to say in his *Philosophical Dictionary* under the heading, "Adultery": "Adultery is an evil only in as much as it is a theft; but we do not steal that which is given to us."[59] However, on at least one subject with moral implications Voltaire takes a position so clear, courageous and compelling that it will resonate through the centuries. That subject is tolerance. He fights persecution of heretics, infidels and nonbelievers of all sorts—even, though with reluctance, Jews.[60]

For instance, Voltaire took up the cause of the family of a Protestant merchant who, in a burst of anti-Protestant hysteria, was tortured and then executed in Toulouse for, in 1761, allegedly murdering his own son.[61] Employing all the considerable forces at his disposal—collecting evidence, publishing pamphlets, importuning influential friends such as the king's mistress—Voltaire campaigned to overturn the verdict. He succeeded. He succeeded so well that that merchant's widow was invited to meet with the king.

On the subject of living and letting live, Voltaire, following Bayle and Locke, was mostly early, often brave and certainly, given his influence on the makers of modern political systems, important:[62]

> What is toleration? It is the appurtenance of humanity. We are all full of weakness and errors; let us mutually pardon each other our follies,—it is the first law of nature.[63]

Lovely. But, since we are discussing a philosopher, we have to ask what the philosophical status is of this "law of nature" upon which Voltaire's morality seems to rest. It turns out to come from above. Voltaire identifies himself with the sort of "theists" who "believe that God gave to man a natural law"—a law found at the heart of all religions but independent of all the petty, superstitious and sectarian nonsense that, in his view, debases all organized religions.

The law to which "all the other rules, so different and so varied, may be referred" should be familiar to those versed in Christianity, the religion Voltaire scorned. The law is, he writes, this: "Do not to another that which you would not have another do to you."[64]* This, thus, is the will of God. And God's will, thus, is the foundation of human morality—from not stealing or killing (but maybe committing adultery) to Voltaire's cherished tolerance.

Or, at least, he *wants* it to be thus. Voltaire's best known epigram on the subject of religion states: "If God did not exist, . . . it would be necessary to invent him."[65] Voltaire does not appear to be taking the "if" clause here very seriously. The poem this line is taken from is an attack on the "author" of *The Three Impostors,* and it is preceded by:

> *If the heavens, stripped of His noble imprint,*
> *Could ever cease to attest to His being.*

---

* This raises the unpleasant question of whether publishing the work of a deceased writer in such a way that he is made to hold a position on the existence of God he did not hold qualifies as doing to him "that which you would not have another do to you."

Voltaire is not raising the possibility of God's nonexistence here. He is stating that he believes God's indubitable existence is "necessary" to give people a reason to behave morally.

John Stuart Mill would argue in the next century that defending religion because it is useful is significantly less compelling than defending religion because it is true.[66] Voltaire is guilty of defending deism, at least in part, because it is useful. "It is certainly the interest of all men that there should be a Divinity to punish what human justice cannot repress," Voltaire writes[67]—echoing, minus the cynicism, Critias' point on religion serving "as terror for the bad." The threat of such heavenly punishment is, it might be noted, in the interest of the opulently outfitted Monsieur Voltaire and those in his class. "I want my attorney, my tailor, my servants, even my wife, to believe in God," Voltaire announces (presumably with some levity, especially since he has no wife), "and I fancy that as a result I shall suffer from less theft and less cuckoldry."[68]

Jean Meslier did not share Voltaire's levity, condescension or view that God is "necessary." The atheist priest and the deist philosopher do agree that organized religion, rather than a force for good, has been "a fatal source of trouble."[69] But Meslier does not believe some sort of disorganized religion, some lingering notion of God, is "necessary" to keep people— including tailors, servants and wives—acting morally. For Meslier was convinced that men and women can and will behave morally on their own. Meslier's book, in fact, sketches out a possible future in which people might be much kinder to each other—without any hint of a God.

And there was another point on which Meslier diverged from Voltaire: his book is addressed to the masses, to the mostly uneducated farmers and other working people who were his parishioners and with whom he had spent his life. Voltaire's hero John Locke had written, stirringly, of the right to "life, liberty, health and property."[70] This principle had been honored to an extent in the "Glorious Revolution" in England, which set England along the road toward a constitutional monarchy in 1689. But the right to "property" wouldn't have meant as much to Meslier's parishioners as it did to the friends of Locke and Voltaire. Meslier wanted more for them. Indeed, although Voltaire left most of this out of his excerpt, this priest went so far as to attack the nobility and "the vexations, the violence, the injustices and the ill-treatment which they commit on poor people."[71] In this priest's lengthy posthumous *Memoir* is an argument that religion had helped institute and preserve those "injustices," that religion has held the poor down.

In other words, Meslier, here on the cusp of the Enlightenment, con-nected religion and political exploitation—the exploitation of the farmers and other working people amongst whom he lived: "On the pretext of be-ing willing to drive you to heaven, they prevent you from enjoying your life on earth in any way; and finally pretending to keep you away in some other life from the imaginary pains of a hell that does not exist . . . they compel you to suffer in this life, which is the only one that you can claim to, the pains of a real hell."[72] To this, too, Meslier wanted his parishioners to open their eyes.

Meslier certainly deployed a *how-can-that-be?* skepticism about reli-gion in his *Memoir.* He was a resourceful thinker—capable of supplying *natural explanations* where necessary to push supernatural explanations aside. And Meslier's complaint that religion prevents his parishioners from "enjoying . . . life on earth" clearly echoes the *anacreontic.* But there is something additional going on here.

He may not have been the first to think it, but let's give Jean Meslier in his extraordinary *Memoir* credit for a fourth, not-so-ancient spur to disbelief: a political analysis of religion focused on that "real hell"—the oppression and injustice here on earth that religion can support. Meslier's analysis was not limited to what Voltaire saw: that the Catholic Church was greedy, corrupt, intolerant, repressive—a "ferocious," blood-sucking "ani-mal." Nor was this just another version of the problem of evil in the world: with oppression and injustice filling the role played by "mice, cockroaches or snakes" in Cicero. This village priest had developed a more sophisticated analysis of religion's complicity in the political and economic oppression of the lower classes.

Meslier realized that fantasies of heaven and hell can distract us from conditions here on earth—the hellish conditions often experienced by the underprivileged, the downtrodden, the scorned. He understood that reli-gion, whatever its moral contributions, can support tyranny and inequity. He realized that priests, ministers, rabbis and imams, through their homi-lies and ancient tales, can discourage people—the poor, in particular—from focusing on the unfairness of their circumstances and thereby sap their will to change those circumstances. He figured out that the comfort religion may provide for suffering can come at the cost of a struggle to alleviate some of that suffering. Meslier concluded that an end to religion might help free humankind—the poor, in particular—to focus on improv-ing its condition here on earth.

This is where the connection between disbelief and the expansion of human liberty—which I promised to deliver but have mentioned so far only briefly—begins to become clear: if religion supports oppression and injustice, a critique of religion is necessary to help reduce oppression and injustice, and make way for democracy, equality, human rights. The political contributions of Voltaire and Locke can be connected to their own efforts to move beyond established religion, with its hypocrisies, intolerance and corruption. Meslier's critique of religion was more sweeping; so was the political change for which he was calling.

This focus on the "real hell" some among us find ourselves in can lead to an angry, even revolutionary variety of disbelief. It has brought violence. It has also given birth to some far-reaching proposals for nonreligious, less oppressive and more just orderings of societies. The corollary to a "real hell," of course, is a utopian vision—a real heaven. Meslier's *Memoir* does imagine a more perfect way for humans to live together: Forty-seven years before the Declaration of Independence, this village priest insisted "that all men are by nature equal."[73] One hundred and nineteen years before the *Communist Manifesto,* he condemned private ownership of property and called for common ownership. (Meslier would become a hero in the Soviet Union—his name inscribed upon an obelisk.)[74] And all this was proposed in the name of nature, of justice, of truth, of humanity—and as a repudiation of the "imaginary God."[75]

We are watching, therefore, atheism and such egalitarian political and economic arguments make a public, unveiled appearance in Western thought together. They would continue to appear and work together in France, in the United States, in Britain, in the Soviet Union and around the world—not always with exemplary results—for a couple of centuries.

Meslier, in words that would be read only after he was gone, faced death in 1729 with the atheist's lack of illusions: "I am scarcely more than nothing," he wrote, "and soon I will be nothing."[76] But Meslier had expressed something that was indeed revolutionary: without God, this priest told eighteenth-century Europe from the grave, a better life for much of humankind is possible.

BOMBS ON THE HOUSE OF THE LORD

THE ENLIGHTENMENT ARGUMENT FOR ATHEISM

In the Dark Ages people found their surest guide in Religion—just as a blind man is the best guide on a pitch-black night. He knows the way better than the seeing. But it is folly to use the blind old man as a guide after day-break.

—Heinrich Heine[1]

TIME FOR AN EXTENDED VISIT TO A FIVE-STORY MANSION ON the Rue Royale in Paris. For, beginning a couple of decades after Meslier's death, this mansion became something new in the Western world: a hotbed of atheism.

The food and wine there were of the highest quality. But what drew a collection of the most distinguished writers, thinkers, scientists—*philosophes*—to the home of Paul-Henri Thiry, Baron d'Holbach, on Thursdays and Sundays for much of the second half of the eighteenth century was the conversation.[2] Yes, it was witty, as was the fashion in this city's salons; yes, it was erudite and wide ranging. However, the discussion here—and it usually lasted from two in the afternoon until seven or eight in the evening—was also weighty, candid and even contentious, in a way that might be considered unseemly at other such gatherings in Paris.

Jean-Jacques Rousseau was an early participant but stopped attending. For he suffered, as he explains in his *Confessions*, from a "natural aversion to disputation." Rousseau, a deist, was also discomfited by one persistent theme in the conversation. "If it is cowardice to allow people to speak evil of one's absent friend," an outraged Rousseau is reported to have announced after an evening with a crowd like d'Holbach's, "it is a crime to allow evil to be spoken about God, who is present."[3]

The German philosopher Georg Wilhelm Friedrich Hegel cautions that "we should not make the charge of atheism lightly, for it is a very common occurrence that an individual whose ideas about God differ from those of other people is charged with lack of religion, or even with atheism."[4] But then Hegel makes such a charge himself—against the Enlightenment: "Here it really is the case that this philosophy has developed into atheism." It was the case, to Rousseau's indignation, at d'Holbach's salon, which could pass for mission control of the Enlightenment in its most radical, most politically potent, most revolutionary incarnation.

In fact, for some of the sort of radical thinkers who attended this salon, Jean Meslier's atheistic manifesto had become, in the words of cultural historian Philipp Blom, "a kind of underground bible." Baron d'Holbach himself cribbed from Meslier repeatedly (although it was still wise to think twice before mentioning Meslier's name, even in anonymous writings). And Meslier also influenced Denis Diderot—d'Holbach's best friend and probably the outstanding regular intellectual presence at d'Holbach's salon; indeed with Voltaire and Rousseau Diderot was among the outstanding intellectual presences of the French Enlightenment. Diderot had borrowed from Meslier in at least one of his early attempts to stake out a position on religion.[5]

Baron d'Holbach hosted his salon—wryly referred to by the regulars as "the synagogue"—for three and a half decades. Along the way, he and Diderot and some other attendees expanded their rejection of religion into a rejection of irrationality, superstition and prejudice in many forms. They followed Meslier and expanded that critique of religion so far that it led to a frontal attack on monarchy and a call for human equality—notions just about as radical at the time as atheism. Indeed, these committed, crusading atheists, having their witty and contentious conversations over fine dinners in a mansion on the Rue Royale, ended up making an outsize contribution to liberty and equality. For the world started listening.

Perhaps the best-known moment in the history of this salon came in 1763 and involved one of the many distinguished international guests invited to join the conversation when in Paris: the great skeptic David

Hume. Diderot told of Hume's visit in a letter written to his mistress: "The English philosopher," Diderot reports, "took it upon himself to say to the baron that he did not believe in the existence of atheists, that he never had seen any. The baron said to him: 'Count how many we are here.'"[6] Eighteen thinkers surrounded the table. "'I am lucky enough to be able to show you fifteen atheists at one glance. The other three have not yet made up their minds.'"

Despite this professed unfamiliarity with atheists, David Hume, more properly labeled a Scottish philosopher, may have done as much damage to the arguments in support of religion as anyone since Carneades.

He made a contribution to the discussion of miracles, for example, that is more subtle than Spinoza's simple declaration that "nature cannot be contravened." Hume noted that since our judgments about the world must be based on our experience and since miracles, by definition, are events that go against all we have previously experienced, they are (almost) always impossible to credit. (As a conscientious skeptic, Hume usually left a little "almost.") "No testimony is sufficient to establish a miracle," he writes, "unless the testimony be of such a kind that its falsehood would be more miraculous than the fact, which it endeavors to establish."[7] An (almost) impossibly high standard to meet.

Hume did not dare apply his analysis to the miracle that had preoccupied Europe for a millennium and a half; he stuck to those of the pagans and the Jews. But his analysis seems designed to apply to the resurrection of Jesus. All our experience with the world indicates that death is irreversible: "It is a miracle that a dead man should come to life," Hume notes, in a different context; "because that has never been observed in any age or country."[8] What possible collection of "experience"—the testimony of how many reputable experts—would be required to overcome this accumulated wisdom on the finality of death, to accept that the resurrection had occurred?

Certainly not—remembering Jean Meslier's stipulation that any witnesses be "worthy of confidence"—a few contradictory and otherwise unsupported reports, written down, by persons unknown, decades, generations, after the fact; certainly not reports by partisans anxious to justify their own commitment to this man's preaching and to persuade others of its validity; certainly not reports intended for audiences with the typical human "inclination," to use Hume's phrase, "to the marvelous" in an age when the laws of nature were less well understood than today and violations of those laws more easily credited. Is it not wiser to conclude—as Hume does not put it—that the New Testament account of Jesus' resurrection might be incorrect than to conclude, based on such testimony, that "a dead man" has somehow "come to life"?

Hume contributed two major works on the subject of religion. The first, *The Natural History of Religion,* is an account of why people believe in religion. Hume published this book in 1757 under his own name, so it is sprinkled with some reassurances such as, "The whole frame of nature bespeaks an intelligent author."[9] But this book is an effort to explain religion by the way humans think, not by any miracles gods may have performed or any clues they may have left in the "frame of nature." That puts it squarely in the anti-religious tradition of Xenophanes, Critias and other Greeks. Indeed, Hume's book probably broke more ground than any contribution ever made to that tradition.

He notes, as anthropologists would note more than two centuries later, the relationship between religion and our weakness for tales of the extraordinary and our propensity for finding "human faces in the moon, armies in the clouds." He sees religion as a response to the "hope and fear" inspired by the vagaries and power of fate and notes that "gamesters and sailors," being even more vulnerable to that power, are more prone to superstitions. Hume concludes: "No wonder, then, that mankind, being placed in such absolute ignorance of causes, and being at the same time so anxious concerning their future fortune, should immediately acknowledge a dependence on invisible powers, possessed of sentiment and intelligence."[10]

That would leave religion, according to this remarkable eighteenth-century philosopher, as merely a psychological phenomenon: "no wonder."

Denis Diderot, the most prominent of the atheists David Hume encountered around Baron d'Holbach's table, was two years younger than the Scottish philosopher.

This former aspiring Jesuit had struggled with the question of religion in a couple of his early books of philosophy—testing out some of Jean Meslier's ideas but still ending up where Voltaire ended up: an opponent of organized religion but a deist. In one of those books, for example, Diderot accepted some version of the argument for design: "Is not the intelligence of a First Cause more conclusively proved in nature by His works," he asks, "than the faculty of reasoning in a philosopher by his writings?" The underground book in which Diderot posed this rhetorical question was treated as the best anti-Christian but pro-deist books were being treated in Paris: it was banned, burned and reprinted in at least seventeen editions in the remaining decades of the century.[11] This undoubtedly helped please Diderot's mistress at the time, who had a taste for money.

But Diderot did not long remain a deist: "Religion retreats to the extent that philosophy advances," he concludes in a letter.[12] His philosophy was advancing. And Diderot did not long remain with that mistress. His next long-term extramarital relationship—with his great love, Sophie Volland—would contribute to the history of philosophy in large part through her taste not for money but for long, expository letters, including the one in which Diderot proclaimed religion's retreat before philosophy and that letter in which he discussed Hume's visit to Baron d'Holbach's salon.

The development of disbelief—the story we are already well into here—certainly does not follow a straight line; humankind often doubles back.[13] Much of what was learned later had also been learned—perhaps with less sophistication but with no less astuteness—earlier: in India, in Greece and Rome, in Baghdad.

Often we know we are following the ancients: David Hume's other major work on the subject of religion—*Dialogues Concerning Natural Religion*—is modeled on Cicero's *The Nature of the Gods,* which was based, in turn, on the ideas of Carneades. In Hume's book, as in Cicero's, three characters are talking—one of whom is a skeptic with views similar, if not identical, to those of the author. In Hume's book, as in Cicero's, the author appears to backtrack from the dialogue's more anti-religious statements at the end and has the narrator proclaim the arguments of one of the more orthodox characters to be "nearer to the truth."[14]

These Cicero-like precautions, if that's what they were, were apparently not enough for Hume. His *Dialogues* was probably drafted by 1751; he did not allow it to be printed until after his death. (Hume died in 1776.) While "some of my Friends flatter me that it is the best thing I ever wrote," Hume once explained in a letter, "I have hitherto forborne to publish it, because I was of late desirous to live quietly, and keep remote from all Clamour." There was sufficient "Clamour" based on his other writings. Hume's reputed "infidelity" led, for example, to him being rejected twice for professorships in Scotland.[15]

Hume's book was probably most important where Cicero's was incomplete: Cicero's had his skeptic offer a direct reply to the argument that the universe, like a well-made house, was "designed," but that section has (conveniently, I have argued) been lost. The argument for design certainly remained formidable in Hume's time. It was Newton's argument. Voltaire employed it. For a time it was Diderot's argument. For those who don't accept faith or revelation as sufficient proof, it remains probably the dominant argument for the existence of God today. In his *Dialogues* Hume offered as strong a response to the contention that "this most elegant system" of the universe shows the hand of a "Supreme Artificer" as had ever been presented. He attacked from a number of directions.

Speaking through his skeptical character, Philo, Hume questions, to begin with, what crediting God as Universe Designer contributes to our understanding since we then would have to know who designed God. Is it "satisfactory," his skeptic Philo asks, "to explain a particular effect"—the universe—"by a particular cause"—God—"which was not more to be accounted for than the effect itself"? He concludes, therefore, that this "hypothesis"—that God "caused" the universe—brings "no advantages."[16]

Philo then recalls the neat arithmetical phenomenon that the digits in all numbers that can be divided by nine add up to nine or to a number that can be divided by nine. (Sixty-three, for instance, can be divided by nine, and six plus three equals nine.) "A superficial observer," he states, seeing "so wonderful a regularity" in our system of numbers might conclude that it was put there by "design" rather than realizing that this is a necessary and demonstrable quality of our system of numbers. Are we not making, he asks, a similar mistake, based on our still superficial understandings, in attributing the "wonderful . . . regularity" of the universe to design?[17]

How vain it is of us, Philo adds in perhaps the most original of these arguments, to see a human-like, anthropomorphic mind as the driving force behind all that is—all that is being a bit grander than a mere house.[18] "What peculiar privilege," he asks, "has this little agitation of the brain which we call thought, that we must thus make it the model of the whole universe." Why, he asks, is the universe compared to a "machine of human contrivance" not to an animal or a "great vegetable"—which might have been seeded naturally, organically, rather than designed? Nature, Philo states, "possesses an infinite number of springs and principles."[19] On what basis do we ignore all these other possible organizing and animating forces and assume the stars and the planets were all laid out and cobbled together by some human-like, though all-perfect, House Builder?

There is much we do not understand of the universe, much we may never understand. But, Hume's point is, what besides prejudice justifies our inserting into that receding unknown an analogy to our own, very small selves?

Hume displays traces of the anacreontic—an appreciation for the importance of "peaceful," "natural pleasures," for example, and a distaste for "the useless austerities and rigours, suffering and self-denial" of the religious.[20] He certainly does with some frequency squeeze out the supernatural by proposing alternative, natural explanations. Nonetheless, he contributes primarily to a skeptical variety of disbelief. David Hume asked some of the most astute versions of the question *how can that be?* that have ever been asked.

Another character in Hume's *Dialogues* says about Philo: "Of all men living, the task which you have undertaken, of raising doubts and objections, suits you best." The same might be said of Philo's author; it might have been said more than nineteen centuries earlier of the Greek skeptics. The doubling back is particularly apparent here: Hume allied himself with a "mitigated" or Academic Skepticism, like that of Carneades.[21] He did not dismiss *all* efforts to understand the world, as had Pyrrho and Montaigne. But, like a good skeptic, like Carneades, Hume was skeptical of all grand theories, all ambitious systems. He was not, consequently, a crusader for radical change—political or otherwise. Hume thought it wiser to rely on our experience and what had been shown to work reasonably well. Here Hume clearly parted company from his acquaintances around d'Holbach's table.

And Hume's great contributions to disbelief tended to be negative arguments: a credible miracle is (almost) a logical impossibility; gods, rather than being real, are the creation of human "hopes and fears"; attributing what order there is in the universe to a human-like mind makes little sense. Hume may have been, again like Carneades, too much a raiser of "doubts and objections" to ever declare himself an atheist—even if it had been safe to make such a declaration in eighteenth-century Britain.

Then where exactly did Hume end up on the question of God? We have more evidence on the subject than we do for Carneades or Cicero, but not much more: Hume was certainly capable of passing himself off in his books, when necessary, as something of a deist. Yet he denied, upon occasion, being one, and it is hard to see what of the God hypothesis—even in its most abstract form—is left standing after Hume's assaults upon it in these writings.[22] Hume trafficked in so much doubt that he might have been an agnostic, had the designation existed then. But Hume's salvos, in these books, seem to be fired almost exclusively in one direction; like Carneades he rarely aims his cannons at atheistic arguments.[23]

Two more personal statements from Hume on the subject of his own beliefs have also survived. The first is something an emotional Hume is reported, second hand, to have conceded to a friend following the death of his mother: "Though I threw out my speculations to entertain and employ the learned and metaphysical world, . . . in other things I do not think so differently from the rest of mankind as you may imagine."[24] The implication was that religion was one of those "other things."

Hume made the second of these statements in a deathbed interview with James Boswell. He apparently referred, then, to belief in an afterlife as "a most unreasonable fancy" and said that "he had never entertained any belief in Religion" after reading a couple of writers, one of whom was John Locke.[25] Boswell initially had difficulty believing Hume, though it is hard to see why a philosopher on his deathbed would pretend to be *less* religious than he was. Boswell, like many in Britain at the time, might simply have assumed that true nonbelievers did not exist.

When he questioned the existence of atheists at Baron d'Holbach's salon, was David Hume, this great debunker of the arguments for religion, being similarly naïve? Or was he using hyperbole or even being ironic?

Actually, d'Holbach himself likely was exaggerating if he did, in fact, proclaim that there were 15 atheists around his table. The most thorough study that has been made of the *philosophes* who customarily graced the baron's salon, by the historian Alan Charles Kors, suggests that—at that time—only three of them, including the host and Denis Diderot, were out-and-out atheists, with three more probable atheists and two other possible atheists.[26] As many as seven other d'Holbach regulars were deists or otherwise religious. Still, it is hard to come up with any other table in the West, since the Greeks, where atheism could make a better show.

Organized religion was under assault all over Paris in the middle of the eighteenth century—particularly in underground manuscripts and publications, prominent among them the works of Voltaire and that book by Meslier. But the sweeping disbelief espoused by some of the participants in Baron d'Holbach's salon, including that of the host, owed much to the influence of one man: Denis Diderot.

Individuals in Europe were gaining a little freedom to discuss their hesitations about religion—if only at a salon or in an underground publication. So it becomes possible to examine their irreligious epiphanies: the moments at which or, more commonly, the processes through which they were converted from believer to nonbeliever. Diderot seems to have left behind deism and found the atheism of which he would be such an influential proponent in part through a consideration of blindness.

Diderot was obsessed with the philosophical consequences of blindness (not blindness as metaphor, as in Heine's epigraph for this chapter). He had a very modern interest in the way the world changed when examined from different perspectives. Diderot also had a not-quite-so-modern (because not sufficiently relativistic) belief that the visual world could distract us from deeper perspectives and that the blind, consequently, perceive "in a much more abstract manner than we." He was particularly taken with the Cambridge mathematics professor Nicholas Saunderson—blinded by smallpox when he was about a year old—who had investigated, of all subjects, optics.[27]

In 1749, Diderot published—without (wink, wink) his name on it—his *Letter on the Blind for the Use of Those Who See.* It featured excerpts from a conversation between Saunderson, on his deathbed, and a minister summoned to comfort him.[28] Diderot was playing upon the continuing European fascination with atheists on their deathbeds—and the popular belief that they would inevitably repent. This particular deathbed dialogue between a blind scientist and a minister is one of the most important conversations in the history of atheism, although—as the police and other of Diderot's interested readers soon discovered—it had never taken place.[29]

In the conversation Diderot invented, Saunderson announces that because he is blind, "If you desire me to believe in God, then you must make me touch and feel Him." To which the minister replies, "Sir, place your hands upon your own body and there you will sense the divinity that resides in the admirable mechanism of your own organs." This is a biological version of the argument for design. To disprove it Diderot first has Saunderson note that not every "mechanism" is so "admirable." "Look well at me," he tells the minister, "I have no eyes." This is akin—assuming we accept a disability as evidence of faulty design—to Cicero's Skeptic Cotta questioning the existence of benevolent gods by pointing to "mice or cockroaches or snakes."

Diderot's Saunderson then offers a cognitive argument: don't all sorts of accomplishments seem "the work of God" when we don't understand them? "If nature presents us with a knot that is difficult to untie," he has Saunderson suggest, "let us leave it as it is; let us not insist on cutting it . . . and on employing for the task the hand of a being who thereupon becomes a knot even more difficult to untie than the first." Newton should not, in other words, have fallen back on an "intelligent and powerful being" when he came upon a mystery even he could not solve. (Diderot's logic here is similar to Hume's in his *Dialogues Concerning Natural Religion*—written at about the same time.)

What follows was more original and more important. Diderot's earlier arguments against religion in *Letter on the Blind* have been primarily *negative:* attacks on the contentions of those who do believe. *Positive* arguments for disbelief may extol mortal life. They may champion the richness and interest of this world or the human capacity to understand it. They may exhort us, in the anacreontic variety of these arguments, to "seize," or enjoy, today. They may demonstrate that we are better off for our flaws, or that the universe functions in part because of its imperfections.[30] Diderot was about to make a positive argument—an important one.

It helped that Diderot himself, as befits the editor of the *Encyclopédie*, had a sophisticated understanding of science. What Diderot did is have Saunderson sketch out a view of an organized, stable, reasonably logical, *godless* universe. His explanation begins with the supposition that matter is in constant motion, continually creating things and beings.[31] Many of the entities formed by this dynamic matter may not be so well configured. But—and here's the point—"motion still goes on, and will always go on, combining conglomerations of matter," Diderot argues through Saunderson, "until they have attained a state of organization that will permit them to endure"—for a time. That's why the world seems well designed; whatever is poorly organized fails to "endure."

This argument is similar, just to show that we are still doubling back, to points made 1,800 years earlier by Lucretius, with whom Diderot, like many of his contemporaries, was fascinated. And this is also, more or less, a Darwinian argument—a century before Darwin would make it.[32] Diderot was helping lift the "clear understanding," natural-explanations denomination of disbelief to a new level. The universe—a godless universe—evolves. There is a kind of natural selection of various possible "arrangements" of matter. Less effective arrangements don't last. Design is not only unnecessary; it would impede the process. Instead, the universe evolves through its strengths and flaws—in a way that some sort of always-perfect universe created by some sort of Always-Perfect Being never could.

Diderot's work, then, along with that of Hume, has great significance for this history. Newton and others had managed to maintain some compatibility between science and some stripped-down version of religion through the notion of design. After Hume, Diderot and the Enlightenment, that would become harder to maintain. Of course, it is foolish to think that the human impulse to imagine a human-like Universe Designer can be totally expunged: plenty of philosophers and scientists would hang onto the argument for design. However, the logic tying cause (God) to effect (the universe) had grown more elusive. After Hume and Diderot, the intricacies of nature could no longer be so easily viewed as advertisements for a deity.

It was the anti-religious argument in *Letter on the Blind* that earned Diderot his three-month stay in the Vincennes prison. It also earned him a letter from Voltaire: "I have read with extreme pleasure your book," the great man cheered the younger philosopher by writing. But Voltaire did make clear, cleverly, that he was concerned by the absence of "an infinitely clever Workman" in Diderot's universe: "I desire passionately to converse with you," Voltaire writes, "no matter whether you think you are one of His works or whether you think you are a necessarily organized portion of an eternal and necessary matter."[33]

Hume and Diderot—who shared Baron d'Holbach's table upon occasion—had together dealt Voltaire's "infinitely clever Workman" a major blow.

So a critique of religion was advancing at a sprightly pace in Enlightenment Europe. According to the argument of this book, that should be accompanied by and directly connected to an increase in learning. Matching causes with effects in history, of course, is something less than a science. But this was among those periods when the case for such a connection was strongest.

Hume was close enough to atheism and active enough in debunking religion that we might count his seminal contributions to modern philosophy—particularly Anglo-American philosophy—among the contributions of disbelief celebrated in this book. Would a man who believed everything in the universe to be the product of an "infinitely clever Workman" have been able to come up with a skepticism so profound and sophisticated that it still haunts philosophers today? Would a more religious man have been able to shuck off grand systems and theories and undertaken such a productive retreat to experience?[34]

Diderot is not read as often as Hume today, but his influence, too, was wide. Diderot's theory of dynamic matter—a step along the road to Darwin—qualifies as an example of how fruitful for thought nudging aside the God hypothesis can be.[35] In fact, his *Encyclopédie* project itself qualifies as a very large example of that.

Consider, for example, the *Encyclopédie*'s article on "Earthquakes." Europe at the time was still reeling from one particular earthquake, which struck Lisbon in 1755 and, with the assistance of fire and a tsunami, probably killed tens of thousands of people. So interest in the subject was high.

Earthquakes—along with lightning strikes, comets and death—are among those natural phenomena that can seem frighteningly unnatural. They are easy, therefore, to ascribe to the supernatural. But the Lisbon earthquake presented formidable difficulties for its religious interpreters: It occurred, to begin with, on All Saints' Day, at a time when—to add death and injury to insult—the churches were crowded.[36] Along with churches and cathedrals, the earthquake managed to wreck most of the city's monasteries and convents, and a disturbing number of sacred images were damaged in the process. If God were partial to Christians, Catholics in particular, he had a mysterious way of showing it.

Religion's exponents diligently set about the task, however, of justifying God's actions in Lisbon and, implicitly, reconfirming His existence.[37] Some miraculous survivals were soon enough found—which Catholics credited to one saint or another. Protestants pointed out that the victims were predominantly Catholic. And the sinfulness of the city's population—available in any city, at any time, as an explanatory factor—was dutifully noted and decried.

Voltaire, the deist, admitted to the difficulty of reconciling this horrible event to his view of a just and rational God. He wrote an anguished poem on the subject:

> *Will you say: "This is result of eternal laws*
> *Directing the acts of a free and good God!"*
> *Will you say, in seeing this mass of victims:*
> *"God is revenged, their death is the price for their crimes?"*

What crime, what error did these children,
Crushed and bloody on their mothers' breasts, commit?
Did Lisbon, which is no more, have more vices
Than London and Paris immersed in their pleasures?
Lisbon is destroyed, and they dance in Paris![38]

This is one of the strongest formulations of the problem of evil—that venerable argument against the existence of God, familiar from Cicero's dialogue. Voltaire's faith in a "necessary Being," may have been shaken by the occurrence of such seemingly unnecessary evil. But his deism survived, although that required that Voltaire's God, and His purposes, grow even more indistinct: "Undoubtedly, everything is ordered by Providence;" he writes in the preface to that poem on the Lisbon disaster, "but for a long time now, it has been all too evident that everything is not ordered for our present well being."[39] And Voltaire persisted in viewing this earthquake as an opportunity for theological, not scientific, discussion.

The article on earthquakes in Diderot's *Encyclopédie*, on the other hand, mostly confines itself to scientific explanations. In Enlightenment historian Jonathan I. Israel's summary, this article "stood open to every hypothesis, reflecting the latest expertise in geology, mineralogy, water flows, electricity, gas chemistry and mining practices"; it "cited several recent scientific papers."[40] The article was written by Baron d'Holbach.

The *Encyclopédie*'s article on earthquakes does have one significant limitation: despite its allegiance to science, despite its efforts to consult the latest research, it didn't get the cause of these violent tremors right: d'Holbach settles upon underground fires as his explanation. But the faulty hypothesis the *Encyclopédie* ended up supporting would lead, through the scientific method's testing and retesting of such hypotheses, to better and better understandings of such natural phenomena. The road to modern science passed through the speculations on that earthquake of Baron d'Holbach—an atheist—in the *Encyclopédie* edited by his friend and fellow atheist, Denis Diderot.

The purposes of the *Encyclopédie*, as outlined by Diderot, were majestic: "to collect all the knowledge that now lies scattered over the face of the earth, to make known its general structure to the men among whom we live, and to transmit it to those who will come after us."[41] Of course, his project, though it harnessed large numbers of the greatest thinkers of the time, fell short of that. Undergirding the project, as late-twentieth-century postmodernists have noted, were arrogant claims for Western knowledge and reason. And, with the benefit of a couple of centuries of hindsight, we can see that the *encyclopédistes* got quite a bit wrong. But a large swath of Western culture was examined and illuminated in the *Encyclopédie's* 71,818 articles. The road to modern philosophy, history, culture and technology, as well as science, passed through this dazzlingly ambitious work.

Could the *Encyclopédie* have been undertaken by individuals who still revered received wisdom and genuflected before the pronouncements of authorities—ecclesiastic or Greek? Could "all"—or at least a lot of—"the knowledge that now lies scattered over the face of the earth" have been collected and analyzed by individuals who believed all important wisdom had already been inscribed in some ancient holy book? Diderot thought not: "The *Encyclopédie* could only be undertaken in a philosophic age, such as has now arrived."[42]

Christians and deists wrote for the *Encyclopédie*. But it is significant that this project was undertaken and directed by an atheist[43]—one who maintained, as Diderot put it in an article in the *Encyclopédie*, that "whoever does not want to reason is renouncing the status of being human."[44] And a number of this atheist's main collaborators were also nonbelievers. D'Holbach alone wrote 400 of the *Encyclopédie's* articles.

These volumes were initially intended for aboveground publication so the nonbelievers had to hide their tracks; still, it is possible to uncover evidence of this semi-secret society of atheists—many of them regulars at Baron d'Holbach's salon—on numerous pages of the *Encyclopédie*. There were many minor jabs at religion.[45] Irony was sometimes employed—subtly mocking, in a way only readers in the know would grasp, arguments in favor of religion or against materialist philosophy. The article on Spinoza, for instance, often denounced him—as was necessary in a openly published text, one that at times was examined by censors—but it did so, to borrow the analysis of Jonathan Israel, by "recycling wholly out-of-date, irrelevant and feeble theological arguments."[46] And flagrantly anti-religious statements were squirreled away in unexpected places. An article on "Ethiopians," for example, includes this highly dangerous assertion: the universe "has formed itself."[47]

Voltaire, despite his considerable capacity for amusement, was among those who were increasingly not amused. He had been a defender of this grand project for the advancement of human knowledge, as well as, after the *Encyclopédie's* alphabetical progression was already up to the "E" volume, a participant in it. However, Voltaire was more and more put off by the philosophy subtly being expressed—a universe that "has formed itself"?—and by the philosophy driving editorial decisions. His hero John Locke, for example, would receive only four columns in the *Encyclopédie*— fewer than the other top philosophers. The atheist's hero, Spinoza, on the other hand, would be accorded 22 columns—however *faux* disparaging. Voltaire was also growing concerned that those scattered digs at religion, and similar swipes at royalty, were making the *Encyclopédie* too danger- ous.[48] In 1757, after the "G" volume was published, he withdrew from the project and encouraged his friends to do likewise.

The *Encyclopédie,* arguably the great intellectual achievement of the eighteenth century, was to an extent the product of atheists and it har- bored, as much as was possible at the time, expressions of atheism. In a sense—to overstate the case a bit—the whole Enlightenment, led by Diderot's *Encyclopédie,* belongs to the story of the accomplishments of disbelief.

That virtuous cycle of disbelief and learning—to return to my central metaphor—was turning and climbing at a rapid rate in France in particu- lar in the middle of the eighteenth century. The advancement of science and philosophy—along with a growing distaste for the church's corruption and hypocrisy—was contributing to a flight from religion—perhaps as rapid a flight as at any other time in the West since Thucydides' day in Ath- ens. And that increase in disbelief—in atheism as well as deism—was, in turn, clearing the way for science and philosophy to advance more rapidly.

Did Denis Diderot bring Baron d'Holbach, who was ten years his junior, to atheism? This question has an interest for a history of atheism simi- lar to that which the question of whether Bob Dylan first introduced the Beatles to marijuana might have for a history of rock and roll.

The only direct piece of evidence here is a tale related by the friend and biographer of a regular attendee of d'Holbach's salon:[49] We're told that d'Holbach, then still "an adorer of God," was trying to get Diderot to ac- knowledge the resemblance of the universe to a machine they were both admiring. As Diderot dismissed, once again, this version of the design argu- ment, d'Holbach suddenly realized he himself could no longer see that cru- cial resemblance. "Diderot's friend, bursting into tears, fell at his feet," the story goes. And "he who fell on his knees a deist, got up an atheist." With or without such a dramatic irreligious epiphany, the baron become an atheist of great conviction, commitment and influence; and it does seem to have happened sometime after he befriended Diderot in about 1750.[50]

Paul-Henri Thiry, Baron d'Holbach, a German, had been raised in Paris and, after attending university in Holland, settled permanently in Paris in 1749, becoming a French citizen. The baron augmented and consolidated a family fortune, originally primarily his uncle's, by marrying one of his second cousins, then, when she died, her sister. (Life *chez* d'Holbach was enlivened when at least two regular members of the salon successively and unsuccessfully declared their love to the second Baronne d'Holbach.)[51]

Baron d'Holbach was, by all accounts, a man of substantial culture, taste, generosity and decency. I haven't even come across reports of a mistress. The baron's temper when losing at cards was, according to Diderot, formidable, but so was his graciousness, his memory, his library and his love of ideas.[52]

D'Holbach had also picked up from his uncle a title (albeit one of recent vintage), and the "Baron d'Heeze, Leende, seigneur de Walperg," as he styled himself, even went so far as to purchase from some of his relatives the additional French title "counselor-secretary to the king" (a transaction that required his parish priest to certify that d'Holbach was a good Catholic).[53] But the baron was also deserving of one additional title: he ranks as one of history's most energetic and effective advocates for atheism.

D'Holbach's claim to this latter title does not rest only on his salon, which despite its nest of unbelievers remained a congenial place for deists and even some Christians to converse (as long as they, unlike Rousseau, were not adverse to spirited argument). One regular, an abbé, does note an occasion when members of d'Holbach's "synagogue" were "saying things to bring down thunderbolts on their heads a hundred times over, if thunderbolts fell for that." Then he reports that another regular, also an abbé, felt the need to respond to such sacrileges: "If I were pope, I'd hand you over to the Inquisition," that man of the church announced; "and if I were king of France, I'd send you to the Bastille; but as I have the good fortune to be neither the one nor the other, I shall come here to dinner again next Thursday."[54] Baron d'Holbach's stripes as a soldier for unbelief were earned in large part through his publishing efforts.

In 1770, the French clergy, meeting in Paris, decided to warn the kingdom of the mushrooming "dangers of disbelief."[55] They had reason for concern. One set of statistics from the city of Toulouse demonstrates the extent to which religious morality was losing its grip on the people of France. The fraction of illegitimate births there had been one in 59 a hundred years earlier.[56] By 1751 it had risen to one in every 7.2 births, and it would jump to one in every four births by 1788.

The clergy immediately identified the source of this steep and shocking decline in moral behavior: underground books. The royal prosecutor-general drew up a list of the most scandalous of the currently circulating anti-religious books. These books were so incendiary that his summary of their content itself had to be banned. Seven books garnered a place on the royal prosecutor-general's list. Six of them were written, edited or translated—clandestinely, of course—by Baron d'Holbach or the member of his salon who had been assisting him in his work, Jacques-André Naigeon. In fact, from 1761 to 1770, d'Holbach, with Naigeon, published—always clandestinely—no less than 30 anti-religious books.[57]

On a continent where irreligious manuscripts and books had only recently begun to trickle out, this barrage was extraordinary. "It is raining bombs on the house of the Lord," an astonished Diderot exclaimed in a letter to Sophie Volland.[58]

Some of the texts d'Holbach published were old, often anonymous, mostly deist attacks on Christianity, perhaps fortified by the editors with a little extra disrespect toward God. Some of the texts, including a short work by Thomas Hobbes, the baron had collected on a visit to England and translated. Eleven of these books the baron had written himself.[59] The most important of those—d'Holbach's two-volume *The System of Nature or the Laws of the Physical and Moral World*—stands as one of the most influential arguments for atheism ever written.

Baron d'Holbach edited, translated and wrote fast. He would usually prepare a draft of each edit, translation or original work and pass it on to be looked over by Naigeon, who then forwarded the manuscript to his brother, a copyist.[60] The original, with its potentially incriminating handwriting, could then be destroyed. The recopied manuscript was sent "in a package covered with two layers of wax-sealed cloth" to a woman in Liège connected with the veteran underground publisher in Amsterdam who would see the book into print. Copies were then smuggled back into France.

None of these books was printed under the name of a living person. With a sly impudence consistent with the conviction that the dead no longer experience pain, the texts were usually falsely attributed to one deceased writer or another. Some of those whose names graced the title page of one of these books (J. B. Mirabaud, a former secretary of the French Academy, for example, who was credited with authorship of *The System of Nature*) had had nothing to do with such sentiments and some (Jean Meslier, for example) had. (Anyone searching for Meslier's writing today will likely come upon a book called *Common Sense*, which was written many decades after his death and is actually an abridged version of d'Holbach's *System of Nature*.)

"I go in fear and trembling lest one of these terrible bombers gets into difficulties," Diderot writes in that letter to his mistress. His friends, the crusading atheists, did not get into difficulties. There is no evidence that the connection of d'Holbach or Naigeon to these books was even being whispered about. Other members of the salon must have known who was launching these bombs, but they appear to have remained scrupulously silent.[61] And even if he had been exposed, it is difficult to imagine a man like d'Holbach suffering much. Others, less well situated, suffered a great deal.

A grocer's apprentice, for example, purchased two copies of one of Baron d'Holbach's books from a peddler and then was foolish enough to resell one of them to his master.[62] After a dispute, the master reported his apprentice to the police. The young man was sentenced, in 1768, to nine years "on the galleys," the peddler to five and the peddler's wife was locked up in a hospital. Not only were the poor easier targets, but authorities shared Voltaire's fear of what might break loose should the upper class' tense debate on the existence of God be overheard by too many grocery boys, peddlers and peddlers' wives.

Baron d'Holbach sometimes achieved a lyricism in his *System of Nature*:

> If their gods are infinitely good, wherefore should we dread them? . . . If they are omniscient, wherefore inform them of our wants, why fatigue them with our requests? If they are omnipresent, of what use can it be to erect temples to them? If they are lords of all, why make sacrifices to them; why bring them offerings of what already belongs to them? If they are just, upon what foundation believe that they will punish those creatures whom they have filled with imbecility? . . . If they are omnipotent, how can they be offended; how can we resist them? If they are rational, how can they enrage themselves against blind mortals, to whom they have left the liberty of acting irrationally? . . . If they are inconceivable, wherefore should we occupy ourselves with them?[63]

There was plenty of criticism of religion in d'Holbach's masterwork. However, by 1770 that had, more or less, been done—done by Spinoza and Jean Meslier, and done by David Hume, who presumably had discussed his ideas at the baron's table, although his book, *Dialogues Concerning Natural Religion*, had not yet been published because Hume had not yet died. Baron d'Holbach, however, had a more lofty goal in mind. D'Holbach was trying to discover and outline a godless "system." The strength of this effort was not the originality of its arguments: "An organic anthology of all the materialistic and atheistic theses of the eighteenth century," Voltaire calls *The System of Nature*, probably with some awareness of the identity of its author.[64]

Derivative it may have been—of Diderot's thinking on dynamic matter, in particular, but also of the work of numerous other seventeenth- and eighteenth-century (and earlier) scientists and philosophers. Still d'Holbach's book stood apart in its scope, its coherence and its audacity. Unlike the treatises of its more wary predecessors, it never flinches: "The author," as Diderot notes, "is not an atheist in one page and a deist in another."[65]

Baron d'Holbach's anonymous synthesis qualifies, in its way, as monumental, for *The System of Nature* contains a grand, positive argument for disbelief—a comprehensive outline of a universe manufactured, sustained, organized and managed exclusively by the workings of "uncreated" nature. With the audacity of a Lucretius, of a Thucydides, Baron d'Holbach has attempted to provide "a clear understanding" of the workings of nature.

Voltaire quotes what he calls an "eloquent though dangerous" selection from *The System of Nature* in a later edition of his *Philosophical Dictionary*. It includes one of d'Holbach's summaries of his argument:

> *Nature is not a work:* She has always existed of herself. Every process takes place in her bosom. She is an immense manufactory . . . : all her works are effects of her own energy, and of agents or causes which she frames, contains and impels. Eternal, uncreated elements—elements indestructible, ever in motion and combining in exquisite and endless diversity, originate all the beings and all the phenomena that we behold; all the effects, good or evil, that we feel; the order or disorder which we distinguish . . . ; and, in a word, all those wonders which excite our meditation and confound our reasoning.[66]

This was not, of course, an argument that Voltaire could accept. He scoffed at the notion that Nature's "immense manufactory" could actually have fashioned one set of the "beings . . . we behold." "Produce without intelligence, beings with intelligence!" Voltaire exclaims. "Is this conceivable?"[67]

Some who acquainted themselves with d'Holbach's *System* found another ground upon which to reject it: the aesthetic. "How hollow and empty did we feel in this melancholy, atheistical half-night," laments one romantic young German poet, "in which earth vanished with all its creatures, heaven with all its stars!"[68] This poet—fearful that earth and stars somehow won't be visible without the candlepower of the supernatural—is Goethe.[69]

The System of Nature became one of the most reviled—and read—books of the eighteenth century.[70] After the year 1770, defenders of religion in France, in Europe and also in America finally found themselves confronting not just phantoms or carefully hedged arguments but the beginnings of an unabashed, full-blown philosophy of atheism.

The French church actually commissioned an answer to *The System of Nature*. The assignment was given to a priest with tip-top scholarly and literary credentials, Nicolas-Sylvain Bergier, in return for a large pension.[71] And he did publish a tough refutation of the book—which Bergier called "the boldest and most terrible that has been printed since the Creation of the world"—but not before showing a section of that refutation, not only to his friend Denis Diderot, but also to his friend Baron d'Holbach, whom he may or may not have suspected of being the author of the book he was refuting.[72] Indeed, the Abbé Bergier, the main theoretical apologist for the Catholic church in France at the time, was himself a fairly regular visitor to Baron d'Holbach's salon.

Voltaire—the deist—was no political radical: he was buddies with monarchs and unable to imagine a political system without them. The distinguished philosopher respected, as did many moderate Enlightenment thinkers in France and England at the time, the English system: a limited, constitutional, parliamentary monarchy. In a letter to a younger philosopher who would become a member of d'Holbach's salon, Voltaire cautioned that the "infamous"—Christianity—must be crushed but only "slowly."[73]

David Hume—the (almost) atheist—had similar politics. Among the grand theories about which he was skeptical was the presumption that "all governments . . . should be . . . founded on popular consent." As a man with little taste for "Clamour," Hume also lacked enthusiasm for experiments with what he called "such dangerous novelties" as a pure republican government. Hume labeled himself "a friend to moderation."[74]

Diderot and d'Holbach—the atheists—however, were growing increasingly political and increasingly radical. That radicalism had begun to be revealed in the first of the books the baron wrote himself (under a pseudonym, of course): *Christianity Unveiled*.[75] Voltaire, just to be clear, announced that this book "is entirely opposed to my principles. This book leads to an atheistic philosophy that I detest."[76] The book would also seem to lead to an anti-monarchical philosophy, which must have also troubled the elitist Voltaire. For it included a chapter on the connection between religion and politics. D'Holbach's rhetoric here is decidedly immoderate:

> The Christian religion, in fact, always makes despots and tyrants of all the sovereigns by whom it is adopted. It represents them as Gods upon earth; it causes their very caprices to be respected as the will of heaven. It delivers mankind into their hands as a herd of slaves, of whom they may dispose at their pleasure.

D'Holbach is not quite saying that monarchy will always be an unacceptable system of government—in 1761, the year when this book was probably printed, that argument was rare indeed. And, appropriately for a baron, d'Holbach does not go as far as Jean Meslier: he is not condemning private ownership of property. But the baron, like Meslier, was inspired by the fourth spur to disbelief: an awareness of religion's role in keeping a large portion of humankind in a "real hell." D'Holbach sees the connection between religion and political repression. And that understanding takes this "counselor-secretary to the king" far indeed: for he has mounted an argument against almost all of the monarchs then ruling Europe.

And d'Holbach's analysis here demonstrates how effectively an attack on religious authority can be turned into an attack on political authority. Take a sledge hammer to the religious foundation stones—divine right, "the will of heaven"—and there's not much upon which a creaky, inefficient, corrupt, intermittently brutal, Old Regime might stand. A king, stripped of the trappings of religion, can easily be revealed as a despot, a tyrant.

The attack upon such despots, such tyrants, did have something upon which to stand. Diderot—also concerned with responding to oppression and injustice, to the "real hell" so many experience—names that basic principle in an *Encyclopédie* entry entitled "Political Authority": "liberty." Diderot is no less enthusiastic about it than Locke: "No man has received from nature the right to command others," he proclaims in that article, one of the 990 articles Diderot wrote for the *Encyclopédie*. We ought to have the "liberty" to govern ourselves. Diderot was plumping in that *Encyclopédie* article for an alternative standard for political authority: the "consent of the people"[77]—and not just European peoples or the wellborn. For Diderot is also a partisan of "equality." Indeed, in another *Encyclopédie* article he adds an additional principle not much mentioned by Locke: "equity" or fairness, which Diderot proclaims part of "natural law."[78]

As analysis of the collusion between religion, oppression and injustice deepened in the eighteenth century, liberty and atheism were beginning a virtuous cycle of their own—also with a vigor not seen in the West since Athens. And Diderot and d'Holbach weren't done.

Baron d'Holbach's *System of Nature*—that summation of eighteenth-century irreligious thought—was not the only subversive and hugely influential book published in 1770 that came out of discussions in his salon.[79] The second book had a nondescript title, *The Philosophical History of the Two Indies,* and, although published anonymously, was generally attributed to a former Jesuit abbé, Guillaume-Thomas Raynal. Raynal, a friend of Diderot's, was a regular at Baron d'Holbach's salon, where the book had mostly been conceived.[80] The major intellectual presence behind *The Philosophical History*—a multi-volume work that appeared in a number of editions—was not Raynal. It was Diderot, and Diderot also pitched in on much of the editing and writing.[81]

The Philosophical History of the Two Indies was a political, economic, anthropological and (before that term was in use) sociological account of the inhabitants of the globe. Before 1789 forty editions of the various updated versions of *The Philosophical History* had appeared in French. Twenty editions were printed in English—some of them in America.[82]

One of the book's most compelling features, for a world just getting to know itself, was a compendium of interesting and useful facts on governments, cultures, customs and trade. A desire to access those facts may explain why Louis XVI's conservative war minister was caught having ordered a copy, while the king was fighting to have the book banned.[83] *The Philosophical History* also had two other attractions, presumably of less interest to Louis XVI's war minister: One was principles—relatively new ideas on how people, all the world's people, ought to be allowed to live. The other was a multitude of examples of what happened around the world when those principles were violated—a compendium, if you will, of places where the oppressed of the world were living, to again employ Meslier's wording, with "the pains of a real hell."

You can see why most European monarchs would have wanted to suppress this book. It argued again and again for "liberty": "the birthright of all men."[84] Indeed it argued for something rare in the world in these years before the American Revolution, "political liberty," which it defined as "the state of a people . . . who either make their own laws, or who constitute a part in the system of their legislation."[85] This book insisted that "a despotic government, with the best intentions in the world, can never do good."[86]

The Philosophical History argued, too—in a world increasingly being dominated by white people, by Europeans—for human equality: "that original equality established by nature among mankind."[87] With great moral passion the book condemned—"I detest, I abhor"—slavery: "You sell them . . . as you would a base herd of cattle!"[88] But its call for equality went further. *The Philosophical History* opposed aristocracy: "Courage, virtue, and genius, belong to all ranks."[89] It was even sensitive to the "oppression of the women," as perpetrated in numerous non-European societies at least.[90] (Diderot and d'Holbach were ahead of their time in believing women ought to have a right to divorce, but it would be hard to argue that their call for equality extended to a full slate of rights for women.[91])

The Philosophical History was not against commerce, private ownership or trade—indeed it argued for free trade.[92] Diderot was not Karl Marx or, in this regard, even Meslier. However, the book was staunchly opposed to exploitation in all forms. It noted the ravages of colonialism: "Savage Europeans! Ye doubted at first whether the inhabitants of the regions you had just discovered were not animals which you might slay without remorse, because they were black and you were white." Indeed, the book had no patience with the colonial system Europe was in the process of imposing on the world: "This is the decree pronounced by fate upon your colonies: you must either renounce them or they will renounce you."[93]

The Philosophical History also advocated for tolerance: "that sacred law of nature, which enjoins all men to tolerate the opinions of their fellow creatures."[94] And it proclaimed the importance of freedom of speech: "In every well-regulated society, there ought to be no matter upon which a freedom of discussion should not be allowed. The more weighty and the more difficult this matter is, the more necessary doth this discussion become."[95]

Jonathan Israel, a history professor at Princeton's Institute for Advanced Studies, is an enthusiastic and erudite champion of the political accomplishments of what he calls the "radical" or "democratic" Enlightenment, which Professor Israel distinguishes from the "moderate" Enlightenment of Voltaire and Hume.[96] Professor Israel's controversial books have been important to me here. For this "radical" Enlightenment was led, he makes clear, by Diderot and d'Holbert. *The Philosophical History of the Two Indies*—"a devastating denunciation of violence, fanaticism, superstition, greed and despotism," Israel calls it—may be the product of their movement that excites this Enlightenment historian most:

> For the first time, all sections of humanity were being drawn into the same discussion about the human condition and its basic characteristics, in a manner apt to transform men's views about government, empire, trade, the relationship between . . . the different races, religions and genders . . . . Here was a text more widely read than any other Enlightenment work, offering all men "philosophy" stressing basic equality and the right to happiness of all.[97]

One would have liked, from a twenty-first-century perspective, to have seen in *The Philosophical History* more on women if not something on sexual orientation. And it is necessary to acknowledge that most of these ideas had histories that extend back a long way before the Enlightenment. They certainly weren't just French ideas: Greece and Rome had contributed quite a lot to them, as had the Netherlands and certainly England, particularly England's "Glorious Revolution" in 1688. Other thinkers mentioned earlier in this book played a role, including representatives of Jonathan Israel's "moderate" Enlightenment, such as Voltaire and Hume.

No, these democratic ideas were not just born of and nurtured by outright atheists. But they were aided and abetted at many stages in their development—beginning in Athens—by the retreat of hierarchical, sectarian, anti-rational, tradition-preserving religions. And in 1770—right before two revolutions that would, violently, unleash these ideas upon the world—it wasn't Christians who began to crystallize them in a book; it wasn't deists. It was a group of mostly atheists.

With *The Philosophical History of the Two Indies* Denis Diderot, Baron d'Holbach and their coterie laid out a vision of a more equitable world that would eventually—after many setbacks and much bloodshed—be shared by most of the world.[98]

8

THE BEAST LET LOOSE

REVOLUTION IN AMERICA AND FRANCE

Nor is any reconcilement possible between free thought and traditional authority. One or other will have to succumb after a struggle of unknown duration, which will have as side issues vast political and social troubles.

—Thomas Henry Huxley[1]

N AN ALMANAC FOR THE YEAR 1751, A PRINTER, WRITING UNDER a pseudonym, in a town out on the edge of Britain's empire, brought a lively metaphor to the discussion of the consequences of atheism—a major concern of this turbulent chapter:

Talking against Religion is unchaining a Tiger;
The Beast let loose may worry his Deliverer.[2]

The town was Philadelphia, the pseudonym "Poor Richard."

By the time the eighteenth century drew to a close, anti-religious talk had intensified—particularly in France. And it appeared for a time as if a "Beast," as Benjamin Franklin had predicted, had indeed been "let loose." One early piece of evidence of that, later seized upon by horrified conservative commentators, was a particularly notorious piece of irreligious and anti-royalist rhetoric composed in that country.[3]

Voltaire used a similar image, on a slightly different subject, as early as 1761, but the political view expressed in the sentence in question is too radical to have been Voltaire's.[4] Baron d'Holbach's religious and political views were radical enough. But the tone of this sentence seems rather grisly for the gracious baron.

The Marquis de Sade, who will soon appear as a character in this tale, was sufficiently anti-religious and anti-authoritarian—and more than sufficiently clever, ghoulish, fierce and nasty—to have fashioned the sentence. He must have heard it. He must have enjoyed it. But it has not been attributed to him. Nor do the various revolutionary leaders who guillotined each other in Paris in the 1790s have a legitimate claim to authorship.

The line did appear in a poem by Denis Diderot probably written in 1772. But it is not clear that Diderot, who places the words in the mouth of a character, himself supports the sentiment.[5] And Diderot almost definitely borrowed the line's main elements from Jean Meslier's *Memoir*, written much earlier in the century.[6] It is a line that connects atheistic and democratic sentiments—a connection this book wants to honor—but connects them in violence. This is its best known, though not its original form: "With the guts of the last priest let us strangle the last king."

The ideas of Voltaire, d'Holbach and Diderot—if not Meslier—had certainly found their way to Ben Franklin's side of the Atlantic.

"The foundation of our Empire was not laid in the gloomy age of Ignorance and Superstition," recalls George Washington. To the contrary: it was laid, he declares, "in this enlightened Age."[7] The *philosophes* who made the Enlightenment in France and England, in other words, hovered over the uprising Washington led along the eastern seaboard of North America. And for many years they continued to haunt the "Empire"—or nation, as most of its subsequent leaders have preferred to call it—that uprising spawned.

Americans obviously had been inspired by the anti-monarchial strains of the Enlightenment—although the king they shed remained undeposed, unstrangled and out of reach back in Britain. The most direct connection between the radical political ideas being developed in Baron d'Holbach's salon and the American Revolution ran through America's own "radical" Enlightenment figure: the inspirational and influential Thomas Paine.

Paine's *Common Sense* was, historian Eric Foner writes, "unique in the extent of its readership and its influence on events."[8] At least 25 editions of this pamphlet were published in North America, beginning in January of 1776—less than nine months after the first shots of the Revolutionary War. *Common Sense* reached hundreds of thousands of Americans, and it persuaded many of them that this war ought to have two decidedly radical goals: complete independence from Britain and independence from a king. "We were blind," one Connecticut man reported after reading Paine's pamphlet, "but on reading these enlightening words the scales have fallen from our eyes."[9]

And *Common Sense,* according to Enlightenment historian Jonathan Israel's reading, demonstrates that Tom Paine was familiar with and "impressed with" *The Philosophical History of the Two Indies,* which was produced by Diderot and other members of d'Holbach's salon.[10]

Indeed, Paine's writing shares a vocabulary with *The Philosophical History:* "barbarity" (applied to supposedly civilized colonial powers), "prejudice," "superstition," "abuse of power," "oppression" and "tyranny" on the one hand; "mankind," "rights," "freedom," "liberty" and, the key word in *Common Sense,* "independence" on the other. Where *The Philosophical History* speaks of the "defense of those sacred rights which they hold equally by nature's charter," or "the natural equality of man" (itself reminiscent of Jean Meslier's insistence that "that all men are by nature equal"), Paine's *Common Sense* trumpets "the equal rights of nature."[11]

Here are perhaps the most glorious of Paine's lines:

> O ye that love mankind! Ye that dare oppose, not only the tyranny, but the tyrant, stand forth! Every spot of the old world is overrun with oppression. Freedom hath been hunted round the globe. Asia, and Africa, have long expelled her.—Europe regards her like a stranger, and England hath given her warning to depart. O! receive the fugitive, and prepare in time an asylum for mankind.

This image of freedom or liberty, and therefore humankind, requiring an "asylum"—and even of America as potentially offering that asylum—also appears in editions of *The Philosophical History.*[12]

I don't mean to claim too much for the connection between this book, its authors in Baron d'Holbach's salon and American revolutionary thought. I have found no evidence that Jefferson, as he wrote the Declaration of Independence, was—yet—familiar with Diderot's or d'Holbach's thought. Jefferson had read and did respect Paine, but we don't know that when he insists that "all men are created equal," he was echoing Paine and indirectly *The Philosophical History,* rather than just philosophizing himself or expanding on the work of the British thinkers, including Locke, with which he was familiar. Such words and ideas were in the air; they drifted across the Atlantic in many forms from many sources.

Nonetheless, those atheists in Paris had been releasing a lot of radical ideas into the air above these two continents—on politics as well as on religion.

Finding a connection between the anti-Christian, even anti-religious ideas produced "in this enlightened age" and America's Founding Fathers is somewhat easier. This, the first of the two late-eighteenth-century revolutions, did not set about disemboweling or even displacing members of the clergy. But traditional religious notions were being challenged even in this country—a country settled in part by religious groups fleeing persecution.

Benjamin Franklin may have worried about "talking against Religion," but among the books in his library were a version of Diderot's *Encyclopédie*, a copy of Voltaire's *Treatise on Tolerance*, a volume defending David Hume's ideas and an obscure anti-religious tract published by and perhaps written by Baron d'Holbach.[13] Indeed, Franklin had engaged in extended conversations with Hume in Edinburgh in 1771. And while representing America in Paris from 1776 to 1785, Franklin appears to have devoted long, pleasant evenings to repartee and philosophic debate at the baron's salon; he considered Baron d'Holbach a friend.[14] And Franklin's own attitude toward religion was decidedly irregular. Enlightenment books and Paris dining rooms proved more conducive to his moral speculations than what he dismissed as the "dry," "polemic arguments" of a Philadelphia church. Franklin "seldom," as he once explained, "attended any public worship."[15]

Thomas Paine's *Common Sense* includes numerous paragraphs, chockablock with biblical citations, trying to prove—rather unpersuasively—that "the will of the Almighty . . . expressly disapproves of government by Kings." However, this likely was just Paine the master propagandist employing every possible means to persuade; for when John Adams suggested to Paine in 1776 that his "Reasoning from the Old Testament was ridiculous," Paine, in Adams' much later recollection, "expressed a Contempt of the Old Testament and indeed of the Bible at large."[16]

That rings true. Paine, who was originally encouraged to come to America by Franklin, once announced, "My religion is to do good."[17] He was blunt on the subject in his book *The Age of Reason*, written in the

1790s: "I do not believe in the creed professed by the Jewish church, by the Roman church, by the Greek church, by the Turkish church, by the Protestant church, nor by any church that I know of," Paine declared. "All national institutions of churches . . . appear to me no other than human inventions set up to terrify and enslave mankind and monopolize power and profit." The great rhetorician of American independence saw "the exceeding probability that a revolution in the system of government," which Paine's glorious metaphors and insistent logic had helped further in America, "would be followed by a revolution in the system of religion."[18]

And an Enlightenment-inspired religious revolution did appear to have taken place in influential circles in America. A commitment to religious tolerance—Bayle's cause, Voltaire's cause—was enshrined in the new nation's founding documents; at times it protected even nonbelievers. Parts of Europe were beginning to grow more tolerant, too, and America has not always lived up to its principles. Still, there is something wonderful in the fact that there would be no religious Inquisition here, that a Giulio Cesare Vanini would not be strangled, that neither a Menocchio nor a Michael Servetus would be burned, that a reward would not be offered for the arrest or murder of a Diagoras of Melos. Surely, the development and institutionalization of this new form of liberty—freedom of conscience—would be among the greatest of America's contributions to the world.

Not that Americans don't keep fighting about tolerance—for a reason. To be tolerant of another's religion is to entertain the notion, the notion Pierre Bayle asked that we entertain, that there is a chance that your religion might just be wrong. It will take a lot of convincing, for example, to get someone who believes that every word of a holy book is not only literally true but clear and inescapable in its meaning to "tolerate" someone who ignores, contradicts or violates, let alone disparages, those words. It will take a lot of convincing for that person to live peaceably besides such a sinful, devilish infidel.

Tolerance requires that we take a step back from beliefs—from our own beliefs. And it does something else to which the devout might legitimately object: tolerance insists that a realm—another realm—exists into which religion should not intrude. Science was already in the process of becoming such a realm; philosophy was moving in a similar direction. Now, the Constitution of the United States, which itself conspicuously failed to mention God, made it possible for government to be such a religion-free zone, too.

If religion—the teachings of Torah, the good news of the Gospels, the worship of Allah—is all, why should places, including a place as important as the government, be allowed to exist where it is nothing? Such a notion would have been unintelligible in ancient Israel, in Cicero's Rome and in Europe for most of its history. Separation between church and state inevitably means that church has in some sense been diminished:[19] Its sway has been reduced. The government, not the church, is the "leviathan."

By the end of the eighteenth century, the United States had become a beacon of tolerance, a sanctuary for the persecuted, a place where religion and government were to leave each other alone. In the context of this history that was a considerable step forward.

And the "revolution in the system of religion" Paine wanted and predicted in America appeared, for a time, poised to move beyond even this rather radical tolerance. The first five presidents of the United States, like Franklin and Paine, were not traditionally religious. Not that they talked about it much. One reason for their reticence was this new concern that government and religion ought to stay out of each other's business. Given their position in the government it seemed proper to these early presidents to keep their views on religion to themselves. "I inquire after no man's," Jefferson states, "and trouble none with mine."[20] However, the first presidents may have had an additional motivation for such reticence: a concern that their views, molded by first- or second-hand readings in British and French philosophy, might not have played so well with less enlightened members of the voting public. For these five men seem, for the most part, to have been suspicious of organized religion—specifically organized Christian religion.

George Washington, though less philosophically inclined than most of the others, still managed to establish the type: References to Christianity are rare in his speeches and writings. He tends to speak of "Providence," not God. His letters of condolence conspicuously do not mention an afterlife. And Washington allowed himself to die without any effort to obtain the assistance of a clergyman and without any recorded mention of prayer or other manifestations of piety. "I am just going," he is reported to have said.[21]

Thomas Jefferson may have put the most thought into philosophy of any president: by the time he was 28 he had made his way through the works of Bayle, Voltaire and Hume, and, during his own stint representing the United States in Paris, from 1784 to 1789, he became fascinated by

Diderot and d'Holbach.[22] Indeed, Jefferson owned three editions of Baron d'Holbach's *System of Nature*—two in French and one (incomplete) in English[23]—along with a number of the baron's other books.[24]

Jefferson, unlike the other early presidents, let slip in public hints of his unorthodox thinking—and he suffered for it. The evidence that he was an infidel was mostly taken from Jefferson's *Notes on the State of Virginia*, which he had printed while in France. In it Jefferson questions the biblical flood story. (The main sticking point for him being the origin and disposal of all that water.) And in this pamphlet Jefferson makes the case for a very wide-ranging tolerance:

> The legitimate powers of government extend to such acts only as are injurious to others. But it does me no injury for my neighbor to say there are twenty gods, or no god. It neither picks my pocket nor breaks my leg.[25]

"Or no god"? Jefferson sent copies of *Notes on the State of Virginia* to Paris' *philosophes,* some of whom he was in the process of befriending. A regular at Baron d'Holbach's salon worked with him on a translation into French. But copies also found their way to America.

Thus, when Jefferson stood as a candidate in the presidential elections of 1796, 1800 and 1804, accusations of irreligion entered the discourse of the American presidential campaign. "On account of his disbelief of the Holy Scriptures, and his attempts to discredit them," a minister in New York wrote of Jefferson in a pamphlet in 1800, "he ought to be rejected from the Presidency."[26] The shocking phrase, "Or no god," from *Notes on the State of Virginia*, though Jefferson was clearly speaking of an imagined neighbor, causes the writer of this pamphlet to consider "even the charge of atheism against" Jefferson. And this was no lonely crusade. "Is it that we may see the Bible cast into a bonfire," another minister thundered at the thought of a Jefferson presidency, " . . . our children either wheedled or terrified, uniting in chanting mockeries against God? . . . Shall our sons become disciples of Voltaire?"[27] The role of Karl Rove in this campaign was played by Federalist Party leader Alexander Hamilton, who was alerting political allies to the importance of preventing "an *Atheist* in Religion and a *Fanatic* in politics from getting possession of the helm of State."[28] Jefferson overcame these attacks. However, they served as a warning to subsequent candidates, and they shook him. He was careful, thereafter, not to sound too much the infidel.

But Jefferson did leave behind some additional evidence of his questioning spirit. Perhaps his most radical statement is from a letter of advice (private, of course) he wrote to his nephew from Paris in 1787:[29]

> Fix reason firmly in her seat, and call to her tribunal every fact, every opinion. Question with boldness even the existence of a God; because, if there be one, He must more approve of the homage of reason, than that of blindfolded fear.

Unlike Franklin and Voltaire, Jefferson was not concerned about unleashing the "Tiger" of disbelief. He saw it as a mere pussycat. "Do not be frightened from this inquiry," Jefferson advised his nephew, "by any fear of its consequences. If it end in a belief that there is no God, you will find incitements to virtue in the comfort and pleasantness you feel in its exercise and in the love of others which it will procure for you."* Indeed, Jefferson was impressed by the fact that men like Denis Diderot and Baron d'Holbach in Paris had spoken against religion yet still remained virtuous.[30]

After Franklin's death, the man charged with selling off his impressive library, gave Jefferson, then president of the United States, one of Franklin's volumes as a gift: it was that anti-religious tract printed by Baron d'Holbach.[31]

The fourth president, James Madison—Jefferson's disciple and ally, and the main author of the U.S. Constitution and the First Amendment—had contributed as much to the cause of freedom of conscience as had any person. "The Religion . . . of every man must be left to the conviction and conscience of every man," Madison writes in 1785 in his influential "Memorial and Remonstrance Against Religious Assessments" in Virginia. Madison seems also to have questioned "with boldness," though he did it more privately than Jefferson. He studied religion at Princeton and left with considerable wariness of its tendency to stifle free thought: "Religious bondage shackles and debilitates the mind," he writes to a friend.[32] In a letter to Jefferson in Paris in 1787 explaining deliberations on the Constitution, Madison made this cynical claim about

---

* While listening to all this talk of virtue, it must be remembered, of course, that Jefferson, like four of the other five earliest presidents—with Adams the exception—owned slaves.

religion: "Even in its coolest state, it has been much oftener a motive to oppression than a restrain from it."[33]

James Monroe, the fifth president, while he engaged the Episcopal Church in all the appropriate family ceremonies, seems to have himself been remarkably unengaged with religion—failing to mention it where it was almost obligatory: in his own letters of advice to young family members, even in the letters he wrote following the death of his son and the death of his wife.[34]

Of the five first presidents John Adams was probably the most enthusiastic about religion. He labeled himself "a church-going animal." Nevertheless, he also was enough the Enlightenment animal to insist—in a letter to Jefferson, his late-life pen pal—that "we should not believe" in that which is illogical just because we hear of "miracles or prophecies."[35]

America was fathered, in large part, by logic-loving, superstition-resisting, religious-bondage-breaking Enlightenment freethinkers.

But it was not fathered by atheists. There is no evidence that any of these men—even Paine—went so far as to open the last lock on the chain of that "Tiger." Franklin, Paine, Washington, Adams, Jefferson, Madison and Monroe all appear to have found room in their universes, as did Voltaire, at least for a "Creator"—that endower of "certain unalienable Rights" invoked by the Declaration of Independence. Jefferson respected Diderot and d'Holbach and understood their thinking, but he made clear that he disagreed with it (based, primarily, on the argument for design, which lived on despite the logic of Hume and Diderot).[36] Both Franklin and Jefferson, with characteristic self-assurance, prepared summaries of their own unorthodox but real religious views. Jefferson even pasted together his own Bible: the words and life of Jesus minus all the supernatural and metaphysical stuff.[37] And the "religious bondage" that horrified Madison appears, to be fair, to have been that of a state-supported religion.[38]

If there is one faith that might, though not without controversy, be applied to each of these men, it is Voltaire's hazy faith: deism. Paine provided a pretty good summary of it:[39]

I believe in one God, and no more; and I hope for happiness beyond this life. I believe in the equality of man and I believe that religious duties consist in doing justice, loving mercy, and endeavoring to make our fellow-creatures happy.

Paine proclaimed, "My own mind is my own church."[40] Adams, of course, favored the pews-and-steeple variety, but his church was formally or informally Unitarian—probably the form of Christianity closest to deism.[41] "The love of God and his creation—delight, joy, triumph, exultation in my own existence—though but an atom, a molecule *organique* in the universe—are my religion," Adams declares in a letter to Jefferson.[42] Washington, Jefferson, Madison and Monroe all spent considerable time in Episcopal (and other) churches, but they were either very reserved, very private, rather hesitant, "low-church" (liberal, reform-minded) Anglicans or quiet deists.[43]

Jefferson had a thought on why enlightened Americans became deists instead of atheists. Writing to Adams in 1816, he observed that deism was the form "infidelity" tended to take in Protestant countries. Britain was the other obvious example.[44] And it is true that in Britain throughout the eighteenth century it was common to profess disbelief in the existence of outright nonbelievers (as Hume had at d'Holbach's table). "Many people, both ancient and modern, have pretended to atheism, or have been reckoned atheists by the world," an edition of the *Encyclopedia Britannica* did concede in 1771; but then it added: "It is justly questioned whether any man seriously adopted such a principle."[45]

The first published declaration of atheism in Britain was an attempt—under a pseudonym, of course—to answer this widely expressed contention:[46]

> As to the question whether there is such an existent Being as an atheist, to put that out of all manner of doubt, I do declare upon my honour that I am one. Be it therefore for the future remembered, that in London in the kingdom of England, in the year of our Lord one thousand seven hundred and eighty-one a man publicly declared himself to be an atheist.

However, even this profession was not believed since, as one reviewer pointed out, anyone who would claim to be an atheist would have no honor and therefore could not be trusted.[47]

In his letter to Adams, Jefferson explains d'Holbach, *et al.,* in France by noting that atheism is, on the other hand, "a numerous school in the Catholic countries." In the last years of the enlightened eighteenth century, the "Tiger" was indeed unchained back in Catholic France.

Denis Diderot died in 1784. Baron d'Holbach lived until January 1789—half a year before the storming of the Bastille. But their ideas were alive in the revolution that event inaugurated. Indeed, for many who had learned from these men and who shared their ideals, this was a chance to go further than the American "Sons of Liberty."

A "revolution in the system of religion" was high on most to-do lists in Paris in 1789—even those of many members of the clergy.[48] It had grown hard to ignore the hypocrisies and corruption too often displayed by representatives of the state-supported Catholic Church, as well as the vast amounts of untaxed land and wealth controlled by its aristocratic leaders. And it was growing more difficult to justify official persecution of other religions. So there was little protest when the National Assembly, in August of 1789, took away many of the Church's financial privileges.

Thomas Jefferson was in Paris as the French Revolution began. In fact, Jefferson advised his friend, the Marquis de Lafayette, on his draft of the Declaration of the Rights of Man and Citizens.[49] The draft that was finally approved by the National Assembly in France in August of 1789 has, of course, similarities to the Declaration of Independence Jefferson had composed 13 years earlier and an ocean away. But from a religious point of view one difference between the two documents stands out.

In the American declaration God serves as both the "Creator" of "all men" and the endower of those "certain unalienable Rights." In the preamble to the French version God—given a deist sounding name—is merely an observer of and sponsor of the proceedings: "Therefore the National Assembly recognizes and proclaims, in the presence and under the auspices of the Supreme Being, the following rights of man and of the citizen." God had been demoted.[50]

Even this mention was too much for some in Paris. In an address he prepared for the National Assembly in 1790, Jacques-André Naigeon—Baron d'Holbach's publishing partner—protested that reference to "the Divinity" in the Declaration of the Rights of Men and Citizens.[51] Naigeon's was, it must be emphasized, not a veiled, anonymous or posthumous protest. This was an undisguised "Here-I-am!" moment. One consequence of the French Revolution—a significant one for this history—is that the existence of God could now, for the moment at least, not only be questioned but questioned publicly in Europe, by a person who was still alive, under that person's own name. Atheism had stepped out into the open.

And a political program quite similar to that called for in the writings of Diderot and Baron d'Holbach began being instituted. All feudal privileges were abolished by the National Assembly on August 4, 1789, a few weeks before the Declaration of the Rights of Men and Citizens was approved. Other rights of noblemen were eliminated, too—including their special claim to military and civil positions and their special status in court.[52]

The day before Christmas in 1789, the Assembly decreed that all military, judicial and civil positions could be filled by non-Catholics. Sephardic Jews were granted full citizenship on January 28, 1790, Ashkenazi Jews more than a year and a half later. On September 20, 1792, the Assembly approved civil divorce, even if motivated only by incompatible temperaments. It took some time due to economic concerns, but on February 4, 1794, the National Convention abolished slavery in the French colonies.

"The American and French Revolutions of the eighteenth century are probably the first mass political movements in the history of the world [that] expressed their ideology and aspirations in terms of secular rationalism and not of traditional religion," Eric J. Hobsbawm has written.[53] Hobsbawm's thesis here requires a somewhat strict definition of "political movements," but there is considerable truth to it. And is it not significant that the first two major appearances on the world stage of secular rationalism, this alternative to religion, were motivated not by conquest, not by the desire to defend or exalt some tribe or ethnic group? Is it not significant that when secular rationalism finally enters politics it does so in support of representative democracy, in support of tolerance, in support of human equality, in support of what we now call human rights?

Which is not to say it worked out so well in France.

While the Assembly or Convention then governing France was implementing much of the "radical" Enlightenment's political program, the effort to limit the power of the church in France was intensifying. In 1790, the National Assembly adopted the Civil Constitution of the Clergy, which brought the state's established church under state control—eliminating, in the process, many church positions and requiring that church members choose bishops and clergy through, of all things, elections.[54] Pope Pius VI, after some dithering, rejected the arrangement. But the Assembly had also decreed that all clerics had to take an oath of allegiance indicating that they sided with the revolution and accepted the Civil Constitution.

Catholic clergy in France were, in other words, being asked to reject the authority of the pope. Here we can see the beginning of a conflict between distrust of the church and support for tolerance—two key principles for Diderot and d'Holbach as well as for Voltaire. A large number of priests and a small number of bishops took the oath and became associated with what was now known as the Constitutional Church. Many, probably the majority, of France's clergymen maintained allegiance to the Vatican and, as a result, often found themselves labeled traitors and excluded from their churches. "Their religion," an orator insisted in front of the Assembly, "consists in counter-revolution."[55]

And this "revolution in the system of religion" was growing even more severe. A "dechristianization" movement began. Not only did the Assembly pass a series of decrees threatening deportation or arrest for priests who refused to swear their allegiance to the republic, but Constitutional priests, too, began being hounded. In some areas they were practically forced to marry. Occasionally, in mock processions, donkeys were paraded through the streets wearing clerical garb. (This was too much for one leading proponent of dechristianization: degrading, he protested, for the donkeys.) Some recalcitrant Catholic priests were massacred.[56] The French, the *Times* of London concluded from across the channel, were now "loose from all restraints, and, in many instances, more ferocious than wolves and tigers."[57]

King Louis XVI—though he had lost almost all power, though he was not known for taking stands—took a stand against some of these anti-Catholic measures. He was not, of course, strangled—as in that line from Meslier—in the guts of one of those massacred priests. On January 21, 1793, three and a half years after the storming of the Bastille, the king was beheaded by that new, more efficient, reputedly more humane execution technology, the guillotine.

At first the revolution's alternative to Catholicism was a Voltaire-like deism, but, in the fervor to do away with all remnants of "superstition," deism proved insufficiently irreligious. By the winter of 1794, a group of young Parisians would appear before what was now the National Convention and sing a hymn featuring this line[58]:

Henceforth Holy Reason
Will be our Religion.

No religion, in other words, had become the French Revolution's religion.

"We now have no more superstitions, no more prejudices, no more churches," declared, for example, the Revolutionary Committee in one small mountain town in central France.[59] In some places religious dress or public demonstrations of piety were outlawed; in others church bell-towers were torn down so that they would not stand above "the ground level of the nation."[60] Churches all over France were transformed into "temples of reason"—perhaps with "a tree of liberty" in place of a cross, perhaps featuring a statue of that new, secular goddess variously known as "Reason" or "Victory" or "Liberty."[61] (The largest representation of this secular goddess currently stands in New York harbor.) In one region inscriptions were placed on cemetery gates instructing visitors still entertaining the dream of an afterlife that, "Death is an eternal sleep."[62]

On the tenth of November, 1793, a "Festival of Reason" was held in Paris, and France's most important church, the Cathedral of Notre Dame, was consecrated to the new anti-religion. A "Temple of Philosophy" had been constructed within the cathedral, graced with busts of Voltaire, Rousseau and Benjamin Franklin (who had made a good impression in Paris, indeed). A young woman from the Paris opera, dressed in a long white robe, emerged from this "temple," and was enthroned as the "Goddess of Reason."[63]

A historian of atheism wants to pause to recognize this moment. The world, of course, has seen countless festivals to countless supreme beings. Here, finally, was a festival dedicated to the absence of such beings. But this is not an easy moment to linger over: events in France were moving too fast.

Seven days after the Festival of Reason, the government voted to erect a statue of Jean Meslier.[64] Six days after that all the churches in Paris were closed.[65] And the blade of the guillotine was falling with greater frequency.

To slow this story down just a little bit, let's focus on three notable participants in the dechristianization movement. The first was another rich German baron who had found his way to Paris and then to atheism. He had been born Jean-Baptiste Cloots in 1755, but in 1790 adopted a less Christian, more revolutionary name: Anacharsis (after the legendary Scythian wise man) Cloots.[66]

Cloots was a great proponent of cosmopolitanism. He believed the revolution unfolding in Paris at this time belonged not only to the French but to all of humankind. He saw Paris as the capital of a future "Universal

Republic." After an impassioned address to the National Assembly on this theme, the former baron of Gnadenthal gained, or assumed, a new title: "Orator of the Human Race" (a title that lent itself, unfortunately, to satiric uses). The Assembly granted Cloots French citizenship. (Another international revolutionary who had established himself in Paris was given this honor at the same time: Tom Paine.)

Anacharsis Cloots was also a great proponent of atheism. As a young man he had come up with (perhaps after reading Meslier) what he considered an irrefutable proof that all the religions of the world were wrong: If any particular religion were true, Cloots reasoned, wouldn't God have designed it so that all rational people, no matter how simple, could see that truth? All cannot, for any of the world's religions. Hence, no religion is true. Although Cloots had published his proof, Paris' clerics had somehow failed to abandon their calling and Paris' salons had somehow failed to acclaim him the next great *philosophe*.

He did better with a revolution behind him. Anacharsis Cloots was a major force behind the Festival of Reason. He even convinced the archbishop of Paris to abdicate and participate in the Festival. He was the initiator of that plan for a statue of Jean Meslier. And, in what must have been a particularly satisfying moment, Cloots was given an opportunity to acquaint the entire National Convention with his old disproof of all the religions of the world.

"A religious man," Cloots concluded, "is a depraved animal."[67] The "Orator of the Human Race," an ardent and sincere atheist, thought he was witnessing the beginning of the end of that depravity—in Paris, in France and, in time, the whole world. Cloots, in other words, was a dreamy revolutionary, but he was caught up in what was rapidly becoming a nightmarish time.

Jacques-René Hébert is my second example of a leader of the dechristianization movement. He was less dreamy. In fact, he was actually a bit tentative in his dismissal of religion. He led the procession to Notre Dame during the Festival of Reason and reports having been thrilled that the cathedral was "cleansed . . . of foolishness and consecrated to truth and reason." And Hébert does write, "I don't believe anymore in their hell and in their paradise." But then he adds, " . . . If there exists a God, and that is not very clear, He didn't create us to torment us but for us to be happy."[68] "If" is not what we expect from leaders of this stage of the revolution. Some historians even argue that Hébert wasn't an atheist at all but a mere deist.

Atheists would have no difficulty letting him go. For Hébert, in his incendiary and influential newspaper, *Père Duchesne* (named after a blunt, fairground character), was not at all tentative on the subject of what he saw as "the counter-revolution": he writes that it is necessary to "exterminate" it.[69] In fact, it sometimes seemed as if Hébert and those with whom he shared power had become proponents mostly of extermination, of executions.

Père Duchesne styled itself the voice of, and Hébert styled himself the leader of, Paris' increasingly radical *sans-cullottes,* its working class. Under pressure from him, the National Convention agreed to punish "traitors and conspirators" by making "terror the order of the day." *Père Duchesne* often called for the intervention of "Saint Guillotine." And the paper's prayers were usually answered. It became necessary to relocate "Saint Guillotine" a couple of times after neighborhoods complained of the streams of blood.[70] There is no escaping the fact that Hébert—an opponent of religion, whether atheist or deist—had helped start the blood flowing. The tolerance most nonbelievers had previously professed seemed, in Paris in 1793, to have evaporated. (In fairness, the revolution had reason to feel itself under siege: counterrevolutionary forces had organized inside and outside France.)

Another interesting character turned up among the French Revolution's dechristianizers—my third example. He was not a leader of the movement, like Anacharsis Cloots or Jacques-René Hébert, but he was an active participant in these events all the same. He now called himself: Citizen Louis Sade.

Not that the pre-revolutionary Marquis de Sade had displayed much empathy for the lower classes. In his books, Sade was broadminded, to say the least, about sex but not always committed to restricting that sex to the consensual. Those books, though, are fiction. In real life, he did tend to ask and pay. Still, this was a man who had repeatedly used his money and position to subject poor women to whippings and other degradations (though it is true that he subjected himself to similar torments with similar passion). After the complaint of one outraged woman or another landed him back in prison, in a letter to one of his servants Sade seethed at his prosecutors: "They will stand solidly behind a whore and throw a gentleman into jail on her behalf."[71] The marquis had always been very much a partisan of *liberté* but was considerably weaker on *égalité.*

However, Sade did bring to the revolution a healthy supply of rebelliousness and of resentment against his fellow aristocrats and the corrupt, prudish, hypocritical and repressive system that had frequently locked him up. Sade possessed, too, a useful and well-demonstrated talent for conceiving and acting out violent scenarios. And Sade's credentials for the role of revolutionary also included a recent prison term under the Old Regime—a prison term that had lasted more than 13 years. The incident that led to it was hardly an example of egalitarianism: the marquis had convinced two young women to swallow candies laced with a substance he probably intended as an aphrodisiac but which may have made them sick.[72] Nonetheless, until midnight on July 3, 1789, Sade had been among those sainted few locked in that imposing symbol of the Old Regime, the Bastille itself. At one point, angry over the loss of one of his privileges, he could even be heard encouraging the crowds that had begun gathering by the ancient prison to free the prisoners. That proved a useful credential for a marquis, a count in fact, as French society was turned upside down.

Citizen Louis Sade threw himself into his new role. He served as secretary then president of the committee of revolutionaries running his "section" of Paris.[73] He even was appointed, in one of the choicer of the many ironies here, a judge. Sade may have enjoyed the upheaval, although it was his class that bore the brunt of it. He may have found a perverse thrill in the bloodshed, though he knew and mourned some of those whose blood was being shed. He certainly was committed, in these treacherous times, to doing whatever it took for a nobleman to stay alive.

And on one subject Sade appeared to be sincerely and completely in agreement with the direction the revolution was heading. Citizen Louis Sade called Baron d'Holbach's *The System of Nature* "incontestably the basis of my philosophy" and "a book which should be in every library and every head."[74] Indeed, on 25 Brumaire of year II (November 15, 1793)— almost three weeks after the new revolutionary calendar was introduced, five days after Paris' Festival of Reason, two days before Cloots proposed that statue of Jean Meslier, eight days before Paris' churches were all closed—the National Convention was read a petition insisting that "man is finally enlightened" and celebrating the substitution of "Reason" for "Mary in our hearts." It also heard, in that petition, the Catholic religion called "bloodthirsty" and that same Mary, Jesus' mother, labeled "an adulterous woman."[75] This petition was read and mostly written by Citizen Louis Sade.

But—Sade rarely had much luck with this sort of thing—the revolution soon changed direction.

Edmund Burke, the increasingly conservative British political philosopher, was monitoring events in Paris. "We know, and it is our pride to know, that man is by his constitution a religious animal," Burke asserted; "that atheism is against, not only our reason but our instincts; and that it cannot prevail long."[76] Burke was correct about at least one thing: atheism in France during the Revolution—this bloody, intolerant manifestation of atheism—did not long prevail.

Sade's performance before the National Convention was followed, less than a month later by his return to jail. Shortly after that, Anacharsis Cloots was arrested. (Thomas Paine was, too, though the new American ambassador to France, James Monroe, eventually was able to free him.)[77] Jacques-René Hébert was seized two months later. Maximilien Robespierre was running things now, and Robespierre, a partisan of Rousseau, was definitely a deist. He believed the people needed a god. Robespierre executed large numbers of alleged counterrevolutionaries and political rivals, as well as some atheists.

Anacharsis Cloots and Jacques-René Hébert were tried and then guillotined on March 24, 1794. Cloots did not miss the irony in the fact that such dedicated revolutionaries were dying at the hands of the revolution. "You will admit, citizens," he noted before his head was severed, "that it is quite extraordinary that the man burnable in Rome, hangable in London and qualified to be broken on the wheel in Vienna, should be guillotined in Paris, at the high tide of the republic." Cloots impressed observers with his calm and courage as he met his death. Hébert, if it matters, did not.[78]

On June 8, with Robespierre firmly in charge, Paris was the scene of a different kind of celebration, a "Festival of the Supreme Being" staged in the Tuilleries gardens.[79] Robespierre presided, wearing a pale-blue coat, a hat festooned with patriotic ribbons and holding a bouquet of flowers and grain. "The day forever fortunate has arrived, which the French people have consecrated to the Supreme Being," he proclaimed.[80] "Never has the world which He created offered Him a spectacle so worthy of His notice." Then Robespierre grabbed a torch and set fire to effigies depicting crimes and vices—with a representation of "atheism" looming large among them.

Sade's trial and inevitable execution were scheduled for July 27, 1794, but somehow—a mistake? a bribe?—the bailiff failed to locate him in jail that day.[81] Robespierre was ousted suddenly in a *coup d'etat* and was himself executed the next day, allowing the frenzied guillotining to finally cease. So Sade survived, although he would still spend most of the rest of his life locked up by the revolution and then by Napoleon.

What had happened in France at the end of 1793? For this brief moment—and perhaps for the first time since classical Athens—nonbelievers were in charge of a country and streams of blood ran in the streets. Had a "Tiger" indeed been unchained? Did this not bring to mind Athens' nonbelieving, bloody tyrant Critias? Is this what happens when "everything is permitted"? How did all this killing square with this book's argument that the rise of atheism has encouraged a rise in liberty? Was there not evidence in France during the terror in 1793 that disbelief unleashed, instead—as many had predicted—immorality?

The movement Diderot and d'Holbach had helped inspire provided a home for individuals of suspect morality like Sade and Hébert—individuals who might, dare we say, have benefited from some homilies on doing "unto others." Diderot and d'Holbach had been great proponents of tolerance: "that sacred law of nature, which enjoins all men to tolerate the opinions of their fellow creatures," as *The Philosophical History* put it.[82] But tolerance is always easier to support when you need to be tolerated than when you are being asked to tolerate. And Diderot and d'Holbach also seem to have believed that violent revolution might be necessary to achieve political reform.[83] Well, this violent revolution—as often enough happens—got out of control.

The historian Jonathan I. Israel wants to pin the terror on Robespierre and his Rousseau-inspired deism—letting Diderot and d'Holbach off the hook. The guillotine did accelerate under Robespierre. And it is true that Jacques-André Naigeon, a former member of d'Holbach's salon who was active in the revolution, withdrew in disgust after Robespierre's ascendency.[84] But Naigeon had apparently still been active when Hébert—another aficionado of the guillotine, if not as ruthless as Robespierre—wielded power.[85] I don't think the atheists' fingerprints can be removed from the terror. I don't, however, believe the move away from religion caused the terror.

One answer to the charge that the guillotine demonstrated atheism's immorality is that the religious have at times—too many times—done worse: to nonbelievers, to heretics, to each other, often enough for their own personal gain. Indeed, it is hard to come up with any forms of sexual abuse, thievery, torture, slavery or murder that some among the religious have not at some point permitted themselves. But, since we are trying to earn atheism special status in this book as a force for human understanding, this answer seems inadequate. Another possibility is to note that many movements behave badly when first intoxicated by power. But that too undercuts the effort to claim special status for this particular movement.

Perhaps the most effective way to wipe the blood of the guillotine off "secular rationalism," however, is to note to what extent this "mass political movement"—when it was at its least tolerant—resembled a religion, suffused with sectarianism, fanaticism and unwillingness to abide the fact that some saw things otherwise. Tom Paine was among those at the time who commented upon this. "The just and humane principles of the Revolution, which philosophy had first diffused, had been departed from," he observes in a preface to the second part of *The Age of Reason*. "The intolerant spirit of church persecution had transferred itself into politics; the tribunals, styled Revolutionary, supplied the place of an Inquisition; and the guillotine . . . out-did the fire and faggot of the church."[86]

What was morally wrong with the religion of no religion that was briefly institutionalized during the French Revolution, as Paine argues, was not that it was too profane but that it was too orthodox. As the religious often had, these true believers in "Holy Reason" divided populations into the good and the evil. Disagreement became a sin.

All four of the varieties of disbelief introduced so far in this book—there is still one to come—have their pitfalls. Skepticism can slide into cynicism: into a status-quo-tolerating politics similar to that of a David Hume. The anacreontic can, if overdone, become the dissolute: Sade, when out of prison, tended to head in that direction. Those who hunt for natural explanations, for "a clear understanding of what happened"—the heroes of the first half of this book—risk, perhaps, a dry pedantry. But the dangers have proved greater with the fourth variety: the political analysis that sees religion as one of the sentries at the gates of humankind's "real hells" and that is prone to dreaming that, should we manage to free ourselves from religion, we might find real heavens. This is perilously black and white, worryingly absolute. People get violent over absolutes.

There was work to do, consequently, before it became possible to apply what was learned from an analysis of the politics of religion without sending people to the guillotine—or the gulag. It was necessary to become less devout about egalitarianism, to stop crusading against clerics, if not against clericalism. It was necessary to once again write "reason" with a lower-case "R."

In other words, those infused with this fourth variety of disbelief needed to scale down their anger and their aspirations—as has often been required in the modern world. They needed to restrict themselves to gentler and more realistic goals. They might hope instead, for example, that we will see the day when a new constitution has stripped power from the last king; and that then, perhaps in retirement in the south of France, the last king will reminisce over a Bordeaux with one of the few remaining priests.

After order finally returned to France, there was a rush to restore the chains around various Tigers, including popular sovereignty, radical reform and atheism. In the first years of the new century, Napoleon and a new pope, Pius VII, negotiated an agreement—the Concordat—and France once again had a strong, though not as strong, Catholic Church. That early, unfortunate and brief experiment with institutionalized atheism—conducted, to be sure, under the most extreme conditions—was over.[87] It certainly lent support to the conclusion that an atheistic society would have trouble prevailing and remaining civil. More experiments were to come.

And the long experiment with uninstitutionalized atheism continued.

But many of the egalitarian policies espoused by Diderot and d'Holbach—the political program of Enlightenment atheism—survived. Napoleon did reinstitute slavery in the French colonies, but it would be abolished again in 1848 under the Second Republic. The nobility did not regain their privileges in Napoleon's France, though neither did the advantages of wealth and breeding disappear, and Napoleon did hand out new hereditary titles. The French church, despite the Concordat, had lost quite a bit of its power. Civil divorce remained legal. The Jews retained their citizenship, though upon occasion in the next century and a half their situation in France would become precarious—or worse.

And as Napoleon conquered much of Europe he spread these reforms. Some of them lasted there, too. The rest eventually were reinstituted.

At the end of the eighteenth century, that tumultuous time for unbelief in Europe and parts of North America, William Wordsworth composed a poem that provides an alternative way of looking at the excitements and terrors of those decades.

Wordsworth was a poet of ambiguous religiosity. But this poem, a preface to *The Excursion*, can be read as asserting that God is not the dominant source of the "fear and awe" in our world:[88]

> *Jehovah—with his thunder, and the choir*
> *Of shouting Angels, and the empyreal thrones—*
> *I pass them unalarmed. . . .*

Instead, we find that "fear and awe":

> *. . . when we look*
> *Into our Minds, into the Mind of Man—*
> *My haunt, and the main region of my song.*

William Blake read Wordsworth's poem this way; it made him, Blake reports, ill: "Does Mr. Wordsworth think his mind can *surpass* Jehovah?" Blake asks.[89] I suspect that Wordsworth is entertaining that thought. Guillotines, after all, are designed and deployed by "the Mind of Man"; ambitious collections of all the world's wisdom and grand advances in human freedoms are conceived there, too. I suspect that many people then and even more so now find their "fear and awe" primarily in human minds.

France's revolution had ended for a while; its churches had been restored. The Republic was no more. But the terrible, incredible drama that had played itself out there was increasingly seen not as apocalypse or divine retribution but as a human drama. This was a revolution in perspective. And it did not end.

The attacks on religion in eighteenth-century Europe of Jean Meslier, David Hume, Denis Diderot and Baron d'Holbach helped inspire and clear the way for a series of political reforms in America and Europe—reforms that have continued. Those reforms would not have been possible without the growing conviction that men and women—not gods—are responsible for this world. This is another sense in which God was demoted in the eighteenth century.

THIS GLORIOUS LAND OF FREEDOM

ABOLITION, SUFFRAGE AND FREETHINKING

The joy, the triumph, the delight, the madness!
The boundless, overflowing, bursting gladness,
The vaporous exultation not to be confined!

—Percy Bysshe Shelley, *Prometheus Unbound*[1]

THE UNITED STATES HAS CERTAINLY PRODUCED SOME DISTIN-
guished critics of traditional religion who—unlike Jefferson and
Paine—were also critics of all religion. Some will appear in subsequent
chapters. Ernestine Louise Rose, arguably the most impressive of them, is
the main subject of this chapter.

Rose was born in Poland in 1810.[2] Her mother's last name had been
Susmond; her father's was Potowski. Her mother died when her daughter
was young; those sketchy accounts don't agree on how young. Her father
was a rabbi.

The influence of France upon central Poland, then known as the
Duchy of Warsaw, was strong. As Greek ideas had found their way into
Israel 2,000 years earlier, some Enlightenment ideas probably found their
way into the large Jewish ghetto in Piotrkow where this rabbi's daughter
grew up. Jews were also beginning to find their way out of the ghettos: Napoleon, in his role as propagator of the Enlightenment, allowed them full
citizenship throughout his empire.[3] With assimilation came fuller intellectual involvement. A period of Jewish contributions to European thought,

which were to surpass even those of Spinoza, was about to commence. Atheism was high on the list of areas of thought to which Jews—Marx and Freud, among them—would contribute. Rose, who lived her entire adult life outside of ghettos and outside of Poland, would be a major contributor.

She began by debating religion with her father. "A young girl does not want to understand the object of her creed" but should "accept and believe it," the rabbi is said to have responded.[4] His daughter, however, did insist on understanding. And her questioning—forgetting the gender of the questioner—actually owed something to the Rabbinic Judaism her father, like almost all religious Jews, practiced.

One explanation for the ability of Rabbinic Judaism, irrigated by European Enlightenment thought, to germinate disbelief is its emphasis on intensive, almost obsessive, fine-grained study of religious texts. It is filled with debate on the meaning and significance of those texts. It wants a kind of understanding. Rabbi Potowski's daughter, like some of the prominent Jewish atheists who would follow, took that debate further than intended. When she was 14, she announced that she had stopped believing in the Bible.

Next she escaped from a marriage her father had arranged for her. Different accounts of how the teenager managed this trick have survived. One involves a mix of candor ("I do not love you") and pleas ("Oh! Pray release me!"), then, when that failed, convincing a judge to intercede. Another version of this story features a dramatic wedding-day flight. (Rose herself must have been the source of most of the versions.)

We do know that the young woman soon escaped her father, a stepmother and her country by leaving, presumably alone, for Berlin. She was now 17 and supporting herself by selling chemical sheets, which she had devised, for perfuming rooms. But Berlin could not hold her long. In 1830, when she was 20, Ernestine Susmond (she had shed her father's name) made her way to London, where she purchased an English dictionary and began teaching herself the language.

The struggle for freedom and possibility, set back by the excesses of the French Revolution, had resumed by 1830. London was becoming a major battleground in that struggle. Ernestine's brief stay there provides an occasion to catch up on it.

Nineteenth-century atheism in Britain begins, perhaps, in 1811 with two Oxford students. One, Thomas Jefferson Hogg, had drafted an essay.

That essay was edited, polished and expanded by the other Oxford student, 18-year-old Percy Bysshe Shelley, who was just getting started as a poet but was already an accomplished firebrand. The two young men published their tightly argued work at their own expense.[5] They published it anonymously. The pamphlet's title was *The Necessity of Atheism*. It leaned heavily on Baron d'Holbach's *System of Nature*.[6]

To understand the audaciousness and recklessness of what Shelley and Hogg had done (Shelley was also fond of playing with gunpowder) all that's necessary is to glance back a little more than a century to another young man at university in Britain. Thomas Aikenhead, an orphan, was studying at the University of Edinburgh when he began sharing—openly, brashly, unwisely—the criticisms he had developed of religion. The Scriptures, he was reported to have proclaimed, are "so stuffed with madness, nonsense and contradictions, that you admired the stupidity of the world in being so long deluded by them."

Based on the testimony of some of his fellow students, Aikenhead was convicted of blasphemy. Repentance would have helped, but the young man's efforts in that direction were not entirely convincing, especially when he explained that his errors had flowed from an "insatiable inclination to truth." Thomas Aikenhead was hanged in Edinburgh on January 8, 1697, a few months before his twenty-first birthday.[7]

Shelley's and Hogg's parents were alive and well-connected. The eighteenth century had changed things, even in Britain. Still, these two young men were exploring similar territory to that of Aikenhead—and they did it in print. "God," Shelley and Hogg insist, "is a hypothesis and, as such, stands in need of proof." After attempting to rebut the more common efforts to support that "hypothesis," their essay "earnestly entreats" those who disagree to respond with alternative arguments.[8] The response its authors actually received was somewhat different.

Within twenty minutes of Shelley placing copies in a prominent Oxford bookshop, a minister and fellow of one of the Oxford colleges walked in, saw the pamphlets, looked through a copy, which he saved for evidence, and then ordered all the rest burned at the back of the shop. The next month Oxford expelled Shelley and Hogg. The month after that Shelley's father, a member of Parliament, announced that he was prepared to leave the young man "to the punishment and misery that belongs to the wicked pursuit of an opinion so diabolical and wicked."

Shelley responded by doubling down. The reasoned tone of his college-student essay was replaced two years later—in *Queen Mab*, a long, anti-religious poem—by flashes of fury:

> *And priests dare babble of a God of peace,*
> *Even whilst their hands are red with guiltless blood.*[9]

Shelley's anger was fueled by the intolerance and hostility with which his ideas—anti-religious, republican—were greeted, beginning at Oxford and continuing throughout his short career as a poet. And his lifestyle was no less provocative than his ideas: he was living, for a time, with two teen-aged half-sisters. (He later married one of them, the writer Mary Shelley.[10]) The British Home Office was doing its best to keep tabs on this young radical as he composed *Queen Mab*. When the poem was printed, its nervous publisher removed his own name from the title page. Two-hundred-and-fifty copies of this poem were printed in 1813; eight years later only 70 of those copies had found their way to readers.[11]

In 1818, another publisher withdrew a version of Shelley's poem, *The Revolt of Islam*, until the poet changed 63 lines to remove controversial references, particularly to atheism. "How Atheists and Republicans can die" became, for example, "How those who love, yet fear not, dare to die." Later that year, Shelley (and his odd household) left what he had come to decry as Britain's "stupid tyranny" for exile in Italy.[12]

And that's where he died less than a month before his thirtieth birthday. In 1822, a summer squall in the Gulf of Spezia sank the 24-foot schooner Shelley had purchased, with the poet and two others on board. According to one account, Shelley had refused to leave his boat for the safety of a larger vessel and had even refused to lower his sails in the storm.[13]

The abuse directed at Shelley back in Britain did not end with his death. One London newspaper began its report on the tragedy with this quip: "Shelley, the writer of some infidel poetry, has been drowned; now he knows whether there is a God or not."[14]

Yet something odd had begun happening in Britain shortly before Shelley died: *Queen Mab* was being reprinted and many of the copies were being sold to members of the working class.[15]

In 1830, when Ernestine Susmond passed through London, the pro-republican and anti-religious publisher, Richard Carlile, was not in prison. That in itself was noteworthy.

Carlile's first trial had come in 1819 after he had published Thomas Paine's *The Age of Reason.* The verdict: guilty of, among other charges, blasphemy. That unloosed a storm of indignation from an Englishman then in exile in Italy. "For what was Mr. Carlile prosecuted?" Percy Bysshe Shelley thundered, while bringing the discussion back to a favorite topic: himself. "For impugning the Divinity of Jesus Christ? I impugn it. For denying that the whole mass of ancient Hebrew literature is of divine authority? I deny it."[16] Shelley added, "I hope I am not to be dragged home . . . to be made a sacrifice to the superstitious fury of the ruling sect." Carlile was to spend, on this occasion, six years in prison thanks to that fury.

But Carlile, who shared Shelley's moxie, was not chastened. "ASSOCIATED PROSECUTORS," he declares in an open letter, " . . . Having immured me within the walls of a prison, methinks I see a demonic smile glide over your several cheeks with the glowing expression of 'we have now crushed him.'—Be not too sanguine." In fact, Carlile published two pirated editions of *Queen Mab,* Shelley's atheistic attack on religion, while in prison for publishing Paine's deistic attack on religion.[17] (Carlile's wife had reopened the print shop in his absence, and ended up in the same prison cell for a time.[18])

Shelley's poem was finding readers because the struggle against religion was beginning to gain strength in Britain. Thanks to Diderot, d'Holbach and the *Philosophical History,* thanks to Paine, and thanks now to a firebrand like Carlile, atheism was becoming a plank in the radical platform—another front, to switch metaphors, in the war against privilege, oppression and economic exploitation. "Many faint with toil," Shelley fumes in *Queen Mab.* "That few may know the cares and woe of sloth."[19]

Shelley—thick haired, fine featured and incapable of half measures—brought a quality to the struggle against religion not much available from the A-to-Z-minded encyclopediasts whose cause it had been: romance. Along with anger, Shelley offered intuitiveness, intensity and an intoxication with art. He managed to re-enchant nature, without literally re-divinizing it, through the formidable capabilities of the whimsical, allegorical human imagination.

For a century, maybe two, those who found themselves losing their faith would learn, through Shelley's poems, that they would not also have to lose their wonder, their verve and their joy. Goethe had spoken, of a "hollow and empty . . . atheistical half-night." Shelley saw it differently: "How beautiful this night!" he exclaims in *Queen Mab,* " . . . . so cold, so bright, so still"[20]:

How bold the flight of passion's wandering wing,
How swift the step of reasons' firmer tread,
How calm and sweet the victories of life,
How terrorless the triumph of the grave!

Carlile printed another version of *Queen Mab* shortly after he was released from prison. Though the grave had, by then, triumphed over its young author, the poem had become, along with that book by Paine, Carlile's bestselling title.[21] He would return to prison in January of 1831—this time for sedition, this time for almost three years. Yet Carlile—undeterred, irrepressible—continued to see history moving his way:

> All faith is in danger, because faith has no relation to the knowledge of mankind. All faith is in danger, because faith has no relation to the welfare of mankind. All faith is in danger, because it injures and disorders mankind. All faith is in danger, because it is a cheat upon mankind. . . . All faith is in danger, because truth exhibited must triumph over it.[22]

Carlile's fourth edition of *Queen Mab* was published during this jail term.

So the London to which Ernestine Susmond immigrated in 1830 was a place where it was possible for a radical few to begin to imagine "all faith . . . in danger."

The most important influence upon this young woman during her stay in London was a Welsh entrepreneur and mill owner turned utopian socialist, Robert Owen. He, too, had no use for religion—though he was probably too wealthy for that to land him in jail.

In 1830, Owen—a fan of Shelley's—gave a lecture on religion in London:[23] "When religion is stripped of the mysteries with which the priests of all times and countries have invested it," Owen announced, " . . . all its divinity vanishes; its errors become palpable; and it stands before the astonished world in all its naked deformity of vice, hypocrisy and imbecility."[24] This sounded right to one just-arrived rabbi's daughter.

Ernestine Susmond became a follower of Robert Owen. She married another of Owen's disciples, who was three years younger than she: William Rose. Then in 1836, when she was 26, Ernestine Rose, together with her new husband, escaped one more time—this time to a continent swelling with escapees and to a country she would later call, while demanding much more of it, "this glorious land of freedom."[25]

Ernestine and William Rose settled in lower Manhattan. She made some money selling perfumes. According to her biographer, Carol A. Kolmerten, she gave birth to two children, both of whom died in infancy.[26] And Ernestine rapidly began attending meetings, circulating petitions and making speeches. William repaired jewelry and watches. He attended many of the meetings his wife would attend (particularly of freethinkers). He signed the petitions she would sign or draft. He helped fund the lecture tours she would undertake. But he would leave most of the traveling, organizing and speechmaking to her.

I have come upon no physical description of William, but we know that Ernestine was short and thin, that she had brown hair, which "fell in ringlets about her face" and that she wore white gloves and "sober" dresses.[27] We also know that Ernestine Rose was—despite her accent and at a time when few women were so bold as to speak in public—a remarkably forceful orator.

In this she had a role model—another follower of Robert Owen who had also come from Britain to America: Frances Wright. While in America, Wright had become, by some reckonings, the first woman in the United States publicly to take action against slavery: setting up a utopian, interracial—and ultimately unsuccessful—commune near Memphis, Tennessee. Wright also spoke publically in favor of equal rights for women—another American first, some historians assert.[28] And she lectured around the country against what she saw as an additional evil: religion. "The victims of this odious experiment on human credulity and nervous weakness," Wright contends, "were invariably women." On God, she writes, "I see no sufficient evidence of his existence; and to reason of its possibility I hold to be an idle speculation."[29] Wright was one of the publishers of an American edition of *Queen Mab*.[30]

Frances Wright had left America before Rose arrived: she had returned to England to hide an out-of-wedlock pregnancy. But Ernestine Rose would ascend stages to argue—with great forcefulness—in favor of all three of Wright's causes.

Rose spoke first at meetings of the groups of freethinkers beginning to organize themselves in New York and Boston. Religion may have been more intensely felt in the United States than in Europe: since many had crossed the Atlantic precisely for freedom to practice their religion. But some in this land that preached tolerance were looking for freedom *from* religion. These freethinkers had a publication: the *Boston Investigator*, which survived from 1831—half a decade before Rose arrived in the United States—to 1904.[31] They had their meetings, some of which they dubbed "Infidels Conventions."[32] Their great public event each year was a celebration on January 29 of Thomas Paine's birthday.

Paine, like Voltaire and Jefferson, though not quite an atheist, was a hero and inspiration to atheists. They gathered to breathe the religion-free air that seemed to collect around Paine's memory. "He has not only labored to throw off political despotism," Rose proclaimed in one of her paeans to the late revolutionary, "but also that worst kind of despotism—superstition, under whose oppressive thralldom all other freedom becomes stifled."[33]

That last line was crucial for Ernestine Rose. Her atheism was in part skeptical: one of her sayings was that "superstition is religion out of fashion, and religion is superstition in fashion."[34] But Rose's atheism belonged primarily to the fourth variety of disbelief: like Meslier, like Diderot, like d'Holbach, she saw religion as "despotism"—as an "oppressive thralldom" that stifles all other freedoms. It may have had to do with living after, not before, a revolution; it may have had to do with being an American, though one of recent vintage; but Rose's emphasis in expressing this fourth variety of disbelief—perhaps even more than Meslier's, Diderot's or d'Holbach's—was on freedom.

Rose argued and fought, in other words, for what became possible after the overthrow of that "oppressive thralldom"—for the human freedoms she believed to be inherent in atheism. Paine's influence could certainly be felt here, Jefferson's, too. If any text had been sacred for Rose, it would have been the Declaration of Independence—with the deletion of "by their Creator" from the magnificent first sentence of its second paragraph, and with Rose's interpretation of "all men," in that sentence: "which means all human beings, irrespective of sex."[35]

A Unitarian minister once told Rose, "You are the only person I have ever met who believes less than I do." She believed, it is true, neither in Trinity, nor Son of God, nor God the Father, nor Yahweh, nor Supreme Being; but Rose did believe strongly in freedom. Shelley had written about an "unpavilioned sky."[36] Ernestine Rose, too, saw atheism as leaving our view of the sky unobstructed, as leaving humankind unbound. Hers was a liberation anti-theology.

Soon Rose was speaking against slavery, alongside abolitionists like William Lloyd Garrison and the former slave Frederick Douglass, and earning more than her share of hissing and catcalls—as a woman, as a white woman who shared a stage with a black man, as a Jew, as an immigrant, as an atheist.

Abolitionists were often furious with the churches. "I . . . hate the corrupt, slaveholding, women-whipping, cradle-plundering, partial and hypocritical Christianity of this land," Douglass wrote.[37] In their frustration that, as Garrison put it, "the sanctity of religion is thrown, like a mantle, over the horrid system," he and some other leading abolitionists did encourage their followers to "come out" of the churches, but most of them still believed they were acting as Christians. "I love the pure, peaceable and impartial Christianity of Christ," Douglass made clear, as he was decrying the slaveholders' churches. Garrison was continually fending off the charge that the abolition movement was full of "infidels."[38] And, indeed, many abolitionists saw themselves as fighting a "holy war."[39] But there was often at least one infidel up on the stage. Here, as elsewhere, Rose was the exception.

Soon she was also mounting platforms to decry what she chose to label, to the chagrin of some of her abolitionist allies, domestic slavery. In fact, Susan B. Anthony was Rose's closest political comrade. They sometimes traveled together, with Anthony handling most of the business arrangements and Rose doing most of the lecturing.

Rose gave three formal speeches at the first national woman's rights convention in Worcester, Massachusetts, in 1850, and she may have given the *New York Herald* an excuse for reporting on the proceedings under the malicious, though at least partially true, headline: "Bible and Constitution Repudiated." The *Herald* also chose to mock her accent: "Mrs. Rose spoke at length, saying among other things, dat woman is in de quality of de slave." The *New York Tribune*, however, labeled Rose, accent and all, the most "eloquent" speaker there.[40]

Paulina Wright Davis, who presided over the second such national convention, states that Rose's speech on woman's rights there "has never been surpassed." After another such speech, a journalist wrote: "She is one of the best speakers we have ever heard; and we can only regret that a woman of such brilliant intellect should be wasting her energies in a cause for which there is not a shadow of hope."[41]

This was a movement in which an "infidel" might feel more at home. The patriarchal aspects of religion are rather hard to ignore, which may help explain why the women's movement has often been led by women who have surrendered traditional religious beliefs. This was true in the twentieth century: Simone Beauvoir was an atheist, and Betty Friedan and Gloria Steinem were, for much of their lives, dismissive of religion.[42] It was true in the nineteenth century, too.

Elizabeth Cady Stanton, who became Susan B. Anthony's main partner in the struggle for women's suffrage, was almost six years younger than Rose and a little more than four years older than Anthony. Stanton was a schoolgirl during one of the periods of renewed religious fervor—"Great Awakenings"—the United States has periodically been said to be undergoing.[43] She reports having lost her religion after being terrified by some particularly energetic preaching:

> After many months of weary wandering in the intellectual labyrinth of "The Fall of Man," "Original Sin," "Total Depravity," "God's Wrath," "Satan's Triumph," "The Crucifixion," "The Atonement," and "Salvation by Faith," I found my way out of the darkness into the clear sunlight of Truth. My religious superstitions gave place to rational ideas based on scientific facts, and in proportion, as I looked at everything from a new standpoint, I grew more and more happy, day by day.[44]

Stanton would later use a new, late-nineteenth-century term to label her disbelief: "agnostic."

Susan B. Anthony, too, by Stanton's account, was an agnostic—but one who seemed to lean, in her uncertainty, more toward the perhaps-there-is side than the "rational ideas based on scientific facts" side.[45] Anthony was, at least, careful not to criticize religion and thereby offend Christian women who were interested in joining their struggle. Stanton wasn't so careful: "You may go over the world and you will find that every form of religion which has breathed upon this earth has degraded woman . . . ," she declared in a speech. "Man, of himself, could not do this; but when he declares, 'Thus saith the Lord,' of course he can do it."[46]

So two of the leaders of the struggle for equal rights for more than half the population of the United States in the nineteenth century were agnostics, and two others, first Frances Wright and then Ernestine Rose, were atheists.[47]

Throughout the 1850s and into the 1860s, despite lapses in her health, Rose kept "agitating"—at various conventions, through countless lectures. Rose had only been in the United States eight years when she was included in the same lecture series as Ralph Waldo Emerson and Henry David Thoreau. By the time she had been in the United States 20 years, Rose—traveling by train, stagecoach and foot—had lectured in 23 states.

She spoke and fought mainly for three causes: woman's rights, abolition and freethinking, but she took the opportunity to weigh in, where possible or necessary, on some other issues, too: for immigrants, for fairer divorce laws, for prison reform, against anti-Semitism. "Human rights include the rights of all, not only man, but woman, not only white, but black," Rose proclaimed; "wherever there is a being called human, his rights are as full and expansive as his existence, and ought to be without limits or distinction of sex, country or color . . . and only ignorance, superstition and tyranny—both the basis and influence of the Bible—deprive him of it."[48]

Atheism never lost its prominent place on Rose's list of causes. Religion in the view of this champion of freedom is "mental bondage," escape from the delusion of God is freedom. And Rose believed that humankind could accomplish great things after securing that freedom: "We may have," she enthuses, "all the power, goodness and love that we have been taught belongs to God himself."[49]

William Lloyd Garrison, although a dedicated Christian, saw how religion can slow political progress. "Religious opprobrium," Garrison noted, has been inflicted upon "every great reformatory movement in every age."[50] If that is the case, then the shucking off of religion can further such "reformatory" movements and aid, as Rose put it, "the human rights of all." Without an attempt to push back against religion and its promiscuous, reform-stifling "opprobrium," little would have changed. Without exceptions like Ernestine Rose—prepared to lay the groundwork for such a critique of religion—little would have changed.

Rose helped pick up the banner—trampled and bloodied by the French Revolution—of the Enlightenment atheists and carry it forward. Others, as that century progressed, would continue to march under that banner.

Susan B. Anthony stood in some awe of Rose's militancy, resoluteness and vision. "Mrs. Rose is not appreciated, nor can she be by this age," Anthony wrote; "she is too much in advance."

Indeed, Rose was hated by many of her contemporaries: "A thousand times below a prostitute," was the characterization of an editor from

Maine. For a minister from Charleston, Rose was "this female devil." But Walt Whitman came through with a more generous appraisal. He calls Rose "big, rich, gifted, brave, expansive—in body a poor sickly thing . . . but with a head full of brains—the amplitude of a Webster."[51]

Those ample brains were deployed untiringly, unrelentingly, unbendingly. It was, at the time, fashionable for educated people to play at hypnotism or to have a go at a séance. When someone made the mistake of inviting Rose to a party at which this was among the entertainments, she immediately set about, Anthony tells us, cross-examining the chief participant in order to unmask the "deception."[52]

Rose liked to debate; in a freer world, she acknowledged, she would have become a lawyer. While still in her twenties, she walked into a church to hear a minister lecture on education. We have a newspaper account of what happened when that minister dared stray from his topic into an attack on disbelief: "A young, beautiful and interesting Lady with uncovered head, and fine flowing locks, arose in the gallery opposite the speaker, and, saying . . . a sense of duty and regard for truth induced her to rise . . . , she humbly begged permission of the chairman to ask the gentleman . . . a question." Shouts and hisses followed. That minister refused to take the question, saying he had been taught never to fight with a lady. Rose then turned and stared down the audience "with a look which seemed to pierce the soul."[53]

Like Shelley, Carlile, Wright and most of those who publically questioned religion in these centuries, Rose was not the sort to lower her sails. There was, for another instance, the time in 1853 when Rose visited South Carolina and spoke against slavery—a significant act of bravery in itself—and was asked by a "gentleman" for her impression of his state. "You are a century at least, behind," Rose replied, with astonishing bluntness, "in that the only civilization that you have exists . . . among your slaves." He responded that she was lucky she is a woman or he would have her tarred and feathered. She shot back that she always feels lucky to be a woman.[54]

Rose clearly was disputatious. She could be sarcastic. She could be stern. She could be indelicate: once when accused of slighting the Bible, she retorted "that it is utterly impossible to ridicule a thing so sublimely ridiculous as the whole account of the flood in the Bible."[55]

Rose was also easy to disappoint: Woe to the abolitionist who chose to ignore the "bondage" of women! Woe to the supporter of woman's rights who asserted that Christianity could set women free! Woe to the freethinker who accused "even the modern Jews" of being "bigoted, narrow, exclusive"![56] And Rose was not particularly open to intimate female friendships, as Anthony, who often traveled and worked with her, understood. She remained "Mrs. Rose" to many of her comrades.

"If, in expressing my opinions, I have been severe alike on friend and foe," Rose wrote in an open, uncharacteristically apologetic letter to her acquaintances, "it is because in principle I know no compromise."[57] Had she been less "severe," more willing to compromise, could Rose have traveled so far and remained so true to such a collection of controversial principles?

Rose's apologetic open letter preceded a trip she and William took, in May of 1856, to France and, after 20 years absence, back to Britain. Religious practice in Britain was in the midst of a dramatic change.

Five years earlier England had conducted its first "religious census." It employed a simple methodology: the seats in all of England's churches that were actually filled on one particular Sunday were counted. The census found, to no one's great surprise, that religious loyalties had become quite divided: About half of England's churchgoers attended services other than those of the established Anglican church—the Church of England. Catholicism, though still relatively small, had made a bit of a comeback in England. Other less liturgical denominations—Methodists and various evangelical churches—had grown large.

What was news in the 1851 religious census was the fact that a significant percentage, perhaps more than half, of the men and women of England could not be found in any church that Sunday.[58] In a country in which religious observance had once been mandatory, much of the population now was staying away from church. And church attendance was even lower in the large cities: among the poor and working class. Most simply preferred to spend Sunday morning with the family, in a park or in a pub. "We are in an age of weak beliefs," the political philosopher John Stuart Mill concluded at the time.[59] However, some individuals in Britain—poor and working-class individuals prominent among them—were more than just tired, bored or otherwise engaged; they were beginning to reject religion.

In 1851, the year of that census, George Jacob Holyoake, another Owenite, had founded the London Secular Society. Holyoake scrupulously avoided the term "atheist," with all the odium attached to it. He was merely a "secularist." The word "secular" is from Latin and means, belonging "to the world," as opposed to the church. Holyoake is credited with the first use of this word as the name for a doctrine.[60] "Secularism is not an argument against Christianity," he insisted; "it is one independent of it. It does not question the pretensions of Christianity; it advances others."

Holyoake—for the moment Britain's most visible nonbeliever, under any name—served only a total of six months in prison, for blasphemy. That was progress, given the experiences of Richard Carlile only a couple of decades earlier. Britain's "stupid tyranny" was beginning to ease slightly. Indeed, the opponents of religion were becoming so well organized in Britain that the Roses' impending visit had been announced in advance—in *The Reasoner*, Holyoake's newspaper.[61] Holyoake, along with other secularists and Owenites, made sure the couple was properly welcomed, honored and feted.

Ernestine and William Rose returned to New York in November of 1856.

The attack on Fort Sumter on April 12, 1861, began the war that would lead, after horrific bloodshed, to a degree of success for the most pressing of the causes of Ernestine Rose. Still, in Boston two days earlier, Rose had taken the time to give a speech in support of another of them. It was entitled "A Defense of Atheism" and would become the best known of her talks.[62] Few have expressed as eloquently the case for a godless humanism and defended as eloquently a post-religion morality:

> The Atheist says to the honest, conscientious believer, Though I cannot believe in your God whom you have failed to demonstrate, I believe in man; if I have no faith in your religion, I have faith, unbounded, unshaken faith in the principles of right, of justice and humanity. Whatever good you are willing to do for the sake of your God, I am full as willing to do for the sake of man.

(Again Rose would want us to interpret "man" here as "all human beings.")

The women's movement split after the Civil War, with Rose, alongside Susan B. Anthony, in the more radical faction—unwilling to accept the postponement of female suffrage until after Negro male suffrage. Anthony and her ally, Elizabeth Cady Stanton, were reduced to opposing giving the vote to black men if it meant continuing to deny the vote to white and black women—with Anthony and Stanton, but not Rose, resorting to some racist rhetoric.[63] It was a bitter split and an ugly debate. In June of 1869, William and Ernestine Rose left for Europe again—more or less permanently. In the summer of 1870, they settled in Britain.

William Rose died of a heart attack in London in 1882. Ernestine lived on for ten years, apparently unenthusiastically. She felt she had lost her ability to contribute to the struggle for various freedoms. "It is no longer necessary for me to live," Rose told George Jacob Holyoake, "I can do nothing now."[64] However, her comment to the secularist leader, now her friend, did not end there: "But I have lived!" Rose added. She died after a stroke in 1892.

The slaves were freed in the United States 29 years before Rose's death. Women finally won the vote 28 years after her death. "Mental" freedom—Rose's third major cause and the one that made her exceptional—has been slow to experience such a success. That may help explain why Ernestine Rose's name is not as well known today as that of William Lloyd Garrison, Frederick Douglass, Susan B. Anthony and Elizabeth Cady Stanton. The age that might fully appreciate Ernestine Rose has, perhaps, still not come.

10

FREE ROVERS ON THE BROAD, BRIGHT, BREEZY COMMON OF THE UNIVERSE

WORKING-CLASS ATHEISM IN NINETEENTH-CENTURY BRITAIN

If error and ignorance have forged the chains of peoples, if prejudice perpetuates them, science, reason and truth will one day be able to break them.

—Baron d'Holbach[1]

IN 1880, VOTERS IN NORTHAMPTON, A SHOEMAKING TOWN NORTH of London, elected a new member of Parliament. It took almost six years before Charles Bradlaugh was actually allowed to take his seat. Nonetheless, the moment is worth savoring. For 183 years after young Thomas Aikenhead became the last atheist executed in Britain, the people of Northampton had chosen as one of their representatives the world's most notorious atheist.

Bradlaugh had first begun questioning religion while in Sunday school. His father was a clerk in a law office in London. And Charles himself had been working full-time since the age of 12: first running errands in that law office, then as a cashier for some coal merchants. So Sunday school was the only school Charles Bradlaugh was able to attend. Diligence and good sense had already earned this 14-year-old boy a chance to teach a Sunday school class of his own. Then—the year was 1848—Charles was selected for another honor: representing his church in a confirmation ceremony the bishop of London himself was to conduct.

In order to prepare, the Rev. John Graham Packer instructed his young Sunday school teacher to make a close study of the *Thirty-Nine Articles* of the Church of England. He did. He also reread the Gospels. And the teenager noted with some perplexity that those texts include apparently contradictory accounts of Jesus. He wrote a letter to the vicar asking for help in making sense of such contradictions.[2]

That letter does not survive. The apparent contradictions in these documents do. Article III of the Anglicans' 39, to pick one example, suggests that Jesus, after his death and before ascending to heaven, "went down into Hell" and Matthew has him spending "three days and three nights in the heart of the earth." However, another of the Gospels, Luke, has Jesus, while on the cross, suggesting that he will be in "paradise" that same day.[3] The Gospels, of course, also differ widely among themselves in their accounts of Jesus' behavior before his death.

The young instructor never received a reply to his request for help in working this out. Instead, Reverend Packer suspended him from Sunday school and characterized Charles' questions, in a letter to his father, as "atheistical."

Reverend Packer's reaction proved counterproductive. Charles used his free Sundays to wander to a place not far from his home where issues were being freely argued: a corner of Victoria Park in London known as Bonner's Field. Speakers would set up there. Crowds would gather to cheer, hiss or answer back. Charles had already visited Bonner's Field on weeknights, when the topic generally was politics—radical politics. Revolution was, at the time, sweeping through Europe. On Sunday the topic in this open-air, rent-free opinion market was religion.

And among the preachers and tract distributers with their various takes on Christianity, Bradlaugh came upon representatives of a new addition to the country's theological potpourri: freethinkers. At first Charles, ever one for a debate, had drifted to that section of Bonner's Field to challenge the speakers with arguments in favor of the "true religion"—Christianity. But after a particularly intense engagement with one leading freethinker, Charles was unable to escape the conclusion that he had lost. His position in the debates switched, for a time, to an abstract deism.

Meanwhile, Reverend Packer had become a regular visitor to the Bradlaugh home; he even succeeded in enticing Charles' father to church on Sundays. To straighten out the son, the vicar advised tacking edifying quotations on the wall, including one, placed directly across from where Charles sat for meals, from the fourteenth Psalm: "The fool hath said in his heart, There is no God." This too proved unhelpful. Charles was not the sort to accept assertions in lieu of reasoning. The suspension stretched on.

Then young Charles sent Reverend Packer, with a request for comment, a tract printed by Richard Carlile he had come upon, questioning the early history of Christianity and including this apposite statement: "To suppose . . . any man morally better or worse for belief or unbelief is to assume that man has . . . a power of making himself believe, of being convinced when he is not convinced."[4] This communiqué certainly was not innocent. And it also failed to draw the vicar into a discussion. Instead, the infuriated Reverend Packer persuaded Charles' father to threaten the teenager with the loss of his job and, by extension, his right to stay in the house if he did not stop his questioning within three days.

Charles responded, on the third day, by packing, kissing his younger sister goodbye and leaving home. He was 16.

Young Charles Bradlaugh, exiled from his parents' home, was reading—voraciously, rapidly, widely. He was educating himself, and—on the subject that most interested him that had become easier.

By the middle of nineteenth century in Britain, France, the United States and some other countries, discussion of disbelief was, finally, beginning to flow more freely—no longer under the shadow of the stake, the noose or the guillotine. Some in and out of power certainly were offended by these outbreaks of open conversation and did their best to obstruct them. Still, it had become possible for the son of a clerk—too poor to finish school—to encounter the Athenian Enlightenment, Hobbes, Spinoza, Hume and the French Enlightenment. It had become possible for such a young man to have the benefit of numerous editions of Shelley's *Queen Mab* and Paine's *The Age of Reason,* to have the benefit of forums like Holyoake's London Secular Society and Bonner's Field.

Of course, few autodidacts had Charles' intellectual hunger and his discipline. He was, for example, also teaching himself languages—French, of course, Hebrew, a few others. And soon this tall, desperately skinny teenager, with a cockney accent, was himself climbing the soapbox and holding forth before the crowds at Bonner's Field. Bradlaugh's position had evolved into a carefully worked out atheism. He was billed as a former Sunday school teacher.

"The stump orator for the real scoffing party," one unenthusiastic member of the audience wrote in a British newspaper, "is an overgrown boy of seventeen with such an uninformed mind that it is really amusing to see him sometimes stammering and sputtering on in his ignorant eloquence. . . . He is styled by the frequenters of the park as the 'baby'; and I believe is listened to very often more from real curiosity to know what one so young will say, than from any love the working men have to his scoffings."[5]

Soapbox speeches were not, of course, remunerated, and the budding orator required a place to live. Most nights Charles made do with half a bed in a house that doubled as a meeting hall for freethinkers. (It was run by the woman who had been the late Richard Carlile's common-law wife.) But there was also the question of food, which made unavoidable the question of money. Charles supported himself for a time by selling coal. However, his best customer, a baker's wife, dropped him after someone informed her that her supplier was "an infidel." "I should be afraid," this woman explained, "that my bread would smell of brimstone."[6] Young Bradlaugh sometimes went hungry.

And this particular teenager was not easy to treat to a meal. There is a story of Charles fleeing a coffee house upon realizing that an invitation to a discussion was a pretext to buy him some food. "I got very poor and at that time was also very proud," Bradlaugh later admitted.[7] He fell into debt: just four pounds, fifteen shillings of debt—an impossible-to-imagine-repaying four pounds, fifteen shillings of debt.[8]

So Charles did what many young working-class men did in such circumstances: he joined the Army for the enlistment bonus, which was six pounds, ten shillings. (The regular meals must also have been an inducement.) His parents, who had had no contact with him in the many months since their showdown, invited their son over for a half-hearted Christmasday reunion before he shipped for Ireland.[9]

On the ship some other recruits broke into Charles' suitcase, where, to their amusement, they found books, which, to their further amusement, they employed as footballs. The largest book made the best football and was, consequently, the most heavily damaged. It was a Greek lexicon.[10]

Charles' father died while he was in the army.[11] That left the family with no means of support. His two youngest siblings were put in an orphanage. After three years of participating in the British army's activities in Ireland, of which he was no fan, Charles tried to get home to pitch in.

An aunt died. Thirty pounds of the money she left were used to buy the family's only remaining working-age male out of the army.

Back in London Charles found a job with an open-minded lawyer and eventually earned enough to return the thirty pounds to his mother and help out. In the evenings, on weekends, Bradlaugh engaged in other work. He campaigned against the monarchy and for a truly republican Britain. He campaigned in favor of compulsory national education (which certainly would have helped him as a child). He campaigned for freedom for the Italian, Polish, Indian and, with first-hand knowledge, Irish peoples. He campaigned for women's suffrage and birth control. Bradlaugh was championing, in essence, an updated version of Denis Diderot's and Baron d'Holbach's, Tom Paine's and Ernestine Rose's, liberty-freedom platform. But Bradlaugh was best known as an advocate of atheism.

Bradlaugh was certainly not Britain's only outspoken atheist in the middle of the nineteenth century. The movement—a radical protest against religion and the social and political system it supported—was growing. In fact, after he left the army, Charles married Susannah Lamb Hooper—the daughter of Abraham Hooper, another prominent working-class nonbeliever. Yet, despite his lack of formal education and while still in his mid-twenties, Bradlaugh was elected to replace George Jacob Holyoake as president of the country's main organization of nonbelievers: the London Secular Society. Under his leadership it became the National Secular Society. Charles Bradlaugh had quickly become Britain's leading atheist.

In 1858 a series of debates began in cities across Britain.[12] On one side would be a minister, religious-association leader or religious scholar— occasionally with somewhat unconventional views, more commonly with traditional beliefs and an equally traditional outrage that anyone would dare question those beliefs. On the other side of the stage stood a long-limbed, thin-lipped man in his twenties. So as not to embarrass the lawyer for whom he worked, Charles Bradlaugh used the pseudonym "Iconoclast."

Among the propositions put forward in the first of those debates, in Sheffield on June 7, 1858, was the following: "The God of the Bible, revengeful, inconstant, unmerciful and unjust."[13] The debate continued the next night and then was resumed for two more nights the next week. There were never fewer than 1,100 middle-class and working-class people in the audience.

Yes, working-class people. We tend to think of atheism as emanating primarily from the educated classes. Bradlaugh, himself, and his audiences disprove that. Similar crowds gathered for similar, multi-night debates in Northampton, Wigan, Liverpool, Bradford, Halifax, Glasgow and in Paisley, where the local paper reported that the audience was the largest it had ever seen in the hall. Not everyone present was poor, powerless, disenfranchised and uneducated, but many were. And not everyone there agreed with Iconoclast, but they were there to hear religion challenged. The working-class interest in atheism that had surfaced in Britain with reprints of Shelley's *Queen Mab* was intensifying.

And these large audiences heard this young man marshal evidence, logic and rhetoric in an attempt to demonstrate that the religion they had been told all their lives was the height of wisdom and goodness was actually the height of absurdity and perilously unreliable as a moral guide. This was a time and in a country where the gulf between the classes remained impassable and the condition of many lives remained impossible—as evidenced by what had happened to two of Bradlaugh's siblings when their father died. Iconoclast was telling the working-class men and women in his audiences that religion was a major part of the social and political system that made their existences so difficult.

Jean Meslier had never stood before a crowd of farmers and mechanics and argued that religion was holding them down. Such an event would have been unimaginable for Denis Diderot or Baron d'Holbach: they held forth only in clandestine books or fancy salons. Indeed, a public debate on religion before a large audience would probably have been impossible anywhere in Europe or America before the start of the French Revolution. Perhaps Anacharsis Cloots—"Orator of the Human Race"—had attracted such a crowd during the wildest days of that revolution.

But things were changing: Robert Owen had given public talks in Britain in which he attacked religion. Ernestine Rose, a truly accomplished orator, did, too—in the United States and also in Britain, when she passed through in 1856. And, in 1858, Charles Bradlaugh—himself the son of a clerk—was drawing some of the largest crowds a critic of religion had ever drawn.

As a self-taught expert on and critic of religion's history, Bradlaugh was familiar with all the basic arguments against religious belief. He contributed to many of them—though less, perhaps, to the anacreontic, which had difficulty gaining a toehold in Victorian Britain.[14] Bradlaugh lived at a time of continuing injustice and oppression—in the form of social and political inequality, colonialism and exploitation of women and workers. So he was probably most important as a spokesman for the fourth, more political, variety of disbelief. He had gotten a first-hand glimpse of the "real hell" religion supported in poorer areas of Britain.

Men starve, Bradlaugh liked to assert, "because pulpit teachers have taught them for centuries to be content with the state of life in which it has pleased God to [place] them. . . . Men starve because the teachers have taught heaven instead of earth, the next world instead of this."[15]

Bradlaugh was helping develop as thoughtful and rhetorically powerful a formulation of the doctrine of the Enlightenment atheists as the world had seen—with one exception. That exception was a man also based in London at the time who had encapsulated the Meslier-Diderot-d'Holbach argument on the politics of religion into a sentence: "It is the opium of the people."

A theism has had its great eras, its great moments: Athens in Thucydides' day, Paris during the Enlightenment. Charles Bradlaugh's time in Britain belongs on any such list. Indeed, one year there might be so honored.

In Britain in 1859, the German refugee Karl Marx was researching and just beginning to publish his most serious analyses. Marx, of course, shared Bradlaugh's concern for the working class and his belief that religion was furthering their oppression. Marx called Diderot his favorite writer.[16] His ideas would lead in the next century to perhaps the most sweeping attempt at economic transformation the world has seen. It would also lead to a form of atheism being, of all things, established as a kind of state "religion"—in, among other places, Russia, Eastern Europe, China and Southeast Asia. Because of his significance for the twentieth century, Marx will be discussed further in the next chapter. Besides, 1859 was not an exceptional year for Karl Marx. The case for the importance of this year in the history of atheism does not rest on his work.

In Britain in 1859, John Stuart Mill published probably the greatest argument for tolerance, freedom of speech and intellectual freedom ever written: *On Liberty*. "If all mankind minus one were of one opinion, and only one person were of the contrary opinion," Mill states, in perhaps his grandest pronouncement, "mankind would be no more justified in silencing that one person than he, if he had the power, would be justified in silencing mankind."[17]

Mill, however, is doing more than making a broader demand for liberty; he is endowing this demand with an extraordinary new justification: Mill—leaping beyond Bayle, Voltaire and Madison—does not want even the most outlandish-sounding "contrary opinion" just to be tolerated because, as Jefferson put it, "it does me no injury"; he insists that it be welcomed because it does us good. For challenges to widely held understandings, Mill is arguing, are *necessary* if we are to evaluate, invigorate, improve, update, correct or replace our understandings. "He who knows only his own side of the case," he asserts, "knows little of that."[18]

And Mill made clear that he was calling even for challenges to religion. Indeed, he himself later linked this principle specifically to the opinions of Charles Bradlaugh: "If you will do me the honor to read my little book *On Liberty,*" he writes in a letter, "you will at once understand why I think such men as Mr. Bradlaugh ought to be allowed to say what they have got to say."[19] Of course, it hadn't been that long ago in Britain and most of the rest of the world that "such men as Mr. Bradlaugh" could be executed for saying "what they have got to say." Now Mill was asserting that criticism of religion not only should be permitted but encouraged.

Tolerance and encouragement—those were two great gifts Mill's book offered atheists. But it contained a third large gift: it is an attack—radical and modern—upon authority, certainty and faith, pillars of religion. "The beliefs which we have most warrant for have no safeguard to rest on but a standing invitation to the whole world to prove them unfounded," Mill writes, in another splendid sentence. While many among the religious have been more hospitable to questioning, even doubt, than, say, Bradlaugh's old antagonist, Reverend Packer, no religion wants to be treated as a perpetual target—repeatedly interrogated about its history, assumptions, inconsistencies and contradictions. No faith wants to be seen as, in effect, merely another hypothesis. But that's the status to which Mill's relentlessly questioning liberalism, if honored, would reduce all such beliefs. Mill was, in essence, arguing for a radical skepticism—a society invigorated by perpetual exposure to the question, *How can that be?* In *On Liberty* "authority" and "certainty" are pejoratives, while "contradicting" and "disproving" are held heroic.[20]

Mill's argument could also, of course, be applied to atheists. Wouldn't some atheists, too, benefit by being a little less certain? Shouldn't they, too, send "a standing invitation to the whole world to prove" their ideas "unfounded?" Shouldn't atheists, too—particularly on those occasions when they find themselves wielding power—tolerate and even encourage dissenting views? If only Jacques-René Hébert, for whom the guillotine had been the proper response to dissenting views, had been able to read Mill. If only Karl Marx had placed more importance on freedom of speech—before and after the "dictatorship of the proletariat."[21]

Charles Bradlaugh did not waver in his atheism, but he was open and tolerant. He certainly believed in freedom of speech and the other basic political liberties. He had no interest in violent revolution. He was always game to test his ideas in debate. And, although I have found no evidence that the two men ever met, Bradlaugh saw the contribution Mill was making to his cause. He had eight books by Mill in his library, *On Liberty* prominent among them.[22]

In Britain also in 1859, Charles Darwin published his radical, revelatory and still-accepted explanation of the development of life: *On the Origin of Species by Means of Natural Selection.* Many defenders of religion immediately saw the threat Darwin's book represented: one religious newspaper at the time characterized the book as "standing in blasphemous contradiction to biblical narrative and doctrine."[23] By demonstrating that living things evolve naturally—rather than having been created, all at once, supernaturally—Darwin's book did as much to further disbelief as any book ever written. It was, with Newton's *Principia Mathematica,* the greatest demonstration humankind has seen of the power of natural explanations—of "a clear understanding"—to push aside supernatural explanations.

However, Mill's book and Darwin's book also *benefited* from the growing disbelief of the age. They were written by nonbelievers. Probably they had to be written by nonbelievers. And Mill and Darwin would have had difficulty thinking their revolutionary thoughts and publishing their revolutionary books without the intellectual freedom and the comfort made possible by the ongoing struggle against religion in Britain in the middle of the nineteenth century.

Mill's father, the political philosopher James Mill, raised him as an atheist. "I am thus one of the very few examples, in this country," he explains in his autobiography, "of one who has not thrown off religious belief but never had it."[24] Mill is also one of the few examples of that in this book.

Perhaps a religious version of John Stuart Mill could still have called as eloquently for tolerance and even encouraged, as persuasively, dissenting views. But could a Mill with any sort of faith in any sort of god, promulgating any sort of truth, have produced his call for a permanent intellectual revolution against all "authority" and "certainty"? *On Liberty* is very much the product not only of an atheist but of atheism. The same might be said of *On the Origin of Species.*

Darwin, unlike Mill, first had to cast off his religion, which had been, as he puts it, "quite orthodox." That happened shortly after he returned from his specimen-gathering, around-the-world trip on the *Beagle.*[25] It does not seem to have been what he learned on the *Beagle* about the variety of species that finally extinguished Darwin's faith; according to his own account, it was what he learned about the variety of religions.[26] Seeing how seriously those other faiths were taken had exposed Darwin to what this book has called the pathogen of relativism, which tends to weaken religious belief. The result was an outbreak of skepticism. "I had come, by this time," he recalls in a short memoir, "to see that the Old Testament . . . was no more to be trusted than the sacred books of the Hindoos."

Darwin was undoubtedly helped in coming to this conclusion by the spread of the same ideas that helped young Bradlaugh question Christianity. We know, for example, that Darwin read Shelley's poems and essays, along with the work of Hume and a number of other thinkers who challenged traditional views of religion.[27] "Disbelief crept over me at a very slow rate," Darwin himself explains, "but was at last complete."[28]

Darwin's theory of natural selection also began creeping over him in those years. "The great naturalist did not abandon Abrahamic and other religious dogmas because of his discovery of evolution by natural selection, as one might reasonably suppose," the biologist Edward O. Wilson concludes. "The reverse occurred. The shedding of blind faith gave him the intellectual fearlessness to explore human evolution wherever logic and evidence took him."[29] Genesis, the point is, had to have been left far behind before a theory of natural selection could arise.

Achieving the fearlessness to actually publish that theory was another matter. It took 21 years before Darwin allowed his ideas on evolution into print. Much of this delay stemmed from wariness. And that wariness stemmed from his theory's unavoidable odor of atheism. "I know how much I open myself to reproach, for such a conclusion," he wrote in a letter in 1845.[30] The fact that Darwin's wife was religious may have contributed to his hesitations. At one point in a notebook he considers a way he might propose his theory and still "avoid stating how far I believe in Materialism."[31]

Darwin's decision finally to publish *On the Origin of Species* owed a lot to his realization that Alfred Russel Wallace had come up with the beginnings of a similar theory, but it was made easier by the growth of the anti-religious movement in Britain during those 21 years.[32] "Materialism" still opened one to reproach, but a number of Darwin's contemporaries— Bradlaugh the most prominent among them—had hazarded that reproach and survived it.

There is no evidence that Darwin—an upper-class, reserved, Cambridge-educated scientist—and Bradlaugh, who was none of that, ever met. But Darwin did count Harriet Martineau, who sometimes lent her name to Bradlaugh's causes, among his friends.[33]

Martineau, the daughter of a manufacturer, had been a political crusader and a writer of religious books, when, in her mid-forties, she undertook a trip to the Middle East to learn more about religion. She returned in 1847 a political crusader and an outspoken atheist. Martineau had visited the biblical sites and grown convinced that she had seen there not a religion that had been revealed by God in a moment but a religion that had been developed by humans over history. "I recognized the monstrous superstition in its true character," Martineau explains, before adding a stirring positive statement of disbelief, "and found myself . . . a free rover on the broad, bright, breezy common of the universe."[34] Despite having detached herself from religion, Martineau, as Darwin undoubtedly noticed, was able to continue writing successful books and articles.

I n Britain in 1859, as Darwin and Mill were publishing their monumental books, Charles Bradlaugh was frequently out on the stump—sometimes in debate, often speaking alone, consistently attracting large working-class crowds and always arguing forcefully for what it had long been impermissible to argue.

News of an upcoming visit by this proselytizing atheist proved, not surprisingly, distressing for the burghers of a town. In March, for example, Bradlaugh was scheduled to speak at the Guildhall in Doncaster, to the north of London.[35] In response, a group calling itself "Friends of Religion" felt called upon to issue a "caution to the public" in which it advised the town's population to make sure Bradlaugh would gaze "on the unpeopled interior of the Guildhall." In fact, the interior of the Guildhall in Doncaster, when Bradlaugh mounted the stage, was "crowded to excess," according to the *Doncaster Herald,* which nevertheless dubbed Bradlaugh's talk a "frantic panegyric in honour of hell."

Another newspaper, the *Doncaster Chronicle,* conceded, "He is a person possessing great fluency of speech, of ready wit, and the declamatory style of his oratory is well calculated to excite and carry away a popular audience." Bradlaugh returned to Doncaster later that year. This time the "Friends of Religion" were better organized: He was denied use of any of the town's halls. So Bradlaugh spoke outdoors on a temporary platform erected under the roof of the corn market. The "popular audience" in this larger space that evening included, according to one report, 4,000 people.

The city quickly forbade Bradlaugh from speaking in the market, so the next evening he spoke from a wagon in an open area near the market. The subject that night, a standard Bradlaugh critique, was the "History and Teaching of Jesus Christ." More than 7,000 people turned out to hear it.

One defender of Christianity that evening managed to hit Bradlaugh in the head with a stone as he made his way back to his lodgings. Nonetheless, some percentage of the people of Doncaster clearly had an interest in the subject of atheism. Some percentage of the people evinced a similar interest in cities all across Britain in 1859. And soon Bradlaugh would be lecturing to similar crowds and causing similar consternation as far away as India, as well as on the Continent and in America. (Bradlaugh became a late-life friend of Ernestine Rose.)

For that virtuous cycle was operating in this as in all great eras of atheism. The spread of disbelief in the supernatural helped make possible new kinds of thinking about human society and the natural world—such as that of Mill and Darwin. Hugely important new kinds of thinking: Darwin's theory is, of course, the foundation of modern biology, and the case can be made that Mill's variety of liberalism, with or without its implications honored, has become the dominant political philosophy in the modern world. (However, the work of that other atheist in London at the time, Karl Marx, would certainly give Mill's theory a run for the money in the twentieth century.) Then these new kinds of thinking also contributed to the spread of disbelief in the supernatural.

None of this came without strife.

The summer after the publication of *The Origin of Species*, the theory it expounded and its theological implications were hotly debated at a meeting in Oxford of the British Association for the Advancement of Science. Darwin, too sickly and timid to stand up to the unrelenting religious assault that followed the book's publication, was absent. As he often would in coming years, Thomas Henry Huxley, an up-and-coming biologist with a fierce allegiance to what he saw as truth, stepped into the breach.

The bishop of Oxford, Samuel Wilberforce, launched the best known of the meeting's attacks. Along the way, he said something (accounts differ) to this effect: "If anyone were to be willing to trace his descent through an ape as his *grandfather*, would he be willing to trace his descent similarly on the side of his *grandmother?*" Huxley, already assuming the role of Darwin's main defender, saw an opening in this ungallant remark. "If then . . . the question is put to me would I rather have a miserable ape for a grandfather," he replied (carefully leaving the lady out of it), "or a man highly endowed by nature and possessed of great means of influence and yet who employs those faculties and that influence for the mere purpose of introducing ridicule into a grave scientific discussion, I unhesitatingly affirm my preference for the ape." This retort was much remembered (though not by all who were actually there; accounts differ). A woman in the audience (by a couple of accounts) promptly fainted.[36]

Huxley, who earned the sobriquet "Darwin's bulldog," proclaimed himself committed "to untiring opposition to that ecclesiastical spirit, that clericalism, which in England, as everywhere else, . . . is the deadly enemy of science." A couple of months after his face-off with Wilberforce, Huxley's beloved eldest son died, and an acquaintance implied, gently, that he might, in his grief, profit from the comforts of religion. Huxley's response was staunch and unbending: "Truth is better than much profit," he wrote. "If wife and child and name and fame were all to be lost to me one after the other as the penalty, still I will not lie."[37]

Truth is a standard before which atheists often genuflect. But Thomas Henry Huxley was not prepared to call himself an atheist:

> When I reached intellectual maturity and began to ask myself whether I was an atheist, a theist, or a pantheist; a materialist or an idealist; a Christian or a freethinker—I found that the more I learned and reflected, the less ready was the answer; until, at last, I came to the conclusion that I had neither art nor part with any of these denominations, except the last. The one

thing in which most of these good people were agreed was the one thing in which I differed from them. They were quite sure they had attained a certain *gnosis*—had, more or less successfully, solved the problem of existence; while I was quite sure I had not, and had a pretty strong conviction that the problem was insoluble.[38]

The word Huxley coined in 1869—so, as he puts it, he too could have "a label to cover himself"—was "agnostic." (*Gnosis* is "knowledge" in Greek; *a* means "without.")

Agnostics profess a deep humility: "The little light of awakened human intelligence," suggests Huxley, "shines so mere a spark amidst the abyss of the unknown and unknowable."[39] Agnostics could, consequently, disbelieve—or mostly disbelieve—with an agreeable air of caution and reserve: "In matters of the intellect do not pretend that conclusions are certain which are not demonstrated or demonstrable," Huxley advises.[40] Darwin latched onto the term to cover his own wary unbelief.

Darwin's bulldog was not at all timid, but he does repeatedly characterize himself as being "hopelessly ignorant concerning a variety of matters about which metaphysicians and theologians, both orthodox and heterodox, dogmatize with the utmost confidence."[41] Huxley here seems to want not only to challenge ideas by attempting to "prove" them "unfounded" but not to hold those ideas in the first place. In such statements it is hard not to hear the Greek Skeptic Pyrrho, whose professions of intractable ignorance—"no more this than that"—and whose belief that we should be "without judgment" were widely known in Europe two millennia later. Agnosticism rests upon and promotes a skeptical withholding of judgment.

Charles Bradlaugh was watching all these efforts among the educated classes to deal with what seemed to some of them as the increasingly manifest absence of God. Bradlaugh had great enthusiasm, of course, for Mill's ideas and Darwin's theory. He was less impressed by Huxley's retreat, however strategic, to some sort of ultimate ignorance. And Bradlaugh was against mincing words. He was no fan of "agnostic" or even "secularist"—terms he considered watered-down, defensive and cowardly. He thought someone who didn't think that religion was true was an "atheist," nothing less.

Bradlaugh's own views—which he had no trouble fitting under that traditional label—were not particularly dogmatic: he was always careful not to pretend to what he considered indemonstrable conclusions.

According to a newspaper account of one of his debates in 1859, Iconoclast did not "deny" in some general or abstract sense "that there was 'a God,' because to deny that which was unknown was as absurd as to affirm it." Bradlaugh would return to this point many times. It was among his more original contributions to the growing body of thought on atheism. "The Atheist does not say," he explained, "'there is no God,' but he says, 'I know not what you mean by God; I am without idea of God; the word *God* is to me a sound conveying no clear or distinct affirmation. I do not deny God, because I cannot deny that of which I have no conception.'"[42]

That was one reason Bradlaugh was so infuriated by the "watch story."[43] "The well-known Atheist Bradlaugh, at a public meeting in London," is how one newspaper presented its version of the story in 1870, "is reported to have taken out his watch, with these words, 'If there be a God in heaven, I give him five minutes to strike me dead.'"[44] This anecdote was regularly repeated about Bradlaugh and occasionally about other atheists, though no reliable witness could ever be found who had been there when a watch was taken out and such a dare was given. Bradlaugh labeled the story a "monstrous lie" and went to court when a member of Parliament and then a newspaper failed to retract it.

For Bradlaugh was in no way disposed to challenging or showing up a deity of whom he could not conceive. "I cannot war with a nonentity," is how he once put it.[45] He was not in the habit of addressing such a deity. Nor was Bradlaugh trying, through some cheap carnival trick, to prove that there was absolutely no chance whatsoever that something of which he had "no conception" might exist.

However, Bradlaugh—whose skepticism while not formally Academic was certainly not Pyrrhonian[46]—was able to make judgments on specific religions. He had no difficulty denying—on logical, historical, evidentiary, scientific, textual and moral grounds—the plausibility of the world-creating, flood-causing, Son-begetting God that Christians worshipped. According to a newspaper's account of one of his debates, "as an atheist" Iconoclast was eager and ready to disprove the existence of "the God of the Bible, of the Koran, of the *Vedas*" or of any other holy book of which he knew.[47] Here he differed substantially with Thomas Henry Huxley.

Atheist and agnostic have at times squabbled—albeit not with the violence with which Catholic and Protestant, Sunni and Shiite, have at times squabbled. Bradlaugh, in the end, was unhesitating in his dismissal of Huxley's neologism. "A mere society form of atheism," he sneered.[48]

Certainly, in mid-nineteenth-century Britain atheism seemed the rougher, less humble, more dangerous movement—in part because of the social class of its leader and its audience.

The scenes Charles Bradlaugh had been enacting all across Britain were the realization of a nightmare for many upper-class men: a working-class crusader weaning audiences, thousands-strong, of laborers, shop-keepers, clerks and women from religion. For many centuries the educated, the landed, the wealthy, whatever their own views, had been obsessed with keeping any suspicion that God might not exist away from the ears of, as Voltaire put it, tailors, servants and wives—for fear of immorality if not insurrection. Look what happened in Paris! But in the era of Mill, Darwin and Bradlaugh, such suspicions had become impossible to contain. Consider the case of Annie Besant, the young wife of the Rev. Frank Besant—vicar of a church in Lincolnshire.

Their infant daughter had fallen ill. The doctor said she would die. Annie spent her days and nights at the tiny girl's bedside trying to nurse her through severe coughing spells. The baby recovered after some desperate weeks, but her illness had left Annie's faith severely shaken. Why had this evil happened to her beloved little girl? This vicar's wife was wrestling, in other words, with the problem of evil—a problem Cicero has wrestled with in his book *On the Nature of the Gods:* how could an all-powerful God allow the world to be filled with so much suffering, so much evil?[49] In an attempt to quiet her mind and quell her doubt Annie read and spoke with a variety of theologians.

Explaining why an all-good, all-powerful God would make, for example, innocent babies sick is such a complex and considerable undertaking for theologians that this branch of their discipline has its own name: theodicy.[50] We do not know exactly what Besant found in her researches. The three standard theological answers to the problem of why God permits such suffering, however, are that a sin—which God is, justly, punishing—was committed somewhere (by the infant?); that the suffering is a test or a route to redemption (for the infant?); or that all will finally be made right by God in the end (but why would it have been made wrong in the first place?).[51] If these responses prove unconvincing, the religious are wont to fall back on the ever reliable: "God works in mysterious ways." (God's behavior is, of course, seen as quite intelligible when something good happens.)

Whatever Besant read or heard did not prove reassuring or persuasive. Annie Besant's spiritual crisis—her growing skepticism—led to a physical breakdown, to a suicide plan and then to what was becoming in Britain in the second half of the nineteenth century a more and more common conclusion: that the religion she had been taught was wrong. Besant felt it impossible to believe in God's beneficence or the notion that He had a son who died for our sins.

Annie Besant was not the type to keep her thoughts to herself. Eventually, the vicar's wife refused to participate in Holy Communion and joined the anti-religious movement swelling around her. She published a pamphlet, credited only to "the wife of a beneficed clergyman," questioning "the Deity of Jesus of Nazareth." The separation agreement in 1873 gave Reverend Besant custody of their son, Annie their daughter.

Annie Besant supplemented the small income she received under the agreement by writing more pamphlets. The essay in which she finally came around to dismissing the notion of God entirely was ready to be published when she attended her first lecture by Charles Bradlaugh.

Bradlaugh and his wife had two daughters and a son, but their marriage was not a success. Until he visited France and began to allow himself a little wine, Bradlaugh did not drink. His wife did—to excess.[52] The couple separated. The great love of Charles Bradlaugh's life would be Annie Besant.

Besant was 26, 14 years younger than Bradlaugh, when she attended that lecture by Britain's leading atheist. For her it seems to have been love at first sight and hearing:[53]

> The grave, quiet, stern, strong face, the massive head, the keen eyes, the magnificent breadth and height of forehead. . . . His knowledge was as sound as his language was splendid. Eloquence, fire, sarcasm, pathos, passion, all in turn were bent against Christian superstition. . . . The great audience, carried away by the torrent of the orator's force, hung silent, breathing soft, as he went on, till the silence that followed a magnificent peroration broke the spell, and a hurricane of cheers relieved the tension.

Besant invited Bradlaugh to visit. He protested that, as she recalled, "he was so hated by English society that any friend of his would be certain to suffer." She repeated the invitation: Besant, like Bradlaugh, could be headstrong. Bradlaugh's two daughters took an early and lasting dislike to her, after she, with eyes only for him, ignored their presence in a room.[54] But Bradlaugh, himself, was impressed. Soon Besant was working at his weekly, the *National Reformer*. She edited and wrote. She organized. She began to lecture. "Probably the best speech by a woman to which we have ever listened," Bradlaugh, increasingly smitten himself, wrote of her debut. She participated in the anti-religious, political, journalistic and legal enterprise he sometimes referred to as, "The Bradlaugh."[55] (He no longer required that day job working for an attorney.) They became a team.

Charles Bradlaugh and Annie Besant usually spent their days and evenings together, working on their various projects in the sunny study of her home. He would leave at about ten to sleep at the house he had purchased nearby. The term Besant uses for their relationship is "friendship," but there seems little doubt it was love. He uses the word in reference to their relationship in at least one letter. She claimed at one point that "Mr. Bradlaugh and myself are engaged to be married," but then was forced to admit that it was not true but that she "hoped it would be true."[56]

It could not be true. Neither of them was legally divorced nor could get legally divorced. Bradlaugh's wife died in 1877. But Besant remained and had to remain technically married to Reverend Besant, since adultery (by the woman), cruelty and desertion were the only accepted grounds for divorce. Matthew quotes Jesus as saying, "Whoever divorces his wife for any reason except sexual immorality causes her to commit adultery; and whoever marries a woman who is divorced commits adultery"[57]—which, like the British marriage laws based upon it, did not leave much hope for victims of bad marriages.

Bradlaugh and Besant certainly were not entirely approving of Victorian morality. They opposed those restrictive, religious divorce laws—particularly their unfairness to women.[58] And in 1877, Bradlaugh and Besant republished together a thinly veiled, admittedly rather clumsy birth-control manual for married couples—knowing it would lead to a prosecution.[59] (Bradlaugh unsuccessfully tried to call Darwin as a scientific witness at their trial.) The jury concluded that "the book in question is calculated to deprave public morals." Bradlaugh and Besant were each sentenced to six months in prison. But the decision was set aside on a technicality.

Despite these forward-looking efforts, neither Bradlaugh nor Besant was prepared to risk respectability by openly advocating or openly engaging in a sexual relationship unsanctioned by marriage. Here they were at pains to demonstrate how traditionally moral they could be. "Although

Mr. Bradlaugh gives prominence to his disbelief," wrote a British newspaper, "it is his belief in many essential elements of Christian morality which gives him his power."[60] Whether Annie and Charles had a consummated sexual love appears impossible to determine: their letters to each other were destroyed.[61] But in public, at least, there was no lapse in propriety.

The way Bradlaugh and Besant behaved with each other was, to be sure, being carefully scrutinized by their many enemies—in particular by detectives hired by her husband. Indeed, Reverend Besant eventually won custody of the couple's daughter, too, on the grounds that her mother had been denying her a religious education.[62] "It is a pity there isn't a God," Annie Besant said after losing that most important of court battles, "it would do one so much good to hate Him."[63]

Bradlaugh had one additional reason to demonstrate propriety: he was considering running for office.

Even the mostly sycophantic biographies acknowledge that Bradlaugh was unwavering, ambitious and proud. He worked hard, for example, to rid himself of his cockney accent. He was also pugnacious.

Bradlaugh sometimes found himself at the same meetings in London as that other crusader against religion and for the working class, Karl Marx. But Marx and Bradlaugh saw things differently. For all his concern for the proletariat, Bradlaugh—a staunch, small-"r" republican—was unpersuaded by socialism and alarmed by the violent revolution that appeared to stand between the current situation and Marx's communism. In 1871 the two men had a loud falling out.[64]

Even friends acknowledged that Bradlaugh's temper could be formidable. After he assumed (mistakenly) that the German had been behind an attack on him, Bradlaugh's anger was unleashed upon Marx. "I feel indebted to Karl Marx for his enmity," Bradlaugh announced. "If I were one of this own countrymen he might betray me to his government; here he can only calumniate." Marx—having just been calumniated pretty good himself—roared back, calling Bradlaugh, not without some truth, "that huge self-idolater." The German also accused the Englishman, in a phrase unworthy of this champion of working people, of "the low cunning of a solicitor's clerk." Bradlaugh suggested they arbitrate their dispute. Marx sensed a trap. "I have done with Mr. Charles Bradlaugh," he announced, "and leave him to all the comforts he may derive from the quiet contemplation of his own self."

Bradlaugh had a history of breaking, acrimoniously, with former allies. Probably the most painful of these disputes was that occasioned by the conversion of his closest associate, after more than a decade of working side by side, to a kind of religion: Annie Besant had taken up Theosophy.

Besant had already put some distance between herself and Bradlaugh personally when she began spending much of her time with a recent re-cruit to their movement: a charismatic fellow a couple of years younger than she.[65] However, her greatest betrayal may have been Theosophy—a kind of spiritualism, which claims access to the essence at the heart of all religions. At the last meeting of the National Secular Society she attended, Besant insisted that she was receiving letters from the dead.[66]

Bradlaugh, of course, was quick to distance himself from such talk. "An Atheist certainly cannot be a Theosophist," he felt compelled to point out.[67] Bradlaugh and Besant saw little of each other after that. By then he had focused his energies on an even more public and more political role for himself.

In 1868, Charles Bradlaugh ran as the "radical" Liberal candidate for one of the seats in Parliament from Northampton, a town north of London dominated by shoe factories. He stood for compulsory national educa-tion; he stood for greater rights for workers, land reform, women's suffrage and complete separation of church and state. John Stuart Mill was among those who contributed to this notorious atheist's campaign (a contribu-tion that, when it became known, may have cost Mill his own seat in Par-liament).[68] Bradlaugh came in fifth out of six candidates for the two seats from Northampton—ahead only of the temperance candidate.

But Bradlaugh was obstinate. Britain's best-known atheist ran for Par-liament again in Northampton in the next election, in 1874, although he was lecturing in America at the time and unable to campaign. An alphabet-ical campaign ditty served to remind any voters who had not been paying attention with whom they were dealing: "A stands for 'Atheist,'" it began. "M" was for "Murderer of God's word."[69] Bradlaugh came in fifth again, but this time he received 567 more votes.[70]

When one of the two winners in Northampton died, Bradlaugh ran for the vacant seat and, splitting the vote with the "moderate" Liberal can-didate, helped the Conservative win in what had been a Liberal constitu-ency. Then, before the election of 1880, the radical and moderate Liberals in Northampton finally managed to make a deal to support each other's candidate in an attempt to share the two seats.[71]

As it became clear that Bradlaugh might actually get elected, the attacks intensified. One poster asked, "Can any Christian vote for Bradlaugh?" and then quoted (probably accurately) "Iconoclast's" words:[72]

Bradlaugh on God: "A bloodthirsty Deity."

Bradlaugh on Christianity: "A cursed, inhuman Religion."

Bradlaugh on the Bible: "Immoral book, I denounce it."

Another poster described the radical candidate (again, with some validity) as "THE GREATEST ENEMY OF GOD AND OF HIS TRUTH NOW LIVING AMONGST MEN." The churches weighed in: at least one minister asserted that Jesus would say, "Well done!" to Liberals who voted against Bradlaugh (a statement whose accuracy is more difficult to confirm).[73]

On April 2, 1880, Northampton voted. The moderate Liberal candidate received 4,158 votes, Bradlaugh 3,827—675 votes more than the top Conservative candidate and, therefore, enough to give God's "GREATEST ENEMY" Northampton's second seat in Parliament.[74]

Bradlaugh's election is an important milestone in this history—an early and, from an American perspective, stunning victory in the struggle for acceptance of atheism. But that struggle, of course, was far from over. Indeed, Bradlaugh's own struggle to enter Parliament had only begun.

Members of Parliament were required to take an oath before they took their seats, and this oath was sworn on a Bible and included the phrase, "So help me God."[75] Bradlaugh had led a successful fight to gain nonbelievers the right to testify in British courts—and, therefore, defend their rights— by "affirming" that they would tell the truth under penalty of law, rather than swearing to God.[76] Upon arriving in the House of Commons, Bradlaugh asked that he be allowed to affirm instead of taking the oath. (The right of officeholders to affirm rather than take an oath had been written into the United States Constitution in the previous century.)[77]

A select committee was appointed to decide if this would do. It decided, by a one vote margin, that it would not. So Bradlaugh agreed to take the oath even though it included "words of idle and meaningless character." Another select committee was appointed to mull that possibility over. "Admit the Atheist and you will have, in course of time, Atheistical legislation," warned a member from Ireland. "Thus came the excesses of the French Revolution." Queen Victoria was among those lobbying for a negative decision, pointing to Bradlaugh's "known atheism" and dismissing him as a "disgrace."[78] This committee decided he should not be allowed to take the oath, since Bradlaugh had already indicated that "an oath would not, as an oath, be binding on his conscience."[79]

Various other possibilities were explored, with Bradlaugh even being allowed to sit in Parliament for a short time, before being forcibly removed and briefly imprisoned. The courts got involved. Finally Parliament voted that Bradlaugh's seat had been "vacated" and that Northampton must hold a new election. Bradlaugh won that election, by 132 votes, but the struggle continued.

Before he was finally allowed to take the oath and, therefore, take his seat in 1886, Bradlaugh would win three more such elections in Northampton, lose at least a half-dozen more votes in the House of Commons, win and lose various suits in various courts, wrestle with a sergeant-at-arms trying again to evict him from the House of Commons and inspire a protest rally of 15,000 people in Trafalgar Square.

Bradlaugh did well, by most accounts, when he finally was seated as a member of Parliament from Northampton: working thoughtfully and effectively for causes like reform of aristocratic privileges and against imperialism but also weighing in with reason and force on other issues of the day. In fact, Bradlaugh was asked to consider a position as a minister in the next Liberal government.[80] However, before that could happen Charles Bradlaugh, suffering from kidney failure, died—on January 30, 1891, at the age of 57.

The death of an atheist remained a dramatic moment in the popular imagination: wouldn't such an individual, facing Hell's fires, recant? To put a stop to the inevitable rumors, Bradlaugh's daughter, Hypatia Bradlaugh Bonner, secured "signed testimony" from those who were with him at the end. They swore that while ill Bradlaugh never said a single word "either directly or indirectly bearing upon religion or any religious subject."[81]

After Karl Marx had died eight years earlier, 17 people gathered for his burial. Extra trains were added to accommodate the thousands of mourners who came to London for Bradlaugh's funeral, though he had insisted that nothing be said at his grave. The death of Karl Marx commanded a paragraph—full of factual errors—in the *Times* of London. That newspaper accorded Charles Bradlaugh, member of Parliament, about 1,500 words.[82]

Within a few years of his death a seven-and-half-foot-tall white, terracotta likeness of Charles Bradlaugh was erected atop a pedestal in Northampton, where it still stands. He looks forthright. He looks stern. This is a statue of a consistent, unhesitating, principled and, in some circles, revered atheist.

11

TO WIPE AWAY THE ENTIRE HORIZON

CREATING THE TWENTIETH CENTURY

Speaking the wisdom once they could not think,
Looking emotions once they feared to feel,
And changed to all which once they dared not be

—Percy Bysshe Shelley, *Prometheus Unbound*[1]

N 1882, A CHARACTER IN A BOOK BY A THEN OBSCURE GERMAN philosopher makes a portentous announcement. The character is described as a "madman." Initially, this book, like the other books Friedrich Nietzsche is writing, is mostly ignored; only 200 copies sell in four years. The announcement—crucial in my story of the development of atheism—is that "God is dead."[2]

The madman proclaims this in a marketplace before, Nietzsche tells us, "many . . . who did not believe in God." Crowds of that composition had become more common in the last decades of the nineteenth century—after Mill, after Darwin. The speeches, the debates, the conversations and the writings of proselytizing nonbelievers—more and more open in Europe and America in that century—had also had their effect. Many had weighed the arguments, looked around them and begun to see things Ernestine Rose's way, Charles Bradlaugh's way. Together these atheists or agnostics added up to a significant minority—an influential minority.

As Nietzsche's madman pronounced God dead, Bradlaugh was being reelected to Parliament in Northhampton (though he had not yet been

allowed to take his seat). And new, often outspoken disbelievers were ap-
pearing. We might gather our own group of them—a group of the makers
of the twentieth century—to puzzle out the significance for that century of
what was happening to God.

K arl Marx had died, at the age of 64, in London the year after Nietzsche's
book was published. At his sparsely attended funeral, the task facing Marx's main eulogist, Frederick Engels was arguing for his historical,
philosophical and political significance. Engels did not hold back: "On the
fourteenth of March, at a quarter to three in the afternoon, the greatest
living thinker ceased to think."[3] Engels did not feel called upon to note the
absence of any deathbed religious conversion: Karl Marx had forcefully
denied the existence of God, and insisted that thought ceases with death,
all his adult life.

Both his grandfathers had been rabbis.[4] But Marx's father, Herschel
Levi, was a secular man, who became, in stages, Heinrich Marx. When
the Prussian government made it impossible for Jews to practice law,
Heinrich, a successful lawyer in the old German city of Trier, was forced
to switch his religion as well as his name. His conversion was made less
painful by the fact that he had stopped believing in the Jewish religion
long ago and was now, in actuality, an Enlightenment-loving deist. Karl
Marx was born in 1818, just about when Heinrich Marx officially became
a Protestant.

Karl was baptized at the age of six. In one surviving school essay the
young Marx writes of the "happiness . . . which only one bound uncondi-
tionally and childlike to Christ, and through him to God, can know."[5] Such
sentiments, whether sincere or not, do not recur.

"Criticism of religion is the premise of all criticism," Marx wrote in
an essay published when he was 26. That is an amplified version of one of
the theses of this book. Marx's own "criticism of religion" was unsparing:
"Man makes religion; religion does not make man," Marx concludes in
that essay.[6]

The next step beyond the "criticism of religion" is to figure out *why*
"man makes religion." Here Karl Marx, in that same essay, uses a series of
metaphors: "Religion is the sigh of the oppressed creature, the heart of a
heartless world." Then he adds, memorably: "It is the *opium* of the people."
This is the punchiest and best-known formulation of the fourth spur to
disbelief: the realization that religion, by dulling the "pains" of the "real

hell" in which the masses often find themselves, helps preserve those hellish conditions. I have found no solid evidence that Marx read Jean Meslier,
but on this, and much else, they concurred.[7]

One goal of further criticism, following this logic, becomes determining the route "the people"—the mass of oppressed people—might follow toward a world that could be borne without need for such an opiate.
"Thus," Marx writes, "the criticism of heaven turns into the criticism of the
earth . . . and the criticism of theology into the criticism of politics."[8] It did
for Meslier, for Denis Diderot and Baron d'Holbach, for Ernestine Rose
and for Charles Bradlaugh. It certainly did for Marx.

Karl Marx is the oldest of the influential nonbelievers we have gathered to hear of God's demise and help clarify the relationship of that
event to the twentieth century. That relationship seems clear enough with
him. Marx's Hegel-influenced, history-divining, materialistic, proletariat-
championing "criticism of politics" would transform the political and economic systems under which a large part of humanity lived for much of
the twentieth century. If we take Marx at his word, the twentieth-century
political and economic transformations in Russia, Eastern Europe, China,
Cuba and Southeast Asia can, therefore, be traced back precisely to "criticism of heaven," to "criticism of theology"—to God's death.

Nietzsche himself—born in 1844—is the next nonbeliever whom we
might place in the crowd that will hear of god's death—whom we might
place, in other words, in this scene that he himself has drawn. His analysis
of the struggle between religion and irreligion is complex, but Nietzsche's
anger at religion is, nonetheless, intense: "Whoever has theologian blood
in his veins has a wrong and dishonest attitude towards all things from the
very first," he writes. "What a theologian feels to be true must be false: this
provides almost a criterion of truth."[9] Nietzsche was born with even more
"theologian blood" than Marx. Not only were both his grandfathers Lu-
theran pastors, so was Nietzsche's father, who died when his son was four.
Nietzsche was expected to become a pastor as well.

But by the age of 17 he had made a decisive break with the theologian's
"attitude." Nietzsche set sail, with a boldness that made him tremble, upon
what he called a "boundless ocean of ideas."[10] He began asking himself
what the world would look like if people had not been "led astray by a
vision," by religion. "The curtain falls," he wrote at the time, "and man re-
discovers himself . . . like a child awakening at dawn and laughingly wiping
his awful dreams from his brow."[11]

Nietzsche would soon contribute his own, characteristically startling explanation for humankind's enthusiasm for this "vision," these "dreams": religion—Christianity in particular—is a way, Nietzsche argues, for the weak to limit the strong.[12] And with his madman Friedrich Nietzsche would explore the consequences of awakening from "dreams" of religion—the consequences not just of God's nonexistence but, since we are talking about something humans created and then destroyed, of His death. Criticism of religion, along with an insistence upon complicating that criticism, might be said to be the premise of Nietzsche's philosophy.[13]

Irreligion was so common among the twentieth century's inventors that it might also be useful to list those among them who were *not* atheists. Among the individuals who helped make that century who were well disposed toward religion we would have to count Gandhi—a Hindu (although while in London Gandhi attended Charles Bradlaugh's funeral).[14] Martin Luther King Jr. was a Baptist minister. Inventors like Guglielmo Marconi and Wilbur and Orville Wright also practiced religion. We'll leave them out of this crowd the madman has gathered.

Werner Heisenberg, the physicist most responsible for quantum mechanics—and, therefore, for the theory that the universe is, at bottom, random—was a churchgoer. He suggested an analogy between religious concepts and a couple of seemingly self-contradictory, perhaps even "imaginary," but tremendously useful concepts from mathematics: infinity and the square root of negative one. "Hence we must be skeptical about any skepticism" on these matters, Heisenberg concludes.[15]

One the most interesting and influential philosophers of the century, Ludwig Wittgenstein, was once asked by a minister whether he believed in God. "Yes I do," he answered, "but the difference between what you believe and what I believe may be infinite."[16] Wittgenstein's God, glimpsed mostly through self-loathing, appears to have been a stern, deeply ethical force whose existence could barely be spoken of, let alone proven. Not that Wittgenstein was looking for proof: "The point is that if there were evidence," he writes, "this would in fact destroy the whole business."[17]

Some of the contributors to the century's great movements in art and literature, which fall under the heading *modernism*, were also religious or "spiritual": most notably the experimental composers Igor Stravinsky and Arnold Schönberg, and the pioneering abstract painter Wassily Kandinsky.[18] Andy Warhol arrived relatively late in the twentieth century but still succeeded in affecting its direction. When asked if he believed in God, Warhol answered, "I guess I do." Warhol was characteristically curt and flat in his explanation: "I like church."[19]

And, in a century that gave new breadth and scope to genocide, one of its leading practitioners, though not a practicing Christian, seems to have had a god: "I believe I am acting in accordance with the will of the Almighty Creator," Adolf Hitler writes in *Mein Kampf*; "by defending myself against the Jew, I am fighting for the work of the Lord."[20]

Nonetheless, an impressive number of the creators of the twentieth century belong, with Karl Marx and Friedrich Nietzsche, in our crowd of "those who did not believe in God." Thomas Edison, who illuminated the century with electric light and entertained it with recorded sound, declared himself an agnostic. Sigmund Freud was an unabashed atheist. The list of nonbelievers also includes: Bertrand Russell, Wittgenstein's mentor for a time, who helped introduce analytic philosophy; Simone de Beauvoir, the existentialist and early feminist; and John Maynard Keynes, the century's predominant non-Marxist economist. Five path-breaking modernists were also professed nonbelievers:[21] Pablo Picasso, James Joyce, Virginia Woolf, Albert Camus and Adolf Loos, whose crusade against ornamentation in architecture was connected in his mind to a crusade against God.[22]

Alan Turing, the Cambridge mathematician who imagined the computer, was unusually forthright, for his time, about his homosexuality and his atheism. That Turing ended up killing himself in 1954, just before his forty-second birthday, is a tragic sign that such candor was not easy in his time. And the list of scientists who had no use for the hypothesis of God is a long one, stretching from Marie Curie to both of the co-discovers of DNA: Francis Crick reports that he was about 12 when he became "a skeptic, an agnostic with a strong inclination toward atheism."[23] James Watson is blunter about his disbelief: "I have no religious component," is how he recently put it. He is also blunt about how wide the gulf between science and religion had grown by the end of the twentieth century: "I don't want to speak for others, but I don't have a single colleague who is religious."[24]

Should the man who was perhaps the twentieth century's top scientist be invited to join that crowd of nonbelievers? Albert Einstein did enunciate God's name fondly upon occasion—as in his famous response to Heisenberg's quantum mechanics, with its insistence that the most basic elements of the universe can be known only through probabilities: "God does not play dice with the universe." But if Einstein ever indeed had a God, it would appear to have been either mostly synonymous or entirely synonymous with nature, with the universe, with the laws of physics (or is it the Laws of Physics?). At one point, Einstein expressed a belief in "Spinoza's God"—that Nature God who has always been easy to confuse with no God.[25]

However, in a recently uncovered letter to a philosopher, written near the end of his life, Einstein disparages religion: "The word god," he states in 1954, "is for me nothing more than the expression and product of human weaknesses"; then he dismisses all religions as incarnations of "the most childish superstitions."[26] This would appear to have settled the question.

The day has just broken when Nietzsche's madman, carrying a lantern, runs into the market place, amid that crowd of "many of those who did not believe in God." His message is not that God has expired peaceably after a long illness: "We have killed him," he cries—"you and I. All of us are his murderers."[27]

To call the nonbelievers we are gathering here "murderers" of God is, of course, rather harsh. Most did abandon the religion into which they were raised. (Virginia Woolf, whose father Leslie Stephen had become an outspoken agnostic, is an exception.) But most abandoned it hesitantly and with anguish.

For some the break came when they realized, as had so many before them, how deeply imperfect is the world said to have been created by that said-to-be-Perfect Being (the venerable problem of evil). Alan Turing, for example, became a nonbeliever when a fellow student with whom he had developed a friendship, and upon whom he had a crush, took sick and died.[28]

Maria Sklodowska experienced something perhaps even more tragic. Manya, as she was called, was born into a Catholic family in Russian-ruled Poland in 1867. When she was nine, an elder sister died of typhus, then, despite all the young girl's prayers, her churchgoing mother died from tuberculosis. That's when Manya began losing her faith.[29]

In 1895, after she had finally found her way to Paris and an education, Marie, the name she now used, married another physicist, Pierre Curie. Two traditional elements were missing at their wedding: Marie did not wear a white dress: she owned only one other dress and wanted the new one to be practical enough so that she could wear it in the laboratory. And they did not have a religious ceremony: both bride and groom were committed nonbelievers. Marie and Pierre Curie had two daughters together—both raised without religion.[30] Together, too, they helped discover the nature of radioactivity and shared the Nobel Prize in physics. (She won a second Nobel Prize, in chemistry, after Pierre's early death.)

James Joyce—born in 1882, the year Nietzsche published his madman's revelation—was raised a Catholic in Ireland. The break for him came after a sexual encounter with a prostitute on the way home from the theater.[31] Joyce was 14. His initial reaction to that encounter was repulsion—with himself—intensified by the prospect of burning in hell. He attended confession. He prayed. His sister saw him walking to school fingering a rosary.

But then the teenager, always prone to rebellion, began to think things over. Joyce concluded that what he took for piety was just panic. He evaluated his own insistent sexuality, and realized abstinence—a holy purity—was beyond him. The choice: religion and a life of guilt or irreligion. In choosing the latter he grew furious at the former. "I left the Catholic Church," he explains in a letter to his future wife six years later, "hating it most fervently. I found it impossible for me to remain in it on account of the impulses of my nature."[32]

Bertrand Russell's loss of religion was more cerebral, but it also appears to have been more painful. Maybe, since Russell was a dedicated diary keeper, we just know more about his suffering or maybe his young life was just filled with an unusual amount of suffering.

Bertrand, born in 1872, was the grandson of Lord John Russell—a staunch Liberal and reformer who was twice Queen Victoria's prime minister.[33] He was the godson of John Stuart Mill, whose radical politics and friendship his parents shared. Russell's father wrote a book arguing for a vague version of deism.

When Bertrand was two, his older brother, Frank, came down with diphtheria. Frank recovered but was brought home while still contagious. Bertrand's mother was infected and died. His sister, the middle child, died five days later. A year and a half later his father succumbed to other causes, perhaps exacerbated by despair. Bertrand Russell, now an orphan, was raised by his politically liberal but impeccably proper, desperately reserved and conventionally religious grandparents. He was educated on their estate, with little in the way of companionship. The best moment of this childhood may have been when Frank introduced him to Euclid's geometry. "I had not imagined," he later recalls, "that there was anything so delicious in the world." His brother rebelled against this repressive upbringing and eventually escaped to school. Bertrand kept his rebellions secret. "Till he went to Cambridge he was an unendurable little prig," Frank reports.[34]

The young Russell found his atheism through his readings and in guilty conversations with his diary. "I have been irresistibly led to such conclusions as would not only shock my people, but have given me much pain," he writes at the age of 15. Alone with those thoughts, he contemplated suicide: "I have the very greatest fear that my life may hereafter be ruined by my having lost the support of religion." That fear would be eased, eventually, by further reading: of Shelley's poetry.[35] But in Russell's initial anguish we do get the sense that something has died. And in his guilt we do, perhaps, sense that disbelief in God might be experienced as a crime—even by a man who would go on to become an international spokesman for atheism.

One impetus to abandoning belief in God at this time was relatively new: the theories of Karl Marx. No one was more responsible for whatever happened to God in the twentieth century than Marx. The fourth variety of atheism—a political analysis of the "real hell" religion supported—was central to the rhetoric, rallies and revolutions of his followers. Then it became central to the societies created when their revolutions, remarkably, succeeded. Indeed, the political and economic system that men like Fidel Castro, Ho Chi Minh, Mao Zedong, Stalin and, of course, Lenin instituted, Soviet Communism, was accompanied by the largest effort to erase all forms of traditional religion the world has known.

In his writing, Lenin went at least as far as Diderot, whom he had read and complemented.[36] "Every religious idea, any idea of any god, any flirtation with the idea of a god," Lenin declares, "is an unspeakable vulgarity."[37] In practice Lenin and the others went further. The idea of "murder" comes to mind more easily here.

Of course, religion was in no way dormant during the twentieth century. Its effects upon lives and societies—every society, even Soviet societies—remained profound. And others would, no doubt, produce different lists of the century's creators—including, perhaps, more believers. Still, it is hard to dispute the fact that twentieth-century thought, culture and politics were conceived in part—in large part—by nonbelievers. (Whether this is a century for which you would want to take credit is another matter.)

This high concentration of influential nonbelievers is a sign, first, that it had become somewhat easier by the late nineteenth and early twentieth century to declare yourself a nonbeliever. It is a sign, too, that Spinoza,

Voltaire, Meslier, Hume, Diderot, d'Holbach, Shelley, Rose, Darwin, Mill, Bradlaugh and all the others had had an influence on individuals who would themselves prove influential.

But there is a larger point to be made here: that the murder of God, if you will, helped give us a particular kind of twentieth century.

Sigismund Schlomo Freud received, like Marx, at most a tepid introduction to religion from his family. He was born in Moravia in 1856 but was raised mostly in Vienna—his father's third child, his mother's first. Young Sigmund participated in Passover Seders but apparently was given no Bar Mitzvah.[38]

"My parents were Jews," Freud notes in a short autobiography. "I, too, have remained a Jew."[39] But he never was the traditional sort of Jew: the sort who attends synagogue and believes in God. Freud wavered only once: at university, under the influence of a philosophy professor—a "genius," Freud called him—who had once been a priest and who did believe in God. "I am no longer a materialist, also not yet a theist," Freud explains in a letter written at the time. He never did, as his biographer Peter Gay points out, make it to theist. Soon Freud was back to being a thoroughly atheistic, Diderot-quoting, champion of the Enlightenment. "Neither in my private life nor in my writings," Freud states, late in life, "have I ever made a secret of being an out-and-out unbeliever."[40]

Which raises a question; Freud asks it himself in a letter to a friend and colleague who was a minister: "Why did none of the devout create psychoanalysis? Why did one have to wait for a completely godless Jew?"[41] For this book the interest is in the "godless" not the Jewish half of that question, and it needs to be asked not just about psychoanalysis but about Marxism and aspects of modern art, politics, philosophy, science and technology.

Sigmund Freud occupies an interesting place in the history of thought. Few modern thinkers have been as insistent as he on the limitations of reason. Our own minds, according to the compelling drama he outlines, face continual rebellion by the twisted, desperate forces of a seething unconscious. Our understandings, Freud asserts, are undermined by insistent absurdities, which we believe in part because they are so childishly, stubbornly, angrily, enticingly absurd: daddy has taken mommy from me!

Yet Freud—"the specialist in unreason," Peter Gay calls him—remains, nonetheless, a partisan of beleaguered, often ineffectual reason.[42] We talk.

We decode our dreams. And eventually our Tertullian-like, "because-it-is-absurd" neuroses and the self-destructive strategies they fuel are brought to the surface and defused by *analysis*.[43] Through psychoanalysis, reason can fight back against unreason. And Freud was not shy about drawing an analogy between an individual's unreasonable and counterproductive fantasies and those of a society.

In 1927 Freud published a book called *Future of an Illusion*. Religion—belief in God—is the "illusion," composed of "fairy tales."[44] "The universal obsessional neurosis of humanity," Freud calls it. God, he suggests, is the feared but just father we long for in our helplessness. And the illusion's future? Freud reports himself "optimistic enough to suppose that mankind will surmount this neurotic phase, just as so many children grow out of their similar neurosis."[45]

Unreason had its moments in the twentieth century—some of them almost incomprehensible in their magnitude and horror. But a major part of the story of the century is a continuation and intensification of a seventeenth-, eighteenth- and nineteenth-century story: the spread of learning, particularly training in science, to more places and more levels of society, with a concomitant increase in life expectancy and living standards. Freud himself gives one of the stauncher statements of the Enlightenment conviction that this learning will undercut unthinking belief: "In the long run nothing can withstand reason and experience, and the contradiction which religion offers to both is all too palpable."[46]

It is not just that "reason and experience" can encourage individuals to "surmount" religion; it also works—as in the virtuous cycle for which I have been arguing—the other way: as religion contracts, types of learning are better able to expand. Superstition and unthinking belief must be gotten out of the way.

Heading into the twentieth century, most thinkers, it is true, no longer had to worry about incorporating into their theories the biblical pronouncement that the sun stopped for Joshua. Many members of the clergy had grown more hesitant to weigh in on the subject of how heaven goes. The more heavy-handed aspects of God had been "denounced." Nevertheless religion, even if it often did try to mind its own realm, remained capable of interfering with various kinds of thinking, scientific and otherwise. It still imposed meanings, strictures, truths, moralities. It still had its scruples. It still held certain things sacrosanct.

For most artists, scientists and revolutionaries bent on challenging traditional understandings in the twentieth century, this wouldn't do. For most thinkers committed to reevaluating life's purposes or society's hierarchies in the twentieth century, even this less intrusive religious worldview was too constricting.

At the very beginning of the century, the philosopher William James, an aficionado of the "religious experience," provided a summary of its essence: "It consists of the belief that there is an unseen order, and that our supreme good lies in harmoniously adjusting ourselves thereto."[47] But even this plain, relaxed-fit version of religion—devoid of any particular mythology—was probably too tight to allow the new century to breathe. A "supreme good"? An "order"—an ancient order—to which we had best adjust? That didn't leave much room for assaults on accepted notions of truth, beauty and the way society is organized, and the twentieth century would be full of such assaults. The century would also throw up some versions of truth and beauty that were not at all harmonious, well adjusted or orderly. For that to happen—for men and women to gain, to borrow another phrase from Shelley, "wisdom once they could not think"[48]—wasn't it useful for God and His "unseen order," His "supreme good," to expire?

Not every advance required rejection of religion, of course: Guglielmo Marconi had no difficulty reconciling his development of "wireless telegraphy" with his tepid and intermittent Catholicism. The flights made by the Wright brothers, sons of a bishop of the United Brethren Church, did not rise high enough to challenge the cosmology of early-twentieth-century Protestantism (though it is true that after air travel God was less frequently depicted lounging on clouds). Gandhi actually borrowed the trappings (or lack of trappings) of Hindu asceticism in his nonviolent anti-colonial struggle. The Rev. Martin Luther King Jr. regularly transferred rhetoric from sermons to speeches: "We will not be satisfied until 'justice rolls down like waters, and righteousness like a mighty stream.'"[49]

Karl Marx did see in history something of an "unseen order." His familial acquaintance with Judaism, his schoolboy exposure to Christianity, may have shaped his rhetoric and colored his philosophy. I would argue that a lingering dream of a heaven contributed to his utopian view of what society might look like beyond the "dictatorship of the proletariat." But could a Karl Marx who had hung on to Judaism or Christianity have exalted material conditions and conceived of an "unseen order" that was about the triumph of an economic class and not a group of believers? This is the sort of question—and, given the difficulty of proving these "could"s, it is best to stick to questions—that, if we are to understand the contributions of atheism, needs to be asked.

Einstein uncovered an astounding, previously unrecognized order, but wasn't his curved space something that could be quantified and even, in the orbit of Mercury, observed? Wasn't it eminently natural? And if Einstein really had in mind not, at most, Spinoza's more-or-less-the-same-as-Nature-itself God but some sort of bearded, biblical Creator who keeps tabs on all that is, could he have imagined a universe devoid of privileged vantage points, uniform space or unvarying time?

When Manya Skodowska, aged 19, is facing yet another death—that of a cousin's newborn child—she concedes, in a letter to that cousin, that the religious can obtain consolation from saying to themselves, "God willed it." But then Manya makes clear that this consolation is not available to her: "The more I recognize how lucky they are," she writes her cousin, "the less I can understand their faith, and the less I feel capable of sharing their happiness." In this same letter Manya says she has a "respect" for "sincere religious feelings" but then adds, not entirely respectfully, "even if they go with a limited state of mind."[50] Could Marie Curie have experimented, analyzed, theorized and discovered with such brilliance if she had not long ago left behind that "limited," fatalistic "state of mind"?

In a report written in 1948, Alan Turing considered the arguments against the then radical idea he was propounding: that it is "possible for machinery to show intelligent behavior." One of those counterarguments, he notes, was "a religious belief that any attempt to construct such machines is a sort of Promethean irreverence." Another counterargument, acknowledged by Turing, was the suggestion "that God, having created his Universe, has now screwed the cap on His pen." The final counterargument echoed the belief Locke and Voltaire challenged: that, as Turing puts it, "thinking is a function of man's immortal soul"—and therefore is unavailable to a machine.[51] Could anyone who credited any of these religion-inspired counterarguments, have conceived, as Turing did, of a "universal computing machine"?

Could a Freud more comfortable with biblical cosmology have set off to explore a territory, the unconscious, unmentioned there? Maybe floating somewhere among the turbulent swamp of infantile instincts, desires and neuroses that he found in this unconscious was a hint of original sin. But could a religious Freud have made do without locating a soul—befouled but still transcendent—somewhere inside us? Maybe there is a mythological element in Freud's Id, Ego and Superego. But could a religious Freud have been so even-handed about the most Yahweh-like member of this trinity: the Superego? Certainly Freud preached, in William James' terms, harmonious adjustment, but to what he saw as "reality," not to any heavenly plan.

And what of James Joyce? Like Freud, like Virginia Woolf, like Wordsworth, the "main region of" his "song" was the "Mind of Man" and Woman. Yes, Joyce allowed himself the occasional oddly angled affirmation—here in the last lines of the lusciously human run-on sentence with which Molly Bloom ends *Ulysses:*

> . . . and I thought well as well him as another and then I asked him with my
> eyes to ask again yes and then he asked me would I yes to say yes my moun-
> tain flower and first I put my arms around him yes and drew him down to me
> so he could feel my breasts all perfume yes and his heart was going like mad
> and yes I said yes I will Yes.

But, no: no God is officiating at this affirmation. Could the perfumed breasts and beating heart of "as-well-him-as-another" love have achieved such nobility if Joyce acknowledged the reign of a lawgiving, sin-defining God? Could this celebration of the heroically common, this symphony of "well"s and "and"s, this feast of wondrous flaws, have occurred if its author worshiped the perfect and deferred to the immortal? Could this new, non-narrative, out-of-kilter, inconclusive, but no-less lovely art—made of the sputter and drift of human thought—have appeared in the realm of a watchmaker God or even of a run-of-the-mill, harmonious, unseen order? Surely there is much that is astonishing here, but—yes—its origin is adamantly human.

The English poet T. S. Eliot declared his faith in God, the Catholic God, in 1927, after he had written *The Waste Land*.[52] By 1934, Eliot was bemoaning the consequences of his contemporaries' lack of faith. "What I do wish to affirm," he writes, is that the whole of modern literature is corrupted by what I call Secularism, that it is simply unaware of, simply cannot understand the meaning of, the primacy of the supernatural over the natural life."[53] Was Eliot not correct to conclude that much of modern literature was influenced, if not "corrupted," by a tendency to turn away from such supernatural meanings?

And what of modern painting? Could a Picasso have conjured up the fractured, almost monstrous half-hidden reality of cubism if he believed in the ideal, transcendent hidden-reality of Catholicism? This argument runs into some trouble here, however: for Kandinsky—the first of the modernists to surrender any hint of representation in painting—precisely did see himself as escaping to the "non-material" and providing glimpses of inner "spiritual life," otherwise obscured by outer shapes and forms.[54] However, Kandinsky, for all his spirituality, remains oddly reticent on the subject of God.

Arnold Schönberg is even more of a problem. For he managed to create atonal compositions that were boldly dissonant, undeniably out of kilter, while taking his relationship with God quite seriously: Schönberg converted from Judaism to Lutheranism and then back.[55] And Andy Warhol—what to make of this ironic, surface-loving, celebrity-obsessed, quintessential last-half-of-the-twentieth-century character, praying every Sunday in a Catholic church on Manhattan's East Side?[56] The stubborn religiosity of Schönberg and Warhol means that any attempt to insist on a tight connection between modernism and atheism must fall back on the view that disbelief was simply in the air these artists breathed.[57] It was. But maybe it's wiser to insist on a less-tight connection between modernism and atheism.

Those hugely creative scientists and philosophers who didn't entirely reject religion are also a problem for this theory. But let's keep asking questions: If Heisenberg had contemplated in church not a God as enigmatic as the square root of negative one but a God who has positioned every grain of sand, every electron, could he have suggested that both the position and momentum of an electron can never be known? And how might we harmoniously adjust to the square root of negative one? If Wittgenstein had not conceived of a religion "infinitely" different from that revealed in religious texts, if he truly believed in an "unseen order," could he have come up with an understanding of language that denies that words necessarily get their meaning from something beyond themselves?[58]

The twentieth century produced painting, music, architecture, literature, science and philosophy obsessed by what it is not possible to say. Wasn't one reason for this because it has become more difficult to say the one thing that art and philosophy had usually gotten around to saying: that *life* gets meaning from something beyond itself?

The murder of God is an event of almost incomprehensible significance for Nietzsche's madman: "Who gave us the sponge to wipe away the entire horizon?" he asks. "What were we doing when we unchained this earth from its sun?"[59] One thing they were doing, these nonbelievers, was making it possible to think in new ways.

"We philosophers and 'free spirits,'" writes Nietzsche, "feel, when we hear the news that 'the old god is dead,' as if a new dawn shone on us. . . . At long last our ships may venture out again, . . . the sea, our sea, lies open again; perhaps there has never yet been such an 'open sea.'"[60]

The twentieth century featured the rise of a series of revolutionary movements: Communism, psychoanalysis, relativity, futurism, cubism, Bauhaus, surrealism, abstract expressionism, analytic philosophy, phenomenology, quantum mechanics, existentialism, pop art, anti-colonialism, structuralism, civil rights, poststructuralism, feminism, postmodernism, gay liberation and deconstruction. Didn't all these demands for change—inconsequential or profound, frivolous or overdue, brutal or wonderful—require at least a glimpse of what Nietzsche called the "open sea"? Isn't the contemplation of that "open sea"—possible only after we get word that "the old god is dead"—what it means to be *modern?*

Perhaps all the questions asked here might support a statement: if the horizon had remained in place, if the earth were still chained to the sun, if the sea had not opened, if God had survived, we would not have had anything remotely like this twentieth century. Criticism of religion was its premise.

Indeed, in the desire to sail off on an open sea—in the characteristically twentieth-century desire to make a new kind of art, institute a new politics, think new kinds of thoughts—we can see a fifth and final spur to disbelief. In order for many of the artists, philosophers, scientists and political thinkers who made the twentieth century to help invent this modern world, they needed a freedom from commandments, doctrines, traditions, mores, customs, conventions, myths and values; they needed a freedom from religion. This final spur to disbelief is the yearning for an open sea—the need for God to be dead.

Another question must be asked about the role of disbelief in the twentieth century—the century in which atheism attained and, for many decades, maintained vast political power. It is the moral question—similar to that raised by Jacques-René Hébert and other devotees of "Saint Guillotine" during the French Revolution's bloody dechristianization movement and terror. The twentieth-century version of this question is this: did not the atheism shared by some of the century's most ruthless leaders—Lenin, Stalin, Mao and Pol Pot—contribute to some of this century's great crimes? The open sea is a place for dreamers, creators, visionaries, but is it not also—given the absence of law and lore—perilous?

Consider atheism's role in the first of the regimes inspired by Karl Marx's theories: the Soviet Union. "Economic slavery," stated Lenin, following Marx, is "the true source of the religious humbugging of mankind." Hence, the end of economic slavery should, according to Marxist theory, *by itself* bring about the end of religion.[61] "Economic slavery" supposedly ended in Russia sometime after the Communist Revolution in 1917. Religion, as was readily apparent to anyone who looked around, did not end. This was among the largest of the many disappointments true believers in Marxist theory faced in the new Soviet Union. Lenin and his fellow Bolsheviks—committed atheists all—felt they had no choice but to help nudge along religion's demise themselves.

First, in late 1917, Lenin's new and tenuous government issued a series of orders eliminating religious privileges and putting marriages and divorces under civil control. Then the draft of a new decree was released that would end the ancient connections among the Russian state, its schools and the Orthodox Church.[62] "Every citizen may adhere to any religion or adhere to none," it proclaimed. This decree also stated, in a somewhat less tolerant spirit, that all church property now belonged to the state.[63] The patriarch of the Orthodox Church, Tikhon, responded by pronouncing an anathema on the godless Bolsheviks. He did not mince words: "That which you do is not only a cruel deed: it is verily a Satanic deed, for which you are condemned to hell fire in the future life."[64] The battle was joined (though the two sides did not have equal respect for each other's weapons).

Initially, the Bolsheviks, whose forces were physically stronger, contented themselves primarily with giving monastic lands to the peasants and with such propaganda measures as opening silver sarcophagi to demonstrate that the bodies of supposedly "incorruptible saints," said to have been perfectly preserved inside them, were in fact made of wax. An atheist journal was begun. Numerous priests, bishops and monks were, to be sure, imprisoned or murdered, but this was a time when huge numbers of those who held power under the old regime were being imprisoned and murdered and millions were dying in a civil war between the revolution's supporters and its opponents, with their international support.[65] There was no organized effort to destroy the church.

It was only after famine, in the early 1920s, left tens of millions without sufficient food that Lenin did launch an organized campaign against religion.[66] Orthodox churches, Roman Catholic churches, synagogues and mosques were ransacked (with a larger portion of the spoils going to the government and the party than to feeding the hungry). Many more were killed during this campaign. Tikhon was arrested.[67]

Such violent efforts to help along the overdue withering away of religion continued to come and go in the Soviet Union—as party leaders searched for an effective strategy to wean the recalcitrant masses from their gods without alienating those masses. Meanwhile, nonviolent efforts intensified.

For a couple of years, beginning in 1922, the Communist Youth League experimented with its own Christmas celebration, a kind of Festival of Reason. It featured films, skits, parodies, red Christmas trees and atheistic carols. Officials, however, were concerned by the preponderance of frivolity, even hooliganism, and the scarcity of lectures and reports. Or perhaps they were concerned that the public did not seem sufficiently engaged. They ended the experiment.[68] Still, Christmas and other religious holidays remained battlegrounds—with party leaders trying everything from scheduling work or classes on those days to holding alternate festivities (presumably less frivolous) in an attempt to keep the truly or vaguely pious from their traditions. They even distributed alternative Christmas "sermons": "The legend about Christ the Savior appeared in the minds of Roman slaves and paupers crushed by inhuman exploitation. . . ."[69]

At the same time, atheism began to be treated with an official respect it had not before enjoyed. Lenin, in an article written in 1922, encouraged study of its history, so Soviet scholars dutifully began coming out with monographs on the subject: "Atheism in Ancient Greece and Rome" or "On Materialism and Atheism in Ancient India."[70] The Communist Party, the government and quasi-government organizations started periodicals with names like *The Antireligious, The Atheist, Village Godless* and *Godless at the Workbench;* they established museums of atheism, often in former churches or monasteries; they presented lectures in factories, featuring disquisitions on Spinoza, Darwinism and the "origins of religion in the light of Marxism-Leninism"; they included atheism and its history in the curriculum in schools and universities; they published in one decade, by one count, 40 million copies of pro-atheistic books and pamphlets; and they began an organization called the League of the Godless—later renamed, under Stalin, the League of the Militant Godless. Nevertheless, in 1928, even in Moscow, more than half of all births and two-thirds of all burials were still accompanied by a religious ceremony.[71]

Still, under this barrage of propaganda and persecution by what was probably the world's first long-lived anti-religious system of government, religion did appear to decline; the number of atheists, or mostly atheists or professed atheists did appear to grow. Proving this statistically is nearly impossible: the Soviets, perhaps afraid of what they might find, did not ask about religious affiliation, or lack of same, when they conducted their censuses. The consensus guess by historians seems to be that perhaps half the population of the Soviet Union had broken in some significant, maybe even honest, way with religion.[72]

But perhaps the best evidence that religion declined in the Soviet Union and under Soviet Communism in general is that some of that decline has persisted. According to one early-twenty-first-century survey, of the 15 countries with the highest rates of atheism in the world, all but three (Sweden, Uruguay and France) are former or current Communist countries.[73]

But what about—in these atheistic or at least partially atheistic states—that moral question? Millions, and not just priests, died in the Soviet Union under Lenin and Stalin—from famine, during purges. Countless others were sent to gulags. China under Mao Zedong was at least as brutal—particularly during the Cultural Revolution of the 1960s. And the genocide engaged in by Pol Pot's Communist Party in Cambodia in the 1970s ranks among history's worst; almost a quarter of the country's population died. In any reckoning of the political consequences of atheism, don't those millions of deaths appear on the debit side of the ledger? Didn't the loss of religion in the twentieth century lead to a loss of restraint?

Adolf Hitler—perhaps the century's greatest murderer, if one can rank such monsters—is a possible answer to the question of whether religion might have prevented the gulags and the mass killings of the various communist parties. Hitler managed to hang onto a God and exterminated in industrial fashion many millions. Too many church officials approved, condoned or at least looked away from the policies that led to those exterminations.

And certainly the twentieth century suffered from enough of the sort of religion-inspired mass killings that have desecrated most centuries: the massacre of Armenian Christians in the mostly Muslim Ottoman Empire in 1915 and 1916 is an example, as is the genocide perpetrated in the 1990s by Christian Serbs against Bosnian Muslims.[74] If "the religious did it, too" is an answer, then we have that answer.

However, perhaps the best response to the charge that the absence of religion contributed to the Communists' atrocities is the argument that, like Hébert and other members of the cult of the guillotine in 1793, Lenin, Stalin, Mao and Pol Pot *were* in a sense religious. Orthodox believers in Communism killed because of the revelations in which they *did* believe— about history's inexorable direction, about the inevitable withering away of the state—more than because of the "thou shall not"s in which they did not believe.

If the decline of religious certainties contributed to the brutalities of communism, it did so in large part because it sent people scurrying to find other certainties. Getting rid of gods is not as simple a business as it might have appeared to Jean Meslier or Baron d'Holbach or even Charles Bradlaugh.

Some of the nonbelievers who helped make the twentieth century were alert to the tendency for substitute or watered-down faiths to move in after more traditional religions had begun to move out. Most of these replacement gods are relatively benign. Let's deal with them first.

Sigmund Freud was particularly critical of the amorphous, deist God of, among others, Voltaire, Jefferson, Karl Marx's father and so many of Freud's, and our, educated contemporaries—Heisenberg and Wittgenstein perhaps among them. Freud accuses these deists of a confusion of terms. Their "God" is "nothing more than an insubstantial shadow," Freud notes, and yet It is referred to by the same name as "the mighty personality of religious doctrines." Indeed, many sophisticated believers use the uncertainty of modern physics or the humility of modern philosophy to provide hiding spaces for their vague gods—gods the opposite of those old paragons of certainty and authority. For Freud these "shadow" Gods are just a way of "pretending to oneself or to other people that one is still firmly attached to religion, when one has long since cut oneself loose from it."[75]

When Nietzsche first mentions God's demise—shortly before his madman takes the stage—he, too, speaks of a "shadow": "God is dead; but given the way of men, there may still be caves for thousands of years in which his shadow will be shown."[76] That is one way of looking at square-root-of-negative-one gods, at cannot-be-spoken-of gods, at laws-of-physics gods—that they are shadows of God, shadows that linger after His death.

The square root of negative one may be enigmatic, even mysterious; the laws of physics may seem awe-inspiring, even transcendent in their beauty or precision. It is one thing to credit them to some sort of enigma-loving or law-giving Being—as an eighteenth-century deist might have (despite Hume's example of numbers divisible by nine). But what does it mean to try to elevate them into deities or attributes of deities themselves? How do we justify implying that something analogous to the square root of negative one or the laws of physics might play a role in imposing morality, choosing our fate or conveying purpose?

And God's shadows are not all called "gods." New kinds of belief—sometimes not ostensibly religious—tend to spring up when old kinds are eradicated. They usually arrive just in time to redraw some sort of horizon, to restore some sort of meaning—human beings having a tendency to hanker after some sort of meaning. The urge to believe proves devilishly difficult to suppress. "One *wants* by all means," Nietzsche explains, "that something should be firm."[77]

Nietzsche lists among these shadow gods what he calls "petty aesthetic creeds."[78] "Petty" or not they would come—a profusion of "aesthetic creeds" in the twentieth century. Woolf, Joyce and Nietzsche himself were vulnerable to the cult of art.[79]

Engagement—cathartic, decisive, political, occasionally violent action—can also provide investment opportunities for belief, as can the metaphysical wonders of disengagement—detached, austere, meditative, nonviolent inaction. Some profess a faith in progress (a faith to which the author of this book may, at times, be guilty of subscribing), while others proclaim an end-of-days conviction that we are in hopeless decline. Asceticism of any sort—even absent a demanding deity—can serve as a shadow god, but so can a mad, holy dissipation. Many, particularly in the seventh decade of the twentieth century, worshiped love—of the "all you need is" variety.

Baron d'Holbach is among those vulnerable to the charge of having created a shadow god out of Nature: "Show us, then, O Nature!" d'Holbach writes in the final passage of *The System of Nature*, "That which man ought to do."[80] Nature certainly is lovely, powerful and omnipresent, but once again this effort to anthropomorphize "Her" seems highly questionable and the effort to find in "Her" a morality rather strained. John Stuart Mill deftly dismissed this notion of Nature as some sort of moral force. "In sober truth," he observes, "nearly all the things which men are hanged or imprisoned for doing to one another are Nature's everyday performances." Mill's example: "killing, the most criminal act recognized by human laws,

Nature does once to every being that lives; and in a large proportion of cases, after protracted tortures."[81]

However, the belief to which Mill and most crusading nineteenth-century disbelievers subscribed, utilitarianism—that we should do what is best for the majority of humankind—might also be labeled a shadow god. Mill himself dubbed it the "Religion of Humanity."[82]

Political principles are easy to kneel down before in some satisfying approximation of the old rituals. Patriotism, an old intoxicant to be sure, is among Nietzsche's examples of alternate creeds—one that certainly would have a robust enough life in the twentieth century (and beyond). And with patriotism we have arrived at the non-benign substitute gods—much more dangerous than "insubstantial" shadows. These are beliefs, for which some have slaughtered. By 1935—before the worst of the horrors they would perpetrate—Bertrand Russell was among the many talking about both Fascism and Soviet Communism as religions.[83]

They were religious in insisting that "something" is "firm." They were religious in, as one early Russian anti-Communist put it, taking "possession of the whole soul" and calling forth "enthusiasm and self-sacrifice"—in demanding *total* allegiance and *total* control.[84] And, of course, they promised the elect, as do most religions, a utopian future—an escape from hell, a "real" heaven. (Political principles that encourage disagreement and debate—democracy, for example, or human rights—generally fail to exhibit such utopian or fanatical elements.) Fascism and Soviet Communism so exalted a cause that their apostles—Hitler, Lenin, Stalin, Mao, Pol Pot—felt no compulsion against killing or asking adherents to martyr themselves for that cause. (A giant banner hung outside a camp for Hitler youth in Germany in 1934; it read: "WE WERE BORN TO DIE FOR GERMANY!"[85]) Indeed, Fascism may have produced, in the industrialized execution of millions of Jews and other outcasts, history's most terrible *auto-da-fé*.

And despite the erudite philosophical and historical analyses its German founder constructed, communism, in this view, was, in many ways, less a product of what Eric Hobsbawm labeled "secular rationalism" than of secular religion. The similarities between the persecution of the religious in the Soviet Union and the persecution of the insufficiently religious that had been so widespread throughout history was hard to miss. By the middle of the twentieth century, it would become common to label Marxism "the god that failed."[86] Might we not reasonably move its brutalities and horrors from disbelief's ledger to that of substitutes for religion?

In the twentieth century, humans demonstrated an impressive ability to project on the walls of their caves a variety of looming shapes before which they might prostrate themselves. Most were relatively harmless. Some caused unprecedented levels of slaughter. Even if this way of looking at the twentieth century's horrors weakens the attempt to pin them on atheism, it leaves the religious with another argument. Do they not have a right to yell "gotcha!" here because the implication is that even nonbelievers end up believing in something? The twentieth-century theologian Karl Barth had the pleasure of making this point: "There is no man who does not have his own god or gods as the object of his highest desire and trust, or as the basis of his deepest loyalty and commitment."[87] In other words, Barth might say, you nonbelievers think you are too smart to believe in God, but you end up imagining your own Edens; you end up committed to your own dreams of perfection; you end up insisting upon your own contests between good and evil. Barth was onto something.

"When will all these shadows of God cease to darken our minds?" Nietzsche asks.[88] Merely murdering God, in other words, may not be enough. Doesn't the committed nonbeliever also have to take a knife to the various unsupported attempts to give the universe, and our lives, extrinsic meaning that have taken His place?

Freud, too, could see that religion was often replaced by secular fantasies. "Having recognized religious doctrines as illusions," he writes in 1927, "we are at once faced by a further question: may not other cultural assets of which we hold a high opinion and by which we let our lives be ruled be of a similar nature?" Since he lived in the twentieth century, Freud acknowledged the existence of "political" illusions, like Fascism and Communism. Since he was Freud, he acknowledged the existence of "erotic . . . illusions." But the "cultural asset" that would be most interesting—and distressing—to expose as an illusion, as just another shadow of the deceased God, would be what Freud refers to as "the use of observation and reasoning in scientific work."[89]

And science—or "scientism," as some of its detractors call it—does have a couple of things in common with religion.[90] Its practitioners certainly display reverence, "enthusiasm and self-sacrifice." And, if you dig deep enough, it may be possible to find an assumption resembling faith at the bottom of science.[91] What ultimately can justify the belief that an experiment will continue to work just because it has always worked? What justifies, for that matter, our faith that the sun will rise tomorrow? Nietzsche sees an unquestioned assumption, too, in the "unconditional faith . . . that truth is more important than any other thing."[92] Science and this book are, without question, populated with knights of that faith.

However, the evidence for having "faith" in the sun continuing to rise each day appears considerably stronger than the evidence for the existence of a Being who might stop the sun in the sky. The "faith" behind science leans heavily, to reference Hume, upon what has proven our most reliable guide: experience; the faith involved in most religions often directly contradicts experience. And science has had "numerous and important successes," as Freud points out: demonstrable successes such as, to use his examples, the discovery of penicillin and the invention of radio. If religion has had many such successes, they have not been readily apparent. Science is also pretty good at reexamining its conclusions and correcting itself when necessary.[93] Religions certainly have evolved, but the ability to test and, where evidence warrants, reject their doctrines has never been among the strong points of such belief systems.

Moreover, to say that "science is crucial for understanding the world" or "love is all you need" is really more—*pace* Barth—to express an opinion on its significance than to accept, as most religions require, a whole metaphysical scheme. And, while science has often been employed in war, history is short on examples of people starting wars to defend the importance of science, art, progress or love. That sort of thing has usually been left to partisans of gods or their more tangible, more Manichean shadows.

Nonetheless, this critique of even seemingly gentle, opinion-like shadow gods does show how difficult it is to find something that is truly "firm" once God and his various imitators have passed away, once metaphysics has been removed from the equation. Nietzsche—demonstrating the capacity of philosophy to swallow its tail—lists one last way in which the desire "that something should be firm" expresses itself: "nihilism," which he defines as "belief in unbelief."[94]

Alfred North Whitehead worked with Bertrand Russell at Cambridge. His observation that "the progress of religion is defined by the denunciation of gods" was quoted earlier in this book.[95] However, we might propose, here, another observation: if irreligion is not just to end up with each of us still worshiping, in Karl Barth's words, our own "object of . . . highest desire and trust"; if the end of this narrative of disbelief is not just to be a switch to belief in different kinds of illusions; then the "progress" of

irreligion may turn out to be defined by the "denunciation" of the more irrational, demanding and intolerant of these shadow gods.

The French philosopher Henri Bergson may have been better known
in his time than Nietzsche, Whitehead and Russell were in theirs (which
overlapped his). But the twentieth century, in the end, did not prove kind
to Bergson's more mystical, more religious ideas. Bergson announced that
"the essential function of the universe" is as "a machine for the making of
gods."[96] Perhaps the "essential function" of modern culture—its "progress,"
its "premise"—is to kill them off.

Nietzsche's madman ends up concluding—back in 1882—that his audience is not ready to hear what he has to say: "I have come too early," he
mutters in despair. " . . . Deeds, though done, still require time to be seen
and heard."[97]

In April 1966, to be sure, the cover of *Time* magazine (hardly a radical tract) in the United States (hardly an atheistic country) would be filled
with three red words and a punctuation mark against a black background:
"Is God Dead?"[98] But that was 84 years after Nietzsche wrote. And even if
the deed in question—the main subject, in essence, of the second half of
this book—is finally becoming visible and audible, it still remains difficult
to grasp the magnitude of this murder.

For in the great edifice that is our culture religion lies near the foundation. Most of our conclusions about what is good and what is worthwhile
can be connected in one way or another to myths, revelations, commandments, prophecies, gospels or interpretations thereof. Lose them and it is
hard not to lose our way. The news Nietzsche's madman brought is that we
have lost them.

"Are we not plunging continually?" he asks. "Backward, sideward, forward, in all directions? Is there still any up or down? Are we not straying
as through an infinite nothing?"[99] Hard news to hear, this; hard news to
accept. We pursue our various goals; we entertain ourselves; we express an
opinion on this or that. At certain moments in the course of a week, or the
course of a lifetime, we can be found sitting reverently, if a bit restlessly,
before various fading shadows in various increasingly moldy caves. The
"infinite nothing" is, thus, possible to overlook.

The madman's audience, therefore, just stares at him. It is difficult
to imagine Karl Marx, Sigmund Freud, Marie Curie or Bertrand Russell
paying him much mind either. Thanks perhaps to the shadow gods of

dialectical materialism or science, they all hung on to a sense of up and down.

Nonetheless, the "infinite nothing" wormed its way into twentieth-century art and thought. And at least one member of the group of mostly nonbelievers we have gathered might have understood why it made this madman so distraught.

Virginia Woolf was born, like Joyce, the year Nietzsche presented this announcement of the death of God. The news that God was gone had echoed in her ears since she was a child. In her novel *To the Lighthouse*, Woolf paints a haunting portrait of a character, Mr. Ramsey, based on her father, Leslie Stephen—a well-known proponent of disbelief.[100] Mr. Ramsey is smart and forthright: "He was incapable of untruth," Woolf writes. Mr. Ramsey takes "pleasure" in "disillusioning": even when he is merely standing upright in a boat, his son imagines him saying, "There is no God." Mr. Ramsey demands that we face the extinction of our "brightest hopes" with "courage." And Mr. Ramsey, at least after the death of the much warmer Mrs. Ramsey, is a needy, pushy mess: "Every time he approached," another character reports, " . . . ruin approached, chaos approached."

Woolf did not disagree with her father about the absence of God. Indeed, while he officially settled for agnosticism, she went further: "Certainly and emphatically there is no God," Woolf would state in a late memoir.[101] She was not kind to T. S. Eliot after his religious conversion: "I was really shocked," Woolf writes her sister. " . . . I mean there's something obscene in a living person sitting by the fire and believing in God."[102] Nonetheless, Woolf is not cavalier about disbelief. She recognizes how cold, disorienting and terrifying such a journey "through an infinite nothing" can be. Without God or even a shadow of God, what is to keep us from "plunging continually"? What is to hold off "chaos" and "ruin"? Maybe art, *To the Lighthouse* wants to say. Maybe.

"You will never pray again, never adore again, never again rest in endless trust," Nietzsche warns a fellow nonbeliever or perhaps warns himself; "you do not permit yourself to stop before any ultimate wisdom, ultimate goodness, ultimate power . . . ; there is no longer any reason in what happens, no love in what will happen to you." Then Nietzsche asks a crucial question: "Man of renunciation, all this you wish to renounce? Who will give you the strength for that? Nobody yet has had this strength!"[103]

But maybe such strength can be found. There would, for those grappling with such matters, be two twentieth centuries: The first was concerned with the death of God and the adventures of His numerous and resilient shadows. The second twentieth century would be devoted to finding some way to do what Mr. Ramsey failed to do: carry on with some grace and contentment in a post-God world, a world that lacks an "up or down," a world in which the horizon has been wiped away.

THE PASSIONS OF THIS EARTH

LIVING WITHOUT GODS

And our singing shall build,
In the Void's loose field,
A world for the Spirit of Wisdom to wield.

—Percy Bysshe Shelley, *Prometheus Unbound*[1]

BACK IN HADES, SISYPHUS—WHO REBELLED AGAINST THE gods, who gave away the secrets of the gods—remains where we left him: still "grappling his monstrous boulder," as Robert Fagles words it in his translation of *The Odyssey*; still "thrusting the rock uphill toward the brink"; and still watching "the ruthless boulder . . . bound and tumble down to the plain again."[2] Sisyphus is destined to keep at this grueling and futile task for, assuming places like this outlive worship of the gods[3] who administer them, all eternity.

Perhaps a hundred generations of listeners and then readers have felt the horror in this punishment. In the early 1940s, however, Albert Camus, whose generation was seeing horrors on a scale few others would see, proclaims that "one must imagine Sisyphus happy."

In so doing, Camus was taking a stab at the problem of how we might live without God. He wasn't the only one in Paris in those years wrestling with this problem.

Jean-Paul Sartre and Albert Camus would have been sitting where we would want them to have been sitting: at a Parisian café—probably the Café de Flore on the Boulevard Saint-Germain. Camus undoubtedly would be waving a cigarette, a Gauloise, in the air. Sartre might have been sucking on a pipe or a Gauloise of his own.[4] They would have begun drinking. By this hour—it was perhaps 6:30—they would usually have begun drinking.

Most likely the evening—let's make it early in the summer of 1944—also would include a visit to a bistro, a bar or someone's apartment or hotel room, but the festivities would either have had to end before midnight due to the curfew or to have continued until 5:00 a.m., when it was possible to be out on the streets again.[5]

Camus, at the age of 30, was starting to become something of a literary star. Both *The Stranger,* his first novel, and his collection of essays, *The Myth of Sisyphus,* had recently been published. Sartre, eight years his senior and already a significant Parisian intellectual, had reviewed the novel: "The sentences in *The Stranger* are islands," he writes. "We bounce from sentence to sentence, from void to void."[6]

This was, to be clear, meant as a complement—a generous one. The disappearance of God had placed the highest urgency on the exploration of voids—especially at this terrible time in human history when the monstrous seemed ascendant and humanity seemed on the verge of plunging into the abyss. Camus had already credited Sartre with important work on this subject—in the "fundamental absurdity" revealed in his novels *Nausea* and *The Wall,* which Camus reviewed while still living in Algeria.[7] (He was a *pied noir*—a Frenchman born in Algeria.) What was "absurd" for Camus is the muteness of the universe in response to our pleas for coherent meaning and higher purpose.[8] He believed Sartre, too, heard this silence.

The Germans continued to occupy Paris as the summer of 1944 began. (Camus' publisher insisted, therefore, that his essay on Franz Kafka, who was Jewish, not be included in *The Myth of Sisyphus,* and it was not.) But the Allies had just landed at Normandy and their approach could be felt. Camus had become active in the Resistance. He got a late start—perhaps due to his struggles with tuberculosis or his lifelong suspicion of military solutions.[9] (Before Camus was a year old his father had been killed in the First World War.) But now Camus was helping edit the underground paper *Combat.* And Camus had recruited Sartre to write for that paper.

Simone de Beauvoir, a philosopher and novelist, would likely have been with Sartre at the café. Otherwise some young actress might have been sitting beside him. There would probably have been a young actress next to Camus, too—most likely Maria Casares. His second wife Francine was back in Algeria, now under the control of the Allies.

Sartre was small and not particularly handsome, but he was magnetic. Camus was cool and attractive. "His mix of casualness and enthusiasm made him really charming," Beauvoir explains.[10] Camus was impressed, as many were, by Sartre's exuberant intelligence. Sartre was inspired, as many were, by Camus' courage and commitment in his work for the Resistance. They shared, along with outsize literary and philosophical ambitions and that taste for young actresses, a weakness for what Sartre calls "dirty stories."[11] The conversation would, consequently, have been not only intense and erudite but funny. The evening, likely as not, would have succeeded in becoming boisterous.

However, a matter of contention—one that would eventually lead to an irreparable rupture in the Sartre-Camus friendship—could already be detected behind the repartee. They were both declared atheists; they both had important things to say on the consequences of atheism; but each believed the other to have had lingering and embarrassing religious inclinations.

Before celebrating Sisyphus in his book, Camus turns his attention to rehabilitating Don Juan—a character with whom he has an obvious affinity. His Don Juan, like Molière's is, of course, an indefatigable seducer of women. But in his essay Camus, unlike Molière, sees Don Juan as moving from woman to woman not because he loves shallowly but because he loves too deeply. Camus' Don Juan falls profoundly for one woman but then must be untrue to her because he has fallen just as profoundly for another. And then, soon enough, he'll be overwhelmed with love for another woman. This Don Juan is aware of what he is doing—"lucid," in the argot of the Left Bank; he is aware that his passions conflict and that his situation, therefore, is absurd. That, for Camus, is the point. (How painful the women involved might find this is not Camus' point.)

His Don Juan, like Molière's, has no use for an afterlife or a god. And, unlike Molière, Camus refuses in his essay to imagine Don Juan actually receiving any sort of punishment, however cartoonish, for his licentious behavior: no bolts of lightning strike him; the ground does not open to swallow him. If, when it comes time to sort out the consequences of our behavior, we look for supernatural help we will find none. The absurdity is unrelieved.

Jean-Paul Sartre and Albert Camus were back at the Café de Flore late in October of 1945—a year and two months after the liberation of Paris, a year after Camus' wife Francine had finally been able to join her husband in Paris. Beauvoir described Francine as "very blond, very fresh, lovely in her blue-gray suit."[12] Recently she was also very pregnant. This evening Francine was home with the twins.

Maria Casares was not sitting beside Camus. Upon realizing, with his wife's return, that she couldn't have "all" with Camus, she chose "nothing." He was heartbroken, but managed to fill the void—and not only with Francine. The intensity of Camus' eye for attractive women was considered characteristically French by Americans, characteristically *pied noir* by Parisians and rather extraordinary even by his fellow French Algerians.[13]

Camus' romantic adventures were certainly not hurt by his growing fame. *Combat,* the sporadic underground newspaper, had become an aboveground daily, with Camus as one of the top two editors. He continued, in his editorials, to interpret for the French—at least for the left-leaning, noncommunist French—the various cataclysms that were hitting France. And Sartre was keeping up. He was about to begin publication of his own literary review: *Les Temps modernes.* It would become France's leading intellectual journal. Sartre and Camus were now, with so many discredited for having collaborated with the Nazis, among France's leading intellectuals—torchbearers of the spirit of the Resistance, although Camus had come late to the Resistance and Sartre had little role in it. The two of them were also writing books, writing and producing plays, imagining, at the Flore or maybe the Café des Deux-Magots next door, a new France, a new Europe, a new world.

But what new world? Sartre and Camus probably were not discussing, as they drank and greeted admirers, their growing differences. "One had the feeling," Sartre later recalled, "that there might be a clash if we touched on certain things, and we didn't touch on them."[14] Therefore, as they sat at the Flore, Sartre and Camus likely were somewhat circumspect on the two subjects most discussed at the time at Left Bank cafés: philosophy, particularly how to deal with the void; and politics, particularly how condemnatory to be of the Stalinists. But they were each about to speak out on these subjects—and their pronouncements would be repeated and mulled over in numerous other cafés in Paris and around the world.

Sartre believed that his thought, which had been receiving so much attention, had been misunderstood. On October 29, 1945, he took the Metro to the Marbeuf stop to deliver a lecture at the Salle des Centraux in which he would try to explain himself. As he walked toward the hall, Sartre saw a crowd in the street. "Probably some Communists demonstrating against me," he later reported having thought. Instead it was the overflow. The box office had been overrun. It took Sartre more than a quarter of an hour just to squeeze through the crowd to the platform from which he was to speak. The newspapers, later full of excited accounts, would report "elbow fights," "thirty broken chairs," "a mob rather than an audience," "police," "fifteen fainting spells."[15] (It was a warm evening in Paris.) What had drawn this overlarge and overheated audience of perhaps as many as 300 people? What had created one of the few dozen twentieth-century events that can claim to be the first of the "modern 'media events'"?[16] Jean-Paul Sartre had promised to deliver a lecture with the not obviously electric title: "Existentialism is a Humanism."

After some initial reluctance, Sartre, Beauvoir and members of their circle had reconciled themselves to the designation: "existentialist." (The term was a nod to the work on "Being," on *Existenz*, of the German philosopher Martin Heidegger.) Sartre had already detailed his own philosophy in a lengthy, technical disquisition, *Being and Nothingness*. Here, speaking without notes to this audience or "mob," he kept it (relatively) simple: "existence," Sartre explains, "precedes essence."[17] This may not seem a subversive observation, but it is.

When we make something—a paper knife is Sartre's now quaint example—our idea of what it should be, its "essence," precedes its "existence"; we have a conception of the purpose of that paper knife (opening letters or cutting the pages of books) before we manufacture it, before we create it. And we, too, would have a purpose if we, too, were created—by God. But we weren't, so we don't. Sartre was very clear about that. The absence of God was the premise of his philosophy. It means that men and women have no initial purpose, no initial essence. Unlike paper knives and other created things, we exist first, *then* we try to figure out what to do with ourselves.

Jean-Paul Sartre dubbed himself a representative of "atheistic existentialism." And along with Camus and others of the individuals mentioned in the previous chapter, he was contributing to the twentieth-century development of atheism. Of course, no such development would be necessary or possible were disbelief as simple an idea as many of its critics believe it to be: merely a curt, harsh, unsubtle negation. But irreligion, as this book has been trying to demonstrate, is no simpler than religion.

If believers try to find God everywhere in the universe, nonbelievers must contemplate the consequences of His absence from everywhere in the universe—not just from the motion of the stars and development of life, but from our short, clumsy existences. Nonbelievers must struggle, without the crutch of divine intervention or heavenly purpose, to produce new understandings of such phenomena as nebulae, earthquakes, tsunamis, adultery and the exploitation of the working class. Quite a bit must be constructed atop the void.

Disbelief gets complicated. It has depth. It comes in varieties. It raises issues. In the jammed and sweltering Salle des Centraux, Sartre was dealing with two of the more important of those issues.

The first was our tendency to substitute secular gods for the old-fashioned variety. Sartre was among those twentieth-century thinkers with a contribution to make to the shadows-of-God-eradication project—an important project if atheists are to do more than simply replace religious ideals with other ideals. Here he appeared to have eradicated a lot: any notion that we arrive with a purpose, that we are alive for a reason, that our lives have some sort of extrinsic meaning. If existence precedes essence, we're not here to serve God, but we're also not here to further Nature's objectives, to celebrate the workings of the Universe, to devote ourselves to the betterment of Humankind or, even, to drink and love exuberantly. We're just here.

That doesn't mean, however, that our lives are *meaningless.* The second issue upon which Sartre had a contribution to make was the charge that embracing atheism is like letting loose a beast. As Thomas Jefferson did, Sartre had some thoughts on how people might behave ethically without the punishment or rewards of religion. Essence comes after existence but, Sartre insisted on this warm October evening, it still comes. In fact, it can't help but come. We can do what we want: "Everything," as Dostoevsky put it, "is permitted." But we, therefore, have some decisions to make. And in deciding what we want to do we are giving our life meaning; we are giving ourselves some sort of "essence."

Sartre tells his audience of one of his students who came to him during the war with a moral dilemma: His brother had been killed by the Germans, and he wanted to fight them by joining the Free French Forces then gathering in England. However, his father had left his mother, who was already devastated by the loss of her other son, and if he went off to England and took the chance of himself dying in combat, this young man felt that it would "plunge her into despair." Should he stay or should he go?

Sartre's point, in part, was that there was absolutely no way his student could escape answering this question *by himself*. There's no God to help with the answer. Nor is there any other sort of preexisting, inherent, clear-cut or unwavering moral law to which the young man might appeal. Advice can't even help, because in choosing where to seek advice we are already making a kind of decision. (Sartre realized that the student came to him in part because he knew Sartre would support a decision to stay home with mama.) We are not only free to make our own moral decisions; we are *condemned to be free* to make our own moral decisions. That's the rest of Sartre's point in sharing this story. Existence precedes essence, but then we choose—we *must* choose—our own essence. This student decided to become the sort of young man who values his mother's feelings over the need to fight the Nazis.

Existentialism is a humanism because it emphasizes our very human condition: that we humans must each determine what our lives are going to mean. And in some ways the moral stakes are much higher now that we have no holy books, no priests upon whom to foist off these moral decisions. It's all on us. The "beast," the "tiger," of atheism doesn't devour morality, Sartre was arguing, it intensifies it.[18]

Jean-Paul Sartre had reason to believe a bunch of Communists might be picketing his lecture. All his talk of freedom and purposelessness did not, on the face of it, seem to provide much support for revolutionary solidarity with the working class. Freedom to choose your own essence seemed, instead, rather self-indulgent and individualistic. It seemed, in other words, rather *bourgeois*. And in the eyes not only of the Communists but of the other left intellectuals who filled the Salle des Centraux that steamy evening in 1945—with the fascists defeated and a new world to be fashioned—little could be less attractive than to seem staid, middle class and concerned with one's own comforts.

Sartre was no party-line Communist, but he was as committed to the rise of the proletariat as the next Left-Bank philosopher. So, in this lecture he came up with some guidelines on how we might choose our "essence." It turned out there is a limit to our freedom: "When we say that man is responsible for himself," Sartre explained in the Salle des Centraux, "we do not mean that he is responsible only for his own individuality, but that he is responsible for all men." That is one hefty responsibility. And our existential responsibility then gets more burdensome still. For it turned out Sartre did not consider "quietism" or "inaction" to be "authentic" essences for us to choose for ourselves. We have to be out there working for all humanity. Existentialism is also a humanism, then, because it is dedicated to some revolutionary, anti-capitalistic scheme for elevating humanity.

So we choose our own essence but we *should* choose a political essence—a left political essence. This had the virtue of keeping Sartre in the struggle for economic fairness and collective ownership, shoulder to shoulder with the proletariat; this had the virtue of putting Sartre on the right side of "history"; this had the virtue, in other words, of helping Sartre's philosophy seem less bourgeois. But Sartre's insistence that we ought to use our freedom to further radical political change had the drawback of seeming just another invocation of a shadow God.

Albert Camus was remarkably consistent in his attitude toward philosophers. He liked them when they demolished others' theories—as Patrick McCarthy, one of his biographers, notes—not when they set about constructing new theories of their own.[19] Camus respected Sartre's philosophy when it was proclaiming our inescapable, absurd freedom, not when it was telling us how we *must* use that freedom.

This disagreement was kept in check as Sartre and Camus sat and drank and partied together. But Camus' sense that Sartre and his fellow existentialists had gone too far in building a system came out in an interview he gave that fall. "They no longer believe in God," Camus told that interviewer, "but they believe in history." Camus sees this Marxist conviction that history has a direction as an embarrassing religious inclination. He mutters about "divinization" and worries that Sartre is coming a little too close to worshipping Communism.[20] Did Sartre believe the universe is saying something after all—something about revolutionary engagement on behalf of the proletariat?

A year later, Camus arrived late at a party attended by Sartre and Beauvoir and their disagreement, finally, exploded. The specific irritant was an article Sartre had printed in his journal that, in Camus' view, appeared to justify Stalin's show trials of Soviet dissidents in Moscow.[21] Sartre defended the article. Camus slammed the door and left. They did not speak for months.

In 1948, Camus and Maria Casares ran into each other and resumed their relationship. She had decided to accept his offer of something "between the all and the nothing": "seventy-five percent," they called it.[22] Given the presence of Francine Camus and the twins, plus various young actresses, her share of Camus probably was not that high. However, Casares remained his mistress, companion, friend for the rest of his life.

Camus and Sartre also had, for a time, resumed speaking and drinking with each other. They could be seen once again in the evening at the Café de Flore—with friends, disciples and some combination of Beauvoir, Casares, Camus' wife or actresses. But their reconciliation did not last.

The final split between Camus and Sartre was provoked by Camus' extended essay, *The Rebel*, published in 1951. In it Camus championed those who rebel but rejected, for the most part, those who rebel violently and then continue to repress and murder after they seize power. This was, then, Camus' staunchest attack on the Communists and on the intellectuals who, in their eagerness to forgive "the party of the proletariat," act as their enablers. At about this time, Sartre was moving in the other direction and increasingly positioning himself as such an intellectual. Indeed, he experienced, in these years, what he called, "in the language of the Church . . . my conversion"—a conversion to an acceptance of revolutionary violence, a conversion to support for the Communists as the proper, freely chosen "essence" and a conversion to the view that—as Sartre rather unphilosophically put it—"an anti-Communist is a dog."[23]

After a long delay, Sartre's journal, *Les Temps modernes*, published a lengthy, nasty review, not written by Sartre, of Camus' new book. In it Camus, who had been as involved in the issues of his time as any writer, is accused of wanting "to be done with history," and in the review Camus was accused of an embarrassing religious inclination.[24] This last critique stemmed from Camus' undeniable obsession with God—with God's impotence, with God's lack of concern, with God's infuriating, unconscionable nonexistence.

Camus responded to the review with an indignant letter, also lengthy: "Why criticize a book if one has decided to pay no attention to what can be read in it?" Sartre published the letter and his own similarly lengthy, very personal response. It began: "My Dear Camus: Our friendship was not easy, but I will miss it." Sartre's broadside picked up the political and religious charges: "When a child died, you blamed the absurdity of the world and the deaf and blind God. . . . But the child's father, if he was unemployed or an unskilled laborer, blamed men." And Sartre also let loose with some extremely unfriendly personal criticism, including such lines as: "You have become the victim of a dismal self-importance, which hides your inner problems."[25] Camus, less secure than Sartre, was devastated. The two would never share an evening in a café again.[26]

The political break between them may have been inevitable: Camus, born poor and once a member of the Communist Party, long ago became unable to abide its thuggishness. Sartre, born bourgeois, needed the grit and legitimacy offered by the proletariat and its struggle. Their philosophic differences also stretched far back. Sartre was always looking for a way to bridge the void, a way to locate an essence, an escape of some sort from the absurd. Camus wasn't. Though he was less the abstract philosopher than Sartre, he did not believe such an escape was possible. Instead, he suggested, we must learn to live with the absurd. This position dates back to Camus' first book of essays, written before he met Sartre.

Sisyphus was a great rebel: Camus celebrates the tricks he had played on the gods. But by the time he landed in Hades for good, Sisyphus had run out of tricks. No amount of cleverness, no act of violence, no alliance with the proletariat, no rebellion or revolution was going to free him from that "ruthless boulder." And that Sisyphus—who "watches the stone rush down"—is the one in whom Camus was most interested. "Sisyphus," he writes, "is the absurd hero. . . . His scorn of the gods, his hatred of death and his passion for life won him that unspeakable penalty in which the whole being is exerted toward accomplishing nothing."

Accomplishing nothing? "This," Camus concludes, "is the price that must be paid for the passions of this earth."[27] Sure we want to do what we can to prevent poor children from dying, to make the world fairer or smarter or prettier, but we shouldn't pretend that the boulders we work so hard to push up hills will stay there. They will fall back; we will push them up again. We will rebel; our rebellions will fail; we will rebel again. Don Juan loves one woman but then abandons her (or 75 percent abandons her) because he has fallen for another. Even if we are not Don Juans, even if we love only once, it may, at some point, prove to be too much; we may find ourselves caring too deeply or not deeply enough. Such are "the passions of this earth."

Sounds grim, but Camus denied that it is. For without gods and their shadows, without all those persistent illusions, something interesting happens: "In the universe suddenly restored to its silence, the myriad wondering little voices of the earth rise up."[28] Unlike that boulder with which Sisyphus is condemned to struggle, we and he are conscious. We hear and see. We wonder. We feel; we hurt; we delight. We can, however imperfectly, try to assist our fellow humans. We do, however imperfectly, love. Passion is something.

It is a question similar to the one Voltaire found so obnoxious. The religious ask it aggressively. Those who find themselves losing their religion may confront it on their own—perhaps with some hesitation, perhaps resolutely, perhaps sadly. The question is what could replace God.[29]

One answer, once His various shadows have faded, is *nothing:* no creator, no regulator, no judge, no parental figure in the sky, nothing omnipotent or omnipresent, nothing perfect, no pure benevolence, no design, no meaning, no prior essence; mountains and trees, stars and space with nothing to say. "I find myself quite unable to discern any purpose in the universe and still more unable to wish to discern one," announces Bertrand Russell, a twentieth-century philosopher of a different stripe than Sartre or Camus.[30]

"Nothing" is the answer the religious hear, the answer from which the religious flee. It certainly is a valid answer to what might replace religion. It is the skeptic's answer—hard won in the difficult struggle against the fanciful, the supernatural. *How can that be?* It can't. Yet "nothing"—the "nothing," in Wallace Stevens' formulation, "that is not there and the nothing that is"—leaves something to be desired as an answer.[31] It opens the pit of nihilism. And this not entirely satisfactory answer can be said to have led to a not entirely satisfactory era—of tongue-tied art, architecture, politics, books and philosophy. In the last half of the twentieth century, nothing did, indeed, sometimes seem to be filling—or intensifying—the vacuum left by God's disappearance.

But there are other, less empty possible answers to the question of what replaces God: *knowledge,* for one. For wishes and fantasies we substitute understanding, we substitute science—the bullheaded effort to make tentative sense of what we can. This corresponds with the variety of disbelief that is based on natural explanations for the workings of the universe and society—on "a clear understanding." The absence of purpose, even certainty, in the universe does not mean that no patterns or regularities present themselves. We can come up with a "plausible" explanation of what particles are composed of what; we can come up with a "plausible" explanation of what organic chemicals do what; we can route much of the world's knowledge to a device carried in our pocket—even if we cannot explain what is here for what reason.

Freedom—Ernestine Rose's answer—is also a possible and rather encouraging response to the question of what might replace God. We now know that oppression and injustices—Jean Meslier's "real hell"—do not automatically disappear, as the political-analysis variety of disbelief tends to assume, once people escape the "oppressive thralldom" of "superstition." Soviet Communism offered a persuasive example of that, though Sartre was among those shamefully slow to take the lesson. Still, that shouldn't negate all the other twentieth-century evidence of the importance leaving religion's "oppressive thralldom" behind can have for freedom.

The role of religion was mixed in the civil rights and anti-colonial struggles that followed the end of World War II. It would be difficult to find internationally prominent atheists—such as Sartre, Camus, Russell—who were not on the right side of such struggles. Nonetheless, many of the leaders of these liberation movements were religious. Criticism of religion played a more crucial role in the slower-to-develop women's movement.

Indeed, few demonstrated the connection between atheism and liberty as clearly as the woman who often shared a table with Jean-Paul Sartre and Albert Camus—and whose political contribution has proven larger than either of theirs. Simone de Beauvoir—like Ernestine Rose and Elizabeth Cady Stanton—grasped the connection between religion and the subjugation of women. Her 1949 book, *The Second Sex,* as important a contribution to feminism as any that has been written, includes numerous examples of religion's leading role in that subjugation. Beauvoir quotes a line from a Jewish morning prayer: "Blessed be the Lord our God, and the Lord of all worlds, that has not made me a woman." She quotes Paul from the New Testament: "For the husband is the head of the wife, even as Christ is the head of the church." And Beauvoir quotes Tertullian, that early Christian thinker who also represented himself poorly in chapter 3: "Woman! You are the devil's gateway. . . . It is your fault that God's Son had to die. You should always dress in mourning and rags." Beauvoir concludes that "for Jews, Muslims and Christians," among others, "man is the master by divine right." And she makes clear that religion not only establishes this repression but enforces it: "Fear of God," Beauvoir writes, "manages to stifle the slightest inclination of revolt in the oppressed."[32]

The oppressed in this case being more than half the world's population, this liberation movement surely was among the most important of the twentieth century (though it left plenty of work for the next century).

By this point in this book, we should not be surprised that its great manifesto was written by an atheist.

In recent decades, various manifestations of orthodox religion have continued to play a leading role in efforts around the world to limit the rights of women and have continued themselves to severely limit those rights—with shaved heads, veiled bodies and faces, exclusions from the priesthood and continued subservience to husbands. Orthodox religion has also too often lined itself up with resistance to equal rights for lesbian, gay, bisexual and transgender people—among the last and most difficult of the liberation struggles that began in the twentieth century.

Meanwhile, since the fall of Communism and with the exception of a couple of vestigial Communist states, secularism has continued to follow the path of Simone de Beauvoir and has been associated with the struggle for greater human rights. It has fought for political and social freedom as an alternative to religion-justified oppression and injustice. So, yes, religion and its ancient strictures might be replaced with openness and tolerance.

Humankind can also achieve, as Rose envisioned, a greater *freedom of thought* by exiting the one-truth town of religion. The fifth variety of disbelief—inspired by Nietzsche's "open sea"—comes into play here. We begin to see possibility—in art, in science, in philosophy. We may even begin to feel, with Sartre (the not-yet-Communist Sartre), free to determine our own "essence" in the world. Virginia Woolf describes a strong mind—unburdened by "the Deity," not "shut in" by "faith"—as "unroofed and open to the sky."[33] That is both a remarkable expression of the fifth variety of disbelief and a rather exhilarating alternative to life with a god.

A variety of *irony*—the use of humor to express an awareness of the limits of the meanings to which we subscribe—can also help replace God. Might we have expected the universe to offer more meaning than it does? Yeah. Silly us. Still, we must carry on with our projects—knowing that, without God or His shadows, those projects don't have any ultimate or absolute significance. Irony is pretty good at capturing such shades of significance, as when we describe some charitable or political endeavor to a friend as "saving the world." An age of reduced belief, the point is, requires a language of modulated seriousness. It is as if we constantly are, in Woolf's phrase, "sharing a joke with nothingness."[34] "For the present," Nietzsche wrote in 1882, "we still live in the age of tragedy, the age of moralities and religion." He saw how that might change: "For the present," Nietzsche adds, "the comedy of existence has not yet 'become conscious' of itself."[35] Now it has.

But there is another important answer to the what-might-replace-God question—one upon which some of the most lyrical, hopeful and noble varieties of atheism are based: in Albert Camus' silent universe God is replaced by *everything*—by the dirt, the plants, the sky, the sun; by our fellow creatures; by women and men; by our inextinguishable passions; by "the myriad wondering little voices of the earth." This is the anacreontic variety of disbelief in one of its most beguiling forms. Indeed, with the help of the world and its small pleasures, nihilism—the vortex of "belief in unbelief"— might even be said to have been evaded here.[36] With *everything* atheism resurfaces as champion of all the flawed glory of the mortal; as champion of the wondrously messy excessiveness that surrounds us and is us.

Camus lived through the Holocaust, through Stalinism. He watched, with great pain, his people, the *pieds noir,* losing their homes in Algeria in the name of an anti-colonialism that he mostly supported; he suffered with the violence on both sides. And Camus was not, for all his adventures and accomplishments, a particularly satisfied man. Even winning the Nobel Prize for Literature in 1957 (seven years before Sartre would) proved mostly a torment: stuffy ceremonies, political disputes and the implication that his best work was behind him. "I'm castrated!" Camus complains to a friend.[37] Yet Camus wanted to see in us—frustrating as our projects may be, absurd as our lives surely are—a happiness. If it could be found in Sisyphus, it could be found in anyone.

He locates Sisyphus in "a universe" that is "without a master" but is "neither sterile nor futile." It is a universe where people—inspired by "the passions of this earth"—try, where people struggle. He imagines Sisyphus, at the bottom of his hill, facing his rock, content. "The struggle itself toward the heights," Camus insists, "is enough to fill a man's heart."[38] Sisyphus has the world (or at least Hades); he has life (though this too is a bit of stretch, since Sisyphus is, technically, dead); and he has consciousness. Is that not everything?

B y the middle of the twentieth century in many parts of the world, France certainly among them, it became difficult to avoid the detritus from humankind's numerous denounced, destroyed gods. Jagged remnants of shattered belief systems littered the earth—prejudices, judgments and moralities now free of the mythologies and metaphysics that once supported them.[39] It was difficult to spend an evening in a café or in front of one of the newly proliferating television sets without encountering the wreckage.

Camus came as close as anyone to gaining perspective on this rubble-strewn landscape. His last novel, *The Fall*, is, among other things, an account of the power guilt can retain even after the religious frameworks in which it once functioned have fallen into disrepair. Camus writes specifically of the persistence of a belief in "sin" unrelieved by a belief in "grace."[40] However, such insights did not prevent Camus from tripping over the detritus himself. Indeed, in his writing and philosophizing he never seems to get far from the carcass of God.

Camus, consequently, is not yet a truly post-religious thinker: he suffers too much from the loss of God. Like many in preceding and succeeding generations, Camus sometimes seems as obsessed with God's absence as others had been with His presence. He can be accused, to use his own phrase, of "kneeling before a void."[41] And Camus, as Sartre and company couldn't help noting, is not a particularly thorough or subtle philosopher.[42] (Sartre himself would be subject to similar criticism.)

Religion is old; these thoughts on how to live without religion are relatively young, probably immature. Still, Camus is a path-breaker in his struggle to reject, in the name of absurdity, gods and shadows of gods and shadows of shadows of gods. "Atheism," Sartre writes, "is a cruel and long-range affair."[43] Camus had a real go at it.

Camus was a path-breaker, too, in attempting to think out life without God and His shadows: how we go forward without there being any direction that qualifies as forward; how we continue to try despite having so often failed; how we live in the face of the fact that we will soon die. This will be a very long, very demanding, perhaps cruel investigation. With Camus' *Sisyphus*, it has, at least, begun.

Camus had expected his own death to come early—from tuberculosis. It did come early: Albert Camus died just four days into the 1960s, at the age of 46, but in a car crash. It happened near the small town of Villeblevin. Camus was not at the wheel; a friend, also killed in the crash, was driving him back to Paris from southern France. Absurd. Reporters descended upon Villeblevin.

In Camus' briefcase was a draft of a new novel, a revealing journal and a copy of Nietzsche's *The Gay Science*, which features that discussion of God's death.[44]

13

THE GODS ARE BEING DRIVEN FROM THE EARTH

SECULARISM IN EUROPE AND AMERICA

Give me the storm and tempest of thought and action, rather than the dead calm of ignorance and faith! Banish me from Eden when you will, but first let me eat of the fruit of the tree of knowledge!

—Robert Green Ingersoll[1]

IN AUGUST 1960, THE SUMMER AFTER CAMUS DIED, MADALYN Mays traveled to Paris with her two boys—one fourteen, the other five.[2] Her purpose wasn't to see sights or sit in cafés. Much of her time was spent at the Soviet Embassy. Mays' efforts to obtain permission to emigrate to the Soviet Union had failed in Washington; she thought she might have better luck in Paris.

The United States had certainly lost its attraction for Mays. She was tired of its hypocritical morality, to which she hadn't much bothered to conform: both her boys had different fathers, neither of whom was the man to whom she had, briefly, been married. "I see social mores that are wrong, stupid, immoral," Mays fumes in her diary.[3] She was tired, too, of America's narrow, stifling politics. And Mays was furious that her eldest son, William Murray Jr., had been forced—like many, probably most, public-school children in the United States—to read the Bible and say a prayer each morning in his Baltimore public school.[4]

All of these complaints would have been received sympathetically at the Café de Flore. But Mays had the disadvantage of being an aggressive woman a decade before the women's movement (despite the best efforts of Simone de Beauvoir) got off the ground. She had been questioning conventional beliefs not on the Left Bank but in America, in the 1950s and early 1960s, where and when those who indulged in that sort of thing, male or female, were more likely to have the tires on their cars slashed and the windows on their houses smashed than to lecture before overflow crowds. France and the rest of Western Europe were beginning to accelerate their long slide away from religion. The United States, from which Madalyn Mays had fled, was not sliding in that direction in any obvious way—for reasons her story can help illuminate.

The fact that she couldn't speak Russian did not help her case at the Soviet Embassy in Paris, nor did those two fatherless boys. Mays returned to Baltimore, further abashed. This was a woman who could put up with, and had to put up with, a lot of being abashed. She was 41, living with her parents and a failure by most of the standards of her society. However, Madalyn Murray—she had begun using her former lover's last name—was on the verge of a large, notorious success.

The word "secular" has come to be understood in two related but distinct ways:[5] The first of these definitions is: "not religious"—not believing in or, at least, not practicing a religion. The second meaning of "secular" refers not to the rejection of religion on the part of members of a society but to the way a society is structured: keeping religion separate from more worldly institutions—particularly those associated with government. The distinction between these two meanings is often obscured, but to understand what happened to religion in Western Europe and the United States in the 1960s and beyond that distinction must be recognized.

For in those years Western Europeans were becoming significantly more secular—in the first sense. Consider the Netherlands as an example: In 1947, according to a Gallup Survey, 68 percent of the Dutch believed in life after death.[6] By 1961, the percentage of believers in an afterlife had slipped a little, to 63 percent. By 1968, it had plummeted to 50 percent. And in Britain, Sweden and West Germany, the percentage telling Gallup they did believe in life after death in 1968 was even lower—in France only 35 percent.[7] This basic religious belief, in other words, was rapidly becoming a minority belief. Most measures of religiosity in Western Europe, from the end of World War II through the 1980s, produce similar graphs—graphs you could ski down, with the 1960s providing a particularly fast slope.

Something very different, however, happened in the United States in these decades. According to the same Gallup Surveys, in 1947, 68 percent of Americans said they did believe in life after death—the exact same percentage as in the Netherlands that year.[8] But in the United States by 1968 that percentage had actually nudged up slightly: to 73 percent. America, in other words, does not appear to have become more secular—in the first sense of that word.

Why? Why at this time, when the cultural connections between the continents were strong, did so many Europeans lose their religion while most Americans did not? Answers to this question may help reveal whether we are heading toward a future of diminished belief or a future of something closer to the smorgasbord of spiritual beliefs that has characterized America in recent decades.

That spiritual smorgasbord developed in part because the United States, since the days of Jefferson and Madison, has been one of the most secular countries on earth—in the second sense of that word. In the name of tolerance, religion and government have been kept imperfectly but still remarkably separate. And that separation became more rigorous in the 1960s.

In October of 1960, Madalyn Murray, just back from Paris and her failed attempt to emigrate to the Soviet Union, called Woodbourne Junior High and was transferred to an assistant superintendent. Some of the details of this story, as with much having to do with Murray's life, are in dispute, but she says the call was made at her son William's behest.[9] Murray announced, on the phone, that William was going to stop participating in the school's morning "devotionals": readings from the King James Bible and recitation of the Lord's Prayer ("Our Father which art in Heaven . . ."). She asked that William be allowed to stay away from the room during these religious exercises. "This is part of our history and our culture . . . ," responded that assistant superintendent. He added: "I never had a request like this in my life."[10]

However, such requests were beginning to be made. Students or parents were protesting religious readings with sufficient insistency to lead to legal action at three other schools in the United States in these years. Those cases—one from Pennsylvania, one from Florida and one from New York—were beginning or about to begin to hopscotch through the courts.

In some ways they were echoes of the famous trial in Tennessee in 1925 of John T. Scopes, a high-school biology teacher, accused of violating a new state law outlawing the teaching of evolution. Despite a spirited defense by Clarence Darrow, Scopes lost. (His conviction was later thrown out on a technicality.) But evolution would find its way into classrooms and textbooks. Instead of debating whether science belonged in public schools the question became whether religion did. That was the question in these cases on school prayer.

And the plaintiffs seemed, on the face of it, to have a pretty good argument. The first words of the Bill of Rights, appended to the Constitution of the United States by the first Congress, are: "Congress shall make no law respecting an establishment of religion." That's called the "Establishment Clause." Interpreting "Congress" (with the help of the Fourteenth Amendment) broadly, as the Supreme Court in the twentieth century was beginning to do, it is difficult to see how a government-operated school should be able to ask students to participate in reading the texts and prayers of a religion.

Including some religious instruction in schools may have seemed acceptable when almost all the students came from devout Protestant families. But, as Stephen D. Solomon notes in his impressive history of the legal battle over school prayer, Catholics had been arriving in America; Jews had been arriving; nonbelievers—following in the tradition of Ernestine Rose—had grown more outspoken.[11] Why should their children have to recite passages from a Protestant version of the Bible in a public school?

Madalyn Murray wrote that assistant superintendent a letter[12]:

> When there is a clear violation of the principle of separation of Church and
> State, and when my good conscience as a confirmed and practicing Atheist
> requires that I must rebel against such a flagrant violation of basic constitu-
> tional rights, I am compelled, in an action of civil disobedience, to withdraw
> my son, William, from the Maryland public schools.

And she did.

Next, Murray wrote a letter to the editor of the Baltimore *Morning Sun*[13]:

> Anyone in America can worship this alleged God in his own way. . . . This
> is fine, but please, "include us out." We Atheists and Agnostics want only
> the freedom of our opinion. We desire to be excluded from your collective

madness. We desire not to have this forced upon us against our good conscience and our considered convictions.

The *Morning Sun* sent a reporter. William's picture made the front page. Reporters from the three national television networks and the wire services came next. Madalyn's own formidable ability to withstand the scorn of the community, along with that of her sons and her unenthusiastic parents, was soon tested. The tires on their car were indeed slashed. Windows in their house were indeed smashed. One of their cats was killed. William was ostracized at school, and when some local toughs came upon him at a shopping center, they attempted, unsuccessfully, to push him in front of a bus.

Madalyn had a degree, never used, from South Texas School of Law. She got in touch with civil liberties lawyers. And soon a fourth case was proceeding through the courts—in something of a race to the United States Supreme Court. The New York case got there first and won the first victory. The Baltimore case, that of the Murrays, was decided with the Pennsylvania case and was largely overshadowed by it in the decision.[14] Still, the United States Supreme Court, with eight of the nine justices in agreement, had ruled in favor of William and Madalyn Murray. "In light of the history of the First Amendment and of our cases interpreting and applying its requirements," Justice Tom C. Clark wrote in the majority opinion, "we hold that the practices at issue and the laws requiring them are unconstitutional under the Establishment Clause, as applied to the states through the Fourteenth Amendment." Clark added that "in the relationship between man and religion, the state is firmly committed to a position of neutrality."[15]

That was the end of sanctioned prayer in American public schools. The United States now had a more perfect secularism—in the second meaning of that term. And Madalyn Murray had found her life's work.

In 1966, anthropologist Anthony F. C. Wallace said boldly what some scholars were suggesting quietly: that the "evolutionary future of religion is extinction."[16] Wallace stated that, while it might take several hundred years, "belief in supernatural beings and in supernatural forces that affect nature without obeying nature's laws will erode and become only an interesting historical memory." This was a legitimate point of view then, but it has become, in scholarly circles at least, less legitimate.

For twentieth-century thinkers remained concerned with what it is not possible to say. And beginning in the late 1960s, as Wallace was making his prediction, a group of them—operating, once again, mostly out of Paris—began to turn their attention to what we say about history, to in particular the "grand narratives" we use to make sense out of it and, thereby, draw conclusions about the future.[17] Their argument, which became a tenet of postmodern scholarship, was that such "narratives" are themselves collections of untested, unsupported assumptions, which impose their own moral and political views. An obvious example was the heroic tale of noble Europeans bringing progress to backward peoples—by colonizing them. And another early target of these thinkers was the "Enlightenment narrative," which proclaimed that, with the rise of reason and science, primitive, childish religion has been experiencing a steady and inexorable decline—that humankind has been, as Freud among many others asserted, steadily outgrowing religion.[18] That, these thinkers concluded, is a presumptuous and condescending story!

Wasn't this belief in the glorious triumph of reason and science another shadow god? Indeed, the identification of "grand narratives" can be seen as a part of the shadows-of-God eradication project. And that might be a name for what a few decades worth of poststructuralists, postmodernists and practitioners of deconstruction were up to if that project itself weren't vulnerable to being attacked as a grand narrative. (Perhaps the author can be forgiven if he sometimes wishes he were still writing about the eighteenth and nineteenth centuries, when critiquing religion did not always seem to necessitate also critiquing your critique.)

Now, this book is under suspicion to begin with because it tells, often enough, "stories." It does manage to escape the suspect tale of the steady decline in religion in one important way: by arguing that a certain amount of disbelieving has gone on in *all* societies—preliterate, Indian, Greek, Islamic and, long before the Enlightenment, European. But the argument here has indeed been that disbelief in Europe and America has been growing more public, more consistent, more informed, more formidable and more widespread. There is no doubt that these pages have, consequently, indulged in a fair amount of talk about an intermittent but significant lessening of the sway of religion in the West in the past half millennia or so. And, what is worse from a certain postmodern perspective, this book asserts that a decline in religion has been associated with a rise in science and in attention to human rights—with progress (a concept that is particularly suspect in those circles). The best argument of the scholars who have devoted themselves to debunking this kind of talk may be the strange failure of religion to decline in that science-obsessed, reasonably human-rights-attentive outpost of Europe in North America—the author's home turf: the still truculently churchgoing United States.

A long with preventing "Congress" from the "establishment" of a religion, the First Amendment to the U.S. Constitution prevents it from "prohibiting the free exercise" of religion. The escapees from an often-intolerant Europe who had settled the North American colonies had energetically exercised a wide variety of Christian beliefs. And an even wider variety of beliefs, most of them Christian, have been freely and energetically exercised in the United States by their descendants and successors since they managed to guarantee themselves religious tolerance in that Constitution.

Indeed, American history has been punctuated by that series of "Great Awakenings," when religious fervor has seemed particularly intense and new religions (Mormonism) or new sects (Christian Science, Jehovah's Witnesses) have emerged. Historians have not always agreed on the dates and the number of these somewhat amorphous "Great Awakenings," but by the reckoning of one historian or another such a period of revival and reformation has rarely been that far off in the United States.[19]

Did a Great Awakening begin in the United States in the 1960s as evangelical and fundamentalist churches gained members at the expense of more mainstream denominations?[20] Did a Great Awakening flower toward the end of the twentieth century with the growing political influence of evangelicals and fundamentalists? Certainly, on this side of the Atlantic religion has not appeared to be heading toward "extinction."

I n the 1960s, atheism was represented in France by Jean-Paul Sartre and Simone de Beauvoir. It was represented in Britain and, to some extent, internationally by another distinguished philosopher and *littérateur:* that tall, white-haired, aristocratic Cambridge professor, Bertrand Russell. The United States at the time had some distinguished philosophers. It may even have had some distinguished philosophers willing to risk public opprobrium. But the Sartre-Beauvoir-Russell role remained unfilled.

In these years, atheism was mostly associated in the United States with the Soviets, and an association with Communism—which the country was busy arming against, containing and, often, fighting—could still lead to the loss of a job. "The fate of the world rests with the clash between the atheism of Moscow and the Christian spirit throughout other parts of the world," is how that arch anti-Communist senator Joseph McCarthy had put it before he was discredited for costing many people their jobs with many questionable or false accusations.[21] In the United States, consequently, the public face of atheism rapidly became not a philosopher but someone with the courage and obstinacy to withstand just about any opprobrium, someone who had never held a job all that long anyway: Madalyn Murray.

Murray obtained an honorific from the headline on a 1964 *Life* magazine profile of her: "The Most Hated Woman in America." That article rated her "America's most outspoken and militant atheist." Then it noted that, "in a land where most people believe in God and those who don't keep quiet," fighting for atheism "is as good a way to win public favor as bringing back polio."[22]

After her triumph in the school prayer case, Murray sued to force Maryland's churches to pay taxes and lost.[23] She threatened a suit over the words "under God" in the pledge of allegiance, which American school children were (and still are) asked to recite. She formed the Maryland Committee for State/Church Separation, then the Freethought Society of America, the Society of Separationists and the American Atheists. (The latter organization celebrated its fiftieth anniversary at its annual convention in 2013.[24]) She published a magazine called *American Atheist* (also still around). She employed a lot more profanity than women of her age at that time were expected to employ. She received mail with salutations like, "Dear Heathen Communist Bitch," and criticism along the lines of, "You atheist, you mongrel, you rat, you good for nothing shit, you damn gutter rat. Jesus will fix you, you filthy scum."[25] She was accused of enticing a minor to leave her home after her son William, then 18, took up with, impregnated and soon married a young woman of 17; various incidents stemming from this case eventually landed William in jail and inspired Madalyn to flee to Mexico, from which she was soon deported and put back on a plane for the United States.

The United States, of course, had a history of proselytizing nonbelievers. In the last decades of the nineteenth century, Robert Green Ingersoll, known as "the Great Agnostic," carried on in the tradition of Ernestine Rose on the lecture circuit—at a time when suspicion of religion seemed to have grown.[26] In 1872, Ingersoll delivered a lecture entitled "The Gods" in which he attempted to explain why disbelief seemed to be on the rise:

> We have heard talk enough. We have listened to all the drowsy, idealess, vapid sermons that we wish to hear. We have read your Bible and the works of your best minds. We have heard your prayers, your solemn groans and your reverential amens. All these amount to less than nothing. We want one fact. . . . We know all about your moldy wonders and your stale miracles. We want a this-year's fact.[27]

Ingersoll espoused what was not yet called the "narrative" of decreasing religious belief: "The people are beginning to think, to reason and to investigate," he proclaimed. "Slowly, painfully, but surely, the gods are being driven from the earth."[28]

Yet this American nonbeliever, almost a century before Murray, was no pariah. Indeed, he was sufficiently well respected to become one of the leaders of the Republican Party. In 1876, Ingersoll delivered the nominating speech at the Republican convention for James G. Blaine. Ingersoll could grab and hold a room. His eloquence almost won Blaine the nomination.[29]

It is impossible to imagine the support of Madalyn Murray being useful to any major-party political candidate in the 1960s or beyond. America had found the atheist it now wanted—an atheist it could marvel at, chuckle at, disparage and dismiss.

Meanwhile, Western Europe was doing its best to uphold that grand narrative. Consider what the sociologists label "religious participation": By 1981, according to the World Values Survey, only 14 percent of the population of Britain attested to going to church or another religious service at least once a week; in France 11 percent said they went that often; in Sweden 6 percent; in Denmark 3 percent.[30]

Coming up with theories to explain why churchgoing plummeted in Western Europe in and after the 1960s is not difficult (though there are definite chicken-egg problems in any such list).[31] Increased secularization—in the second sense—had weakened the hold of Europe's various national churches on education, the health professions and the media. At the same time, science—its prowess demonstrated by antibiotics, transistors, bombs and such—was strengthening its hold on classrooms, hospitals and informed opinion.[32] After Freud, to pick one significant example, when people hit rough patches, the therapist increasingly replaced the priest as healer of choice. Even crime began to be looked upon less as sin and more as a subject for analysis by those new hybrids: social scientists.

An improving economy also played a role. After decades of depression and war, people on the whole found themselves better off. Economic insecurity, like health worries, tends to inspire people to pray.[33] A higher standard of living not only removes that motivation but tugs people away from religious activities. For many in Europe in the 1960s there were things to buy; for many there was fun to be had. As life in this world became, perhaps, more pleasant; otherworldly escapes from it became not only less necessary but less tolerable.

Many religions—Christianity is a classic example—call on people, in the philosopher Charles Taylor's haunting phrase, to "detach themselves from their own flourishing."[34] With the postwar boom in ways of flourishing, such detachment became still less attractive—even on Sundays.

On those Sundays, churches now not only faced competition from pubs, parks and cafés but from numerous new diversions—diversions often reached by automobile, watched on television or listened to on phonographs. And those cars, TVs and record players were increasingly transporting the young away from the locales, traditions and beliefs of their elders. Education, media and travel were disbursing nontraditional ideas. A "counterculture" full of such ideas established itself not only in garrets and cheap flats but, often enough, right down the hall: in the bedrooms occupied by the increasingly independent young.

However, all of these factors were also present in the United States, where, by 1981, 43 percent of the population, according to that World Values Survey, still reported attending religious services at least once a week—a percentage three times greater than in Britain.[35] Something else must have been going on.

It may have had a little to do with the nature of the counterculture. The drugs and music were the same; hippies and radicals could be found on both sides of the Atlantic. Nonetheless, scruffy, blue-jeaned young men and women in the United States probably were a little more likely to "groove on nature" and meditate on the "Cosmic All." Scruffy, blue-jeaned young men and women in France a little more likely to study Marx and erect barricades in the streets.[36]

After America loosened up in the 1960s, Madalyn Murray O'Hair (she remarried) became something of an institution—a dependable source for a lively quote, an entertainingly outrageous guest on talk shows, a regular and visible litigant. An astronaut said a prayer for peace; O'Hair sued NASA, unsuccessfully, to stop public displays of religion in space. A Dallas teacher was fired for announcing that he was an atheist; she fought, unsuccessfully, for his rights. Since her continuing efforts to revoke the tax exempt status of churches had failed, O'Hair very loudly set up her own church: "We're going to take every exemption," O'Hair declared, with her usual mix of zealotry and humor plus, maybe, an eye for a good racket.[37]

"Once a person is bitten by the Atheism bug, that person stays an Atheist for the rest of his or her life," O'Hair wrote in 1968.[38] But her son William Murray, who was at the center of the school prayer case, did not stay an atheist. William had been drifting in and out of his mother's orbit—alternately working with her, competing with her and trying to put some distance between himself and her outsized, domineering personality. Three marriages had failed. He had a drinking problem. Then in 1980, William found Jesus Christ in a dream. He even wrote a letter to the *Baltimore Sun:* "I would like to apologize to the people of the City of Baltimore for whatever part I played in the removal of Bible reading and praying from the public schools."[39] William became active in the religious right.

His mother, however, had not wavered. In a photograph from 1982 she can be seen picketing the White House, holding a sign with a quote from Charles Bradlaugh: "Liberty's chief foe is theology." But the now prayer-reciting, apostate son made O'Hair an even more convenient representative of atheism for most Americans, who continued to subscribe to one of the country's plethora of religious denominations.

According to those Gallup Surveys, in Denmark, the Netherlands, France, Sweden, Britain and West Germany the percentage of the population believing in life after death dropped some more by 1990 to somewhere between 29 and 44 percent—as would have been predicted by the grand narrative of religious decline.[40] Yet, in the United States—by some measures the most modern society on earth—70 percent continued to believe death is not the end. Surely this was not all because American hippies had spent the late sixties in the woods chanting, "Om."[41]

Could the explanation be that secularism in the second sense actually weakens secularism in the first sense? Separating church and state, some sociologists have argued, turns out to be a good thing for churches. Most European countries have or had a single "established" church—favored by the government. This led, so the theory goes, to a couple of negative consequences for religion: first, as with many government-protected enterprises, an established church—Catholic in France, Anglican in Britain—tends to grow fat and lazy; it tends to be taken for granted if not resented. Second, the development of other churches is hindered. The great theoretician of capitalism, Adam Smith, himself argued that religions that compete in a free marketplace would be more "vigorous."[42] And that is what seems to have happened: with "establishment of religion" prohibited in the Constitution, the United States has produced perhaps the most wide-open, free-market, free-for-all of formidable Christian churches—along with some synagogues, mosques, temples, ashrams and meditation centers—the world has ever seen.

This theory has its weaknesses:[43] Critics have noted, for example, that Poland, where the Catholic Church has long been established, remains relatively religious.[44] Critics have noted that Britain had gotten less religious in the twentieth century even though competition among religions has significantly increased. And critics have noted that the United States is partly a patchwork of areas dominated by one faith—Baptists in many counties down south, for example—and that pockets of intense religious fervor are often found in those more homogeneous areas, not where there is a great bazaar of competing alternatives.

But surely there is something to this theory that a healthy variety of religions can foster religiosity.[45] Consumers do seem to respond well to the opportunity to choose among multiple flavors of ice cream or varietals of red wine, and some of the various U.S. religions have indeed demonstrated entrepreneurial energy. They not only revive; they also innovate: drive-in churches, come-as-you-are services, cyber-prayer lists, etc.[46] In the large, open American market, some churches have, with great effectiveness, started their own radio and television programs, even their own cable networks; many (not just the Catholic Church) have founded their own educational institutions, even evangelical law schools.[47]

Immigration, of which America has been a major beneficiary, also fosters religiosity. Not only do immigrants bring religious traditions; a desire to preserve their ethnic identities in the melting pot often inspires them to hold even tighter to those religious traditions in the New World than they did back in the Old.[48]

The finding that people who worry about money tend to be more open to religion may also, according to the sociologists Pippa Norris and

Ronald Inglehard, help explain the higher religious participation in the United States.[49] There are more rich people in the United States than in European nations, but this country also has, of course, quite a large number of people who are poor. The poor are more likely to pray. And income inequality itself correlates with frequency of prayer in postindustrial societies—perhaps because of the pressure the relatively poor feel to keep up with their neighbors who are much richer. No major postindustrial society has more income inequality than the United States. It also lagged behind in creation of a welfare state, so, Norris and Inglehard suggest, its citizens, even if they currently have some money, have been more likely to worry about the economic consequences of getting sick or losing their jobs:[50] "Our Father, which art in heaven, please make sure my family. . . ." In Western Europe the state is more likely to make sure. And churches in the United States occasionally shoulder some of the burden of helping people out during hard times that the government shoulders on the other side of the Atlantic.

In the summer of 1995, Madalyn Murray O'Hair, now 76 years old and using a walker, disappeared.[51] Gone with her were her younger son, 41-year-old Jon Garth Murray, and her 30-year-old granddaughter, Robin Murray, daughter of O'Hair's elder, apostate son. The three had lived together and worked together on O'Hair's enterprises.

A colleague visited their home and discovered that they had left with their breakfasts unfinished. Jon Garth's Mercedes was sold by someone who did not resemble Jon Garth. Then the IRS reported that more than $600,000 was missing from the assets of American Atheists. Yet—and perhaps this was a testament to the public attitude toward atheists or the reputation of this particular family of atheists—the police seemed uninterested in the case. "Where's Madalyn O'Hair?" the Omaha World Herald smirked nine months after their disappearance. "It seems God only knows."[52] Only after a persistent reporter dug into the case did the truth begin to come out.[53]

On January 28, 2001, David Waters, a former employee of American Atheists who had been fired for stealing money, led investigators to a spot on a Texas ranch where they dug up the skulls of Jon Garth and Robin Murray and the skull and artificial hip of Madalyn Murray O'Hair. The evidence indicated that they had been kidnapped, forced to withdraw money, murdered and dismembered.[54] Waters had already served time in connection with a murder and with assaulting his mother. (O'Hair liked to hire ex-cons.)

After a legal battle, William Murray—the God-fearing and long-estranged son, brother and father of the victims—won control of their remains. He claimed that he did not give them the Christian funeral Madalyn so dreaded. "You cannot pray them out of hell," William was quoted as saying.[55]

Madalyn Murray O'Hair, of course, scoffed at hell, heaven and all that was associated with them. She fought with great vigor against religion, and she fought with great vigilance, and even some success, to keep government apart from religion. She crusaded, in other words, for both kinds of secularism. But to understand fully what happened to disbelief in the second half of the twentieth century and what is happening now it is necessary to introduce a third kind of secularism—one for which O'Hair did not fight.

THIS BREACH OF NAÏVETÉ

RELIGION UNREGARDED

The Sea of Faith
Was once, too, at the full, and round earth's shore
Lay like the folds of a bright girdle furled.
But now I only hear
Its melancholy, long, withdrawing roar,
Retreating, to the breath
Of the night-wind, down the vast edges drear
And naked shingles of the world

—Matthew Arnold, "Dover Beach"[1]

"DO YOU BELIEVE IN GOD?" A RESEARCHER ASKED SOMEONE in England in the late 1960s. "Yes," was the response. "Do you believe in a god who can change the course of events on earth?" that researcher then inquired. "No," the subject answered, "just the ordinary one."[2]

This response points to another possible end, or at least a pause, for the narrative of religious decline: God is not denied, rejected, dismissed or killed off; He is just diminished, deprived of consequence, made "ordinary." Most members of society, in this scenario, do not go so far as to become atheists; they just become *indifferent* to religion: "Yeah, I probably believe in god. So what?" In Britain, writes the sociologist Grace Davie, "widespread indifference . . . remains the norm."[3] Plenty of that has settled over the United States, too. There are signs here of a third kind of secularism[4]—in which religion isn't just separate from government but separate from most of what matters in our lives.

Let's take another look at post–World War II American religion—which has been given much of the responsibility for countering the narrative of religious decline worldwide. In 1952 the pastor of the Marble Collegiate Church in New York City wrote a book in which he attempted, as he later explained, to "describe . . . in the language and thought forms understandable to present day people" the "teachings of Jesus Christ." The book would be translated into 41 languages and has sold, to date, more than seven million copies. It was called *The Power of Positive Thinking.* The biblical "paths of righteousness," writes Dr. Norman Vincent Peale, include "paths of right-mindedness," and he presents some "practical steps" for getting our minds right. Here's one: "for the next twenty-four hours deliberately speak hopefully about everything."[5]

This certainly seems a different kind of Christianity from the one that had inspired adherents to flagellate themselves, practice celibacy or surrender worldly goods; a different kind of Christianity from the one that—in Jesus' words, according to Matthew—rewards with "everlasting life" those who have "left houses, or brothers and sisters or father or mother or wife or children or lands, for My name's sake."[6] Peale's Christianity is significantly more modest in its demands: "Put yourself in God's hands," he writes. "To do that simply state, 'I am in God's hands.'"[7] The result: "a happy, satisfying and worthwhile life," Peale explains—no detachment from "flourishing" required.[8]

Peale had predecessors and lots of followers in his efforts—bestselling efforts—to fashion God into more of a Heavenly Helpmate and religion into something that might provide salvation in *this* world.[9] Was this religion "lite"? It certainly appeared as if the God of the Gospels, in some such twentieth-century American versions of Christianity, had Himself been reduced to just another "shadow God"—a chummy champion of a feel-good, self-help psychology, with the anger and off-putting injunctions, the negativity, subtracted.

Many denominations were falling back on a less harsh, less demanding God in the second half of the twentieth century. In a large number of entrepreneurial American churches, as Steve Bruce, the sociologist, writes, "asceticism was out. Churchgoers no longer gave up smoking, drinking, dancing or going to the theater. They wore the same clothes as other people, lived in the same kinds of houses. . . . They got divorced." In 1951, 98 percent of evangelical young people in a survey had judged drinking alcohol sinful; in a survey of a similar group in 1982, only 17 percent thought it was "morally wrong." In 1951 almost all those young evangelicals had agreed that "social" dancing was "morally wrong all the time"; in 1982, none thought that it was wrong.[10] Some evangelical churches may have taken a well-publicized step back toward sterner beliefs and stricter morality in recent decades. Most probably haven't. Many probably have drifted, with considerably less publicity, in the opposite direction.

And among the great mass of non-evangelical but still-religious Americans moral strictures certainly seemed to be easing in other ways: premarital sex became the rule not the exception; out-of-wedlock births skyrocketed; the importance of "respectability"—of moral rectitude, traditionally defined—tumbled.[11] God in America may not have been dead, but he was less strict, less of a killjoy, more pleasant to have around—to the extent that He was even felt to be hanging around.

So while the readiness of Americans to profess religious belief may not have weakened, the religious beliefs that they were professing did weaken. It often wasn't necessary to commit as much, to inconvenience yourself as much, to fear as much. Americans, in fact, were becoming somewhat less likely to believe in hell—a non-feel-good concept if there ever was one. Christian Americans in the 1980s still believed in the divinity of Jesus Christ and in heaven, in more or less the same high percentages as in the early 1950s.[12] But, while in 1964, 65 percent in the United States believed the Bible to be "literally true," 20 years later, Gallup reported, only 37 percent did.[13]

"Orthodox Christians . . . are now content with the very smallest fragment of all that once they were positive was true," wrote Clarence Darrow, the lawyer who defended the right of John T. Scopes to teach evolution in Tennessee in 1925.[14] In the decades since Darrow's death, in 1938, that fragment has continued, in significant ways, to shrink.

Even the venerable, tradition-celebrating Catholic Church was loosening up. After the Second Vatican Council in the 1960s, it was, for example, okay in most places to eat meat on most Fridays. Meanwhile, a plurality of American Jews belonged to Reform congregations that did not require that they honor the traditional dietary laws or the strict prohibitions against doing work or even driving on the Sabbath.[15] And most new-age beliefs—as popular in the United States, particularly on the West Coast of the United States, as anywhere—are often even looser in their requirements.

Thus in the United States we have a situation in which people mouth all the right things, even sometimes join some community in some form of worship, perhaps congratulate themselves on some sort of relationship with some sort of god, but feel and believe significantly less than their grandparents might have.

Even on the seemingly straightforward question of church attendance the pollsters may be exaggerating our religiosity. When cars in parking lots or backsides in pews are actually counted, it becomes clear that Americans tend to exaggerate the frequency with which they actually show up in church or another place of worship. "Over-claiming" this is called. Studies have found claims of attendance in particular churches in particular communities in the United States that were 47 percent, 83 percent, 101 percent higher than actual attendance. And the evidence is that Americans are "over-claiming" more than they used to—thereby masking a decline in church attendance not nearly as steep as in Europe but still probably significant.[16] That certainly would be consistent with a growing religious *indifference.*

Overall, my point is, there is evidence that even in the United States the degree and content of religious belief declined in the late twentieth century.

This is not, of course, how most observers were seeing it. In the United States, the news was filled, at the end of the twentieth century, with tales of a strengthening religious right, trying, in particular, to roll back abortion rights and inject prayer, biblical morality and religious displays into various corners of American life—private and public. In a handful of towns and states, a "divine Creator" was trying to sneak back into biology classes. In many families a cousin here, a sister there returned to the faith. Talk of God was plentiful in the bookstores, on the airways (where He even appeared in prime time)[17] and, most definitely, in politics. And in the year 2000 the United States elected a president, George W. Bush, who had recommitted himself to Christianity and who gave it considerable credit for the success he had had in overcoming alcoholism and getting his life on track. Indeed, in those years the United States appeared to have undergone yet another of its periodic "Great Awakenings." Orthodox belief, at least as measured by clamor, seemed to have made a grand comeback.

Globally, the fall of Soviet Communism ended that long, inglorious experiment with state-sponsored atheism, and there were reports of churches in these countries being rebuilt, of church attendance there doing something it has not often done in recent centuries anywhere: increasing.

Meanwhile, conservative, even radical, forms of Islam had taken over two more countries: Iran and then Afghanistan. The novelist Salman Rushdie can be seen as the canary who had demonstrated the danger in that intrusion of a medieval, intolerant theocracy into the modern world. Rushdie, born into a Muslim family in India, had lost his religion early. "God, Satan, Paradise and Hell all vanished one day in my fifteenth year, when I quite abruptly lost my faith," Rushdie has explained. "Afterwards, to prove my new-found atheism, I bought myself a rather tasteless ham sandwich."[18]

In 1988, Rushdie published a novel, *The Satanic Verses,* that spoke with some levity about the communication between the angel Gabriel and Muhammad. The next year Ayatollah Ruhollah Khomeini of Iran issued a *fatwā* calling for the execution of Rushdie and those associated with the publication and sale of the book. Its Norwegian publisher was shot three times but recovered. The Japanese translator of *The Satanic Verses* was stabbed to death in his office. Rushdie himself lived in hiding, with armed guards, for a decade.

And then, in what seemed conclusive proof of the power of ancient faiths to impact upon the modern world, two large airliners knifed into the World Trade Center buildings in New York City. Those planes had been hijacked by men who had spent considerable time in the West. Yet, the 19 men on the total of four hijacked planes that day and their masters back in Afghanistan were not at all indifferent about religion. They had chosen—in what certainly appeared to be the ancient, naïve tradition—to sacrifice thousands of civilian lives and all possibility of their own "flourishing" in this world to a belief, perverse and malevolent most would call it, in a warrior god and another world. They appeared to be secular in no sense. At the beginning of the twentieth century, New York City—a center of modernity—had been thrust into the middle of an Islamic holy war.

In 2006, President George W. Bush explained that he based "a lot" of his "foreign-policy decisions," which included the decision to go to war in Afghanistan and Iraq, upon his belief in the "Almighty" and His "great gifts."[19]

"Atheism is . . . the spiritual drama of our time," Pope John Paul II had stated, with appropriate chagrin, in 1980.[20] Had that changed by the first decade of twenty-first century? In the decades after the pope spoke did the spiritual drama of the time become religion's resurgence?

Consider—for this history has finally arrived at our own time—an early-twenty-first-century, middle-class life—European or American: Our subject, born into some ancient faith, enjoyed its rituals, its profundities, its certainties. But doubts arose. At university, politics—a desire to right wrongs here, now—beckoned. After graduation, the attractions were a job, maybe a love. Our subject, not done with searching for something, decided it was wrong to eat meat. Then a class in yoga—attended with impressive regularity—led to some instruction in meditation, which proved calming for a time. A book by one or another long-bearded guru even appeared on the night table. Parenthood revived thoughts of that ancestral religion, but only (the other parent having had different ancestors) thoughts. Perhaps our subject happened upon an argument for atheism: they have been growing increasingly easy to find. Perhaps, as the years passed, some more traditional religious notions seeped back; they often do.

This is not a secular life in the first sense. Religions, of various sorts, appear frequently enough in it. But what is remarkable about this life—and characteristic of many lives in the West today—is the ease with which religions tiptoe in and out. That is one cause of this new kind of secularism.

There have been cultures in which practicing a particular religion was so thoroughly entwined with being a member of a society that there was no word for religion. There have been times when a person's relationship with authority, a person's standing in a community and a person's shot at eternal salvation all hinged on the intensity of commitment to one religion. That is not how it generally is in Europe, North America, much of Asia and many other parts of the world today.

Now we have, and cherish, pluralism. One of the most newsworthy results of a large survey of attitudes on religion in the United States conducted by the Pew Forum on Religion in Public Life in 2007, was that only about a quarter of Americans believe that their "religion is the one, true faith leading to eternal life."[21] Indeed, according to a Pew survey the next year, "about half of American adults have changed religious affiliation at least once during their lives."[22] Now there are many possible faiths—all tolerated, all valued, all there to be selected or rejected should the inspiration arrive; none looking all that inescapably true. It grows harder to avoid wondering about each of their claims.

And alternatives to religion are also available to provide fellowship and purpose, alternatives that extend well beyond a Charles Bradlaugh–like crusading atheism: we can define ourselves and our moral position by choosing to become, for example, environmentalists, libertarians, social activists or epicureans, in the modern usage of that term—devoted with exceptional fervor and discrimination to food, wine and other aspects of our own "flourishing." We can express our ethical concerns through vegetarianism, animal rights or completing a five-kilometer run to raise money to combat some illness. Now "even for the staunchest believer," as the philosopher Charles Taylor explains, "faith" has become "one human possibility among others."[23]

A religion that is merely *an* alternative, the point is, is different from a religion that is the *only* alternative. Do we believe as fully knowing there are many other possible beliefs or ways of being engaged—a few of which we might ourselves have tried out? It certainly requires exemplary focus and enthusiasm to believe as fully when a few years ago you fully believed in something else. The discussion of heresies and the Reformation in the third chapter of this book noted how "contestation" among religions tends to encourage skepticism and weaken the hold of religions. Today such contestation has grown exponentially and the pathogen of relativism it releases has become epidemic.

"When the oracle speaks with a single clear voice," sociologist Steve Bruce explains, "it is easy to believe it is the voice of God. When it speaks with twenty different voices, it is tempting to look behind the screen."[24] It is tempting, in other words, to ask *how can that be?* As a result of the multiplicity of contemporary beliefs, it has become difficult for us not to see that whatever way of looking at the universe we may adopt at the moment is only one of many possible ways of looking at the universe. We, large numbers of us, must live with what Taylor calls: "this breach of naïveté." An old-fashioned, one-truth "naïveté" is, this philosopher contends, "now unavailable to anyone, believer or unbeliever alike."[25]

Taylor pronounces this "a titanic change in our Western civilization." Obviously, as he notes, it does not affect all the "societies, sub-societies and milieux" that make up "modern civilization." Plenty still spend their lives believing deeply and desperately in one faith. But "this breach of naïveté"—an inability to be entirely carried away by a religion or any other philosophy—is, Taylor argues, affecting "more and more of" our "societies, sub-societies and milieux." This, Taylor writes, is "secularity three"[26]—that third variety of secularism.

One of the problems with presenting the conflicts recounted in this book as struggles between nonbelievers and their antagonists is that it is thereby possible to ignore the internal struggles that rage between the nonbeliever and believer inside individual minds.[27] Once those internal struggles had to be kept quiet. In most parts of the world that is no longer required. Once those struggles were mostly binary: faith—a single faith—struggled to overcome doubt. Now they can be fought on multiple fronts between multiple forces. Inside the mind of John Lennon, for example.

Lennon's mother, who did not raise him, was killed by a car when he was just 17, and Lennon attempted to contact her by organizing a séance with his friends.[28] That was only the beginning of his flirtation with the supernatural. In his too short, too famous, often avant-garde adulthood, Lennon experimented with varieties of beliefs (some drug inspired). They ranged from a well-publicized stay in India (along with the rest of the Beatles) with the Maharishi Mahesh Yogi, a popularizer of Hindu meditation; to a brief fascination with extraterrestrials; to a Druid-style ceremony of his "remarriage" to Yoko Ono.[29] He wrote a song about karma (of a particularly fast-acting variety) and a song that included the Hindu mantra, "Om."

Yet, Lennon inspired some Americans to smash Beatles' records by predicting, in a 1966 interview, that "Christianity will go. It will vanish and shrink."[30] He wrote an insistent "I don't believe . . ." song, which announced his disbelief in "magic," "mantra," "Bible" and "Jesus" as well as "Beatles," and which included this intriguing, Karl Marx-like line: "God is a concept by which we measure our pain."[31] John Lennon also wrote one of the better irreligious stanzas of all time, suggesting that we "imagine there's no Heaven . . . above us only sky."[32]

Nonetheless, Lennon still upon occasion imagined he might experience life after death and might then communicate with those still mired in life before death. "He said if anything happened to him," Lennon's son Julian recounts, "he'd send a sign back to say he was okay. He said he'd make a feather float down the room."[33] (Julian, at last report, was still looking for such a feather.) John Lennon remained intermittently susceptible to beliefs many of the heroes of this book might dismiss as poppycock.

Secularism in the second sense gave John Lennon the freedom to experiment with a variety of possible convictions: dressing up as a guru one month, a "working-class hero" the next. Secularism in the first sense filled the culture with particles of anti-belief—always threatening to collide with and annihilate those convictions. The half-life of Lennon's beliefs, consequently, was short. And Lennon believed and disbelieved with irony mostly intact. He seemed never, through his various permutations, to have entirely lost that "nothing is real" (to use his phrase) awareness of "sharing a joke with nothingness" (to use Virginia Woolf's). He seemed never to have entirely lost an alertness to the "comedy of existence" (Nietzsche's phrase). With all these potential beliefs and unbeliefs warring inside of him, Lennon seemed never to display, in Taylor's formulation, all that much naïveté.

When we believe, it has become difficult not to feel as if we're in a play (to borrow a phrase from a verse Paul McCartney says Lennon helped him write).[34] This self-conscious feeling of making believe, as we try on for the moment one of the numerous varieties of spiritualism or anti-spiritualism—this inability to give ourselves fully, naïvely, to a religion—is one of the factors that has left so many in the first decades of the twentieth century with indifferent, undemanding, "ordinary," watered-down, half-hearted, for-the-moment, I-guess, beliefs. These are beliefs that are difficult to distinguish from disbelief. They are characteristic of this third variety of secularity.

This book has tried to demonstrate that atheism helped create the modern world. But, once again, it has worked the other way, too: modernity—with its self-consciousness, relativism, cynicism and possibility; modernity—with its affronts to naïveté; has furthered if not full-blown atheism than at least a profound weakening of religious belief. Disbelief and progress—or "progress"—have once again formed a virtuous cycle.

Despite the clamor caused by various forms of fundamentalism at the start of the twenty-first century, traditional, orthodox religion was, if anything, in retreat. There was political pressure in the name of religion; there was terrorism in the name of religion; but the evidence indicates that there was no religious resurgence—globally or in the United States.

Indeed, listen for a moment to the true believers who were imposing their sometimes-violent dramas upon us and it becomes clear that they were haunted by a fear of the idea that there is no God. The events of September 11, 2001, were, in Osama bin Laden's ugly words, "blessed strikes against world atheism and its leader, America." He speaks of a world "split . . . into two camps: the camp of belief and the camp of disbelief."[35] It is not necessary to accept bin Laden's ravings on who is in what camp, let alone his method of conducting the struggle, to suspect that some version of this split remains, to recall the pained conclusion of Pope John Paul II, the "spiritual drama of our time." In the twenty-first century, many orthodox believers fear if not the rise of outright atheism than at least a profound weakening in the reach and hold of religion.

As well they might. Outright atheism remains the exception, but it is on the rise: Worldwide the number of "convinced atheists" was up to 13 percent in 2012, according to a WIN-Gallup International poll that year.[36] And a less firm withdrawal from religion is much more common and is also increasing. Globally the percentage of individuals describing themselves as "a religious person" dropped from 77 to 68 percent from 2005 to 2012. That seems, for such a short period of time, a sharp drop.

And religious belief is strongest among the poor and uneducated. If the world's population continues to get better off and more educated, that should speed up the decline in religion. The young are also less likely to be religious than the old.[37] Already in China (where religion continues to face government restrictions), Japan, the Czech Republic, Turkey, Sweden, Vietnam, Australia, France, Hong Kong, Austria, Netherlands, Azerbaijan, Canada and Ireland less than half that poll's respondents described themselves as "religious." "In Britain, according to a poll last year," the New York Times reported in 2013, "more people believe in extraterrestrials than in God."[38]

And, as the new century progressed, there were signs, as well, that the religious right was slipping in the United States—on issues such as gay rights, as I'll note in the epilogue, but also in political heft nationwide. There were signs that the country was becoming measurably less religious. The percentage of hard-line nonbelievers in the United States remains small: only 5 percent of Americans were willing to declare themselves atheists in 2012, according to that WIN-Gallup poll. However, that's 4 percent more than were willing to accept that designation in the United States seven years earlier. And, even with our increasingly attenuated and undemanding versions of religion, the percentage of Americans calling themselves religious dropped sharply in those years: from 73 percent in 2005 to 60 percent in the 2012 poll.[39]

Here's a similar number from another, earlier survey: 56 percent of American adults, according to that Pew survey in 2007, said that religion is very important in their lives.[40] For America—held up as the great counterexample to the narrative of religious decline—that does not seem such an impressive number—especially since the indications are that it is shrinking.

And a flurry of books promoting atheism even ascended the bestseller lists in the U.S. in George W. Bush's last term as president. They included *The End of Faith* (2004) by Sam Harris, *The God Delusion* (2006) by Richard Dawkins and *God Is Not Great* (2007) by Christopher Hitchens. Those books, unlike the one you are currently reading, are not histories of atheism. (Few of the individuals celebrated here are mentioned there.) Instead, those books are powerful arguments against religion. Dawkins, as Baron d'Holbach did, deploys science against religion; this renowned evolutionary biologist is particularly scathing on the argument for "intelligent design." Hitchens disputes religion's historical and moral claims, as Jean Meslier did. As Charles Bradlaugh and Ernestine Rose often did, Harris underlines the connections among various contemporary outrages and religions, particularly Islam (not the main target of those eighteenth- and nineteenth-century Europeans).

These early twenty-first-century authors, in other words, "durst . . . speak" astoundingly "boldly." Their books were written under their real names and published while they were still alive. Their atheism wore no veils. And the books—often surprising, I suspect, even their publishers— sold extremely well *in the United States.*

I first contemplated writing a history of atheism and its accomplishments a couple of decades ago. I was distracted then by other projects. But I must admit I considered at that time what the reaction to such a book might be. Should I fear protests? Would I be invited to promote the book on the air? Now, in the United States in the second decade of the twenty-first century, such fears seem quaint.

Harris, Dawkins and Hitchens were writing in part in response to all the noise or trouble being caused by religious fundamentalists at the beginning of this century. But, my point is, that noise and trouble were themselves a reaction. Indeed, it no longer looks as if we were undergoing another "Great Awakening." Instead it appears we were witnessing in the United States and around the world a reaction by increasingly impotent and outnumbered orthodox groups to a growing secularization—or, at least, a growing loss of religious naïveté or a growing indifference to religion. (Perhaps that's what "Great Awakenings" have always been: reactions, as the world continues to shed its staunchest religious beliefs.)

Religion's defenders—along with those postmodern critics of the narrative of religious decline—rebel against any notion of inevitability here, but isn't what is happening becoming clear?

Denounce enough aspects of God; excise most of the otherworldliness from religion; make a life of faith into something that increasingly resembles just a life; see the world as offering a variety of possible belief systems; feel as if you're in a play as you move from one to the other; lose enough naïveté; and isn't this where you end up: with religion watered down to the point where it blends into no religion?

Educate a society; make it more comfortable; saturate it with irony; overwhelm it with entertainments; make available therapists and anti-depressants; and maybe the result isn't so much lots of Charles Bradlaughs but lots of people who often have better things to do with their Sundays (no matter what they tell the pollsters), who have more effective salves for their hurts, who have more interesting subjects for their thoughts than that "ordinary God." The question of whether He or She or It is or isn't is no longer *the* question, just *a* question (surprisingly rarely brought up in conversation in my experience).

An "ordinary God" does not often inspire, insist or interfere. It is Itself mostly indifferent to us and our behaviors—in the manner of Epicurus' too-perfect-to-care Gods. We realize It isn't likely to present us with *an* answer. We realize It isn't likely to disturb us with anything, as John Lennon puts it, "to kill or die for." Go to church, as many in the United States still do. Steer clear of church, as is increasingly the fashion in Europe. Whatever. Do someone a good turn or go have some fun. Suit yourself. Maybe this "ordinary God" supplies a hint of purpose, meaning or guilt upon occasion, maybe It comes through with a little reassurance or hope when things look grim. Or maybe even this is too much to ask of It. For many in the twenty-first century, God just floats somewhere: wan, vaporous, barely alive—Freud's "insubstantial shadow," no longer deserving of that once awe-inspiring, once terrifying old name.

This God, the indifferent God of the indifferent, no-longer-naïve believer, presides over, the argument goes, this era of the third secularism—both in Europe, where It is no longer much discussed, and even to a large extent in the United States, where Its name often still comes up. Secularism, in this third sense, is a condition in which religion matters less and less.

Two hundred years ago, Shelley predicted something along these lines: he saw religion not being "o'erthrown" but simply becoming "unregarded." Most of Shelley's fellow crusading nonbelievers—the stars of this book—dreamt instead of an overthrowing. But, if for many Americans and many more elsewhere around the world religion is now more or less "unregarded," that is a substantial accomplishment for disbelief—this great breacher of naïveté.

Charles Bradlaugh was one crusading nonbeliever who more or less agreed with Shelley. "No religion is suddenly rejected by any people," he once cautioned; "it is rather gradually outgrown. None see a religion die; dead religions are like dead languages and obsolete customs: the decay is long and—like the glacier march—is perceptible only to the careful watcher by comparisons extending over long periods."[41] Not everywhere, of course, but at least in certain "societies, sub-societies and milieux," we may be watching such a slow death—not just of a religion but of religion.

The process of weaning ourselves from gods—and shadows of gods—is far from complete. It may never entirely be completed. And we are still—often enough—prone to foolishnesses, unskilled at joy, resistant to truths, late in recognizing rights and fearful of open seas. But, oh what a start we have made!

EPILOGUE

ABOVE US ONLY SKY

The ability to think has proved itself oppugnant to and destructive of the reckless desire to worship.

—Charles Bradlaugh[1]

N A LITTLE TRIANGLE OF GRASS ON NORTHAMPTON'S ABINGTON Street, shortly after it ceases to be the town's main street, that seven-and-half-foot-tall white, terracotta likeness of Charles Bradlaugh stands atop its pedestal. And Bradlaugh is not the only nonbeliever to be similarly, as it were, immortalized.

The church where Jean Meslier preached—or did his best not to preach—still exists in Etrépigny, a tiny town in northeastern France. But Meslier would have been pleased to learn that it is now used only for weddings and funerals. And the quiet, grassy traffic circle in front of the church has been renamed: a few plaques announce that it is now "Place Jean Meslier." Meslier also has his name inscribed upon that Soviet obelisk.

A statue of Denis Diderot stands in the Place Saint Germain des Prés in Paris, and President François Hollande, a man of the left, announced that he would move Diderot's body—symbolically; the exact whereabouts of his bones is unclear—to the Panthéon on the occasion of his three-hundredth birthday in 2013.[2] Baron d'Holbach's old mansion—site of his salon—still graces the Rue Royale in Paris, but the baron's bones, too, have been lost within a local church.[3] A white-marble likeness of Percy Bysshe Shelley as his body was found in Italy—nude and drowned—lies atop a plinth in the Oxford college from which he was expelled.

No monument was erected honoring Ernestine Rose, but a bronze, life-sized statue of Robert Green Ingersoll, who picked a more congenial time to be a freethinker in the United States, was unveiled in his birthplace, Peoria, Illinois, in 1911. Clarence Darrow, born 24 years after Ingersoll, has a bridge named after him in Chicago. Madalyn Murray O'Hair picked a much worse time to espouse disbelief in the United States and may have done a less stellar job of it. She, of course, was not accorded any such honor—even the place where her remains were deposited has remained her son William's secret. Religion would have to suffer a worse fate than being "unregarded" before O'Hair earns a statue. (By then we might consider monuments to martyrs like Giulio Cesare Vanini and Thomas Aikenhead, too.)

The Bradlaugh statue depicts him with a stern look and with his right arm and index finger extended, as if, with characteristic intensity, making a point. Once Bradlaugh's points riled up Northampton and dozens of other towns. However, when the author of this book made a pilgrimage to this statue on a spring afternoon some years ago, he noticed that, as happens with aging monuments, no one was paying it any mind.

Down the road to the statue's right stood a "Jesus Center"—an example of one of the more entrepreneurial of Britain's potpourri of struggling churches. To Bradlaugh's left, the Urban Tiger Gentleman's Club advertised "Stockings and Suspenders Night." A young man with spiked hair sipped at a can of beer as he walked by. A woman in a maroon burqa pushed a pram in front of the statue. The newsagent directly to Bradlaugh's right sold African and Caribbean newspapers, football and skin magazines, but no secularist publications of the sort to which Bradlaugh contributed.

Perhaps such publications are no longer as needed. Perhaps much of their work has been done. Things may not have changed all that much inside a Jesus Center or under a burqa. However, elsewhere in Northampton, in Britain, in Europe, in much of Asia, even in the United States, God has survived these centuries of attack only by becoming more mutable, more abstract, more amorphous, less judgmental and, therefore, less consequential. As a result, most of the battles fought by Bradlaugh, Meslier, Diderot, d'Holbach, Shelley, Rose, O'Hair and the others have been won.

Fundamentalists once were able to keep scientific explanations out of schools in the United States. Now they must content themselves with trying to sneak biblical interpretations into schools, and still they often fail. On December 20, 2005, for example, Judge John E. Jones, a Republican, ruled that the requirement instituted by the school board in Dover, Pennsylvania, that teachers read a statement presenting "intelligent design" as an alternative to evolution was unconstitutional and characterized by "breathtaking inanity."[4] Our scientists, now overwhelmingly nonreligious, can say what they like about the heavens or anything else. And science, once brought to a halt in the West by religion, now brings surprising new knowledge and remarkable new devices into being at a rapid pace.

European colonialism, which had often been justified as a way to spread Christianity, began to disappear from its last strongholds in Asia, Africa, the Middle East and the Caribbean in the middle of the twentieth century.

The burqa has made a comeback among some Muslim women. Hasidic Jews still often segregate and restrict women, but in most other cultures women's freedoms have expanded well beyond those allowed by ancient holy books. Biblical morality continues to animate one side in the battle over abortion in the United States and has reduced women's access to abortion in some states, but abortion is now legal in the United States, in all of Europe except Ireland, and in most of the world. Despite the pronouncements of the Gospels, divorce is permitted in an increasing number of countries. Europe and the United States are finally confronting their prejudices against gay, lesbian and transsexual people; in the West they rarely have to worry any more about legal prosecution, let alone the biblical insistence that they be "put to death."[5] The task now is making sure they will be accorded *all* the same rights as others.

Religious stories, as Salman Rushdie put it near the end of his decade in hiding, had "come to feel inescapable, not in the way that the truth is inescapable, but in the way that a jail is."[6] Those stories are still being accorded more respect than a Sam Harris, a Richard Dawkins or a Christopher Hitchens might consider appropriate, but they are more and more being escaped.

Religious differences can still explode in violence. In 2002, Rushdie analyzed one such incident: the death of hundreds of people in Gujarat, India, when mobs of angry Hindus attacked Muslims, after some Muslims had reportedly attacked some Hindus. "What happened in India has happened in God's name," Rushdie concluded. "The problem's name is God."[7] Nonetheless, in numerous countries and even some continents today, that "problem" has faded, and religion, in this new wispier incarnation, no longer inspires killings or starts wars.

Blasphemy remains a crime in parts of the Muslim world and elsewhere: those who criticize religion can be thrown in jail or even threatened with death. But that, too, is true in fewer and fewer places. When an earthquake, tsunami, hurricane, terrorist attack, fire or plague destroys lives, some still see signs of heavenly retribution. But they are in the minority and are often mocked. Our thinkers, for the most part, are free to think. Our artists, for the most part, are free to challenge conventions and set out for parts unknown.

In Northampton, in Britain, in Europe, in much of Asia, even in the United States, the point is, we can study, we can investigate, we can propose, we can experiment we can challenge, we can imagine, we can push ahead with the difficult, invigorating work of creating the modern world, without worrying about offending the followers of a supernatural Being or contravening some line in their holy texts. And we owe this freedom, in part, to Bradlaugh, Meslier, Diderot, d'Holbach, Shelley, Rose, O'Hair and the others; we owe it, in part, to our skepticism, to our inclination toward the anacreontic, to our pursuit of natural explanations; we owe it, in part, to atheism.

Liberty and learning continue to experience some setbacks. The development and spread of the idea that we live without gods (or God) is hardly the only explanation for their erratic but evident growth. However, it is a significant explanation.

Charles Bradlaugh's finger, as he stands atop that pedestal in Northampton, is pointing into the void in front of him.

Humankind is still accustoming itself to facing that void. That may not be an issue for the woman in the burqa pushing her pram in front of Bradlaugh's statue. But it may very well weigh upon that young man with spiked hair sipping a beer and upon some of the patrons and performers at the Urban Tiger Gentleman's Club.

Religion, where it has faded, is surely sometimes missed. That can be seen in the peripatetic journeys from one belief system to another many still undertake. We continue to dream, some of us, that we might come upon a revelation, preferably timeless and otherworldly, that might bestow some order upon our messy existences.

But increasingly that is all it is: a dream. We live, more and more of us, in *this* world on *this* day. We understand that our lives are flawed. We sense that our purposes are provisional, homemade. We recognize that we are mortal. We content ourselves, as we try to work things out, with the "plausible." These have been hugely productive realizations. But surrendering, in this sense at least, our naïveté has not been easy.

We still have plenty of thinking to do if we are to live comfortably without Yahweh, God the Father, the Holy Trinity, Allah, Brahma, the Supreme Being or the First Cause—and without an afterlife. This is thinking that began with *Gilgamesh,* with the Cārvāka, with Thucydides. But it remains incomplete.

We are, I would argue, still learning to dance without a caller, to play without someone keeping score. We will need to revisit and then revisit again the question of how humankind might best live together—not "under God," or sheltered by one or another shadow god, but looking up, in John Lennon's words, to "only sky."

We have, similarly, just begun to tackle the question of how to find meaning without relying upon some external dispenser of meaning. Albert Camus, in my view, contributed some insights, into how, "in the universe . . . restored to its silence," we still might enjoy "the myriad wondering little voices of the earth" and still experience a full range of "the passions of this earth." Others have contributed insights, too. Nonetheless, this remains, perhaps, the question of our time.

Still, let's not underestimate how far we have come. An increasing number of men and women around the world now can think things through and work out their obligations to their fellow humans and to the planet without having to worry about the diktats of some ancient, jealous, vengeful god. They can, restrained only by their biological and social circumstances, create their own lives.

Salman Rushdie has earned the right to the last word. "Imagine there's no heaven," Rushdie writes, "and at once the sky's the limit."[8]

NOTES

OPENING EPIGRAPH

1. "Montaigne; or *The Skeptic*," in Ralph Waldo Emerson, *Selections*, ed. Stephen E. Whicher (Boston: Houghton Mifflin, 1960), 288-89.

PROLOGUE: EVERYTHING MUST BE EXAMINED

1. Albert Camus, *The Myth of Sisyphus, and Other Essays*, trans. Justin O'Brien (New York: Random House, 1983), 87.
2. This account is based on that in Lester G. Crocker, *The Embattled Philosopher: A Biography of Denis Diderot* (London: Spearman, 1955), 48-53.
3. Ibid., 76-91.
4. Quoted in ibid., 50.
5. Alan Charles Kors, *D'Holbach's Coterie: An Enlightenment in Paris* (Princeton, NJ: Princeton University Press, 1976), 14.
6. Denis Diderot, *Political Writings*, ed. John Hope Mason and Robert Wokler (Cambridge: Cambridge University Press, 2001), 25.
7. Peter Gay, *The Enlightenment: An Interpretation: The Rise of Modern Paganism* (New York: Norton, 1977), 142. For the thinly veiled puncturings of religion in the *Encyclopédie*, see Robert Darnton, *The Business of Enlightenment: A Publishing History of the Encyclopédie* (Cambridge, MA: Harvard University Press, 1979), 7-8.
8. Quoted in Gay, *The Enlightenment*, 399.

CHAPTER 1: HOW CAN THAT BE?

1. Denis Diderot, "Thoughts on Religion," in *Faith in Faithlessness: An Anthology of Atheism*, ed. Dimitrios Roussopoulos (Montreal: Black Rose Books, 2008), 8.
2. The account here is based on that in A. B. Drachmann, *Atheism in Pagan Antiquity* (London: Kessenger Publishing, 1922, reprinted 2003), 31-34; Jonathan Barnes, *The Presocratic Philosophers* (London: Routledge & Kegan Paul, 1979), 151-53.
3. Drachmann, *Atheism in Pagan Antiquity*, 5; see R. Bracht Branham and Marie-Odile Goulet-Cazé, *The Cynics* (Berkeley: University of California Press, 1996), 54.
4. *Chāndogya Upaniṣad,* an early Indian religious text thought to date back to somewhere between the seventh and fifth centuries BCE, does contain an intriguing discussion of a group with distinct irreligious habits: "the followers of Asura are said to be the ones who never give away anything, have no faith and never perform any sacrifice"; quoted in Debiprasad Chattopadhyaya, ed. *Carvaka/Lokayata: An Anthology of Source Materials and Some Recent Studies* (New Delhi: Indian Council of Philosophical Research), 1990, 3-6; see also K. P. Bahadur, *The Wisdom of the Upanishads* (New Delhi: Sterling Publishers Private Limited, 1989), 134-36; Patrick Olivelle, *Upanishads* (Oxford: Oxford University Press, 1998), 171-74; Sarvepalli Radhakrishnan, *The Principal Upanishads* (London: Unwin Hyman, 1989), 501-6. For a discussion of dating, see Olivelle, *Upanishads*, xxxvi.
5. *Sāmaññphala Sutta;* in Chattopadhyaya, *Carvaka/Lokayata*, 48. For dates see Debiprasad Chattopadhyaya, *Lokayata: A Study in Ancient Indian Materialism* (New Delhi: People's Publishing House, 1959), 510-12.

6. Heinz Bechert, ed. *When Did the Buddha Live? The Controversy on the Dating of the Historical Buddha* (Delhi: Sri Satguru, 1995), 262; George Erdosy, "The Archaeology of Early Buddhism," in *Studies on Buddhism in Honour of Professor A. K. Warder,* ed. N. K. Wagle and F. Watanabe (Toronto: University of Toronto, Center for South Asian Studies, 1993), 40-56. See Jennifer Michael Hecht, *Doubt: A History* (San Francisco: Harper San Francisco, 2003), 94-101.

7. The *Brhaspati-sūtra* and the *Lokāyata-Śāstra;* P. T. Raju, *The Philosophical Traditions of India* (Pittsburgh: University of Pittsburgh Press, 1972), 86; Dakshina Ranjan Shastri, *Charvaka Philosophy* (Calcutta: Purogami Prakasani, 1967), 13; Chattopadhyaya, *Carvaka/Lokayata,* 73; G. Tucci, "A Sketch of Indian Materialism," in *Proceedings of the First Indian Philosophical Congress,* ed. Satischandra Chatterjee (Calcutta, 1927), 36.

8. *Sarva-siddhāntā-samgraha;* in Sarvepalli Radhakrishnan and Charles A. Moore, *A Source Book in Indian Philosophy* (Princeton, NJ: Princeton University Press, 1957), 234. For date, see Chattopadhyaya, *Carvaka/Lokayata,* 380.

9. This is from an eleventh-century-CE allegorical drama. Krsnamisra's *Prabodhacandrodaya;* in Radhakrishnan and Moore, *Source Book in Indian Philosophy,* 247. For other, less pretty, if more literal, translations, see Sita Krishna Nambiar, *Probodhacandrodaya of Krishna Mishra* (Delhi: University of Delhi, 1971), 39-47; and Chattopadhyaya, *Carvaka/ Lokayata,* 344-48.

10. *Sarva-siddhāntā-samgraha,* in Radhakrishnan and Moore, *Source Book in Indian Philosophy,* 235.

11. "It is only a people of ripe civilization who develop scepticism," insisted the renowned historian James Henry Breasted a century ago, in *Development and Thought in Ancient Egypt* (New York: Harper & Row, 1959), 181. Breasted speaks for many historians and anthropologists, then and now. Oxford historian and theologian Alister McGrath maintains in a recent book that the "rise" and "decline" of atheism can be "framed by two pivotal events": "the fall of the Bastille in 1789 and that of the Berlin Wall in 1989"; Alister E. McGrath, *Twilight of Atheism* (New York: Doubleday, 2006), xii, 1. Statements by Lucien Febvre and John Stuart Mill on the impossibility of atheism in earlier and less developed societies are quoted and disputed in chapter 4.

12. John Martin, *An Account of the Natives of the Tonga Islands,* 2 vols. (Edinburgh: Constable, 1827).

13. John Martin, *Account of the Natives of the Tonga Islands,* vol. I, 307n-308n; 338-39; vol. II, 27, 129, 134. See also J. M. Robertson, *A History of Freethought in the Nineteenth Century,* vol. I (London: Dawsons, 1969), 47.

14. Viktor Lebzelter, *Native Cultures in Southwest and South Africa,* vol. 2 (Leipzig: Hiersemann, 1934), 42.

15. A. B. Ellis, *The Tshe-Speaking Peoples of the Gold Coast of West Africa* (Chicago: Benin Press, 1964), 137.

16. See Mitchell Stephens, *The Rise and Fall of the Image the Fall of the Word* (New York: Oxford University Press, 1998), 51-57.

17. Martin, *Account of the Natives of the Tonga Islands,* vol. I, 105, 288-96, 306, 307n-8n; 338-39; vol. II, 27, 129, 134; Robertson, *History of Freethought,* vol. I, 47. The surmise on poisoning is Robertson's, based on Mariner's more circumspect report.

18. Weston La Barre, *The Ghost Dance: Origins of Religion* (London: Allen and Unwin, 1972), 69; Scott Atran, *In Gods We Trust* (Oxford: Oxford University Press, 2002), 4, 13.

19. Charles Bradlaugh: "I mean by religion every form of belief which accepts or asserts the supernatural"; *Humanity's Gain from Unbelief* (London: Freethought Publishing, 1889), 3. This definition might exclude some forms of Buddhism or other Indian religions. Steve Bruce manages to include the notion of *karma* by adding, "or impersonal powers or processes possessed of moral purpose . . . which can set the conditions of, or intervene in, human affairs"; *God Is Dead: Secularization in the West* (Oxford: Blackwell, 2002), 2. Jacques Derrida notes that the word "religion," of Latin origin, is without cognate in other early Indo-European languages, raising the question of whether it is appropriate to extract the term from its Roman and European context and apply it to the spiritual practices of societies that may have a less institutional and less self-conscious view of their forms of worship or spirituality; *Acts of Religion,* ed. Gil Anidjar (New York: Routledge, 2002), 71-73.

20. Roy Franklin Barton, *The Religion of the Ifugao* (Menosha, WI: American Anthropological Association, 1946), 169-85.

21. Pascal Boyer, *Religion Explained: The Evolutionary Origins of Religious Thought* (New York: Basic Books/Harper Collins, 2001), 210-11.

22. Pascal Boyer, *Religion Explained*, 20-21. See also James Thrower, *The Alternative Tradition: Religion and the Rejection of Religion in the Ancient World* (The Hague: Walter de Gruyter, 1980), 139.

23. Pascal Boyer, *Religion Explained*, 10-18. "The metaphysical need is not the origin of religions . . . but merely a late offshoot"; Friedrich Nietzsche, *Gay Science* (New York: Vintage Books, 1974), 196.

24. B. F. Skinner, "'Superstition' In The Pigeon," *Journal of Experimental Psychology*, 38 (1948): 168-72. Skinner's attempts to explain most human behavior as the result of stimulus-response programming have been discredited, but his experiments are still of interest.

25. Thomas Hobbes saw this explanation for religion more than 300 years before it became fashionable: humans, he writes, "are very apt . . . to take casual things, after one or two encounters, for prognostics of the like encounter ever after"; *Leviathan; Or, The Matter, Form, and Power of a Commonwealth Ecclesiastical and Civil* (London: Routledge, 1885), 56-58, 61.

26. Ralph Waldo Emerson: "We are born believing. A man bears beliefs as a tree bears apples"; cited George Kateb, *Emerson and Self-Reliance* (Lanham, MD: Rowman and Littlefield, 2002), 91.

27. This raises the question of whether disbelievers are, hence, not evolutionarily successful. The answer would have to be either that they are sufficiently brilliant to overcome their biology or, more humbly, that the impulse to believe, while there in all of us, is not that difficult to overcome, just as we manage, most of us, to overcome the impulse to procreate continually. See David Martin, "Does the Advance of Science Mean Secularisation?," a lecture at Emmanuel College, Cambridge, November 3, 2005, http://www.st-edmunds.cam.ac.uk/faraday/CIS/martin/David%20Martin%20-%20lecture.htm.

28. See Atran, *In Gods We Trust;* Boyer, *Religion Explained;* Daniel C. Dennett, *Breaking the Spell: Religion as a Natural Phenomenon* (New York: Viking Penguin, 2006).

29. John Stuart Mill, too, sees something like this at the bottom of religion. *Three Essays on Religion* (New York: Greenwood Press, 1969), 100-101.

30. Boyer, *Religion Explained*, 330.

31. Clifford Geertz, *The Interpretation of Cultures* (New York: Basic Books, 1973), 119; see also Evans-Pritchard, *Witchcraft, Oracles and Magic Among the Azande* (Oxford: Clarendon Press, 1937), 20. For an opposing view, see Boyer, *Religion Explained*, 9-10. Geertz also wrote: "If the anthropological study of religious commitment is underdeveloped, the anthropological study of religious non-commitment is non-existent"; "Religion as a Cultural System," in *Anthropological Approaches to the Study of Religion*, ed. Michael Banton (New York: Praeger, 1966), 43.

32. This is an actual report of apparent fraud by a witch doctor. The anthropologist E. E. Evans-Pritchard collected many such reports while he was living with the Azande tribe in the Sudan between 1926 and 1930; Evans-Pritchard, *Witchcraft, Oracles and Magic*, 188-89, 193. For other such tales, see A. B. Ellis, *Tshe-Speaking Peoples*, 128-29; John Lee Maddox, *Medicine Man: A Sociological Study of the Character and Evolution of Shamanism* (Whitefish, MT: Kessinger, 2003), 103-7; E. J. Glave, "Fetishism in Congo Land," *Century Magazine* (April 1891): 836; Moffat, *Missionary Labours and Scenes in Southern Africa* (New York: Johnson Reprint Corp., 1969), 314. Marshall McLuhan wrote: "There never was a sceptic or an agnostic in a pre-literate society"; *Culture Is Our Business* (New York: McGraw-Hill, 1970), 162. McLuhan here was wrong.

33. Skinner, "Superstition' in the Pigeon."

34. Samuel White Baker, *The Albert N'Yanza: Great Basin of the Nile and Explorations of the Nile Sources* (London: MacMillan, 1962), 178-81. Baker is the only witness we have to this debate. However, while he was often clumsy and insensitive, Baker's writing seems to have been respected in the nineteenth century, and there is no evidence that he was a liar. Indeed, Herbert Spencer quoted this particular dialogue in his *The Principles of Sociology* (New York: Appleton, 1896), 672-73. Nietzsche, too, made use of this dialogue; *Nietzsche Briefwechsel Kritische Gesamtausgabe*, vol. III (Berlin: De Gruyter, 2003), 611; Andrea Orsucci, *Orient, Okzident: Nietzsches Versuch einer Lösung Vom Europäischen Weltbild* (Berlin: de Gruyter, 1996), 220. And Charles Darwin quoted a number of Baker's observations; see *The Descent of Man and Selection on Relation to Sex* (New York: Appleton, 1896), 380, 536, 540-41, 574, 575.

35. See Marcus Tullius Cicero, *The Nature of the Gods,* trans. P. G. Walsh (Oxford: Clarendon Press, 1997), 29-34, 38. For a longer version of this argument, see Sextus Empiricus, *Against the Physicists, Against the Ethicists* (Cambridge, MA: Harvard University Press, 1987), 139-82. For the connection between the argument and Carneades, see Eduard Zeller, *Outlines*

of the History of Greek Philosophy (Bristol, England: Thoemmes Press, 1997), 548n; Jennifer Michael Hecht, *Doubt*, 43.

36. For a possible connection between the seminal Greek Skeptic, Pyrrho, and India, see Everard Flintoff, "Pyrrho and India," *Phronesis* XXV, 1 (1980): 88-108.

37. Baker, *Albert N'Yanza*, 181.

38. Redford, *The Oxford Encyclopedia of Ancient Egypt* (Oxford: Oxford University Press), 2001, III, 95; Richard H. Wilkinson, *The Complete Temples of Ancient Egypt* (New York: Thames & Hudson, 2000), 12; Erik Hornung, *The Ancient Egyptian Books of the Afterlife* (Ithaca, NY: Cornell University Press, 1999), 1; James P. Allen, *The Ancient Egyptian Pyramid Texts* (Leiden, The Netherlands: Brill, 2005), 1. For an earlier date see Rosalie David, *The Ancient Egyptians: Beliefs and Practices* (Brighton: Sussex Academic Press, 1988), 70-71, 253; Allen, *Ancient Egyptian Pyramid Texts*, 1.

39. Allen, *Ancient Egyptian Pyramid Texts*, 52, 56, 87, 135; Mircea Eliade, *A History of Religious Ideas*, vol. 1 (Chicago: University of Chicago Press, 1978), 94-97; David, *The Ancient Egyptians*, 71-72.

40. The citations here are from John L. Foster, *Ancient Egyptian Literature: An Anthology* (Austin: University of Texas Press, 2001), 179-80. For additional commentary and translations, see Breasted, *Development and Thought in Ancient Egypt*, 179-84; Charles F. Horne, ed., *The Sacred Books and Early Literature of the East* (New York: Park, Austin, & Lipscomb, Inc., 1917), 87-88; Nathaniel Edward Griffin and Lawrence Hunt, *The Farther Shore: An Anthology of World Opinion on the Immortality of the Soul* (Boston: Houghton Mifflin, 1934), 1-3; Adolf Erman, *The Ancient Egyptians: A Sourcebook of Their Writings* (New York: Harper & Row, 1966), 182-84; Thrower, *The Alternative Tradition*, 249-50.

41. See Stephen Mitchell, *Gilgamesh: A New English Version* (New York: Free Press, 2004), 1; Robert Pogue Harrison, *Forests: The Shadow of Civilization* (Chicago: University of Chicago Press, 1992), 14; Danny P. Jackson, *The Epic of Gilgamesh* (Wauconda, IL: Bolchazy Carducci, 1992), ix.

42. Gilgamesh citations from N. K. Sandars, *The Epic of Gilgamesh* (London: Penguin, 1972), 93-97.

43. Mitchell, *Gilgamesh*, 2, 5-7; Sandars, *Epic of Gilgamesh*, 7-9, 13.

44. Citations from Sandars, *Epic of Gilgamesh*, 100-102.

45. Cited Mādhavācārya's *Sarvadarsana-samgraha;* in Radhakrishnan and Moore, *Source Book in Indian Philosophy*, 228.

46. Only fragments of those poems survive. Patricia A. Rosenmeyer, *The Poetics of Imitation: Anacreon and the Anacreontic Tradition* (Cambridge: Cambridge University Press, 1992), 15-21, 37-49; see also C. M. Bowra, *Greek Lyric Poetry: From Alcman to Simonides* (Oxford: Clarendon Press, 1961), 273, 282.

47. Quotation from Walter Petersen, *The Lyric Songs of the Greeks* (Boston: Badger, 1918), 84.

48. Horace, *Carpe Diem*, ed. David West (Oxford: Clarendon Press, 1995).

49. Thrower, *The Alternative Tradition*, 253.

50. Israel Finkelstein and Neil Asher Silberman, *The Bible Unearthed: Archaeology's New Vision of Ancient Israel and the Origin of Its Sacred Texts* (New York: Free Press, 2001), 243-46, 275-80; for early efforts of the "Yahweh-alone" movement, see pp. 246-50. For additional thoughts on the role of monotheism in the long-term development of secularism, see Bruce, *God Is Dead*, 5-7.

51. Ecclesiastes 8:15, 9:10; Tremper Longman III, *The Book of Ecclesiastes* (Grand Rapids, MI: Eerdmans, 1998), 107, 226. For dates, Dominic Rudman, *Determinism in the Book of Ecclesiastes* (Sheffield: Sheffield Academic Press, 2001), 12; Robert Gordis, *Koheleth, The Man and His World* (New York: Jewish Theological Seminary of America), 1951, 68.

52. See Louis H. Feldman, *Jew and Gentile in the Ancient World: Attitudes and Interactions from Alexander to Justinian* (Princeton, NJ: Princeton University Press, 1993), 3-24.

53. Ecclesiastes 11:9. For the debate on this, see Michael V. Fox, *Ecclesiastes* (Philadelphia: Jewish Publication Society, 2004), 75. For some of the puzzles of Ecclesiastes, see Martin A. Shields, *The End of Wisdom* (Winona Lake, IN: Eisenbrauns, 2006).

54. A radical obliviousness to future consequences is found in Molière's mostly suppressed play, *Don Juan;* see Francis L. Lawrence's reading of the play in "Don Juan and the Manifest God: Molière's Antitragic Hero," *PMLA* 93, 1 (January 1978): 86-94.

55. *Sarvadarsana-samgraha;* in Radhakrishnan and Moore, *Source Book in Indian Philosophy*, 233; *Naisadhacarita;* in Krishna Kanta Handiqui, *Naisadhacarita of Sriharsa* (Poona: Deccan College Monograph Series, 14, 1965), 250.

56. *Naisadhacarita;* in Handiqui, *Naisadhacarita of Sriharsa*, 250.

57. Mādhavācārya's *Sarvadarsana-samgraha;* in Radhakrishnan and Moore, *Source Book in Indian Philosophy,* 229.

58. Ecclesiastes 9:9.

59. Ecclesiastes 1:2. *Tanakh: The Hole Scriptures. The New JPS Translation, According to the Traditional Hebrew Text* (Philadelphia: Jewish Publication Society, 1985), 1441. The word translated as "futile" here is *hebel,* הבל, which appears in more than thirty passages in Ecclesiastes; Longman, *Book of Ecclesiastes,* 32; Douglas B. Miller, "Qohelet's Symbolic Use of lbh," *Journal of Biblical Literature* 117, 3 (Autumn 1998): 437-54. Numerous other translations have been proposed for this word: from "vanity" (though not our current understanding of "vanity" as a kind of mirror fixation) to "meaninglessness," "absurdity," "insubstantiality," "transience," "foulness," "unreality" or "emptiness." A more literal translation of *hebel* would be "vapor," which seems to cover, metaphorically, most of those other possible meanings; Miller, "Qohelet's Symbolic Use of lbh"; W. E. Staples, "The "Vanity" of Ecclesiastes," *Journal of Near Eastern Studies* II, 2 (April 1943): 95-104. The word is used earlier in the Bible in association with the worship of gods other than Yahweh; Deuteronomy 32:21; II Kings 17:15; Jeremiah 8:19. So in stating that "all is *hebel,*" Koheleth may be implying that *everything* is as useless and foolish as worshiping Baal, *et al.,* which, since that *everything* would include worship of Yahweh, would have atheistic implications.

60. See for example the "scoffers" in 2 Peter 3.

61. David J. Kalupahana, *Ethics in Early Buddhism* (Honolulu: University of Hawaii Press, 1995), 16-18; Chattopadhyaya, *Lokyata,* 514.

CHAPTER 2: A CLEAR UNDERSTANDING OF WHAT HAPPENED

1. Percy Bysshe Shelley, *Prometheus Unbound* (Seattle, WA: University of Washington Press, 1959), 4.420.

2. A. C. Pearson, *The Fragments of Sophocles* (Amsterdam: Hakkert, 1963), I, 184.

3. *The Iliad,* trans. Robert Fitzgerald (New York: Farrar, Straus and Giroux, 2004), book VI, 153.

4. Pearson, *Fragments of Sophocles,* I, 184.

5. Camus, *Myth of Sisyphus,* 120.

6. *The Odyssey,* trans. Robert Fagles (New York: Penguin Classics, 1997), XI, 681-89.

7. Hyginus, *The Myths of Hyginus,* trans. Mary Grant (Lawrence: University of Kansas, 1960), 62.

8. Camus, *Myth of Sisyphus,* 120.

9. Camus, *Myth of Sisyphus,* 119; Apollodorus, *The Library of Greek Mythology,* trans. Keith Aldrich (Lawrence, KS: Coronado Press, 1975), 17, 79; Diodorus of Sicily, *The Library of History: Books IV.59-VIII,* trans. C. H. Oldfather (Cambridge, MA: Harvard University Press, 1993), 341. Revealing the gods' secrets was also included in the indictment against that other inhabitant of the lower reaches of Hades: the perpetually thirsty Tantalus, whom Odysseus sees surrounded with water "that reached his chin" but which he is unable to drink; *Odyssey,* book XI. "The Greeks . . . were rather closer to the notion that sacrilege, too, might have some nobility"; Nietzsche, *Gay Science,* 188 (#135).

10. Herodotus implies that it was an eclipse of the sun in *The Histories,* trans. Aubrey De Selincourt (London: Penguin Classics, 2003), I, 74. However, Thomas Worthen makes a case for this having been a lunar eclipse, the prediction of which would have been more within the capabilities of a Greek philosopher in "Herodotos' Report on Thales' Eclipse," in *Electronic Antiquity: Communicating the Classics III,* no. 7 May 1997; Digital Library and Archives, University Libraries, Virginia Tech, http://scholar.lib.vt.edu/ejournals/ElAnt/V3N7/worthen.html. Nonetheless, one rough method of calculating solar eclipses, that they are *possible* twenty-three and a half months after lunar eclipses, might have worked in this case; see Patricia F. O'Grady, *Thales of Miletus* (Burlington, VT: Ashgate, 2002), 126-28, 140-41. O'Grady is among those who note that Thales may have studied Babylonian records.

11. Diodorus of Sicily, *Library of History,* 341.

12. Aristotle, *Metaphysics,* trans. Richard Hope (Ann Arbor: University of Michigan Press, 1966), i.3.983b20.

13. See Nietzsche, *Twilight of the Idols and the Anti-Christ* (London: Penguin, 2003), 175-77.

14. Cited G. S. Kirk and J. E. Raven, *The Presocratic Philosophers* (Cambridge: Cambridge University Press, 1966), 362-63; Sider, 158.

15. See Perez Zagorin, *Thucydides: An Introduction for the Common Reader* (Princeton, NJ: Princeton University Press, 2005), 8-9, 20; Simon Hornblower, *Thucydides* (Baltimore, MD:

Johns Hopkins University Press, 1987), 3, 112, 120, 129, 130; and Drachmann, *Atheism in Pagan Antiquity,* 29.

16. Thucydides, *The Peloponnesian War,* trans. Martin Hammond (New York: Oxford University Press, 2009), II, 54.

17. Cited Zagorin, *Thucydides,* 147.

18. Thucydides, *The Peloponnesian War,* II, 47-54.

19. Cited Zagorin, *Thucydides,* 118.

20. Thucydides, *The Peloponnesian War,* V, 84-116; see Hornblower, *Thucydides,* 68.

21. Herodotus, *The Histories,* III, 64-65.

22. Herodotus, *The Histories,* I, 23-24; for the argument that Herodotus includes less "folklore" in the later books of his history, see Hornblower, *Thucydides,* 17.

23. Herodotus, *The Histories,* V, 92.

24. Thucydides, *The Peloponnesian War,* I, 22.

25. Ibid., xxxii.

26. Hornblower, *Thucydides,* 30, 182-84; Thucydides, *The Peloponnesian War,* xliii. For an interesting but less than persuasive attempt to connect Thucydides to religion, see Nanno Marinatos, *Thucydides and Religion* (Königstein, Germany: Hain Verlag, 1981), 56-65.

27. Thucydides, *The Peloponnesian War,* IV, 104-6.

28. Ibid., V, 26.

29. Plato, *Laws. In The Dialogues of Plato.* Vol. V., trans. B. Jowett (New York: Macmillan, 1892), X, 888.

30. E. R. Dodds, *The Greeks and the Irrational* (Berkeley & Los Angeles: University of California Press, 1951), 185.

31. Drachmann, *Atheism in Pagan Antiquity,* 36-44.

32. Cited Zeller, *Outlines of the History of Greek Philosophy,* 81.

33. Cited W. K. C. Guthrie, *A History of Greek Philosophy* (Cambridge: Cambridge University Press, 1969), III, 234. See also Drachmann, *Atheism in Pagan Antiquity,* 89; Thrower, *The Alternative Tradition,* 165.

34. See, for example, Michele Corradi, "Aristotle, Plato and the Epangelma of Protagoras," in *Protagoras of Abdera: The Man, His Measure,* ed. Johannes M. van Ophuijsen, Marlein van Raalte and Peter Stork (Leiden, The Netherlands: Brill, 2013), 74. On the controversy over whether Athens undertook a crackdown on nonbelievers, see I. F. Stone, "Was There a Witch Hunt in Ancient Athens?" *New York Review of Books* (21 January 1988): 37-41; Dodds, *The Greeks and the Irrational,* 189–91; John Burnet, *Greek Philosophy: Thales to Plato* (New York: St. Martin's Press, 1968), 95; Daniel E. Gershenson and Daniel A.Greenburg, *Anaxagoras and the Birth of Physics* (New York: Blaisdwell Publishing Company, 1964), 346–48. Kirk and Raven, writing back in 1957 (decades before I. F. Stone's persuasive defense of Athens), list the prosecution of Anaxagoras for impiety among the few facts about his life about which "there can be no question"; see Kirk and Raven, *The Presocratic Philosophers,* 364.

35. Drachmann, *Atheism in Pagan Antiquity,* 35-38; see also Dodds, *The Greeks and the Irrational,* 182-83; Guthrie, *History of Greek Philosophy,* III, 22-24.

36. Cited Guthrie, *History of Greek Philosophy,* I, 227.

37. Plato, *Laws,* X, 888. For a discussion of Plato's theology, see Friedrich Solmsen, "The Background of Plato's Theology," *Transactions and Proceedings of the American Philological Association* 67 (1936): 208-18.

38. Plato, *Laws,* X, 907.

39. See, for example, Dodds, *The Greeks and the Irrational,* 180; and Andrew Irvine, "David Stove on Enlightenment," in *On Enlightenment,* ed. Andrew D. Irvine (New Brunswick, NJ: Transaction, 2003), xiii-ix.

40. For Asclepius, the god of healing and medicine, and his "Holy Snake," see Dodds, *The Greeks and the Irrational,* 193; Joint Association of Classical Teachers, *The World of Athens* (Cambridge: Cambridge University Press, 1984), 297.

41. Dodds is actually applying a quote from Jacob Burckhardt, writing on nineteenth-century Europe, to Athens; *The Greeks and the Irrational,* 192.

42. Hornblower, *Thucydides,* 182.

43. Thucydides, *The Peloponnesian War,* II, 48-53.

44. See for example Herodotus, *The Histories,* V,92.

45. Joint Association of Classical Teachers, *The World of Athens,* 101, 296-97.

46. For a discussion of Pericles' relationship to Anaxagoras, see Steven V. Tracy, *Pericles: A Sourcebook and Reader* (Berkeley: University of California Press, 2009), 16-17, 135-37; Anthony J. Podlecki, *Perikles and His Circle* (London: Routlege, 1998), 23, 30.

47. Plutarch, *Plutarch's Lives*, vol. 12, trans. John Dryden (New York: P. F. Collier & Son Company, 1909), 12, 40. See Podlecki, *Perikles and His Circle*, 23-31.

48. J. H. Lesher, *Xenophanes of Colophon: Fragments* (Toronto: University of Toronto Press, 1992), 15, 16.

49. Cited Sextus Empiricus, *Scepticism, Man and God: Selections from the Major Writings of Sextus Empiricus*, trans. Sanford G. Etheridge, ed. Philip P. Hallie (Middletown, CT: Wesleyan University Press, 1964), 189-90.

50. For an analysis of the background of this passage, see Drachmann, *Atheism in Pagan Antiquity*, 44-51.

51. Xenophon, *Hellenica*, vols. I-II (Oxford: Clarendon Press, 1888), II, 3.

CHAPTER 3: THEY FORBID RATIONAL SPECULATION

1. Mark Twain, *Following the Equator: A Journey Around the World* (Hartford: The American Publishing Company, 1897), 132.

2. Edward Gibbon, *The Decline and Fall of the Roman Empire*, ed. Hans-Friedrich Mueller (New York: Random House, 2003), I, ii, 19.

3. L.-L. O'Sullivan, "Athenian Impiety Trials in the Late Fourth Century B. C.," *Classical Quarterly* New Series 47, 1 (1997): 145.

4. The founder was Aristippus of Cyrene (a city in North Africa); Tsouna, *The Epistemology of the Cyrenaic School* (Cambridge: Cambridge University Press, 1998), 5-6, 9-20, 26, 134n.

5. Cicero, *Nature of the Gods*, I, 62; III, 11; for the connection of Cicero's outline of this argument to Carneades, see Zeller, *Outlines of the History of Greek Philosophy*, 543n; Sextus Empiricus, *Scepticism, Man, and God*, 183, 191-93.

6. R. J. Goar, *Cicero and the State Religion* (Amsterdam: Adolf M. Hakkert, 1972), 6-7, 31, 45, 108-11, 126-29; Cicero, *Nature of the Gods*, xxiii-xxvii.

7. Marcus Tullius Cicero, *The Letters of Cicero: The Whole Extant Correspondence in Chronological Order* (London: G. Bell and Sons, 1912), I, 141 (To Terentia, F XIV, 4).

8. Cicero, *The Nature of the Gods*, II, 13; III, 65; III, 95.

9. Lucretius, *On the Nature of the Universe*, trans. R. E. Latham (London: Penguin, 1994).

10. "Timon" in Lucian, *Selected Satires of Lucian* (New York: Doubleday, 1962), 243; see Drachmann, *Atheism in Pagan Antiquity*, 124.

11. Lucian, "Icaromenippus, An Aerial Expedition," in *The Works of Lucian of Samosata*, trans. H. W. Fowler and F. G. Fowler (Oxford: Oxford Clarendon Press, 1905), 140; see T. R. Glover, *The Conflict of Religion in the Early Roman Empire* (Whitefish, MT: Kessinger, 2003), 209.

12. Lucian, *Selected Satires of Lucian*, xiii-v. Lucian is hard, too, it should be acknowledged, on philosophy. The classicist A. B. Drachmann makes a connection between Lucian and the Cynics. He also argues that Lucian's satires were possible because in a day with a number of other religious movements, the old, mythological gods were "fair game"; Drachmann, *Atheism in Pagan Antiquity*, 122-26.

13. Lucian, "The Death of Perigrinus," in Lucian, *Selected Dialogues*, ed. C. D. N. Costa (New York: Oxford University Press, 2005), 77.

14. Mark 9:24.

15. Cited Charles Freeman, *The Closing of the Western Mind* (New York: Vintage Books, 2005), 272. Some argue that use of this quote is unfair to Tertullian, who was not consistently anti-reason and is answering here the argument that God was not made flesh, not the argument that God does not exist; however, what he is saying in these sentences seems clear.

16. Nietzsche is much taken with this critique of Christianity: "In God a declaration of hostility towards life, nature, the will to life!" Nietzsche, *Twilight of the Idols and the Anti-Christ*, 140 ("Anti-Christ" # 18). Hume makes a similar point, more gently, a century earlier in his comparison of the "monkish virtues of mortification, penance, humility and passive suffering" with a pagan emphasis on "activity, spirit, courage, magnanimity, love of liberty"; David Hume, *Principal Writings on Religion, Including Dialogues Concerning Natural Religion and The Natural History of Religion* (Oxford: Oxford University Press, 1998), 163-64.

17. Cited Freeman, *Closing of the Western Mind*, 236-37.

18. Matthew 19:12.

19. R. P. C. Hanson, "A Note on Origen's Self-Mutilation," *Vigiliae Christianae* 20, 2 (June 1966): 81-82; Caner, "The Practice and Prohibition of Self-Castration in Early Christianity," *Vigiliae Christianae* 51, 4 (November 1997): 396-415. The church, to be fair, was uncomfortable with such acts, and there is evidence that Origen questioned his own action.

20. Cited Rene Cadiou, *Origen: His Life at Alexandria*, trans. John A. Southwell (Freiberg, Germany: Herder, 1944), 27.

21. Cited Freeman, *Closing of the Western Mind,* 316.
22. Lucas Siorvanes, *Proclus: Neo-Platonic Philosophy and Science* (New Haven, CT: Yale University Press, 1996), 262; Freeman, *Closing of the Western Mind,* 322. Levi ben Gershom (1288-1344) could, if his work challenging Ptolemy's epicycles qualifies, reduce this period by a couple of centuries; see Hecht, *Doubt,* 247-48.
23. Freeman, *Closing of the Western Mind,* 269; Siorvanes, *Proclus,* 28.
24. Richard E. Rubenstein, *Aristotle's Children: How Christians, Muslims and the Jews Rediscovered Ancient Wisdom and Illuminated the Middle Ages* (Orlando, FL: Harcourt, 2003), 40-41, 78. For the argument that the loss of most of Aristotle's works in the West, was really the fault of the Romans for never having bothered to translate them into Latin, see Frances Gies and Joseph Gies, *Cathedral, Forge, and Waterwheel: Technology and Invention in the Middle Ages* (New York: HarperCollins, 1994), 35-36. I would object that while some educated Romans, such as Cicero, went out of their way to *learn* Greek, such learning was remarkably uncommon in Christian Europe. It does deserve to be noted, however—as Daniel Lazare has reminded me—that the works of Aristotle and other Greek thinkers did better in the Greek-speaking Eastern Roman Empire.
25. Cited Étienne Gilson, *Reason and Revelation in the Middle Ages* (New York: Charles Scribner's Sons, 1966), 9; Rubenstein, *Aristotle's Children,* 50-51.
26. Edmund Boleslaw Fryde, *The Early Palaeologan Renaissance 1261–C. 1360* (Leiden, The Netherlands: Brill, 2000), 192; Rubenstein, *Aristotle's Children,* 35; Roy M. MacLeod, ed., *The Library of Alexandria: Centre of Learning in the Ancient World* (London: I.B. Tauris, 2004), 81. See Freeman, *Closing of the Western Mind,* 315-16. Cicero borrowed a style for his dialogues from Aristotle's; Robert T. Radford, *Cicero: A Study in the Origins of Republican Philosophy* (Amsterdam: Rodopi, 2002), 15.
27. Cited Gilson, *Reason and Revelation in the Middle Ages,* 9; Rubenstein, *Aristotle's Children,* 50-51.
28. Also lost is a book by Clitomachus' student and Cicero's teacher, Philo of Larisa; not even the titles of the books by Clitomachus and Philo are known; Charles B. Schmitt, *Cicero Scepticus* (The Hague: International Archives of the History of Ideas, 1972), 22.
29. L. D. Reynolds and N. G. Wilson, *Scribes and Scholars: A Guide to the Transmission of Greek and Latin Literature* (Oxford: Clarendon Press, 1991), 50-51.
30. Ibid., 48-49.
31. Ibid., 53. Mary R. Lefkowitz, "'Impiety' and 'Atheism' in Euripedes' Dramas," in *Euripedes,* ed. Judith Mossman (Oxford: Oxford University Press, 2003), 104. See also Solmsen, "Background of Plato's Theology."
32. Cicero's reputation—which remained intact under the hegemony of more than one religion—certainly helped. The fact that *The Nature of the Gods* concludes by deferring to the pro-gods argument also could not have hurt; *Nature of the Gods,* xxxix-xliii. For a discussion of the reasons for the incomplete survival of Cicero's *Academica,* a related work, see Schmitt, *Cicero Scepticus,* 16-17, 20, 24-25.
33. Cicero, *Nature of the Gods,* III, 65 131-33; 207; Arthur Stanley Pease, "The Conclusion of Cicero's De Natura Deorum," *Transactions and Proceedings of the American Philological Association* 44 (1913): 25-37.
34. Reynolds and Wilson, *Scribes and Scholars,* 96, 101-2, 112, 137. See also Annie Leigh Broughton, "Notes on Lucretius," *The American Journal of Philology* 60, 2 (1939): 238-42; Schmitt, *Cicero Scepticus,* 3. For further discussion of the survival and significance of Lucretius' poem, see Stephen Greenblatt, *The Swerve: How the World Became Modern* (New York: W. W. Norton, 2011). The fact that Cicero and Lucretius wrote in Latin must have helped, as knowledge of Greek faded in medieval Europe.
35. Edward Peters, *Heresy and Authority in Medieval Europe* (Philadelphia: University of Pennsylvania Press, 1980), 223.
36. Epiphanius, *The Panarion of Epiphanius of Salamis,* 2 vols. (Leiden, The Netherlands: Brill, 1987), I, xii, xvi-xviii.
37. Ibid., I, 10.
38. Siorvanes, *Proclus,* 18.
39. Philip F. Kennedy, *Abu Nuwas: A Genius of Poetry* (Oxford: Oxford University Press, 2005), 20-22. Kennedy suggests that this is provocation, not unbelief; but the evidence of the flouting of religion by Abū Nuwās, presented in the discussion that follows, seems persuasive. Kennedy quotes the poet, for example, as saying, in response to a theological debate, "Only death and the grave are true!" See Marilyn Robinson Waldman, "The Development of the Concept of Kufr in the Qur'an," *Journal of the American Oriental Society* 88, 3 (July-September 1968): 442-55, for a detailed discussion of the root of the word in the Qur'ān translated

as "unbelievers": *kāfir.* The title of this chapter in the Qur'ān, *Sura* 109, is translated as "The Disbelievers"; however, a subsequent line—"I do not worship what you worship, and you do not worship what I worship"—suggests that Muhammad is speaking to local pagans; see F. E. Peters, *Muhammad and the Origins of Islam* (Albany, NY: SUNY Press, 1994), 131-32.

40. Sarah Stroumsa, *Freethinkers of Medieval Islam* (Leiden, The Netherlands: Brill, 1999), 40-41, 46, 93-99.

41. Anwar G. Chejne, "The Boon-Companion in Early Abbāsid Times," *Journal of the American Oriental Society* 85, 3 (July-September 1965): 327-35.

42. This translation is Cited D. C. W. Bisschops, "Disruption of Desire by Religion," Master's thesis, August 2012, Universiteit Utrecht; for a translation by Philip F. Kennedy, see *The Wine Song in Classical Arab Poetry* (Oxford: Clarendon Press, 1997), 220.

43. Unless otherwise indicated, the translations here are from Jim Colville, *Poems of Wine and Revelry: The Khamriyyat of Abu Nuwas* (London: Kegan Paul, 2005), x, 18, 58, 79.

44. Exiles had continued to teach Aristotle's work in schools, where the Syriac language was used, in Persian territory. In conquering the Persians, the Arabs imbibed this Greek wisdom. By the ninth century, Aristotle's works were being translated from Greek and Syriac into Arabic; MacLeod, *Library of Alexandria,* 81, 139; Philip Henry Wicksteed, *Dante and Aquinas* (London: J. M. Dent and Sons, 1913), 54-56; Stroumsa, *Freethinkers of Medieval Islam,* 126, 128; Rubenstein, *Aristotle's Children,* 77-78; Majid Fakhry, *A History of Islamic Philosophy* (New York: Columbia University Press, 1970), 116-24; Majid Fakhry, *Averroes: His Life, Works and Influence* (Oxford: Oneworld Publications, 2001), 130. Nestorian Christians played the major role in teaching Greek philosophy in Persia. The Islamic world would gain its own school of Aristotelian thought, the *falāsifa.* Avicenna, who lived from 980 to1037 and like al-Rāzī was a physician, was perhaps the most distinguished of Islam's Aristotelian philosophers; see Fakhry, *Averroes.*

45. See Ibn Warraq, *Leaving Islam: Apostates Speak Out* (Amherst, NY: Prometheus Books, 2003), 53.

46. Cited Mehdi Mohaghegh, "Notes on the 'Spiritual Physic' of Al-Razi," *Studia Islamica* 26 (1967): 5-22; Stroumsa, *Freethinkers of Medieval Islam,* 91.

47. Cited Stroumsa, *Freethinkers of Medieval Islam,* 97-99.

48. Ibid., 104, 128-29; Fakhry, *History of Islamic Philosophy,* 118-24.

49. Cited Stroumsa, *Freethinkers of Medieval Islam,* 37-38, 47.

50. Cited Warraq, *Leaving Islam,* 52.

51. Cited Sarah Stroumsa, "From Muslim Heresy to Jewish-Muslim Polemics: Ibn al-Rawandi's Kitab al-Damigh," *Journal of the American Oriental Society* 107, 4 (1987): 768.

52. Stroumsa, *Freethinkers of Medieval Islam,* 47, 127. See Fakhry, *History of Islamic Philosophy,* 114-15. How did al-Rāwandī get away with such statements? There is no evidence that he was thrown in jail. That may be because he had a talent for backtracking from his most inflammatory statements. He was a skeptical fellow who was capable, like Carneades, of weighing in on both sides of an issue or arguing—using the Greek dialogue form—with his own ideas. For his skepticism, see Stroumsa, *Freethinkers of Medieval Islam,* 140-41, 72-74. He may just have been playing with such scandalous ideas. His enemies may have exaggerated the extent of his heresy. However, given the consequences of attacking religion, even in relatively open-minded periods, it is also possible that al-Rāwandī felt called upon to obscure or temper his statements of disbelief.

53. Abd al-Jabbār, cited Stroumsa, *Freethinkers of Medieval Islam,* 127.

54. Stroumsa, *Freethinkers of Medieval Islam,* 68.

55. Amira K. Bennison, *The Great Caliphs: The Golden Age of the Abbasid Empire* (New Haven, CT: Yale University Press, 2009), 158-59. See also George Sarton, *The History of Science and the New Humanism* (New Brunswick, NJ: Transaction Books, 1988), 89.

56. Kathleen Kuiper, ed., *Islamic Art: Literature and Culture* (New York: Britannica Educational Publishing, 2010), 66-67.

57. Stroumsa, *Freethinkers of Medieval Islam,* 240-41. For the debate on the relationship of religion or received wisdom to the decline of the "golden age of Islam," see Ahmad Y. al-Hassan, ed., *Science and Technology in Islam, Part II* (Paris: United Nations Educational Fund, 2001), 648-49; and George Sarton, *Introduction to the History of Science,* vol. I (Washington: Carnegie Institute, 1927), 626.

CHAPTER 4: NOTHING BUT THIS VISIBLE WORLD

1. Cited James L. Crenshaw, *Old Testament Wisdom: An Introduction* (Louisville, KY: Westminster John Knox Press, 2010), 230.

2. Rubenstein, *Aristotle's Children*, 98; Hastings Rashdall, *The Universities of Europe in the Middle Ages* (Oxford: Clarendon Press, 1895), 280-88.

3. The heretics were Lisois and Etienne. This is from a contemporary account by a monk, Paul; reprinted in R. I. Moore, *The Birth of Popular Heresy* (Toronto: University of Toronto Press, 1995), 10-15. See also Jeffrey Burton Russell, *Dissent and Reform in the Early Middle Ages* (Berkeley: University of California Press, 1965), 27-35, 276n.

4. These quotes are from his *Proslogium*, cited Edward Grant, *God and Reason in the Middle Ages* (Cambridge: Cambridge University Press, 2001), 54-56.

5. For an evaluation of this and later ontological arguments, see Nicholas Everitt, *The Non-Existence of God* (London: Routledge, 2004), 31-58.

6. Cited Rubenstein, *Aristotle's Children*, 103.

7. M. T. Clanchy, *Abelard: A Medieval Life* (Oxford: Blackwell, 1997), 19.

8. Cited James Burge, *Heloise & Abelard: A New Biography* (New York: HarperCollins, 2006), 51.

9. Such contentious relationships between master and pupil were, to be fair, not so unusual. The instruction in the cathedral-connected "logical schools" in which William and then Abelard taught emphasized "disputation": students were encouraged to challenge teachers. Abelard's challenges, however, seem to have been especially aggressive and especially effective; see John Marenbon, "Life, Milieu and Intellectual Context," in *The Cambridge Companion to Abelard*, ed. Jeffrey E. Brower and Kevin Guilfoy (Cambridge: Cambridge University Press, 2004), 23.

10. This discussion is based on that in Rubenstein, *Aristotle's Children*, 110-15; on Abelard's own account, "History of My Calamities," in Abelard and Heloise, *The Letters of Abelard and Heloise*, trans. Betty Radice, ed. M. T. Clanchy (London: Penguin, 2003), 3-5; and on Betty Radice's introduction in Abelard and Heloise, xv-xvii.

11. His position apparently owed a lot to another of his teachers, Roscelin, and his "nominalism"; Rubenstein, *Aristotle's Children*, 111-12.

12. William's argument also owed much to Plato, whose thought had long been assimilated into Catholic thought.

13. Grant, *God and Reason in the Middle Ages*, 60-61; and Constant J. Mews, *The Lost Love Letters of Heloise and Abelard* (New York: Palgrave Macmillan, 1999), 130.

14. Cited Gilson, *Reason and Revelation in the Middle Ages*, 12.

15. Cited Clanchy, *Abelard*, 7.

16. The Latin word is *modernus;* Matei Calinescu, *Five Faces of Modernity: Modernism, Avant-garde, Decadence, Kitsch, Postmodernism* (Durham, NC: Duke University Press, 1987), 14-15; Clanchy, *Abelard*, 17.

17. The quotes here are from Letter 2 and Letter 4, both Heloise to Abelard; in Abelard and Heloise, *Letters of Abelard and Heloise*, 51, 54, 68.

18. Cited Jeffrey Richards, *Sex, Dissidence, and Damnation: Minority Groups in the Middle Ages* (London: Routledge, 1991), 23.

19. This story is based on comments uncovered by Emmanuel Le Roy Ladurie, *Montaillou: The Promised Land of Error*, trans. Barbara Bray (New York: Vintage Books, 1979), vii-xvii, 242, 260-61, 320-21, 327-28. The Montaillou area—of which Raymond's town, Tignac, was a part—then officially belonged to the small principality of Comté de Foix but was under French control.

20. Catharism was the heresy. The bishop was Jacques Fournier, later Pope Benedict XII in Avignon. Among his meticulous records are the comments on religion of some wayward Catholics who were not Cathars, such as Raymond de l'Aire.

21. Lucian Febvre, *The Problem of Unbelief in the Sixteenth Century*, trans. Beatrice Gottlieb (Cambridge, MA: Harvard University Press, 1982), 460.

22. Translated by the author from the French edition of Emmanuel Le Roy Ladurie's book, *Montaillou: Village Occitan de 1294 à 1334* (Paris: Gallimard, 1975), 529.

23. Le Roy Ladurie, *Montaillou*, 15, 260, 261, 279, 319, 320, 340, 344.

24. See George Huppert, *After the Black Death: A Social History of Early Modern Europe* (Bloomington: Indiana University Press, 1998), 140-42.

25. This quote is from the introduction to a later English edition of Le Roy Ladurie's book, published by George Braziller in 2008.

26. Le Roy Ladurie, *Montaillou*, 265, 169-70.

27. Ibid., 322.

28. Ibid., 154-57, 158-59, 164. Le Roy Ladurie does acknowledge that "as he grew older, Pierre acquired the repulsive habit of making his influence with the Inquisition serve his conquests," p. 156.

29. Ibid., 320.
30. John A. F. Thomson, *The Later Lollards: 1414-1520* (Oxford: Oxford University Press, 1965), 36, 248. Thomson finds "parallels . . . for some of Semer's beliefs elsewhere" in England at the time, pp. 248-49.
31. Keith Thomas, *Religion and the Decline of Magic: Studies in Popular Beliefs in Sixteenth and Seventeenth Century England* (New York: Oxford University Press, 1997), 159, 169. Thomas' research is based, in large part, on complaints to church courts and therefore, as Steve Bruce explains, notes exceptions not rules. The rule, Bruce argues, was widespread superstition and acceptance of Christian beliefs; Bruce, *God Is Dead*, 47-50, 52-54. Nevertheless, such complaints—admissions of failure—were not easy to make, and these exceptions appear quite significant. Thomas' research is cited by those who argue that religion is not in decline in Britain today because it seems to prove that it was never all that strong; see Rodney Stark, "Secularization, R. I. P." *Sociology of Religion* 60, 3 (1999): 249-273. This debate on the "narrative of decline" is discussed in chapter 14.
32. For a brief discussion of this mechanism, see Nicholas Davidson, "Atheism in Italy, 1500-1700," in Michael Hunter and David Wootton, *Atheism from the Reformation to the Enlightenment* (Oxford: Clarendon Press, 1992), 82.
33. Febvre, *Problem of Unbelief in the Sixteenth Century*, 336, 353.
34. Mill, *Three Essays on Religion*, 80.
35. The historian Carlo Ginzburg speaks of a "peasant religion" that comes from "oral tradition . . . deeply rooted in the European countryside" that is "intolerant of dogma and ritual"; *The Cheese and the Worm*, trans. John and Anne Tedeschi (Baltimore, MD: John Hopkins Press, 1992), 112. Although it is true that the folk disbelief I am talking of often was flavored by sprinklings of the supernatural, I prefer to see in it an ineradicable, level-headed, eyes-open variety of common sense. Ginzburg has been criticized for underplaying the extent to which high-culture ideas filtered down into such folk traditions; see Paola Zambelli, "From Menocchio to Piero Della Francesca: The Work of Carlo Ginzburg," *The Historical Journal* 28, 4 (December 1985): 983-99. However, I believe some of the examples I have discussed—particularly from the anthropological literature—could not have been explained that way.
36. De Lacy O'Leary, *Arabic Thought and Its Place In History* (London: Kegan Paul, 2001), 276-78; for a slightly different version of the Toledo operation and for other such centers in Europe, see Rubenstein, *Aristotle's Children*, 16-21; Clanchy, *Abelard*, 98-99; 245-56. For Abelard, see "The History of My Calamities," in Abelard and Heloise, *Letters of Abelard and Heloise*, 33.
37. Cited Rubenstein, *Aristotle's Children*, 162.
38. Ibid., 40-41. The discussion of Aristotle here is based on that in pp. 40-46, 78-80, 84.
39. Grant, *God and Reason in the Middle Ages*, 237; Rubenstein, *Aristotle's Children*, 180-84.
40. Hilde de Ridder-Symoens, ed., *A History of the University in Europe*, vol. 1, *Universities in the Middle Ages* (Cambridge: Cambridge University Press, 2003), 413.
41. Many seemed drawn from interpretations of Aristotle as much as from Aristotle, particularly those of Averroës.
42. The citations here are from Grant, *God and Reason in the Middle Ages*, 214-15; from V. F. Cordova, "Exploring the Sources of Western Thought," in *Women of Color and Philosophy: Reflections on the Discipline*, ed. Naomi Zack (Malden, MA: Blackwell, 2000), 83; from Gilson, *Reason and Revelation in the Middle Ages*, 64; and from Leo Sweeney, "*Sancti Thomae Aquinatis Tractatus de Substantiis Separatis* by Francis J. Lescoe," *Speculum* 39, 1 (January 1964): 168-71. Grant and Cordova seem to be relying on collections with different numbering systems as well as on different translations. Also very useful is the article by Hans Thijssen, "Condemnation of 1277," *The Stanford Encyclopedia of Philosophy*, 2013, http://plato.stanford.edu/entries/condemnation/. See also Hecht, *Doubt*, 258-60.
43. See Grant, *God and Reason in the Middle Ages*, 216; Hecht, *Doubt*, 258-60.
44. Thomas Aquinas, *Summa Contra Gentiles*, trans. English Dominican Fathers (London: Burns Oates & Washbourne, Ltd., 2013), 1.3.
45. Thomas Aquinas, *Summa Theologica*, vol. 1, trans. English Dominican Fathers (New York: Cosimo, 2013), I.2.iii.
46. Since, Thomas argues, "whatever is in motion must be put in motion by another," and since this chain of one thing being put in motion by another and then that by another, in his view, "cannot go on to infinity. . . . Therefore it is necessary to arrive at a first mover, put in motion by no other; and this everyone understands to be God." Thomas makes a similar case for the chain of causes and effects—that there must be an original "first" cause. He then argues that there also must be an original cause for necessity—for things that have to be—and a pure, ultimate cause for "goodness and every other perfection; and this we call God"; Aquinas,

Summa Theologica, I.2.iii. This last proof is not traditionally included with the cosmological argument; Everitt, *Non-Existence of God,* 59. For an evaluation of cosmological arguments, see Everitt, *Non-Existence of God,* 59-84. For an evaluation of Thomas' effort, see Robert Pasnau and Christopher Shields, *The Philosophy of Aquinas* (Boulder, CO: Westview Press, 2004), 85-95. "It is safe to say that this argument has not convinced many of those who have studied it carefully," p. 88.

47. For an evaluation of teleological arguments, which include the currently important argument for design, see Everitt, *Non-Existence of God,* 85-111.

48. Grant, *God and Reason in the Middle Ages,* 13.

49. "The list of these opinions," writes the French historian Étienne Gilson, "is a sufficient proof of the fact that pure rationalism was steadily gaining ground around the end of the thirteenth century"; *Reason and Revelation in the Middle Ages,* 64. I follow Edward Grant and Hecht in quoting this.

50. Menocchio's story and comments here are from Carlo Ginzburg. Ginzburg has been criticized for de-emphasizing the debt Menocchio owed to books and what he may have picked up from high culture. See, for example, David Levine and Zubedeh Vahed, "Ginzburg's Menocchio: Refutations and Conjectures," *Histoire Sociale* 34 (2001): 437-64; and Zambelli, "From Menocchio to Piero Della Francesca," 983-99.

51. "All was chaos," is how he explained the creation of the universe to the Inquisition, "that is, earth, air, water and fire were mixed together; and out of that bulk a mass formed—just as cheese is made out of milk—and worms appeared in it, and these were the angels." Menocchio also occasionally succumbed to the dream of some sort of "paradise."

52. Levine and Vahed, "Ginzburg's Menocchio," 437-64.

53. Greenblatt, *The Swerve,* 9-10.

54. Cited Davidson, in Hunter and Wootton, *Atheism from the Reformation to the Enlightenment,* 55.

55. Greenblatt, *The Swerve,* 221.

56. Niccolo Machiavelli, *The Prince,* trans. Harvey C. Mansfield, 2nd ed. (Chicago: University of Chicago Press, 1998), XVIII, 70. Machiavelli's view here owed something to Averroës, if not to Critias.

57. Machiavelli, *The Prince,* XXI; see Leo Strauss, *Spinoza's Critique of Religion* (Chicago: University of Chicago Press, 1997), 48.

58. Davidson, in Hunter and Wootton, *Atheism from the Reformation to the Enlightenment,* 63, 65, 67, 75, 79, 80.

59. The *Catholic Encyclopedia,* for which this is an uncomfortable subject, includes some numbers in its article on Tomás de Torquemada; M. Ott, "Tomás de Torquemada," in *The Catholic Encyclopedia* (New York: Robert Appleton Company); retrieved October 7, 2013 from New Advent: http://www.newadvent.org/cathen/14783a.htm. See also Cecil Roth, *The Spanish Inquisition* (New York: W.W. Norton and Company, 1996), 123-24; Elphège Vacandard, *The Inquisition: A Critical and Historical Study of the Coercive Power of the Church,* trans. Bertrand Louis Conway (New York: Longmans, Green, 1908), 197.

60. Cited Carter Lindberg, *The European Reformations* (London: Blackwell, 1996), 268-69; Robert Dale Owen, *The Debatable Land Between This World and the Next: With Illustrative Narrations* (New York: G.W. Carleton & Co., 1872), 66-68.

61. The quotes are from Gilbert Genebrard, in a book published in 1581; cited Don Cameron Allen, *Doubt's Boundless Sea: Skepticism and Faith in the Renaissance* (Baltimore, MD: Johns Hopkins Press, 1964), 227.

62. The doctor was Thomas Browne; Thomas Browne, *Religio Medici: To Which is Added Hydriotaphia, Or Urn-Burial: A Discourse on Sepulchral Urns* (London: H. Washbourne, 1845), 41.

63. Chapelain's reason for wanting a copy: "for disarming impieties"; cited Allen, *Doubt's Boundless Sea,* 230. Silvia Berti, "Unmasking the Truth: The Theme of Imposture in Early Modern European Culture," in *Everything Connects: In Conference with Richard H. Popkin,* ed. James E. Force and David S. Katz (Leiden, The Netherlands: Brill, 1999), 30; Veronica Buckley, *Christina, Queen of Sweden: The Restless Life of a European Eccentric* (New York: HarperCollins, 2004), 136.

64. Sarah Stroumsa takes its existence in the sixteenth century more seriously, and even considers possible connections to Al-Rāzī and al-Rāwandī; Stroumsa, *Freethinkers of Medieval Islam,* 217.

65. See "An Apology for Raymond Sebond," in Michel de Montaigne, *The Essays of Michel de Montaigne,* trans. M. A. Screech (London: Penguin, 1991); Richard H. Popkin, *The History of Scepticism: From Savonarola to Bayle* (Oxford: Oxford: Oxford University Press, 2003), 47.

66. Diogenes Laertius, *Life of Pyrrho,* in Brad Inwood and L. P. Gerson, *Hellenistic Philosophy: Introductory Readings,* 2nd ed. (Indianapolis: Hackett, 1997), 288.

67. From Timon via Aristocles via Eusebius, cited A. A. Long, *Hellenistic Philosophy: Stoics, Epicureans, Sceptics* (Berkeley: University of California Press, 1986), 80-81. This withholding of judgments sounds very Eastern, and Pyrrho was, indeed, said to have traveled with Alexander's army to India, where he is said to have met some *gymnosophists*—"naked philosophers"; see Diogenes Laertius, *Life of Pyrrho,* 285. Were ideas exchanged?

68. Montaigne, *Essays of Michel de Montaigne,* 564.

69. Ibid., 557.

70. Cicero translated the Greek word Carneades used here, *pithanon,* as *probabile;* hence the frequent use of the English word "probable" in discussions of Carneades' epistemology. However, Long gives "persuasive" or "trustworthy," which "plausible" seems to capture, as more literal translations; Long, *Hellenistic Philosophy,* 97. Hankinson gives the argument against "probable" and for "plausible"; R. J. Hankinson, *The Sceptics* (London: Routledge, 1995), 111. For a detailed examination of the pitfalls surrounding *pithanon,* see Richard Bett, "Carneades' Pithanon: A Reappraisal of Its Role and Status," in *Oxford Studies in Ancient Philosophy,* ed. Julia Annas (Oxford: Clarendon Press, 1989), 59-94, VII. "Carneades is closer to the spirit of modern British philosophy than perhaps any other ancient thinker"; Long, *Hellenistic Philosophy,* 106. An earlier head of the Academy, Arcesilaus, contributed to this and other of Carneades' arguments; see Long, *Hellenistic Philosophy,* 92-93.

71. Francisco Sanches, *That Nothing Is Known,* trans. Douglas F. S. Thomson, ed. Elaine Limbrick (Cambridge: Cambridge University Press, 1988), 173.

72. Ibid., 78.

73. Ibid., 289.

74. This account is from ibid., 37-39. See also Clarisse Doris Hellman, *The Comet of 1577* (New York: Columbia University Press, 1944).

75. Sextus Empiricus, *Against the Mathematicians,* in Inwood and Gerson, *Hellenistic Philosophy,* 275-80. See also *The Academia of Cicero,* 26, 40, http://archive.org/details/academicaofcicer00cicerich. For a summary of three stages of determining plausibility, see Long, *Hellenistic Philosophy,* 97.

76. Guy Patin claimed to have seen a copy of this book; Sanches, *That Nothing Is Known,* 4-7, 290, 292.

77. Popkin, *History of Scepticism,* 41.

78. The methods of science were generally not well conceptualized in the early stages of the Scientific Revolution; H. Floris Cohen, *The Scientific Revolution: A Historiographical Inquiry* (Chicago: University of Chicago Press, 1994), 153. Was Sanches himself religious? He mumbled all the appropriate things about Catholicism, even professing a kind of fideism. However, when Sanches quotes the Bible it is, likely as not, that skeptical and mostly irreligious text, Ecclesiastes; Sanches, *That Nothing Is Known,* 185, 224. At least one scholar has suggested that Sanches, like many *Marronos,* maintained a secret allegiance to Judaism. And, as with all those who dared publish controversial philosophic theories in the age of the stake, there is always the possibility—outlined by Leo Strauss—that his Catholicism was insincere, his piety a ploy and that he was not, in reality, a believer of any sort. The best counter to these surmises may be the fact that two of his sons became priests; Popkin, *History of Scepticism,* 43.

79. Sanches, *That Nothing Is Known,* 172, 275-90.

80. Ibid., 276.

CHAPTER 5: HOW HEAVEN GOES

1. Sigmund Freud, *The Future of an Illusion,* trans. James Strachey (New York: W. W. Norton & Company, 1989), 49.

2. David Wootton, *Galileo: Watcher of the Skies* (New Haven, CT: Yale University Press, 2010), 1-6.

3. Philolaus, a Pythagorean contemporary of Socrates, seems to have gotten closest; Carl B. Boyer, *A History of Mathematics* (New York: Wiley, 1968), 71. Carl A. Huffman, ed. and trans., *Philolaus of Croton: Pythagorean and Presocratic* (Cambridge: Cambridge University Press, 1993), 232-44.

4. The list that follows is based on Maurice A. Finocchiaro, ed. and trans., *The Galileo Affair: A Documentary History* (Berkeley: University of California Press, 1989), 15-25. See Edward Rosen, *Copernicus and His Successors* (London: Hambledon Press, 1995), 102.

5. Psalm 93; Joshua 10:12-13.

6. Cited Arthur Cushman McGiffert, *Martin Luther: The Man and His Work* (New York: The Century Company, 1911), 271.

7. Wootton, *Galileo,* 51.

8. "Decree of the Index," March 5, 1616, in Finocchiaro, *The Galileo Affair,* 148-50.

9. Wootton, *Galileo,* 51-56.

10. This discussion of Galileo's hesitations and how he moved beyond them is based on that in Finocchiaro, *The Galileo Affair,* 25-26.

11. Wootton, *Galileo,* 89-92

12. Ibid., 125.

13. Galileo to Castelli, December 21, 1613, in Finocchiaro, *The Galileo Affair,* 49-54.

14. "Consultants' Report on Copernicanism," February, 24 1616, in Finocchiaro, *The Galileo Affair,* 146-47; "Decree of the Index," March 5, 1616, in Finocchiaro, *The Galileo Affair,* 148-50.

15. "Galileo's Letter to the Grand Duchess Christina," 1614, in Finocchiaro, *The Galileo Affair,* 96.

16. James A. Rawley with Stephen D. Behrendt, *The Transatlantic Slave Trade: A History* (Lincoln, NE: University of Nebraska Press, 2005), 15.

17. 1 Timothy 6:1.

18. Titus 2:5; 13. Merry E. Wiesner, *Women and Gender in Early Modern Europe* (Cambridge: Cambridge University Press, 2000), 13.

19. Gerald D. Alpern, *Divorce Rights of Passage* (Gretna, LA: Wellness Institute, 2000), 88. Matthew 5:32.

20. "The Massachusetts Body of Liberties," 8, 1641, http://www.bartleby.com/43/8.html#txt2; Leviticus 18:22.

21. Finocchiaro, *The Galileo Affair,* 32-39; Stillman Drake, *Galileo: Pioneer Scientist* (Toronto: University of Toronto Press, 1990), 192-206.

22. This account is based on Finocchiaro, *The Galileo Affair,* 32-40; Galileo's Fourth Deposition, June 21, 1633, in Finocchiaro, *The Galileo Affair,* 286-87; Galileo's Abjuration, June 22, 1633; in Finocchiaro, *The Galileo Affair,* 292-93.

23. Camus on Galileo: "In a certain sense, he did right. That truth was not worth the stake"; Camus, *The Myth of Sisyphus,* 3.

24. Galileo's Abjuration, June 22, 1633; in Finocchiaro, *The Galileo Affair,* 292-93.

25. William Shakespeare, *Hamlet* (New York: Simon & Schuster, 2012), III, I.

26. William Shakespeare, *King Lear* (New York: Simon & Schuster, 1993), I, II.

27. Shakespeare, *King Lear,* V, III.

28. This quote is from Albert Bermel's translation; Molière, *Don Juan (Also Le Mariage Force)* (Orlando: Houghton Mifflin Harcourt, 2001); see Alan Charles Kors, *Atheism in France, 1650-1729,* Vol. I: *The Orthodox Sources of Disbelief* (Princeton, NJ: Princeton University Press, 1990), 32n.

29. The Prince of Conti, cited Frederick William Hawkins, *Annals of the French Stage from Its Origin to the Death of Racine* (London: Chapman and Hall, 1884), I, 316-17. For reaction to the play, see also Kors, *Atheism in France,* 32n.

30. A modified version in verse by Thomas Corneille was performed after 1677. Mechele Leon, *Molière, the French Revolution, and the Theatrical Afterlife* (Iowa City: University of Iowa Press, 2009), 149n.

31. Cited Robert Alan Schneider, *Public Life in Toulouse, 1463-1789: From Municipal Republic to Cosmopolitan City* (Ithaca, NY: Cornell University Press, 1989), 154.

32. This account of Vanini's execution is from Nicholas S. Davidson, "Science and Religion in the Writings of Giulio Cesare Vanini, 1585-1619," in John Hedley Brooke and Ian Maclean, eds., *Heterodoxy in Early Modern Science and Religion* (Oxford: Oxford University Press, 2005), 60, 66; and John Owen, *The Skeptics of the Italian Renaissance* (London: S. Sonnenschein, 1893), 403.

33. These quotes are from *The Visions of John Bunyan* (though it was probably not written by Bunyan, the author of *Pilgrim's Progress*); and Samuel I. Mintz, *The Hunting of Leviathan* (Cambridge: Cambridge University Press, 1969), 21-22.

34. "Every part of the universe is body," Hobbes writes, "and that which is not body is no part of the universe." For Hobbes on both sides of this issue, see Hobbes, *Leviathan,* 57, 178, 281, 302; 303; Mintz, *The Hunting of Leviathan,* 23. For Hobbes' defense of himself, see Mintz, *The Hunting of Leviathan,* 42.

35. Hobbes, *Leviathan,* 173, 176.

36. Mintz, *The Hunting of Leviathan,* 21-22.

37. Popkin makes a good argument for Hobbes having been at best second, to Isaac La Peyrère. He notes that there is also a rabbinical tradition of mulling over potential contradictions in the Torah; Popkin, *The History of Scepticism,* 223.
38. The twentieth-century philosopher Leo Strauss was a proponent of this latter theory. "Many present-day scholars," he writes, " . . . do not seem to have a sufficient notion of the degree of circumspection or of accommodation to the accepted views that was required, in former ages, of 'deviationists' who desired to survive or to die in peace"; Leo Strauss, "On the Spirit of Hobbes' Political Philosophy," in Keith Cates Brown, ed., *Hobbes: Studies* (Cambridge, MA: Harvard University Press, 1965), 27n. See also: Mintz, *The Hunting of Leviathan,* 44-45.
39. A. P. Martinich, *Hobbes: A Biography* (Cambridge: Cambridge University Press, 1999), 318-20.
40. John Aubrey, *Brief Lives* (Woodbridge, UK: Boydell Press, 2004), 154; Martinich, *Hobbes,* 294-95.
41. The citations and the story are from Steven Nadler, *Spinoza: A Life* (Cambridge: Cambridge University Press, 1999), 1-15; Yirmiyahu Yovel, *Spinoza and Other Heretics,* Vol. I, *The Marrano of Reason* (Princeton, NJ: Princeton University Press, 1989), 3-14.
42. Nadler, *Spinoza,* 11, 13.
43. Philipp Blom, *A Wicked Company: The Forgotten Radicalism of the European Enlightenment* (New York: Basic Books, 2010), 85.
44. Popkin, *The History of Scepticism,* 245; Yirmiyahu Yovel, *Spinoza and Other Heretics,* Vol. II, *The Adventures of Immanence* (Princeton, NJ: Princeton University Press, 1989), x.
45. Baruch Spinoza, *A Theologico-Political Treatise and a Political Treatise,* trans. R. H. M. Elwes (Mineola, NY: Courier Dover, 2013), 82.
46. Joshua 10:12-14.
47. Baruch Spinoza, *Tractatus Theologico-politicus* (London: Trübner, 1862), 59-60.
48. Spinoza, *A Theologico-Political Treatise,* 84.
49. Spinoza, *Tractatus Theologico-politicus,* 132.
50. Letter XXV, February 7, 1676, *Correspondence by Benedict de Spinoza,* http://www.sacred-texts.com/phi/spinoza/corr/corr22.htm.
51. Spinoza, *Tractatus Theologico-politicus,* 69.
52. Popkin, *The History of Scepticism,* 239.
53. Cited Genevieve Lloyd, ed., *Spinoza: Context, Sources, and the Early Writings* (London: Taylor & Francis, 2001), 232.
54. Leo Strauss argues that Spinoza—whose motto was *caute,* "caution"—purposely contradicts himself in a subterfuge intended to fool the "vulgar" into thinking he has religion while providing more sophisticated readers with a thorough critique of religion. *Persecution and the Art of Writing* (Chicago: University of Chicago Press, 1988), 166.
55. These quotations are from Baruch Spinoza, *The Ethics: Treatise on the Emendation of the Intellect,* trans. Samuel Shirley, ed. Seymour Feldman (Indianapolis: Hackett Publishing Company, 1992), 37-43.
56. Alan Donagan, *Reflections on Philosophy and Religion* (New York: Oxford University Press, 1999), 62n. See Nadler, *Spinoza,* 187-88; and J. S. Spink, *French Free-Thought from Gassendi to Voltaire* (New York: Greenwood Press, 1969), 253-55.
57. See Correspondence with Richard Bentley, letter one, in Isaac Newton, *Philosophical Writings,* ed. Andrew Janiak (Cambridge: Cambridge University Press, 2004), 94-97; Patricia Fara, *Newton: Making of Genius* (New York: Columbia University Press, 2002), 1-2, 13-14.
58. See Don Cameron Allen, *The Legend of Noah; Renaissance Rationalism in Art, Science, and Letters* (Urbana: University of Illinois Press, 1949); also Jack Pearl, *A Study of the Interpretation of Noah and the Flood in Jewish and Christian Literature* (Leiden, The Netherlands: Brill, 1978), 116.
59. Allen, *The Legend of Noah,* 94, 102-3.
60. These quotations are from Halley. Halley got into trouble for this calculation and his theory that a comet had caused the flood; see "Further thoughts," in Edmond Halley, "Some Considerations about the Cause of the Universal Deluge, Laid before the Royal Society, on the 12th of December 1694," *Philosophical Transactions (1683-1775)* 33 (1724–1725): 118-23; also Richard S. Westfall, *Science and Religion in Seventeenth-Century England* (Hamden, CT: Archon Books, 1970), 100, 113-14, 134.
61. See Westfall, *Science and Religion,* 100, 113-14, 134.
62. Cited Simon Schaffer, "Halley's Atheism and the End of the World," *Notes and Records of the Royal Society of London* 32, 1 (July 1977): 17-40.

63. In the first edition of *Quaestiones in Genesim;* then withdrawn in the second edition; Cited Owen Chadwick, *The Secularization of the European Mind* (Cambridge: Cambridge University Press, 1993), 9-10, 267n. See Kors, *Atheism in France,* 30.

64. In *The Darkness of Atheism Dispelled by the Light of Nature;* Cited Westfall, *Science and Religion,* 107-8.

65. Perhaps the most interesting contemporary example is Francis S. Collins, head of the Human Genome Project and author of *The Language of God: A Scientist Presents Evidence for Belief* (New York: Free Press, 2006).

66. Cited Westfall, *Science and Religion,* 31.

67. Ibid., 56.

68. Ibid., 52-3.

69. Isaac Newton, *The Principia: Mathematical Principles of Natural Philosophy,* trans. Anne Whitman and I. Bernard Cohen (Berkeley: University of California Press, 1999), 940.

70. Cited Westfall, *Science and Religion,* 197.

71. Robert H. Hurlbutt III, *Hume, Newton and the Design Argument* (Lincoln: University of Nebraska Press, 1885), 5; Newton, *The Principia,* Vol. 2, 668-69.

72. Westfall, *Science and Religion,* 201-3; Max Jammer, *Concepts of Space: The History of Theories of Space in Physics,* 3rd ed. (Mineola, NY: Dover Publications, 2012), 112-13; Alexandre Koyre and I. Bernard Cohen, "The Case of the Missing Tanquam: Leibniz, Newton & Clarke," *Isis* 52, 4 (December 1961): 555-66; Hurlbutt, *Hume, Newton and the Design Argument,* 5, 14. A particularly interesting line of attack, from a modern perspective, is Bishop George Berkeley's criticism of Newton's notion of "absolute" or "real" space. Berkeley, championing a more relativistic conception of place and motion, argues that Newton's view raises the danger of "thinking either that Real Space is God, or else that there is something besides God which is eternal, uncreated, infinite, indivisible, immutable"; *A Treatise Concerning the Principles of Human Knowledge* (Philadelphia: J. B. Lippincott & Co., 1874), 255-59.

73. John Maynard Keynes, a Newton buff: "Newton was not the first of the age of reason. He was the last of the magicians"; from a lecture in 1942; Cited Michael White, *Isaac Newton: The Last Sorcerer* (Reading, MA: Addison-Wesley, 1997), 3.

74. White, *Isaac Newton,* 139-48.

75. One of Newton's Bible-based timelines placed the "end of the great tribulation of the Jews" in 1944, which is intriguing, but then the "second coming of Christ" in 1948. White, *Isaac Newton,* 154-60; Hurlbutt, *Hume, Newton and the Design Argument,* 17-19.

76. Cited Clifford Pickover, *Archimedes to Hawking: Laws of Science and the Great Minds Behind Them* (Oxford: Oxford University Press, 2008), 106.

77. Alfred North Whitehead, *Adventures of Ideas* (New York: Free Press, 1933), 12.

78. See White, *Isaac Newton,* 149-53, 234n; George Burton Adams and Henry Morse Stephens, *Select Documents of English Constitutional History* (New York: Macmillan Co., 1939), 459-62; Hurlbutt, *Hume, Newton and the Design Argument,* 18-19.

79. Newton, *The Principia,* 942; Isaac Newton, *Opticks: Or, A Treatise of the Reflections, Refractions, Inflections and Colours of Light* (London: Dover Publications, 1730), 379; Hurlbutt, *Hume, Newton and the Design Argument,* 18-19; Westfall, *Science and Religion,* 202-4.

80. Popkin, *The History of Scepticism,* 71.

81. Westfall, *Science and Religion,* 216, 218-19.

82. Cited ibid., 208.

83. *The Simpsons,* "Weekend at Burnsies," written by John Vitti, aired April 7, 2002. http://www.simpsoncrazy.com/scripts/weekend-at-burnsies

84. Westfall, *Science and Religion,* 219-20.

85. Newton's friend the philosopher John Locke played a leading role in this; see Westfall, *Science and Religion,* 182-91.

86. Charles Bradlaugh, "Humanity's Gain From Unbelief," in *Theological Essays* (London: A. and H. Bradlaugh Bonner, 1895), 12.

87. Sanches, *That Nothing Is Known,* 65, 70, 171, 172.

88. Cited Popkin, *The History of Scepticism,* 243.

89. Ernan McMullin, "Empiricism and the Scientific Revolution," in *Art, Science and History in the Renaissance,* ed. Charles S. Singleton (Baltimore: The Johns Hopkins University Press, 1967), 333.

90. Ibid., 344.

91. "An Apology for Raymond Sebond," in Montaigne, *Essays of Michel de Montaigne,* 642.

92. For discussions of the complex history of the word *hypothesis* in seventeenth-century Europe, see McMullin, "Empiricism and the Scientific Revolution"; and Westfall, *Science and Religion.* See also: for Newton, Wilbur Applebaum, *The Scientific Revolution and the*

Foundations of Modern Science (Greenwood, NY: Greenwood Press, 2005), 212; for Hooke, Allen Chapman, *England's Leonardo: Robert Hooke and the Seventeenth-Century Scientific Revolution* (Bristol, UK: Institute of Physics Publishing, 2005), 94; and Desmond M. Clarke, *Occult Powers and Hypotheses: Cartesian Natural Philosophy Under Louis XIV* (Oxford: Clarendon Press, 1989), 131-63. Nietzsche: "In science convictions have no rights of citizenship. . . . Only when they decide to descend to the modesty of hypotheses, of a provisional experimental point of view . . . may [they] be granted admission"; *Gay Science,* 280.

93. See H. Floris Cohen, 305–13.
94. Cited McMullin, "Empiricism and the Scientific Revolution," 361, 364.
95. Cited David Brewster, *Memoirs of the Life, Writings, and Discoveries of Sir Isaac Newton* (Edinburgh: Thomas Constable and Co., 1855), 347; Ayval Leshem, *Newton on Mathematics and Spiritual Purity* (Dordrecht, The Netherlands: Kluwer Academic Publishers. 2003), 30-31; Newton, *Opticks,* Query 28 and 31; 344, 373-76.
96. Newton, *Opticks,* Query 28 and 31; 344, 378; correspondence with Richard Bentley, letter one, in Newton, *Philosophical Writings,* 94-97; see Hurlbutt, *Hume, Newton and the Design Argument,* 6-7; Percy Bysshe Shelley, *The Necessity of Atheism and Other Essays* (Buffalo, NY: Prometheus Books, 1993), 37.
97. The philosopher Charles Taylor emphasizes the distinction between "transcendent" and "immanent": "The great invention of the West was that of an immanent order in Nature, whose working could be systematically understood and explained on its own terms"; *A Secular Age* (Cambridge, MA: Harvard University Press, 2007), 15.
98. Michael M. Woolfson, *On the Origin of Planets: By Means of Natural Simple Processes* (Singapore: World Scientific, 2011), 120, 149-50.
99. Sue Taylor Parker and Karin Enstam Jaffe, *Darwin's Legacy: Scenarios in Human Evolution* (Plymouth, UK: AltaMira Press, 2008), 117.
100. Westfall, *Science and Religion,* 198.
101. Alexander Pope, *The Works of Alexander Pope,* ed. Joseph Warton (London: Richard Priestley, 1822), 379.
102. "De-divinization" is another possible translation. Max Weber, the early German sociologist, preferred the more lyrical but more discomfiting "disenchantment"; Mariano Artigas, *The Mind of the Universe: Understanding Science and Religion* (Philadelphia & London: Templeton Foundation Press, 2000), 300-301; Morris Berman, *The Reenchantment of the World* (Ithaca, NY: Cornell University Press, 1981), 69-70.
103. Westfall, *Science and Religion,* 220.
104. This account is based primarily upon Allen, *Doubt's Boundless Sea,* 231-43.
105. Cited ibid., 235.
106. Cited Roger Hahn, "Laplace and the Mechanistic Universe," in *God and Nature: Historical Essays on the Encounter between Christianity and Science,* ed. David Charles Lindberg and Ronald L. Numbers (Berkeley: University of California Press, 1986), 272. Laplace's book is entitled *Treatise on Celestial Mechanics.*
107. Hahn, "Laplace and the Mechanistic Universe," 256. See Herbert H. Odom, "The Estrangement of Celestial Mechanics and Religion," *Journal of the History of Ideas* 27, 4 (October–December 1966): 535n. For the argument that Laplace himself was a practicing Catholic; see Denis Alexander, *Rebuilding the Matrix: Science and Faith in the 21st Century* (Oxford: Lion Publishing, 2001), 150-51.

CHAPTER 6: OPEN YOUR EYES

1. Voltaire, *Voltaire in His Letters: Being a Selection from His Correspondence,* trans. S. G. Tallentyre (New York: G. P. Putnam's Sons, 1919), 232.
2. These citations from Voltaire's letter are from Andrew R. Morehouse, *Voltaire and Jean Meslier* (New Haven, CT: Yale University Press, 1936), 33. See also Meslier, *Oeuvres Complètes des Jean Meslier,* 3 vols., ed. Roland Desné, Jean Deprun, and Albert Soboul (Paris: Anthropos, 1970), lviii.
3. Alfred Owen Aldridge, *Voltaire and the Century of Light* (Princeton, NJ: Princeton University Press, 1975), 93.
4. Ibid., 92-94.
5. Alfred Noyes questions the depth of this emotion and emphasizes the couple's separations. He attributes to Voltaire the conclusion "that he was made not for love but for friendship"; *Voltaire* (New York: Sheed & Ward, 1936), 209. Other biographers, however, are more enthusiastic about the relationship.

6. Voltaire, "Eulogy of Madame la Marquise du Châtelet," in Esther Ehrman, *Mme Du Châtelet* (Leamington Spa, Warwickshire, UK: Berg Publishers, 1986), 84-89. "I feel the full weight of the prejudice which so universally excludes us from the sciences," Emilie acknowledged in a book; cited Ehrman, 61. Emmanuel Kant demonstrated that prejudice when he muttered that "women like Madame du Châtelet might as well even have a beard"; Noyes, *Voltaire*, 209.

7. Cited Amelia Ruth Gere Mason, *The Women of the French Salons* (New York: Century Publications, 1891), 164.

8. Letter XIII, "Voltaire (1694-1778): 'On John Locke,' from *Letters on the English* or *Lettres Philosophiques*," Fordham University, http://www.fordham.edu/halsall/mod/1778voltaire-locke.asp.

9. John Locke, *An Essay Concerning Human Understanding* (Oxford: Clarendon Press, 1894), IV, xviii, 11 (426); Westfall, *Science and Religion*, 182-91.

10. The argument that mind cannot be explained entirely in material terms has returned recently in the philosopher Thomas Nagel's *Mind and Cosmos: Why the Materialist Neo-Darwinian Conception of Nature Is Almost Certainly False* (New York: Oxford University Press, 2012).

11. This account of his life is from Morehouse and Roland Desné's introduction to Meslier, *Oeuvres Complètes*.

12. The French, probably from Voltaire, is in Morehouse, *Voltaire and Meslier*, 15-16; Meslier, *Oeuvres Complètes*, I, xxvii-xxviii.

13. See Meslier, *Oeuvres Complètes*, I, xxix-xxxi

14. Michel Onfray uses a "bomb" image in "Jean Meslier and 'The Gentle Inclination of Nature,'" trans. Marvin Mandell, *New Politics* X-4, 40 (Winter 2006).

15. Reproduced in Meslier, *Oeuvres Complètes*, I, 2; cited Morehouse, *Voltaire and Meslier*, 22n; I have also made use of the translation in Onfray, "Jean Meslier and 'The Gentle Inclination of Nature.'"

16. François-Joachim de Pierre de Bernis, *Memoirs and Letters of Cardinal de Bernis*, Vol. I, trans. Katharine Prescott Wormeley (Boston: Hardy, Pratt & Company, 1902), 113; Gay, *The Enlightenment*, 339.

17. Matthias Knutzen in Jena in 1674 would be another possible candidate, though I have seen no evidence that his name was on his tract; see Jonathan I. Israel, *Enlightenment Contested: Philosophy, Modernity and the Emancipation of Man, 1670-1752* (Oxford: Oxford University Press, 2006), 166.

18. Meslier, *Superstition in All Ages*, trans. Anna Knoop, http://www.gutenberg.org/files/17607/17607-h/17607-h.htm. The selection from "Common Sense" included on this website is by Baron d'Holbach not Meslier; see chapter 7.

19. Jean Meslier, *Mon Testament*, trans. Herve Gourmelon, http://eyler.freeservers.com/Jeff-Writings/jbconv15.htm.

20. Ibid.

21. Ehrman, *Mme Du Châtelet*, 31. See also Jean Orieux, *Voltaire*, trans. Barbara Bray and Helen R. Lane (Garden City, NY: Doubleday, 1979), 3; details on their life at Cirey are on pp. 119-21, 136-39.

22. Orieux, *Voltaire*, 119-21.

23. Emilie Du Châtelet, *Selected Philosophical and Scientific Writings*, ed. Judith P. Zinsser, trans. Isabelle Bour and Judith P. Zinsser (Chicago: University of Chicago Press, 2009), 207.

24. Voltaire, *Épître 41*, "À Madame la Marquise du Châtelet, Sur la Calomnie," 1733. http://fr.wikisource.org/wiki/%C3%89p%C3%AEtre_41.

25. Cited Popkin, *The History of Scepticism*, 296.

26. H. T. Mason, *Pierre Bayle and Voltaire* (Oxford: Oxford University Press, 1963), 16.

27. Cited Ryan Patrick Hanley and Darron M. McMahon, eds., *The Enlightenment* (New York: Routledge, 2010), 14.

28. Perez Zagorin, *How the Idea of Religious Toleration Came to the West* (Princeton, NJ: Princeton University Press, 2003), 281.

29. Cited Zagorin, *How the Idea of Religious Toleration Came to the West*, 274.

30. This discussion is based on that in Chadwick, *Secularization of the European Mind*, 21-24; Zagorin, *How the Idea of Religious Toleration Came to the West*, 272-83; John Kilcullen, *Sincerity and Truth: Essays on Arnauld, Bayle, and Toleration* (Oxford: Clarendon Press, 1988), 89-92.

31. Mason, *Pierre Bayle and Voltaire*, 133-138.

32. Cited Hanley, *The Enlightenment*, 14.

33. Pierre Bayle, *Historical and Critical Dictionary*, 4 vols. (London: Hunt and Clarke, 1826), I, 162-80.

34. The belief that atheists are immoral has been so persistent among the religious that it was news when, in 2013, Pope Francis allowed that they can do good; "Pope Francis Says Atheists Can Be Good," *Guardian,* May 22, 2013, http://www.guardian.co.uk/world/2013/may/22/pope-francis-atheists-can-be-good.

35. Bayle, *Historical and Critical Dictionary,* I, 174.

36. Fyodor Dostoevsky, *The Brothers Karamazov,* trans. Constance Garnett (New York: Random House, 1950), 78-79, 312.

37. Aldridge suggests that another woman, Marie Marguerite, Comtesse de Rupelmonde, a widow, helped Voltaire develop his critique of Christianity. *Voltaire and the Century of Light,* 37-39.

38. Meslier, *Oeuvres Complètes,* I, xlvii-xlviii. In his introduction to this collection of Meslier's work, Roland Desné gives a more precise account than that in Morehouse, *Voltaire and Jean Meslier,* 23, 24.

39. Morehouse, *Voltaire and Jean Meslier,* 36. Earlier, handwritten extracts from Meslier's book had circulated; for an analysis of Voltaire's contribution, see Meslier, *Oeuvres Complètes,* I, lxv-lxix; Morehouse, *Voltaire and Jean Meslier,* 34-37; Ira Owen Wade, *Voltaire and Madame du Châtelet* (Princeton, NJ: Princeton University Press, 1941).

40. Cited Orieux, *Voltaire,* 366.

41. Cited Meslier, *Oeuvres Complètes,* I, lxv: "Je crois que rien ne fera jamais plus d'impression que le livret de Meslier"; Orieux, *Voltaire,* 365; Jean Meslier, *Le Testament de Jean Meslier,* ed. Rudolf Charles (Amsterdam: R. C. Meijer, 1864), lviii, lx.

42. *Testament de Jean Meslier,* nouvelle edition (Geneva, Switzerland: Cramer, 1762, translated for marxists.org by Mitch Abidor).

43. Roland Desné mentions as examples of individuals punished for expressing anti-religious views, Pietro Giannone, who attacked the Catholic Church and spent fourteen years in prison in Turin; he mentions someone named Lefèvre who was burned alive in Reims; and he discusses another French *curé,* Guillaume, who was arrested for atheism; Meslier, *Oeuvres Complètes,* I, xxxviii-xlii. All were contemporaries of Meslier. Desné might have added Thomas Aikenhead, who will be discussed in chapter 9.

44. Jean Meslier, *Testament: Memoire of the Thoughts and Sentiments of Jean Meslier,* trans. Michael Shreve (Amherst, NY: Prometheus Books, 2009), 17.

45. Meslier, *Testament de Jean Meslier.*

46. The citations from Voltaire's version of Meslier are, except where indicated, from Meslier, *Superstition in All Ages,* trans. Knoop, http://www.gutenberg.org/files/17607/17607-h/17607-h.htm.

47. Meslier's logic, though not his conclusions, owes much to Descartes; Michael J. Buckley, *At the Origins of Modern Atheism* (New Haven, CT: Yale University Press, 1987), 269.

48. Morehouse, *Voltaire and Jean Meslier,* 65.

49. Here I have switched to *Testament de Jean Meslier,* nouvelle edition.

50. See Morehouse, *Voltaire and Jean Meslier,* 42-43, 63; Meslier, *Oeuvres Complètes,* I, lxv-lxix. Wade argues in *Voltaire and Madame du Châtelet* that most of these additions to Meslier's text, including the final paragraph, are not Voltaire's but from some earlier handwritten excerpt and some other editor. Morehouse suggests that Voltaire's authorship of most of these passages is "improbable, but possible"; *Voltaire and Jean Meslier,* 34-37, 62-65. However, since there is reason to believe Voltaire was familiar with Meslier's original manuscript, he may at least have known that he was not accurately reproducing Meslier's words or sentiments. Peter Gay, in his otherwise impressive text, writes in *The Enlightenment* that "Voltaire's abstract . . . follows Meslier faithfully," 392n. That, it seems clear, is not correct.

51. See Meslier, *Oeuvres Complètes,* I, lxvii.

52. Cited Gay, *The Enlightenment,* 391. For a gentler view of Voltaire's thoughts on Christianity and the "infamous," see Dennis C. Rasmussen, "Burning Laws and Strangling Kings? Voltaire and Diderot on the Perils of Rationalism in Politics," *The Review of Politics* 73, 1 (Winter 2011): 77-104.

53. Ian Davidson, *Voltaire in Exile: The Last Years, 1753-78* (New York: Grove Press, 2005), 117. See also Orieux, *Voltaire,* 383.

54. These quotations are from "God—Gods," in Voltaire, *A Philosophical Dictionary,* 6 vols. (London: John and Henry L. Hunt, 1824), III, 324.

55. Ehrman, *Mme Du Châtelet,* 50.

56. Voltaire, *A Philosophical Dictionary,* III, 323.

57. Meslier, *Oeuvres Complètes,* I, 21.

58. Nietzsche: "For this is how man is: an article of faith could be refuted before him a thousand times—if he needed it, he would consider it 'true' again and again"; *Gay Science,* 287.

59. Voltaire, *A Philosophical Dictionary*, I, 55.
60. Voltaire is hard to save from the charge of anti-Semitism. This is from his entry on "Jews": "In short, we find in them only an ignorant and barbarous people, who have long united the most sordid avarice with the most detestable superstition and the most invincible hatred for every people by whom they are tolerated and enriched. Still, we ought not to burn them"; *A Philosophical Dictionary*, IV, 214.
61. This account is based on that in Orieux, *Voltaire*, 350-61.
62. For an analysis of distinctions in the views on tolerance of Bayle, Locke and Voltaire, see Voltaire, *Treatise on Tolerance*, trans. Brian Masters (Cambridge: Cambridge University Press, 2000), xvi-xix. For a legal perspective on this history and the limitations of Locke's view, see Michael W. McConnell, "The Origins and Historical Understanding of Free Exercise of Religion," *Harvard Law Review* 103, 7 (May 1990): 1409-1517.
63. "Toleration" in Voltaire, *A Philosophical Dictionary*, VI, 272.
64. Voltaire, *A Philosophical Dictionary*, I, 336.
65. Voltaire, "Epistle to the Author of the Book, *The Three Impostors*," (1768) trans. Jack Iverson, http://www.whitman.edu/VSA/trois.imposteurs.html.
66. Mill, *Three Essays on* Religion, 70.
67. "Atheist" in Voltaire, *A Philosophical Dictionary*, I, 330.
68. Voltaire, *Political Writings*, 190.
69. Meslier, *Superstition in All Ages*, trans. Anna Knoop, http://www.gutenberg.org/files/17607/17607-h/17607-h.htm.
70. Locke, *Two Treatises of Government* (London: C. and J. Rivington, 1824), 133.
71. Cited William Doyle, *Aristocracy and its Enemies in the Age of Revolution* (Oxford: Oxford University Press, 2009), 68.
72. Meslier, *Mon Testament*, trans. Herve Gourmelon, http://eyler.freeservers.com/JeffWritings/jbconv15.htm.
73. John Locke had also referred to "men being, as has been said, by nature, all free, equal and independent," but Locke's emphasis is on how someone "divests himself of his natural liberty" by putting "on the bonds of civil society"; *Two Treatises of Government*, 186.
74. Meslier, *Oeuvres Complètes*, I, xi.
75. Meslier, *Oeuvres Complètes*, I, 24-25; II, 17.
76. Cited Morehouse, *Voltaire and Jean Meslier*, 69; Meslier, *Oeuvres Complètes*, III, 177. Thanks to Neil and Carol Offen for this translation.

CHAPTER 7: BOMBS ON THE HOUSE OF THE LORD

1. Cited Frederic Ewen, ed., *The Poetry and Prose of Heinrich Heine* (New York: Citadel Press, 1948), 653.
2. This account of Baron Holbach's salon is from Kors, *D'Holbach's Coterie*, 12-13; 94-95; and Arthur M. Wilson, *Diderot* (New York: Oxford University Press, 1972), 174-75.
3. Cited Kors, *D'Holbach's Coterie*, 95; Jean-Jacques Rousseau, *The Confessions*, trans. J. M. Cohen (London: Penguin Books, 1953), 463-65; Jean-Jacques Rousseau, *Correspondance Générale*, Vol. V (Paris: A. Colin, 1924–1934), 358-59.
4. Georg Wilhelm Friedrich Hegel, *Lectures on History of Philosophy*, Vol. 3, trans. Elizabeth S. Haldane and Frances H. Simson (London: K. Paul, Trench Trübner, 1896), 387.
5. Blom, *A Wicked Company*, 86. For Denis Diderot and Jean Meslier, see also Diderot, *Philosophie et Mathématique*, ed. Jean Varloot (Paris: Hermann, 1975), 86-87n.
6. Cited Kors, *D'Holbach's Coterie*, 41. For another account of this incident, see Sir Samuel Romilly, *The Life of Sir Samuel Romilly*, Vol. I (London: John Murray, 1841), 131-33.
7. Hume's argument is in Hume, *An Enquiry Concerning Human Understanding* (New York: Barnes & Noble Publishing, 2004), 90-109. John Stuart Mill finds "two apparently weak points in this argument," but ends up in agreement with Hume's conclusion. Mill, *Three Essays on Religion*, 220-39.
8. Hume, *An Enquiry Concerning Human Understanding*, 95.
9. Hume, *Principal Writings on Religion*, 134.
10. Ibid., 136-37, 140-42.
11. Five of these editions were collections of Diderot's work. Wilson, *Diderot*, 55-57.
12. Quoted in Gay, *The Enlightenment*, 399.
13. Freud, while perhaps being overly humble, understood this about his own criticism of religion: "I have said nothing which other and better men have not said before me in a much more complete, forcible and impressive manner"; *The Future of an Illusion*, 45.
14. Hume, *Principal Writings on Religion*, 130.

15. From J. C. A. Gaskin's introduction to Hume, ibid., xiii, xvii.
16. Hume, *Principal Writings on Religion,* 63, 66, 84-85.
17. Ibid., 93.
18. Ibid., 51.
19. Ibid., 50-51, 78-79.
20. See Ryu Susato, "Hume's Nuanced Defense of Luxury," *Hume Studies* 32, 1 (2006): 167-86.
21. Hume, *An Enquiry Concerning Human Understanding,* III, 129; V, I, 34.
22. From J. C. A. Gaskin's introduction to Hume, *Principal Writings on Religion,* ix.
23. See Popkin, *The History of Scepticism,* 291.
24. Alexander Carlyle, *Autobiography of the Rev. Dr. Alexander Carlyle* (Edinburgh: W. Blackwood and Sons, 1860), 273-74. Reverend Carlyle, giving his wife as witness, says he heard the story from Patrick Boyle.
25. Cited J. Noxon, "Hume's Concern with Religion," in *David Hume: Many Sided Genius,* ed. K. R. Merrill and R. W. Shahan (Norman: University of Oklahoma Press, 1976, 59-82), 248; Charles Taliaferro, *Evidence and Faith: Philosophy and Religion Since the Seventeenth Century* (Cambridge: Cambridge University Press, 2005), 161-62. The other writer was Samuel Clarke, who criticized organized religion from a deist perspective.
26. Kors, *D'Holbach's Coterie,* 41-81. Jacques-André Naigeon was the third clear atheist, by this count; Augustin Roux, Jean-Francois de Saint-Lambert and Claude-Adrien Helvétius the probables; with the skeptic Friedrich-Melchior Grimm and the chemist Jean Darcet also possible; Buckley is not persuaded on the probables; Buckley, *At the Origins of Modern Atheism,* 258-59.
27. Buckley, *At the Origins of Modern Atheism,* 211-15.
28. The quotes here from *Letter on the Blind* are from Denis Diderot, *Selected Writings,* trans. Derek Coltman, ed. Lester G. Crocker (New York: Macmillan, 1966), 20-23.
29. Buckley, *At the Origins of Modern Atheism,* 218.
30. In a chapter that has included a visit with a skeptic on the order of David Hume, it is probably prudent to acknowledge that this distinction between negative and positive arguments for disbelief has its limitations. Critiques of religion do, of course, point to positive possibilities, and positive alternatives to religion do, of course, also serve as critiques of religion.
31. This idea was not original to Diderot. It follows, initially, from Newton's notion of inertia and then shows up here and there in eighteenth-century thought. Hume, in his *Dialogues,* actually comes up with a theory quite like Diderot's at about the same time, though his *Dialogues* were not published until much later; see Hume, *Principal Writings on Religion,* 48, 84-87. See also Louis Dupré, *The Enlightenment and the Intellectual Foundations of Modern Culture* (New Haven, CT: Yale University Press, 2004), 29; Buckley, *At the Origins of Modern Atheism,* 223.
32. For an attempt to outline the ways in which Diderot's theory is or is not Darwin's theory, see Crocker, *The Embattled Philosopher,* 97.
33. Voltaire's letter is reprinted in Crocker, *The Embattled Philosopher,* 102.
34. See Nicholas Phillipson, *David Hume: The Philosopher as Historian* (New Haven, CT: Yale University Press, 2011), 32-33.
35. Diderot's theory, as further discussed in his later trilogy—*Conversations with D'Alembert, D'Alembert's Dream* and *Conclusion of the Conversation*—did have, with the benefit of hindsight, a significant limitation: it ascribed a "sensibility" to matter, which subsequent investigators have failed to locate; see Buckley, *At the Origins of Modern Atheism,* 232-33, 236.
36. This discussion of the damage caused by the Lisbon earthquake and reaction to it is based on that in Jonathan Israel, *Democratic Enlightenment: Philosophy, Revolution and Human Rights, 1750-1790* (Oxford: Oxford University Press, 2013), 44-46.
37. Ibid., 47-48. A few Christians did, tentatively, mix scientific explanations—mostly having to do with electricity—with theological speculations, they included Juan Luis Roche and Benito Jerónimo Feijóo.
38. Cited Merry E. Wiesner, Julius Ralph Ruff, and William Bruce Wheeler, *Discovering the Western Past: Since 1500* (New York: Houghton Mifflin, 1993), 69.
39. Cited John T. Scott, *Jean-Jacques Rousseau: Human Nature and History,* vol. 2 (Abingdon, Oxon, UK: Routledge, 2006), 366. Rousseau, another deist, also weighed in on the earthquake.
40. Israel, *Democratic Enlightenment,* 51.
41. Diderot, "The Encyclopedia," in *Rameau's Nephew and Other Works,* trans. Jacques Barzun and Ralph H. Bowen (Indianapolis, IN: Hackett Publishing Company, 2001), 277.
42. Diderot, *Political Writings,* 25.

43. The second editor on the first editions of the *Encyclopédie* was the mathematician and philosopher Jean le Rond d'Alembert—another freethinker who could be found at Baron d'Holbach's salon and who seemingly possessed no belief in a god. But d'Alembert became uncomfortable with the Diderot-d'Holbach brand of materialism as it developed. "D'Alembert was no deist," writes his biographer Thomas L. Hankins. "His religious position was one of extreme skepticism"; *Jean D'Alembert: Science and the Enlightenment* (New York: Gordon and Breach Science Publishers, 1990), 102.

44. Cited Leopold Damrosch, *Jean-Jacques Rousseau: Restless Genius.* New York: Houghton Mifflin Harcourt, 2005), 241.

45. See T. C. Newland, "D'Holbach, Religion, and the '*Encyclopédie*,'" *The Modern Language Review* 69, 3 (July 1974): 523-33.

46. Israel, *Democratic Enlightenment,* 69.

47. Cited ibid., 79.

48. Ibid., 59, 68-70.

49. The attendee of the salon was Jean-Baptiste-Antoine Suard; his friend and biographer, was D.-J. Garat. The story is repeated in Wilson, *Diderot,* 176; and W. H. Wickwar, *Baron d'Holbach: A Prelude to the French Revolution* (London: Allen & Unwin, 1935), 62-63.

50. Wickwar is willing to allow a relatively late conversion. *Baron d'Holbach,* 63-65.

51. Kors, *D'Holbach's Coterie,* 18-19; 158-59.

52. Wilson, *Diderot,* 174-77, 373.

53. Kors, *D'Holbach's Coterie,* 1976, 158-59; Wickwar, *Baron d'Holbach,* 69.

54. Cited Wickwar, *Baron d'Holbach,* 39. The abbés were Morellet and Galiani. See Buckley, *At the Origins of Modern Atheism,* 259.

55. Buckley, *At the Origins of Modern Atheism,* 252-53; Kors, *D'Holbach's Coterie,* 240-42; Wickwar, *Baron d'Holbach,* 86-87.

56. The statistics from Toulouse are in Chadwick, *Secularization of the European Mind,* 3.

57. Buckley, *At the Origins of Modern Atheism,* 252-43; Kors, *D'Holbach's Coterie,* 240-42; Wickwar, *Baron d'Holbach,* 86-87.

58. Cited Wickwar, *Baron d'Holbach,* 85.

59. Ibid., 79.

60. This account is from Kors, *D'Holbach's Coterie,* 83; Wickwar, *Baron d'Holbach,* 84-85.

61. See Israel, *Democratic Enlightenment,* 788-90.

62. This account is from Wickwar, *Baron d'Holbach,* 86.

63. Baron d'Holbach, *The System of Nature,* vols. 1 and 2 (Freethought Archives and Distributed Proofreaders, based on a London translation and edition, 1820-21), 2, part 5, chapter 10. http://www.fullbooks.com/The-System-of-Nature-Vol-25.html.

64. Cited Buckley, *At the Origins of Modern Atheism,* 252. See also Sveinbjorn Thordarson, "Voltaire, d'Holbach and the Design Argument," dissertation in History (University of Edinburgh, 2009), http://sveinbjorn.org/voltaire_d_holbach_and_the_design_argument#113.

65. Cited John Morley, *Diderot and the Encyclopædists,* 2 vols. (London: Macmillan, 1897), II, 156.

66. Cited Voltaire, *Philosophical Dictionary,* III, 217.

67. Voltaire's response to *The System of Nature* is in the final version of his article on "God—Gods"; Voltaire, *Philosophical Dictionary,* III, 322-50.

68. Cited Friedrich Albert Lange, *History of Materialism and Criticism of Its Present Importance,* trans. Ernest Chester Thomas, 3 vols. (London: Trübner & Co., 1881), II, 149.

69. Rousseau takes a similar tack in his novel, *Julie: or the New Héloïse,* when he describes a religious woman walking with her husband, Wolmar, a character widely assumed to have been based on Baron d'Holbach: "the one admiring in the rich and splendid robe of the earth the handiwork and the bounteous gifts of the author of the universe; the other seeing nothing in it all save a fortuitous combination, the product of blind force!"; cited Morley, *Diderot and the Encyclopædists,* II, 162. Goethe's view of religion was complex. In 1772 he writes in a letter: "You look upon the gospel as it stands as the divinest truth: but even a voice from heaven would not convince me that water burns and fire quenches, that a woman conceives without a man, and that a dead man can rise again. To you nothing is more beautiful than the Gospel; to me a thousand written pages of ancient and modern inspirited men are equally beautiful"; cited Joseph Mazzini Wheeler, *A Biographical Dictionary of Freethinkers* (London: Progressive, 1889), 153.

70. On the influence of Baron d'Holbach and other atheistic writers, see Carl Lotus Becker, *The Heavenly City of the Eighteenth-Century Philosophers* (New Haven, CT: Yale University Press, 2003), 75-76.

71. Kors, *D'Holbach's Coterie,* 114.

72. Ibid., 113-17; Israel, *Democratic Enlightenment,* 790.

73. In a letter to Helvétius. Israel, *Democratic Enlightenment,* 68.
74. Cited ibid., 217, 220.
75. These selections are from an 1835 translation into English. Baron Paul-Henri thiry de Holbach, *Christianity Unveiled, Being an Examination of the Principles and Effects of the Christian Religion,* trans. W. M. Johnson (New York: 1835), 117-26.
76. Cited Thordarson, "Voltaire, d'Holbach and the Design Argument," http://sveinbjorn.org/voltaire_d_holbach_and_the_design_argument#113.
77. Denis Diderot, "Political Authority," in *The Encyclopedia of Diderot and D'Alembert, Collaborative Translation Project,* trans. Stephen J. Gendzier (Ann Arbor, MI: MPublishing, University of Michigan Library, 2009). http://quod.lib.umich.edu/d/did/did2222.0000 .062/—political-authority-abridged?rgn=main;view=fulltext;q1=Denis+Diderot#N1.
78. "Natural Law," ARTFL Encyclopédie Project, Robert Morrissey, general editor, http://artflsrv02.uchicago.edu/cgi-bin/philologic/getobject.pl?c.4:258:30.encyclopedie0513. Israel *Democratic Enlightenment,* 639.
79. Israel, *Democratic Enlightenment,* 648.
80. Ibid., 421-22. Jonathan Israel has tried to debunk the assertion that the salons were driving forces in what he calls the "radical" Enlightenment (pp. 4-5). The contributions of Baron d'Holbach's salon to this highly influential book and others would seem to debunk his debunking.
81. Ibid., 3, 421-23. Raynal, an early critic of the excesses of the French Revolution, was not shy about blaming "*la philosophie,*" some of it expounded in the book attributed to him (pp. 734-36).
82. Ibid., 421.
83. Ibid., 431.
84. Abbé Raynal, *A Philosophical and Political History of the Settlements and Trade of the Europeans in the East and West Indies,* vol. II (Edinburgh: Silvester Doig,1792), II, 185.
85. Raynal, *A Philosophical and Political History of the Settlements and Trade of the Europeans in the East and West Indies,* vol. IV (Edinburgh: Mundell and Son, 1804), IV, 101.
86. Raynal, *Philosophical and Political History,* vol. II (1792), 135.
87. Raynal, *A Philosophical and Political History of the Settlements and Trade of the Europeans in the East and West Indies,* trans. J. A. Justamond, 2nd ed., vols. I and IV (London: B. Strahan, T. Cadell Jr. and W. Davies, 1798), I, 124.
88. Raynal, *A Philosophical and Political History of the Settlements and Trade of the Europeans in the East and West Indies,* trans. J. A. Justamond, vol. IV (London: B. Strahan and T. Cadell, 1783), IV, 261.
89. Raynal, *Philosophical and Political History,* vol. IV (1804), 411.
90. Ibid., 266.
91. See Israel, *Democratic Enlightenment,* 920.
92. Raynal, *Philosophical and Political History,* vol. IV (1798), 284.
93. Raynal, *Philosophical and Political History,* vol. IV (1804), 239.
94. Raynal, *A Philosophical and Political History of the Settlements and Trade of the Europeans in the East and West Indies,* trans. J. A. Justamond, vol. VI (London: B. Strahan and T. Cadell, 1788), VI, 428.
95. Raynal, *Philosophical and Political History,* vol. IV (1804), 396.
96. See also Jonathan I. Israel, *A Revolution of the Mind: Radical Enlightenment and the Intellectual Origins of Modern Democracy.* Princeton, NJ: A Princeton University Press E-Book, 2010.
97. Israel, *Democratic Enlightenment,* 418, 420.
98. This is the argument of Israel's *A Revolution of the Mind.*

CHAPTER 8: THE BEAST LET LOOSE

1. Thomas Henry Huxley, *Aphorisms and Reflections,* Selected by Henrietta A. Huxley (London: Macmillan, 1908), 150.
2. Benjamin Franklin, *Poor Richard's Almanack* (September 1751) (Mount Vernon, NY: Peter Pauper Press, 1980), 201.
3. John Nicholas Pappas, *Essays on Diderot and the Enlightenment in Honor of Otis Fellows* (Geneva: Droz, 1974), 405.
4. "Is it not possible that the virtuous and moderate proposal to strangle the last Jesuit in the bowels of the last Jansenist might do something toward reconciling matters?"; cited Morley, *Diderot and the Encyclopædists,* II, VIII, note 202. As is often the case for these writers, it is difficult to say whether Voltaire borrowed the image or was borrowed from.

5. We know Diderot, or at least a character authored by Diderot, used a form of the image it embodies in a poem, probably written in 1772, probably circulated in manuscript and definitely printed in 1795, well after his death: "And his hands would plait a priest's entrails;/ In lieu of a rope for strangling kings." (*"Et ses mains ourdiraient les entrailles du pretre, / Au défaut d'un cordon pour étrangler les rois"*); in Diderot, *Les Éleuthéromanes*, 96. For the argument that the author would not approve of the activity his character describes, see Morley, *Diderot and the Encyclopædists*, II, VIII, note 202; Rasmussen, "Burning Laws and Strangling Kings?" For dates and circulation, see Denis Diderot, *Les Éleuthéromanes* (Paris: Ghio, 1884), 14-21.

6. Meslier is quoting, with approval, someone else: "His wish was that all the rulers of the earth and all the nobles be hanged and strangled with the guts of priests" (*"Il souhaitait que tous les grands de la Terre et que tous les nobles fussent pendus et étranglés avec les boyaux des prêtres."*) Meslier, *Testament*, 37. See Herbert Dieckmann, "The Abbé Jean Meslier and Diderot's *Eleuthéromanes*," *Harvard Library Bulletin* 7 (1953): 231–35.

7. Cited Michael Novak and Jana Novak, *Washington's God* (New York: Basic Books, 2006), 114, 117.

8. Eric Foner, *Tom Paine and Revolutionary America* (New York: Oxford University Press, 2005), xxvii.

9. Ibid., 79

10. Israel, *Democratic Enlightenment*, 421-22, 451-56.

11. Attempts to connect *Common Sense* with *The Philosophical History of the Two Indies* can lead to significant chicken-and-egg issues since the authors of the latter in France were quite alert to goings on in North America and changed later editions to reflect them. Indeed, Diderot lifted wordings—not atypical behavior for him—from Paine's *Common Sense* in a later edition of *The Philosophical History;* see Mary Efrosini Gregory, *Freedom in French Enlightenment Thought* (New York: Peter Lang Publishing, 2010), 106. Three editions of *The Philosophical History* were published in French: in 1770, 1774 and 1780. To demonstrate the influence the work might have had on Paine, whose pamphlet was published in January 1776, I have restricted myself in these comparisons to excerpts translated into English of the North American portions of the book that must have come from the first two editions and which Paine might therefore have seen before writing *Common Sense*. They are: *The Sentiments of a Foreigner on the Disputes of Great-Britain with America,* published by James Humphreys in Philadelphia in 1775, and *A Philosophical and Political History of the British Settlements and Trade in North America,* published in two volumes in Edinburgh in 1776 by C. Macfarquhar but probably based on a translation available elsewhere. To complicate matters further, Paine later wrote a critique of "Raynal's" later accounts of the American Revolution: *A Letter Addressed to the Abbé Raynal on the Affairs of North America, in Which the Mistakes in the Abbé's Account of the Revolution of America Are Corrected and Cleared Up.* As noted in chapter 6, when John Locke speaks of "men being, as has been said, by nature, all free, equal and independent," his emphasis is on how someone "divests himself of his natural liberty" by putting "on the bonds of civil society"; Locke, *Two Treatises of Government,* 186.

12. Abbé Raynal, *A Philosophical and Political History of the British Settlements and Trade in North America,* Vols. I and II (Edinburgh: C. Macfarquhar, 1776), I, 109, 191; II, 168, 172. For a particularly apropos example of the use of the word "asylum" in a reprint of a later edition—one that raises the chicken-egg problem—see Raynal, *Philosophical and Political History,* vol. IV (1804), 137.

13. Edwin Wolf and Kevin J. Hayes, *The Library of Benjamin Franklin* (Philadelphia: American Philosophical Society, 2006), 274, 419, 641, 816. The tract was *Lettre de Trasibule a Leucippe,* attributed, probably falsely, to Nicolas Fréret; see J. Ph. Damiron, "Mémoire sur d'Holbach," in *Séances et travaux de l'Académie des sciences morales et politiques,* vol. XIX (edited collection of a journal, Paris, 1851), 264-69.

14. See Benjamin Franklin and William Temple Franklin, *Memoirs of the Life and Writings of Benjamin Franklin* (London: A.J. Valpy, 1818), 346n, 357n. Philipp Blom considers Franklin's attendance at d'Holbach's salon only likely; Blom, *A Wicked Company,* 286-89.

15. Cited James Parton, *Life and Times of Benjamin Franklin,* 2 vols. (New York: Mason Brothers, 1864), I, 173. See also Walter Isaacson, *Benjamin Franklin: An American Life* (New York: Simon & Schuster, 2004), 451, 467. Kerry S. Walters has produced perhaps the most thorough study of Benjamin Franklin's religious views, though one that is perhaps more sympathetic to his faith than his doubts. Walters sees Franklin as vacillating between a Calvinist Christianity and an Enlightenment deism, unified only by a "theistic perspectivism" or a

sense, as Walters explains, "that humans . . . symbolically represent God to themselves in such a way as to establish some sort of contact with the divine"; *Benjamin Franklin and His Gods* (Urbana: University of Illinois Press, 1998), 8, 10, 150.

16. Cited Alfred Owen Aldridge, *Thomas Paine's American Ideology* (Cranbury, NJ: Associated University Presses, 1984), 97. And these paragraphs in *Common Sense* owe a debt to John Milton's *Paradise Lost*, as Paine, according to John Adams, acknowledged; "John Adams autobiography, part 1, 'John Adams,' through 1776; sheet 23 of 53, January–April 1776," *John Adams Family Papers: An Electronic Archive*, http://www.masshist.org/digitaladams/aea/cfm/doc.cfm?id=A1_23.

17. Thomas Paine, "Rights of Man," in *The Political Writings of Thomas Paine*, vol. II (Boston: J. P. Mendum, 1870), 217.

18. Thomas Paine, *Age of Reason: Being an Investigation of True and Fabulous Theology* (London: R. Carlile, 1826), 4.

19. Sayyid Qutb, an influential twentieth-century Islamist thinker, is among the many who saw the dangers for religion in tolerance. Qutb bemoans the "desolate separation between [the Christian] church and society." He writes, "God's existence is not denied, but His domain is restricted to the heavens and His rule on earth is suspended"; Paul Berman, *Terror and Liberalism* (New York: W. W. Norton & Company, 2004), 80-81.

20. Cited William D. Gould, "The Religious Opinions of Thomas Jefferson," *Mississippi Valley Historical Review* 20, 2 (September 1933): 195.

21. Joseph J. Ellis, *His Excellency George Washington* (New York: Random House, 2004), 151, 269; David L. Holmes, *Religion of the Founding Fathers* (Charlottesville, VA: Ash Lawn-Highland, 2003), 79-89; Novak and Novak, *Washington's God*, 102-8, 120, 130-34; Don Higginbotham, ed., *George Washington Reconsidered* (Charlottesville: University Press of Virginia, 2001), 259-61. Michael and Jana Novak are intent on proving Washington an orthodox Anglican. They produce some evidence that "Providence" might have been a Christian as much as a deist term. Besides the presence at the foot of his bed of his more devout wife, they produce no evidence that Washington's death deserves to be considered, as they put it, "quite Christian in its entire context," though, in fairness, we have only one, rather reserved report on that death, from Washington's secretary, Tobias Lear.

22. Edwin S. Gaustad, *Sworn on the Altar of God: A Religious Biography of Thomas Jefferson* (Grand Rapids, MI: William Eerdmans, 1996), 29.

23. The Jefferson Monticello, "System of Nature," http://www.monticello.org/site/research-and-collections/system-nature. See also Kevin J. Hayes, *The Road to Monticello: The Life and Mind of Thomas Jefferson* (New York: Oxford University Press, 2008), 581.

24. See The Jefferson Monticello, "System of Nature." See also Hayes, *The Road to Monticello*, 581; Blom, *A Wicked Company*, 286-87. In fairness, Jefferson owned a lot of books: 6,487 by one count, when he sold his collection to Congress.

25. Cited Gould, "The Religious Opinions of Thomas Jefferson," 193; Thomas Jefferson, *Notes on the State of Virginia* (Richmond, VA: J. W. Randolph, 1853), 30-31, 170.

26. The Rev. William Linn, "Serious Considerations on the Election of a President," 1800, http://candst.tripod.com/pol1800.htm#Serious; see Gaustad, *Sworn on the Altar of God*, 90-104; Gould, "The Religious Opinions of Thomas Jefferson," 193.

27. Cited Fred C. Luebke, "The Origins of Thomas Jefferson's Anti-Clericalism," *Church History* 32, 3 (September 1963): 344-56.

28. Cited Frank Lambert, *The Founding Fathers and the Place of Religion in America* (Princeton, NJ: Princeton University Press, 2003), 275.

29. Samuel Eagle Forman, *The Life and Writings of Thomas Jefferson* (Indianapolis, IN: Bobbs Merrill Co., 1900), 359-60.

30. Jefferson, *Writings*, 140.

31. Wolf and Hayes, *Library of Benjamin Franklin*, 44-45.

32. Cited Garry Wills, *James Madison* (New York: Times Books, 2002), 17.

33. James Madison, *The Writings of James Madison*, ed. Gaillard Hunt (New York: G.P. Putnam's Sons, 1904), V, 31.

34. David L. Holmes, "The Religion of James Madison," *Virginia Quarterly Review* 79, 4 (Autumn 2003).

35. John Adams, *The Works of John Adams*, ed. Charles Francis Adams (Boston: Little, Brown, 1856), X, 66. See also Norman Cousins, ed., *"In God We Trust": The Religious Beliefs and Ideas of the American Founding Fathers* (New York: Harpers & Brothers, 1958), 100.

36. Bruce Braden, ed., *"Ye Will Say I Am No Christian": The Thomas Jefferson/John Adams Correspondence on Religion, Morals and Values* (Amherst, NY: Prometheus Books, 2005), 221.

37. For Franklin, see Walters, *Benjamin Franklin and His Gods,* 59-68. For Jefferson, see Walters, *Rational Infidels: The American Deists* (Durango, CO: Longwood Academic, 1992), 170-83; Gould, "The Religious Opinions of Thomas Jefferson," 201-3.

38. For a discussion of his attitude toward religion, see Garrett Ward Sheldon, *The Political Philosophy of James Madison* (Baltimore: Johns Hopkins University Press, 2001), xvi.

39. Paine, *Age of Reason,* 3.

40. Ibid., 3

41. See Holmes, *Religion of the Founding Fathers,* 90-95.

42. Cousins, *"In God We Trust,"* 238-41.

43. Strong, though not conclusive, arguments for classifying these four presidents as deists were made by contemporaries and have been made by some historians. David L. Holmes gives the most sweeping version of the argument in *Religion of the Founding Fathers,* 69-71. For Franklin and deism, see Walters, *Rational Infidels,* 68-81; Isaacson, *Benjamin Franklin,* 26, 46, 84-87, 486; Holmes, *Religion of the Founding Fathers,* 72-78. For Washington and deism, see Peter R. Henriques (who might accept the category "warm deist") in Higginbotham, ed., *George Washington Reconsidered,* 257-58; Holmes, *Religion of the Founding Fathers,* 79-89; Joseph J. Ellis, *His Excellency George Washington,* 151; Novak and Novak (who accept only "Christian"), *Washington's God,* 97-98. For Jefferson and deism, see Walters (who labels him a "Christian deist"), *Rational Infidels,* 153-88; George Harmon Knoles, "The Religious Ideas of Thomas Jefferson," *The Mississippi Valley Historical Review* 30, 2 (September 1943): 187-204; and Gould (who insists that Jefferson was not exactly a deist but acknowledges that contemporaries were convinced he was), "The Religious Opinions of Thomas Jefferson," 199-201; Holmes, *Religion of the Founding Fathers,* 96-106. For (the very reticent) Madison and deism, see a late-life letter he wrote, cited by Ralph L. Ketcham in Robert S. Alley, *James Madison on Religious Liberty* (Buffalo, NY: Prometheus Books, 1985), 176; see also James Hutson, *Forgotten Features of the Founding: The Recovery of Religious Themes in the Early American Republic* (Lanham, MD: Lexington Books, 2003), 155-60; Holmes, *Religion of the Founding Fathers,* 107-14; Noll, 135. For (the equally reticent) Monroe and deism, see Holmes, *Religion of the Founding Fathers,* 115-27; Holmes, "Religion of James Monroe." Franklin, Washington and Monroe were also Freemasons, and the Masons had become, by this time, strongly deistic; Holmes, "Religion of James Monroe."

44. Braden, *"Ye Will Say I Am No Christian,"* 164. See Charles B. Sanford, *The Religious Life of Thomas Jefferson* (Charlottesville: University Press of Virginia, 1984), 84.

45. Cited David Berman, *A History of Atheism in Britain: From Hobbes to Russell* (London: Croom Helm, 1988), 1.

46. Ibid., 42-43; for evidence that the contention was widely expressed, see pp. 20 and 42. The writer of this publication was given as William Hammon, who appears not to have existed; it was probably written by Matthew Turner, a physician in Liverpool. Martin Priestman, *Romantic Atheism: Poetry and Freethought, 1780–1830* (Cambridge: Cambridge University Press, 1999), 12-15.

47. Berman, *A History of Atheism in Britain,* 42-43.

48. George Rudé, *The French Revolution* (New York: Grove Press, 1988), 66-67; Paine's book, *The Age of Reason,* in which he called for that "revolution in the system of religion," was actually written in Paris during the French Revolution; see David Freeman Hawke, *Paine* (New York: Harper Colophon, 1975), 292-95.

49. Willard Sterne Randall, *Thomas Jefferson: A Life* (New York: Perennial, 1994), 486; William Howard Adams, *The Paris Years of Thomas Jefferson* (New Haven, CT: Yale University Press, 1997), 285-86.

50. This continues to be noticed, in Islamic lands for example; see Esmaeli Salami, *Islamic Views on Human Rights* (London: Hoda, 2001), 125.

51. Kors, *D'Holbach's Coterie,* 275-76; Wickwar, *Baron d'Holbach,* 81; Edgar Saltus, *The Anatomy of Negation* (New York: Scribner and Welford, 1886), 153-54.

52. Israel, *Democratic Enlightenment,* 902-23, 928.

53. Eric J. Hobsbawm, *Primitive Rebels: Studies in Archaic Forms of Social Movements in the 19th and 20th Centuries* (Manchester: Manchester University Press, 1959), 126.

54. This account is from Rudé, *The French Revolution,* 67-69; Sidney Z. Ehler and John B. Morrall, *Church and State through the Centuries* (Cheshire, CT: Biblio and Tannen, 1967), 237-38.

55. Cited William Milligan Sloane, *The French Revolution and Religious Reform* (New York: C. Scribner's Sons, 1901), 166.

56. Norman Hampson, *A Social History of the French Revolution* (London: Routledge, 1963), 201; Michel Vovelle, *The Revolution Against the Church: From Reason to the Supreme Being,* trans. Alan José (Cambridge: Polity Press, 1991), 105-7; Rudé, *The French Revolution,* 68-69; Sloane, *The French Revolution and Religious Reform,* 168.

57. Cited David V. Erdman, *Blake: Prophet Against Empire* (Mineola, NY: Dover Publications, 1991), 195.

58. Cited Vovelle, *The Revolution Against the Church,* 100.

59. Saint Flour, Cited ibid., 100.

60. Ibid., 129-30.

61. Ibid., 101-3, 116; Sloane, *The French Revolution and Religious Reform,* 198n.

62. J. Mills Whitham, *Men and Women of the French Revolution* (New York: Viking Press, 1933), 368.

63. Vivian Hubert Howard Green, *A New History of Christianity* (New York: Continuum, 2000),187; Sloane, *The French Revolution and Religious Reform,* 198. According to later religious accounts the "goddess" had been "half-naked," see *New Catholic World,* XX (February 1875): 681. Becker suggests that the goddess was Liberty, not Reason; Becker, *The Heavenly City of the Eighteenth-Century Philosophers,* 156-57; see François-Alphonse Aulard, *The French Revolution: A Political History, 1789-1804,* trans. Bernard Miall, 4 vols. (New York: C. Scribner's Sons, 1910), II, 21.

64. Meslier, *Superstition in All Ages,* 34; http://www.gutenberg.org/files/17607/17607-h/17607-h.htm.

65. Alan Forrest, *Paris, the Provinces and the French Revolution* (New York: Arnold Hodder, 2004), 138.

66. This account is based primarily on that in Ernest Belfort Bax, *Outlooks from the New Standpoint* (London: S. Sonnenschien, 1891), 1-37.

67. Cited Morris Slavin, *The Hébertistes to the Guillotine* (Baton Rouge: Louisiana State University Press, 1994), 195.

68. Louis Jacob, *Hébert, Le Père Duchesne* (Paris: Gallimard, 1960), 233-34.

69. Cited Slavin, *The Hébertistes to the Guillotine,* 17.

70. Jacob, *Hébert,* 208, 211; Hawke, *Paine,* 289; Neil Schaeffer, *The Marquis de Sade: A Life* (New York: Alfred A. Knopf, 1999), 447.

71. Donald Thomas, *The Marquis de Sade* (London: Allison & Busby, 1992), 81.

72. Ibid., 108.

73. This account of his activities during the revolution is from Schaeffer, *The Marquis de Sade,* 125-44; 381-82; 394; see also Thomas, *The Marquis de Sade,* 206-21.

74. Marquis de Sade, *Selected Letters,* trans. W. J. Strachan., ed. Margaret Crosland (New York: October House, 1966), 145. See Lawrence W. Lynch, *The Marquis de Sade* (Boston: Twayne, 1984), 15, 24-26.

75. Cited Francine du Plessix Gray, *At Home with the Marquis de Sade* (New York: Simon & Schuster, 1998), 339; see also Schaeffer, *The Marquis de Sade,* 436-37.

76. Cited Berman, *A History of Atheism in Britain,* 40.

77. Paine spent, however, ten months and nine days in Paris prisons. Hawke, *Paine,* 297-306.

78. Georges Avenel, *Anacharsis Cloots, l'Orateur Du Genre Humain,* 2 vols. (Paris: A. Lacroix, Verboeckhoven, 1865), II, 463-74. Slavin, *The Hébertistes to the Guillotine,* 200, 230.

79. This description is from George Henry Lewes, *The Life of Maximilien Robespierre* (London: Chapman and Hall, 1849), 340-46; Charles Franklin Warwick, *Robespierre and the French Revolution* (London: Fisher Unwin, 1909), 324-26; Edmond Dehault de Pressensé and John Power Lacroix, *Religion and the Reign of Terror,* trans. John P. Lacroix (New York: Carlton and Lanahan, 1869), 244-45.

80. Robespierre's speech is in Lewis Copeland and Lawrence W. Lamm, *World's Great Speeches* (Mineola, NY: Dover Publications, 2007), 83-85.

81. Schaeffer, *The Marquis de Sade,* 449-50.

82. Raynal, *Philosophical and Political History . . . East and West Indies,* vol. VI (1788), 428.

83. Israel, *Democratic Enlightenment,* 27, 819-20.

84. Ibid., 947.

85. Ibid. Hébert's name does not appear in Jonathan Israel's 951-page book.

86. Paine, *The Age of Reason,* 55.

87. By the middle of the next century, a liberal and a nonbeliever like John Stuart Mill would speak of the "temporary aberrations" of the French Revolution "the worst of which were the work of a usurping few, and which, in any case, belonged not to the permanent working of popular institutions, but to a sudden and convulsive outbreak against monarchical and

aristocratic despotism"; *On Liberty and Other Essays* (New York: Oxford University Press, 1998), 7.

88. William Wordsworth, *The Excursion* (London: J. M. Dent, 1904), vi. The poem was originally published in 1814 but probably composed by 1800. This interpretation owes much to Priestman, *Romantic Atheism*, 182-83. *The Excursion* itself was intended to be part of a larger poem: *The Recluse.*

89. Cited Henry Crabb Robinson, *Blake, Coleridge, Wordsworth, Lamb, Etc.* ed. Edith J. Morley (Manchester: The University Press, 1922), 5.

CHAPTER 9: THIS GLORIOUS LAND OF FREEDOM

1.   Shelley, *Prometheus Unbound*, 4.320.

2.   Carol A. Kolmerten has done an impressive job of collecting the various incomplete and contradictory versions of Rose's early life. This account of Rose's life is based on that in Kolmerten's fine biography and on the less thorough biography in Annie Laurie Gaylor, *Women Without Superstition* (Madison, WI: Freedom from Religion Foundation, 1997), 63-72.

3.   See Paul R. Mendes-Flohr and Jehuda Reinharz, eds., *The Jew in the Modern World,* 2nd ed. (New York: Oxford University Press, 1995), 113.

4.   Cited Carol A. Kolmerten, *The American Life of Ernestine L. Rose* (Syracuse, NY: Syracuse University Press, 1999), 5.

5.   This incident is detailed in and the quotations, unless otherwise indicated, are from Richard Holmes, *Shelley: The Pursuit* (New York: New York Review Books, 1994), 49-60.

6.   Compare with the selection from Baron d'Holbach's *System of Nature* quoted in chapter 7 this passage from the *Necessity of Atheism:*

> If he knows all, why warn him of our needs and fatigue him with our prayers? If he is everywhere, why erect temples to him? If he is just, why fear that he will punish the creatures that he has filled with weaknesses? . . . If he is all-powerful, how offend him, how resist him? . . . If he is inconceivable, why occupy ourselves with him? IF HE HAS SPOKEN, WHY IS THE UNIVERSE NOT CONVINCED?

Shelley, *Necessity of Atheism.* D'Holbach might have benefited from a translator as lyrical as Shelley. Young Shelley had clearly benefited from reading d'Holbach.

7.   *A Complete Collection of State Trials and Proceedings for High Treason and Other Crimes and Misdemeanors from the Earliest Period to the Year 1820,* compiled by Thomas Bayly Howell, vol. XIII (London: Longman, 1816-1828), 917-38.

8.   These quotes are from Shelley, *Necessity of Atheism.*

9.   Shelley, *Queen Mab: A Philosophical Poem. With Notes,* VII, 44-45, http://www.bartleby.com/139/shel111.html.

10. Holmes, *Shelley,* 230, 242-43, 715, 729-30.

11. Ibid., 200, 208.

12. Ibid., 200, 208, 373, 390-92.

13. Ibid., 715, 729.

14. Ibid., 715, 729-30.

15. Ibid., 660.

16. "Letter to Leigh Hunt on the Trial of Richard Carlile," November 3, 1819, in Percy Bysshe Shelley, *The Works Of Percy Bysshe Shelley in Verse and Prose,* ed. Harry Buxton Foxman (London: Reeves and Turner, 1880), VIII, 291-300.

17. R. Carlile, "A LETTER to The Society for the Suppression of Vice, ON THEIR Malignant Efforts TO PREVENT A FREE ENQUIRY After TRUTH AND REASON," London, 1819, http://www.gutenberg.org/files/40212/40212-h/40212-h.htm. Priestman, *Romantic Atheism*, 207; Holmes, *Shelley,* 209, 660-61; William St. Clair, *The Reading Nation In the Romantic Period* (Cambridge: Cambridge University Press, 2004), 318-20, 680-81.

18. Despite this heroic partnership, their relationship did not last; Carlile's great love, after they separated, would be Eliza Sharples.

19. Shelley, *Queen Mab: A Philosophical Poem. With Notes,* III, 116-17, http://www.bartleby.com/139/shel111.html.

20. Ibid., IV, 1-19; VI, 58-61.

21. St. Clair, *Reading Nation In the Romantic Period,* 680-81.

22. Richard Carlile, *The Lion,* number 9, volume 3, February 20, 1829, in *The Lion,* III, London: 1829.

23. Kenneth Neill Cameron, "Shelley as Philosophical and Social Thinker: Some Modern Evaluations," *Studies in Romanticism* 21, 3 (Fall 1982): 357-366.

24. Cited Priestman, *Romantic Atheism,* 205.

25. Cited Kolmerten, *American Life of Ernestine L. Rose,* 98.

26. Once again I am relying on Kolmerten and, to a lesser extent, Gaylor.

27. Cited Kolmerten, *American Life of Ernestine L. Rose* 147.

28. Celia Morris, *Fanny Wright: Rebel in America* (Cambridge, MA: Harvard University Press, 1984), 1-2, 99.

29. Frances Wright, *Course of Popular Lectures As Delivered by Frances Wright with Three Addresses on Various Public Occasions, And a Reply to the Charges Against the French Reformers of 1789* (New York: Office of the Free Enquirer, 1829), 9. The quote on belief in God being "an idle speculation" is actually attributed to a wise and sympathetic character of Wright's speaking in her novel; Wright, *A Few Days in Athens: Being the Translation of a Greek Manuscript Discovered in Herculaneum* (Boston: Mendum, 1850), 211.

30. James Bieri, *Percy Bysshe Shelley: A Biography: Youth's Unextinguished Fire, 1792-1816* (Cranbury, NJ: Associated University Presses, 2006), 293. Hecht's work on Wright and other early women freethinkers is important and valuable.

31. Founded in 1831 by Abner Kneeland; later edited by Horace Seaver and published by Josiah P. Mendum; Bill Cooke, "*Boston Investigator*" in *The New Encyclopedia of Unbelief,* ed. Tom Flynn (Amherst, NY: Prometheus Books, 2007). See also Frank L. Mott, *A History of American Magazines, 1865-1885* (Cambridge: Harvard University Press, 1938), 88.

32. Kolmerten, *American Life of Ernestine L. Rose,* 207-8. For an example, see Infidel Society for the Promotion of Mental Liberty, *Minutes of the Proceedings of the Infidel Convention Held in the City of New York, May 4th, 5th and 6th, 1845* (J. P. Mendum, 1845).

33. Cited Kolmerten, *American Life of Ernestine L. Rose,* 42.

34. Ibid., 129.

35. Ibid., 267.

36. Shelley, *Prometheus Unbound,* 4.184.

37. Frederick Douglass, *Narrative of the Life of Frederick Douglass, an American Slave* (New York: Random House, 2011), 113.

38. William Lloyd Garrison, "The 'Infidelity' of Abolition," in *The Liberty Bell* (Boston: National Anti-Slavery Bazaar, 1856), 139-158.

39. Cited David Keith Adams and Cornelis A. van Minnen, *Religious and Secular Reform in America: Ideas, Beliefs, and Social Change* (New York: NYU Press, 1999), 98; Kolmerten, *American Life of Ernestine L. Rose,* 58-59, 65, 149-50; Douglass, *Narrative of the Life of Frederick Douglass,* 9113.

40. Cited Kolmerten, *American Life of Ernestine L. Rose,* 81.

41. Ibid., 84, 166.

42. Bettyann Kevles, "A Feminist in the Late '80s," in *Interviews with Betty Friedan,* ed. Janaan Sherman (Jackson: University Press of Mississippi, 2002), 82. Betty Friedan is speaking here about a new interest in Judaism but makes clear that she "was not particularly religious until a few years ago"; Letty Cottin Pogrebin, "Gloria Steinem," in *Jewish Women: A Comprehensive Historical Encyclopedia,* http://jwa.org/encyclopedia/article/steinem-gloria.

43. Lori D. Ginzberg, *Elizabeth Cady Stanton: An American Life* (New York: Macmillan, 2010), 23.

44. Elizabeth Cady Stanton, *Eighty Years and More* (New York: European Publishing Company, 1897), 44. In her biography of Stanton, Ginzberg questions details of this story; Lori D. Ginzberg, *Elizabeth Cady Stanton,* 25.

45. Stanton, *Eighty Years and More,* 161. Susan Jacoby, *Freethinkers: A History of American Secularism* (New York: Metropolitan Books, 2004), 144-45.

46. Cited Jacoby, *Freethinkers,* 197.

47. Ibid., 97-98.

48. Cited Kolmerten, *American Life of Ernestine L. Rose,* 109.

49. Cited Gaylor, *Women Without Superstition,* 65.

50. Garrison, "The 'Infidelity' of Abolition," 139-158.

51. Cited Kolmerten, *American Life of Ernestine L. Rose,* xvii, 153, 271; Gary Schmidgall, *Intimate with Walt: Selections from Whitman's Conversations with Horace Traubel, 1888-1892* (Iowa City: University of Iowa Press, 2001), 223-24.

52. Cited Kolmerten, *American Life of Ernestine L. Rose,* 155.

53. Ibid., 35-36.

54. Ibid., 57.

55. Ibid., 108.

56. This comment was made by Horace Seaver, a long-time ally of Rose's, in the periodical that mostly supported her and her causes, the *Boston Investigator.* Rose responded, with some

heat, in that publication; Sandra J. Berkowitz and Amy C. Lewis, "Debating Anti-Semitism: Ernestine Rose vs. Horace Seaver in the Boston Investigator, 1863-1864," *Communication Quarterly* 46, 4 (1998): 457-71; Kolmerten, *American Life of Ernestine L. Rose,* 238.

57. Cited Kolmerten, *American Life of Ernestine L. Rose,* 181.
58. These numbers are difficult to interpret for a number of reasons and have inspired a number of recent reevaluations. Bruce gives a figure for church attendance on that day of between 40 and 60 percent of the adult population of Great Britain; *God Is Dead,* 63. See also David Martin, *A Sociology of English Religion* (London: Heinemann Educational Books, 1979), 19; Hugh McLeod, *European Religion in the Age of Great Cities: 1830-1930* (London: Routledge, 1995), 12-13, 19-45. Scotland, which tended to be slightly more religious, and Wales were also included in the survey.
59. Mill, *Three Essays on Religion,* 70.
60. Joseph McCabe, *Life and Letters of George Jacob Holyoake,* 2 vols. (London: Watts & Co., 1908), I, 208.
61. Kolmerten, *American Life of Ernestine L. Rose,* 184n.
62. Ernestine L. Rose, "A Defense of Atheism," in Gaylor, *Women Without Superstition,* 73-85. See Hecht, *Doubt,* 388.
63. Carol A. Kolmerten does come upon one statement by Rose that could be interpreted as disparaging toward "Chinaman," "Hottentot," "Calmuck" and Indian, but Rose was generally scrupulous in her defense of immigrants and African-American men; *American Life of Ernestine L. Rose,* 252-53.
64. Ibid., 270.

CHAPTER 10: FREE ROVERS ON THE BROAD, BRIGHT, BREEZY COMMON OF THE UNIVERSE

1.   Cited Israel, *Democratic Enlightenment,* 35.
2.   This tale is told in all the biographies and in the short autobiographical sketch; "Autobiography of Mr. Bradlaugh" in John Saville, ed., *A Selection of the Political Pamphlets of Charles Bradlaugh* (New York: Augustus M. Kelley, 1970). The details are richest and the dates somewhat less hazy in Bradlaugh's daughter's account; Hypatia Bradlaugh Bonner and with John M. Robertson, *Charles Bradlaugh: A Record of His Life and Work by His Daughter,* 2 vols. (London: T. Fisher Unwin, 1908), I, 7-16. Bonner is the main source for the biographical information that follows; but see also Walter L. Arnstein, *The Bradlaugh Case: A Study in Late Victorian Opinion and Politics* (Oxford: Clarendon Press, 1965); David Tribe, *President Charles Bradlaugh, M.P.* (London: Elek Books, 1971).
3.   Matthew 12:40: "For as Jonas was three days and three nights in the whale's belly; so will the Son of Man be three days and three nights in the heart of the earth." However, Luke 23:43 has Jesus, while on the cross, assure a criminal beside him, "Today you will be with Me in paradise." The standard explanation for this apparent contradiction: until Jesus ascended, paradise was located down in Hell, which was similar to the Greek Hades, so Jesus could have been both in Hell and paradise on the same day.
4.   Robert Taylor, *The Diegesis; Being a Discovery of the Origin, Evidences, and Early History of Christianity* (London: Richard Carlile, 1829), 2.
5.   Cited Bonner, *Charles Bradlaugh,* I, 20-21.
6.   Ibid., I, 18.
7.   "Autobiography of Mr. Bradlaugh."
8.   Bonner, *Charles Bradlaugh,* I, 25-27.
9.   Ibid., I, 25-27; "Autobiography of Mr. Bradlaugh" in Saville, *A Selection.*
10. Bonner, *Charles Bradlaugh,* I, 28.
11. This account is based on that in ibid., I, 35-39.
12. This account is based on that in ibid., I, 72-89. Iconoclast's were not the first such debates; in 1853, for example, George Jacob Holyoake, Bradlaugh's predecessor as leader of England's secularists, squared off with the Rev. Brewin Grant, who was one of Bradlaugh's debate partners, for six successive Thursday evenings in London; Edwin Hodder, *The Life of Samuel Morley* (London: Hodder and Stoughton, 1887), 114-15.
13. For a transcript, see *Full Report of the Discussion Between the Rev. Brewin Grant, B.A., and "Iconoclast," in the Mechanics' Hall, Sheffield, on the 7th, 8th, 14th & 15th June, 1858* (London: 1858). Both the debaters approved the transcript; Bonner, *Charles Bradlaugh,* I, 84.
14. An exception was Edward Fitzgerald's lovely and eventually quite popular publication, in 1859, of a translation of the poems of an anacreontic Persian poet: *The Rubáiyát of Omar*

Khayyám, in Edward Fitzgerald, *The Variorum and Definitive Edition of the Poetical and Prose Writings,* ed. George Bentham (New York: Phaeton Press, 1967).

15. Bradlaugh, "Why Do Men Starve?" London, 1882, http://debs.indstate.edu/b811w5_1882 .pdf.

16. Arnold Miller, *The Annexation of a Philosophe. Diderot Studies XV* (Geneva: Librairie Droz, 1971), 32; Andrew S. Curran, "Diderot, an American Exemplar? Bien Sûr!" *New York Times,* January 24, 2013.

17. Mill, *On Liberty,* 21. See Chadwick, *The Secularization of the European Mind,* 28-37.

18. Mill, *On Liberty,* 42.

19. Bonner, *Charles Bradlaugh,* I, 64. John Stuart Mill and Mary Taylor, *The Letters of John Stuart Mill,* vol. II (London: Longmans, Green, 1910), 140.

20. Mill, *On Liberty,* 22, 26, and elsewhere.

21. For the relationship between Marx and Mill, see Womack, "John Stuart Mill, Karl Marx, and Modern Citizenship," *Journal of Cambridge Studies* 7, 4 (2012), http://journal.acs-cam.org. uk/data/archive/2012/201204-article1.pdf.

22. Bonner, *Charles Bradlaugh,* I, 64. For Ernestine Rose on Mill, see Kolmerten, *American Life of Ernestine L. Rose,* 261.

23. Cited Janet E. Courtney, *Freethinkers of the Nineteenth Century* (London: Chapman and Hall, 1920), 150.

24. John Stuart Mill, *Autobiography of John Stuart Mill* (Auckland, NZ: The Floating Press, 2009), 43.

25. The quotes here are from Charles Darwin, *The Autobiography of Charles Darwin* (Amherst, NY: Prometheus Books, 2000), 62.

26. Darwin also mentions as factors in his loss of religion the Old Testament's "manifestly false history of the world" and its notion of God as "a revengeful tyrant."

27. Edward Manier, *The Young Darwin and His Cultural Circle* (Dordrecht, The Netherlands: Reidel Publishing Company, 1978), 69, 86, 88, 89-96; William B. Huntley, "David Hume and Charles Darwin," *Journal of the History of Ideas* 33, 3, Festschrift for Philip P. Wiener (July–September 1972): 457-470; Charles Darwin, *Early Writings of Charles Darwin* (Chicago: Chicago University Press, 1974), 19, 33, 40, 42, 45, 55-56, 61, 65, 88, 99; Darwin, *Autobiography,* 53; Jonathan Hodge and Gregory Radick, *The Cambridge Companion to Darwin* (Cambridge: Cambridge University Press, 2003), 199.

28. Darwin, *Autobiography,* 62.

29. Edward O. Wilson, "Intelligent Evolution," *Harvard Magazine* (November–December 2005). For more complex explanations of the relationship between Darwin's theory and his loss of faith, see Ernst Mayr, *One Long Argument: Charles Darwin and the Genesis of Modern Evolutionary Thought* (Cambridge, MA: Harvard University Press, 1991), 74-75; John Bowlby, *Charles Darwin: A New Life* (New York: W. W. Norton, 1990), 226-28; John Hedley Brooke, "The Relations Between Darwin's Science and His Religion," in *Darwinism and Divinity: Essays on Evolution and Religious Belief,* ed. John Durant (Oxford: Blackwell, 1985), 65; Hodge and Radick, *Cambridge Companion to Darwin,* 199-200.

30. Darwin, *Autobiography,* 186.

31. Mayr, *One Long Argument,* 15. Charles Darwin, *Notebooks: 1836-1844,* ed. Paul H. Barrett, et al. (Ithaca, NY: Cornell University Press, 1987), 291; see also Bowlby, *Charles Darwin,* 212-13.

32. Darwin, *Autobiography,* 186.

33. Darwin, *Early Writings,* 55-56; see Tribe, 55.

34. Harriet Martineau, *Harriet Martineau's Autobiography,* 3 vols. (Cambridge: Cambridge University Press, 2010), I, 116; II, 279-81. Also Cited Hecht, *Doubt,* 384.

35. The account of this and subsequent Bradlaugh visits to Doncaster, and the citations, are from Bonner, *Charles Bradlaugh,* I, 74-77.

36. Based on the various accounts of this meeting, including Huxley's own, cited and discussed by J. R. Lucas, "Wilberforce and Huxley: A Legendary Encounter," *The Historical Journal* 22, 2 (June 1979): 313-30; see also Sheridan Gilley, "The Huxley-Wilberforce Debate: A Reconsideration," in *Religion and Humanism,* ed. Keith Robbins (Oxford: Blackwell, 1981), 325-40.

37. Cited Courtney, *Freethinkers of the Nineteenth Century,* 139, 152.

38. Thomas Henry Huxley, "Agnosticism," in *Christianity and Agnosticism: A Controversy* (New York: D. Appleton, 1889), 36.

39. Thomas Henry Huxley, *Selections from Huxley,* ed. John P. Cushing (Boston: Ginn, 1911), 23.

40. Thomas Henry Huxley, *Methods and Results* (New York: Greenwood, 1917), 33.

41. Cited Arnstein, *The Bradlaugh Case*, 11n.
42. The newspaper account is cited Bonner, *Charles Bradlaugh*, I, 87; the additional quotes from Bradlaugh on God are from "A Plea for Atheism," in Charles Bradlaugh, *Champion of Liberty* (New York: Freethought Press Association, 1934), 121. John Stuart Mill was similarly undogmatic. He did accord the existence of God "one of the lower degrees of probability" in *Three Essays on Religion*, 242. Nevertheless, that slim chance did not deter Mill from making it through life without any "religious belief."
43. This account is based on that in Bonner, *Charles Bradlaugh*, II, 63-75.
44. The newspaper was the *Christian*.
45. George Jacob Holyoake and Charles Bradlaugh, *Secularism, Scepticism and Atheism: Two Nights Public Debate* (London: Austin, 1870), 59.
46. For a general discussion by Bradlaugh of "scepticism," see Bonner, *Charles Bradlaugh*, I, 332-36.
47. Cited ibid., I, 87.
48. Cited Arnstein, *The Bradlaugh Case*, 11. Huxley fought back; see Thomas Henry Huxley, *Agnosticism and Christianity and Other Essays* (Amherst, NY: Prometheus Books, 1992), 102-3. Bradlaugh also had difficulty with George Jacob Holyoake's term, "secularism."
49. The story of Annie Besant's loss of faith and its consequences is from her *Annie Besant: An Autobiography* (Adyar Madras, India: Theosophical Publishing Society, 1908), 64, 71-96.
50. The subject is raised in the Hebrew Bible in the form, for example, of a challenge to the Lord, posed by the prophet Jeremiah: "Yet I shall present charges against You: / Why does the way of the wicked prosper? / Why are the workers of treachery at ease? / You have planted them, and they have taken root, / They spread, they even bear fruit"; Jeremiah 12:1-3.
51. See James Wood, "Holiday in Hellmouth," *New Yorker*, June 9 and 16, 2008.
52. Bonner, *Charles Bradlaugh*, I, 49-51. Note that this is their daughter's account.
53. Besant, *Annie Besant*, 115-16. For a different version of their meeting, see Tribe, *President Charles Bradlaugh*, 157-60.
54. Anne Taylor, *Annie Besant: A Biography* (Oxford: Oxford University Press, 1992), 99-100.
55. Cited ibid., 75.
56. Tribe, *President Charles Bradlaugh*, 179-80.
57. Matthew 5:32.
58. Bradlaugh, however, could sound rather conservative on the sanctity of marriage; see Tribe, *President Charles Bradlaugh*, 70.
59. For this case, see Taylor, *Annie Besant*, 105-23; Arthur H. Nethercot, *The First Five Lives of Annie Besant* (London: Rupert Hart-Davis, 1961), 116-39; and Tribe, *President Charles Bradlaugh*, 172-83.
60. Cited Arnstein, *The Bradlaugh Case*, 11. Nietzsche: "They have got rid of the Christian God, and now feel obliged to cling all the more firmly to Christian morality. . . . In England, in response to every little emancipation from theology one has to reassert one's position in a fear-inspiring manner as a moral fanatic"; Nietzsche, *Twilight of the Idols and the Anti-Christ*, 80.
61. They were, for what it is worth, thought by friends to be chaste. Taylor, *Annie Besant*, 123-25; Nethercot, *First Five Lives of Annie Besant*, 31.
62. Taylor, *Annie Besant*, 128-37; Nethercot, *First Five Lives of Annie Besant*, 140-53.
63. Cited Tribe, *President Charles Bradlaugh*, 183.
64. For this dispute and the Marx/Bradlaugh citations see ibid., 54, 124-27.
65. His name was Edward Bibbins Aveling; see Arnstein, *The Bradlaugh Case*, 264-65; Tribe, *President Charles Bradlaugh*, 227-30; Taylor, *Annie Besant*, 140-44.
66. Taylor, *Annie Besant*, 224, 260.
67. Cited Tribe, *President Charles Bradlaugh*, 270; see also Taylor, *Annie Besant*, 245.
68. Mill, *Autobiography*, 218-20; Arnstein, *The Bradlaugh Case*, 25.
69. "The New Alphabet," October 3, 1874; original at the Northamptonshire Central Library.
70. Bonner, *Charles Bradlaugh*, I, 395.
71. Ibid., 397-400.
72. Undated, original at the Northamptonshire Central Library.
73. Cited Arnstein, *The Bradlaugh Case*, 31; Tribe, *President Charles Bradlaugh*, 189.
74. Adolphe Headingley, *The Biography of Charles Bradlaugh* (London: Remington, 1880), 328-29.
75. This account of Bradlaugh's struggle to take his seat is based on that in Tribe, *President Charles Bradlaugh*, 91-250; Arnstein, *The Bradlaugh Case*, 34-312.
76. In *On Liberty*, Mill pointed out the foolishness of questioning whether atheists who were honest enough to admit that they were atheists could be trusted to tell the truth in court (p. 35).

77. Stephen D. Solomon explains that this was in deference to Quakers, Mennonites and Moravians, not atheists and agnostics. *Ellery's Protest: How One Young Man Defied Tradition & Sparked the Battle Over School Prayer* (Ann Arbor: University of Michigan Press, 2007), 87.

78. Cited Tribe, *President Charles Bradlaugh,* 195; Arnstein, *The Bradlaugh Case,* 54-55.

79. Cited Arnstein, *The Bradlaugh Case,* 69.

80. Tribe, *President Charles Bradlaugh,* 282-85.

81. Hypatia Bradlaugh Bonner, in "Memorial Number" of the *National Reformer,* February 8, 1891.

82. "Obituary. Mr. Bradlaugh," *Times,* January 31, 1891, 12. Francis Wheen, *Karl Marx* (London: HarperCollins, 2012), 382; Philip Sheldon Foner, *When Karl Marx Died* (New York: International Publishers Company, 1973), 122-23.

CHAPTER 11: TO WIPE AWAY THE ENTIRE HORIZON

1. Shelley, *Prometheus Unbound,* III, 57-59.

2. This scene is in Nietzsche, *Gay Science,* 181-82.

3. Foner, *When Karl Marx Died,* 38-40.

4. This account of Marx's early life is from that in Franz Mehring, *Karl Marx, The Story of His Life* (London: Allen & Unwin, 1951), 1-15; David McLellan, *Karl Marx: His Life and Thought* (London: Papermac, 1995), 1-33; Isiah Berlin, *Karl Marx* (New York: Oxford University Press, 1996), 17-60.

5. Cited McLellan, *Karl Marx,* 9.

6. Karl Marx, "Contribution to the Critique of Hegel's Philosophy of Right," in Karl Marx and Friedrich Engels, *On Religion* (Moscow: Foreign Languages Publishing House, 1957), 41-58.

7. For mention, without a citation however, of a Marx-Meslier connection, see "Jean Meslier," Freedom From Religion Foundation, http://ffrf.org/news/day/dayitems/item/14848-jean-meslier.

8. Karl Marx, "Contribution to the Critique of Hegel's Philosophy of Right," in Marx and Engels, *On Religion,* 41-58.

9. Nietzsche, *Twilight of the Idols and the Anti-Christ,* 132.

10. Cited Rüdiger Safranski, *Nietzsche: A Philosophical Biography,* trans. Shelley Frisch (New York: W. W. Norton. 2002), 39. This phrase had been used by Immanuel Kant; Cited Friedrich Paulsen, *Immanuel Kant: His Life and Doctrine* (New York: Scribner's, 1902), 272n.

11. Cited Safranski, *Nietzsche;* Nietzsche, *Gay Science,* 35-39.

12. Nietzsche, *Twilight of the Idols and the Anti-Christ,* 129, 139, 169. Commoro, the "wild, naked savage" introduced in the first chapter makes a similar argument; Baker, *Albert N'Yanza,* 178-81. That may have been one of the reasons Nietzsche was interested in Samuel White Baker's account of his discussion with Commoro; see Nietzsche, *Briefwechsel Kritische Gesamtausgabe,* III, 611; Orsucci, *Orient, Okzident,* 220.

13. See George Allen Morgan, *What Nietzsche Means* (Westport, CT: Greenwood, 1943), 36-37.

14. Rajmohan Gandhi, *Gandhi: The Man, His People, and the Empire* (Berkeley: University of California Press, 2006), 39.

15. Neils Bohr, Heisenberg's partner in developing quantum mechanics, also hesitated to close the door on religion entirely, though he admits to having no "personal God." Werner Heisenberg, *Physics and Philosophy* (New York: Harper Perennial, 2007), 169-78; and "P.S." in Heisenberg, *Physics and Philosophy,* 11-24.

16. Cited Ray Monk, *Ludwig Wittgenstein: The Duty of Genius* (New York: Penguin, 1991), 463.

17. Ludwig Wittgenstein, *Lectures and Conversations on Aesthetics, Psychology, and Religious Belief,* ed. Cyril Barrett (Berkeley: University of California Press, 2007), 56 (note: this book is based on student lecture notes). See Monk, *Ludwig Wittgenstein,* 115-16, 122-23, 410-13; 463-64, 580.

18. See Mikhail Druskin, *Igor Stravinsky* (Cambridge: Cambridge University Press, 1983), 111. Schönberg, Letter to Richard Dehmel, December 13, 1912, in Joseph Henry Auner, ed., *A Schoenberg Reader: Documents of a Life* (New Haven, CT: Yale University Press, 2003), 118-20; 161, 245. Wassily Kandinsky, *Concerning the Spiritual in Art* (Auckland, NZ: The Floating Press, 2009), 30-52.

19. Kenneth Goldsmith, ed., *I'll be Your Mirror: The Selected Andy Warhol Interviews: 1962-1987* (New York: Carroll & Graf, 2004), 258; Jane D. Dillenberger, *The Religious Art of Andy Warhol* (New York: Continuum, 2001), 38, 331.

20. Cited Lucy S. Dawidowicz, *The War Against the Jews: 1933-1945* (New York: Bantam Books, 1986), 21.

21. The views on religion of some seminal twentieth-century figures are more difficult to categorize, among them writers Marcel Proust, Franz Kafka and Samuel Beckett.

22. Miriam Gusevich, "Decoration and Decorum, Adolf Loos's Critique of Kitsch," *New German Critique* 43 (Winter 1988): 97-123.

23. Francis Crick, *What Mad Pursuit: A Personal View of Scientific Discovery* (New York: Basic Books, 2008), 10.

24. Gary Robbins, "Nobel Laureate Watson to Speak at Salk," March 19, 2013, *San Diego Union-Tribune,* http://www.utsandiego.com/news/2013/mar/19/DNA-genome-jameswatson/all/?print.

25. Ronald W. Clark, *Einstein: The Life and Times* (New York: HarperCollins, 1984), 38, 502.

26. Cited James Randerson, "Einstein's Letter Makes View of Religion Relatively Clear," *Guardian,* May 13, 2008, http://www.theguardian.com/science/2008/may/12/peopleinscience.religion. This article also includes a significant, though earlier, quote on the other side from Einstein: "Science without religion is lame, religion without science is blind."

27. Nietzsche, *Gay Science,* 181.

28. Andrew Hodges, *Alan Turing: The Enigma* (New York: Vintage, 2012), 108; see also, Olivia Solon, "Alan Turing's Extraordinary, Tragically Short Life: A Timeline," *Wired UK,* June 19, 2012, http://www.wired.com/wiredscience/2012/06/alan-turing-timeline/.

29. Rosalynd Pflaum, *Grand Obsession: Marie Curie and Her World* (New York: Doubleday, 1989), 9; Eve Curie, *Madame Curie: A Biography* (New York: Da Capo Press, 2001), 29, 51.

30. Curie, *Madame Curie,* 136-37, 268.

31. This account is based on that in Richard Ellmann, *James Joyce* (Oxford: Oxford University Press, 1983), 47-50.

32. Cited ibid., 169. For the argument that Joyce not only remained a nonbeliever but that this was central to his writing, see Geert Lernout, *Help My Unbelief: James Joyce and Religion* (Amsterdam: London, 2010).

33. This account of his childhood is based on that in Ray Monk, *Bertrand Russell: The Spirit of Solitude, 1872-1921* (New York: Free Press, 1996), 5-19.

34. Cited ibid., 17, 25.

35. Ibid., 30-35.

36. Arnold Miller, *The Annexation of a Philosophe. Diderot Studies XV* (Geneva: Librairie Droz, 1971), 34.

37. Cited Paul Gabel, *And God Created Lenin: Marxism vs. Religion in Russia, 1917-1929* (Amherst, NY: Prometheus Books, 2005), 80.

38. Peter Gay, *Freud* (New York: W. W. Norton, 2006), 4-7; Peter Gay, *A Godless Jew: Freud, Atheism and the Making of Psychoanalysis* (New Haven, CT: Yale University Press, 1987), 125.

39. Gay, *Freud,* 6; Gay, *A Godless Jew,* 125.

40. Gay, *Freud,* 29, 526; Gay, *A Godless Jew,* 38, 42.

41. Cited Gay, *A Godless Jew,* 37.

42. Ibid., 65.

43. See Freud, *The Future of an Illusion,* 35.

44. Freud distinguishes between *errors,* such as "Aristotle's belief that vermin are developed out of dung," and *illusions,* such as "Columbus' that he had discovered a new sea-route to the Indies. . . . What is characteristic of illusions is that they are derived from human wishes." Freud accepts "delusion" as another possible characterization of religious belief. Ibid., 37, 39.

45. Ibid., 29-30, 55, 68.

46. Ibid., 69.

47. William James, *The Varieties of Religious Experience* (New York: Barnes & Noble Classics, 2004), 57.

48. Shelley, *Prometheus Unbound,* III, 57.

49. Martin Luther King Jr., "I Have a Dream," speech delivered at the March on Washington, August 28, 1963; Amos 5:24.

50. Curie, *Madame Curie,* 76.

51. "Intelligent Machinery: A Report by A. M. Turing," 1948, in Alan Turing, *The Essential Turing,* ed. B. J. Copeland (Oxford: Oxford University Press, 2004), 409-32. The second counterargument is a quote from Dorothy Sayers.

52. Peter James Lowe, *Christian Romanticism: T. S. Eliot's Response to Percy Shelley.* Youngstown, NY: Cambria Press, 2006).

53. Cited Michael Lackey, "Virginia Woolf and T. S. Eliot: An Atheist's Commentary on the Epistemology of Belief," in *Woolf Studies Annual,* vol. 8 (New York: Pace University Press, 2002), 71.

54. Kandinsky, *Concerning the Spiritual in Art,* 30-52.
55. See Arnold Schönberg, Letter to Richard Dehmel, December 13, 1912, in Auner, *A Schoenberg Reader,* 118-20; 161, 245.
56. Walter Simon, "Show Unveils Andy Warhol's Catholic, Abstract Side," Reuters, June 11, 2010, http://www.reuters.com/article/2010/06/11/us-finearts-warhol-idUSTRE65A43C20100611.
57. See Arnold Schönberg, Letter to Richard Dehmel, December 13, 1912, in Auner, *A Schoenberg Reader,* 118-20.
58. Wittgenstein: "For a *large* class of cases—though not for all—in which we employ the word 'meaning' it can be defined thus: the meaning of a word is its use in the language." Ludwig Wittgenstein, *Philosophical Investigations,* trans. G. E. M. Anscombe (New York: Macmillan, 1968), 20e (43). For Ferdinand de Saussure's somewhat earlier formulation of this idea and later development of it by Jacques Derrida, see Lackey, "Virginia Woolf and T. S. Eliot," 85-86.
59. Nietzsche, *Gay Science,* 181.
60. Ibid., 280.
61. Cited Delos Banning McKown, *The Classical Marxist Critiques of Religion* (The Hague: Martinus Nijhoff, 1975), 95; James Thrower, *Marxist-Leninist "Scientific Atheism" and the Study of Religion and Atheism in the USSR* (Berlin: Walter de Gruyter, 1983), 114. See Sabrina Petra Ramet, ed., *Religious Policy in the Soviet Union* (Cambridge: Cambridge University Press, 1993), 4, 126; see Roland Boer, *Lenin, Religion, and Theology* (New York: Palgrave Macmillan, 2013).
62. William Husband, *"Godless Communists": Atheism and Society in Soviet Russia, 1917-1932* (Northern Illinois University Press, 2002), 46-48.
63. "Decrees and Stipulations of the Soviet Government Relating to Religion and the Church," January 23, 1913, in Julius F. Hecker, *Religion and Communism: A Study of Religion and Atheism in Soviet Russia* (New York: Hyperion Press, 1973), 289-90; also see pp. 202-4.
64. Ibid., 200.
65. Ibid., 204-6; Ramet, *Religious Policy in the Soviet Union,* 6; Gabel, *And God Created Lenin,* 141, 144-46; Husband, *"Godless Communists,"* 51.
66. This account of the implications for religious policy of the famine is based on that in Gabel, *And God Created Lenin,* 206; Dmitri Volkogonov, *Lenin* (New York: Simon and Schuster, 1998), 374-83; Husband, *Godless Communists,* 55-57.
67. Volkogonov, *Lenin,* 383.
68. Husband, *"Godless Communists,"* 58-59, 65; Daniel Peris, *Storming the Heavens: The Soviet League of the Militant Godless* (Ithaca, NY: Cornell University Press, 1998), 39. 297-98; Richard Stites, "Bolshevik Ritual Building in the 1920s," in *Russia in the Era of NEP: Explorations in Soviet Society and Culture,* ed. Sheila Fitzpatrick, Alexander Rabinowitch and Richard Stites (Bloomington, IN: Indiana University Press, 1991), 295-309.
69. Cited Hecker, *Religion and Communism,* 250-51.
70. Thrower, *Marxist-Leninist "Scientific Atheism,"* 137, 290.
71. Husband, *"Godless Communists,"* 60-63; Hecker, *Religion and Communism,* 215, 217-19, 229, 247-48, 254-65; Volkogonov, *Lenin,* 374; 138-86.
72. See Benjamin Forest, Juliet Johnson and Mari_tta Tigranovna Stepaniants, eds., *Religion and Identity in Modern Russia: The Revival of Orthodoxy and Islam* (Burlington, VT: Ashgate Publishing, 2005), 8. More reliable information only became available when the Soviet Union was beginning to crumble. In 1990, a telephone survey of Moscow residents found a relatively low number, just about 22 percent, who said they were sure that God exists, while about 17 percent were sure that there is no such being; Ramet, *Religious Policy in the Soviet Union,* 190.
73. "Most Atheist Nations, 2005," Association of Religion Data Archives, http://www.thearda.com/QuickLists/QuickList_39.asp.
74. See Omer Bartov and Phyllis Mack, eds. *In God's Name: Genocide and Religion in the Twentieth Century* (New York: Berghahn Books, 2001).
75. Freud, *The Future of an Illusion,* 41.
76. Nietzsche, *Gay Science,* 167. Marcel Proust: "When a belief vanishes, there survives it . . . an idolatrous attachment to the old things which our faith in them did once animate"; cited Lackey, "Virginia Woolf and T. S. Eliot," 63-64. Michel Foucault: "The death of God is not merely an 'event' that gave shape to contemporary experience as we now know it: it continues tracing indefinitely its great skeletal outline"; *Religion and Culture,* ed. Jeremy R. Carrett (New York: Routledge, 1999), 59. See Lackey, "Virginia Woolf and T. S. Eliot," 83.
77. Nietzsche, *Gay Science,* 288-89.
78. Ibid.

79. For Woolf, see "A Sketch of the Past," in Virginia Woolf, *Moments of Being* (San Diego: Harcourt Brace Jovanovich, 1985), 72. For Joyce, see Ellmann, *James Joyce*, 50, 66, 96. For Nietzsche, see his *Gay Science*, 123.

80. Holbach, *The System of Nature*, II, 7.

81. Mill, *Three Essays on Religion*, 28.

82. Ibid., 81, 87, 99, 110, 112, 118.

83. Bertrand Russell, *Religion and Science*, Introduction by Michael Ruse (Oxford: Oxford University Press, 1997), xi, xxi.

84. N. Berdyaev, cited Hecker, *Religion and Communism*, 188.

85. Dorothy Thompson, "Good-By to Germany," *Harper's Monthly Magazine*, December 1934. These are not, of course, simple distinctions. Presidents Abraham Lincoln and Franklin Delano Roosevelt also asked armies to die for causes.

86. See, for example, Arthur Koestler, *The God That Failed* (New York: Harper & Row, 1963). For a more nuanced take on this, see Susan Neiman, *Evil in Modern Thought* (Princeton, NJ: Princeton University Press, 2004), 104.

87. Karl Barth, *Evangelical Theology: An Introduction* (Grand Rapids, MI: Wm. B. Eerdmans Publishing, 1979), 3. More from Barth: "There is no philosophy that is not to some extent also theology. . . . The same truth is valid even for a thinker denying . . . a divinity, for such a denial would in practice merely consist in transferring an identical dignity and function to another object. Such an alternative object might be 'nature,' creativity, or an unconscious and amorphous will to life. It might be 'reason,' progress or even a redeeming nothingness into which man would be destined to disappear" (pp. 3-4). See David Martin, *On Secularization* (Burlington, VT: Ashgate, 2005), 126.

88. Nietzsche, *Gay Science*, 168-69.

89. Freud, *The Future of an Illusion*, 43. "Our God *logos* is perhaps not a very almighty one, and he may only be able to fulfill a small part of what his predecessors have promised" (p. 70); see Gay, *A Godless Jew*, 64-65.

90. "Science in many minds is genuinely taking the place of a religion," says William James in *The Varieties of Religious Experience*, 60, 114. William James: "Amid the wreck of every other god and idol, one divinity stills stands upright . . . his name is Scientific Truth"; cited Gay, *A Godless Jew*, 23. The case for religion versus science is often based on its being more holistic, more vital, more intuitive compared with what the philosopher Henri Bergson disparaged as intelligence's sterile "dissolving power"; Dante L. Germino, *Political Philosophy and the Open Society* (Baton Rouge: Louisiana State University Press, 1982), 152-54. For a contemporary attack on "scientism," see Leon Wieseltier, "The God Genome," *New York Times Book Review*, February 19, 2006. For responses to Wieseltier's argument, see the author's blog at WithoutGods.com.

91. See "Faith and Knowledge," in Derrida, *Acts of Religion*, 76, for a particularly searching, though perhaps somewhat Pyrrhonian, discussion of this.

92. Nietzsche, *Gay Science*, 281-83.

93. Freud, *The Future of an Illusion*, 67, 70. Whether psychoanalysis itself has been adept at correcting itself in response to clinical trials is a legitimate question.

94. Nietzsche, *Gay Science*, 289. See Dupré, *The Enlightenment and the Intellectual Foundations of Modern Culture*, 267-68.

95. A few twentieth-century theologians remarkably saw even God's reputed death as a step in the "progress of religion"—a very hazy, existential religion. For a Christian interpretation of that "death," see Thomas J. J. Altizer, *Living the Death of God: A Theological Memoir* (Albany, NY: State University of New York Press, 2006).

96. Henri Bergson, *The Two Sources of Morality and Religion* (New York: Doubleday, 1956), 341.

97. Nietzsche, *Gay Science*, 181-82.

98. *Time*, April 8, 1966. In this story and an earlier one *Time* credited this question not to "a moody French existentialist" but, in part, to "Thomas J. J. Altizer, 38, associate professor of religion at Atlanta's Emory University, a Methodist school"; "The 'God Is Dead' Movement," *Time*, October 22, 1965. Altizer was thoroughly immersed in Nietzsche, but what Nietzsche meant metaphorically Altizer, a Christian, meant perhaps not so metaphorically: he could conceive of God having died with Jesus, died in Jesus, as well as succumbing to the modern age. God's death is, for Altizer, no tragedy: "His death is the gospel, is the 'good news.'" All of this was, as befitted Altizer's understanding of contemporary philosophy, wrapped in tail-chasing paradox: Altizer understood his epiphany on the death of God as having come to him through "the act and grace of God himself"; Altizer, *Living the Death of God*, xiv, 8, 16.

99. Nietzsche, *Gay Science*, 181.

100. Virginia Woolf, *To the Lighthouse* (London: Urban Romantics, 2012), 7, 8, 157, 113.

101. "A Sketch of the Past," in Woolf, *Moments of Being*, 72. Woolf does, however, see a "pattern" "behind the cotton wool" of life. "The whole world is a work of art," she says, in what sounds like a version of the design argument, but then Woolf adds, intriguingly, "there is no Shakespeare, there is no Beethoven." Art without an artist, then.

102. Virginia Woolf, *The Letters of Virginia Woolf*, vol. 3, ed. Nigel Nicolson and Joanne Trautman (New York: Harcourt, Brace, Jovanovich, 1975), 457-58. See Lackey, "Virginia Woolf and T. S. Eliot," 67.

103. Nietzsche, *Gay Science*, 229-30.

CHAPTER 12: THE PASSIONS OF THIS EARTH

1. Shelley, *Prometheus Unbound*, 4.141-43; 153-55.

2. Homer, *The Odyssey*, trans. Robert Fagles (New York: Penguin Classics, 1997), XI, 681-89.

3. Camus, *Myth of Sisyphus*, 123.

4. Herbert R. Lottman, *Albert Camus: A Biography* (Garden City, NY: Doubleday, 1979), 368-69; Annie Cohen-Solal, *Sartre: A Life*, trans. Anna Cancogni (New York: Pantheon, 1987), 201-2; Patrick McCarthy, *Camus: A Critical Study of His Life and Work* (London: Hamish Hamilton, 1982), 182-83, 186, 196; John Tagliabue, "The Ash May Finally Be Falling From the Gauloise," *New York Times*, September 8, 2005, http://www.nytimes.com/2005/09/08 /international/europe/08paris.html?_r=0.

5. Lottman, *Albert Camus*, 296-98; Ronald Aronson, *Camus and Sartre* (Chicago: University of Chicago Press, 2004), 48-50.

6. Cited Harold Bloom, ed., *Albert Camus' The Stranger* (New York: Chelsea House, 2001), 14.

7. Cohen-Solal, *Sartre*, 189-90; McCarthy, *Camus*, 123.

8. Other formulations have, of course, been given of this, but they usually involve being caught betwixt and between two inconceivable, contradictory extremes: "suicide and religion" for Harold Bloom, who was not a fan; Bloom, *Albert Camus' The Stranger*, 2. For Abraham Sagi the extremes can be seen as "rift and separation" and "harmony and unity; *Albert Camus and the Philosophy of the Absurd* (Amsterdam: Rodopi, 2002), 23.

9. McCarthy, *Camus*, 175-77.

10. Cited ibid., 183.

11. Ibid., 206.

12. Cited Lottman, *Albert Camus*, 346.

13. McCarthy, *Camus*, 205-6.

14. Cited Aronson, *Camus and Sartre*, 50.

15. Cited Cohen-Solal, *Sartre*, 249-52; Aronson, *Camus and Sartre*, 47.

16. Cohen-Solal, *Sartre*, 252.

17. The quotes from this lecture are from Jean-Paul Sartre, *Existentialism is a Humanism*, trans. Carol MacComber (New Haven, CT: Yale University Press, 2007), 17-72.

18. Kant: "Man *himself* must make or have made himself into whatever, in a moral sense, whether good or evil, he is or is to become. Either condition must be an effect of his free choice; for otherwise he could not be held responsible for it and could therefore be *morally* neither good nor evil," Cited Robert Erlewine, *Monotheism and Tolerance: Recovering a Religion of Reason* (Bloomington: Indiana University Press, 2010), 88. Jacques Derrida homes in on this notion that God must be absent if we are to behave morally: "Is this not another way of saying that Christianity can only answer to its moral calling and morality . . . if it endures . . . the death of God." *Acts of Religion*, 49-52.

19. McCarthy, *Camus*, 73.

20. Cited Aronson, *Camus and Sartre*, 58.

21. The article was written by the philosopher Maurice Merleau-Ponty; Cited ibid., 66-67.

22. McCarthy, *Camus*, 238.

23. Cited Aronson, *Camus and Sartre*, 128.

24. Aronson, *Camus and Sartre*, 141; McCarthy, *Camus*, 256.

25. Cited Aronson, *Camus and Sartre*, 143-47, 153.

26. Ibid., 178.

27. Camus, *Myth of Sisyphus*, 120.

28. Ibid., 123.

29. Voltaire, having not entirely abandoned God, asked this question instead of the Christian religion and used, since this question is really a criticism, an exclamation mark: "What shall we put in its place!"; cited Gay, *The Enlightenment*, 391.

30. Bertrand Russell, "Is There a God?" in S. T. Joshi, ed., *Atheism: A Reader* (Amherst, NY: Prometheus Books, 2000), 92.

31. Wallace Stevens, *The Snow Man* (Grasse, France: Prometheus Press, 1982). For a fascinating discussion of "the nothing," see Martin Heidegger, "What Is Metaphysics," in *Basic Writings*, 2nd ed., ed. David Farrell Krell (New York: HarperCollins, 1993), 93-110.

32. Simone de Beauvoir, *The Second Sex* (New York: Knopf Doubleday Publishing Group, Kindle ed., 2012), 10-11, 104-5, 649-60.

33. Cited Lackey, "Virginia Woolf and T. S. Eliot," 83.

34. Woolf, *To the Lighthouse*, 97.

35. Nietzsche, *Gay Science*, 74.

36. Lackey writes of "a post-nihilist version of atheism" in "Virginia Woolf and T. S. Eliot," 86. Perhaps this is it.

37. Cited Lottman, *Albert Camus*, 601.

38. Camus, *Myth of Sisyphus*, 120, 123.

39. Bradlaugh: "Traces of obsolete religions may often be found in popular customs, in old wives' stories, and in children's tales"; Charles Bradlaugh, "Humanity's Gain From Unbelief," in Bradlaugh, *Theological Essays*. Such traces can be found elsewhere, too.

40. Albert Camus, *The Fall* (New York: Vintage, 1991), 135.

41. Camus, *Myth of Sisyphus*, 76.

42. Cohen-Solal, *Sartre*, 333, 335.

43. Jean-Paul Sartre, *The Words*, trans. Bernard Frechtman (New York: Vintage, 1981), 253.

44. Lottman, *Albert Camus*, 665.

CHAPTER 13: THE GODS ARE BEING DRIVEN FROM THE EARTH

1. Robert Green Ingersoll, *The Philosophy of Ingersoll*, ed. Vere Goldthwaite (San Francisco: Paul Elder and Company, 1906), 63.

2. This account is based on that in Bryan F. Le Beau, *The Atheist: Madalyn Murray O'Hair* (New York: New York University Press, 2003), 25-42; see also William J. Murray, *My Life Without God* (Eugene, OR: Harvest House Publishers, 2000), 39-47.

3. Cited Le Beau, *The Atheist*, 34.

4. Ibid., 94.

5. Casanova, "Rethinking Secularization: A Global Comparative Perspective," *The Hedgehog Review*, (Spring and Summer 2006). Actually Casanova suggests three connotations of "secularism"; I have collapsed his "privatization of religion" and "differentiation of the secular spheres" into one. See also Taylor, *A Secular Age*, 1-3; Bruce, *God Is Dead*, 2-3.

6. Lee Sigelman, "Review of the Polls: Multination Surveys of Religious Beliefs," *Journal for the Scientific Study of Religion* 16, 3 (1977): 292; Pippa Norris and Ronald Inglehart, *Sacred and Secular: Religion and Politics Worldwide* (Cambridge: Cambridge University Press, 2011), 91.

7. Christie Davies: "It is only from the mid-1950s onward that religion ceased to matter in Britain. During the last forty years of the twentieth century every single index of Christian activity, adherence and religiosity demonstrates collapse"; *The Strange Death of Moral Britain* (New Brunswick, NJ: Transaction Publishers, 2006), 49.

8. Sigelman, "Review of the Polls," 292.

9. This account is based on that in Le Beau, *The Atheist*, 40-56. See Madalyn Murray O'Hair, *An Atheist Epic: The Complete Unexpurgated Story of How Bible and Prayers Were Removed from the Public Schools of the United States*, 2nd ed. (Austin, TX: American Atheist Press, 1989), 18-27. William later claimed the whole thing was his mother's idea; Murray, *My Life Without God*, 53-59.

10. Cited Le Beau, *The Atheist*, 42.

11. Solomon, *Ellery's Protest*, 80-131.

12. Cited Le Beau, *The Atheist*, 43.

13. Ibid., 44.

14. Solomon, *Ellery's Protest*, 288-91; Le Beau, *The Atheist*, 99.

15. Cited Le Beau, *The Atheist*, 87-92.

16. Anthony F. C. Wallace, *Religion: An Anthropological View* (New York: Random House, 1966), 264-65. Steve Bruce argues that this oft repeated quotation is unrepresentative of the work of those who support "the secularization paradigm." Bruce's own, less sensational wording of this paradigm: "The basic proposition is that modernization creates problems for religion"; Bruce, *God Is Dead*, 1-2.

17. See, for example, Jean-François Lyotard, *The Postmodern Condition: A Report on Knowledge*, trans. Geoff Bennington and Brian Massumi (Minneapolis: University of Minnesota Press, 1984).

18. After arguing that faith is at the bottom of knowledge and that "disenchantment" is "the *very resource of the religious*," Jacques Derrida states. "Nothing seems therefore more uncertain, more difficult to sustain, nothing seems here or there more imprudent than a self-assured discourse on the age of disenchantment, the era of secularization"; Derrida, *Acts of Religion*, 98-101. Ouch. Perhaps we might suggest, though, that Derrida is revealing Pyrrhonian tendencies—even fideist tendencies—on these pages, where he emphasizes the unending, unavoidable multiplication of perspectives, of sources, of divisions, of others, through the formula "*n* plus one." Perhaps faith in a miracle can be distinguished in some way—via Carneades' plausibility or Hume's experience—from faith in the sun rising or faith in our ability to communicate. While the inevitable arrival of the "plus one" may prevent us from ever resting on an "*n*," perhaps we can still work it into formulas. Perhaps there are fractions. Or perhaps we historians of secularization should indeed be less "self-assured."

19. For a thoughtful account of these "Great Awakenings," see William G. McLoughlin, *Revivals, Awakenings, and Reform* (Chicago: University of Chicago Press, 1978), 1-11.

20. Robert William Fogel, *The Fourth Great Awakening and the Future of Egalitarianism* (Chicago: University of Chicago Press, 2002), 10, 25-33.

21. Cited Le Beau, *The Atheist*, 59.

22. Ibid., 118-19.

23. This account of Murray's activities and those of her son, William, is from Le Beau, *The Atheist*, 103, 109-111, 125-29, 136, 148, 150, 155, 258-61, 264; Ann Rowe Seaman, *America's Most Hated Woman: The Life and Gruesome Death of Madalyn Murray O'Hair* (New York: Continuum, 2005), 189.

24. American Atheists, http://www.atheists.org/convention2013.

25. Cited Le Beau, *The Atheist*, 122, 151.

26. See Susan Jacoby, *The Great Agnostic: Robert Ingersoll and American Freethought* (New Haven: Yale University Press), 2013.

27. Robert Green Ingersoll, *On the Gods and Other Essays* (Amherst, NY: Prometheus Books, 1990), 36-37.

28. Ibid., 31.

29. David D. Anderson, *Robert Ingersoll* (New York: Twayne, 1972), 61-70.

30. These statistics are from Norris and Inglehart, *Sacred and Secular*, 74. Italy had higher rates of churchgoing than most other Western European countries in 1981; Spain was higher still and Ireland much higher, but churchgoing in Spain and Ireland was about to drop significantly. Rodney Stark argues that the Christianization of Scandinavia was incomplete to begin with in "Secularization, R.I.P."

31. This list is indebted to that in David Martin, "Does the Advance of Science Mean Secularization?," lecture, November 3, 2005, Emmanuel College, Cambridge, http://www.st-edmunds .cam.ac.uk/faraday/CIS/martin/David%20Martin%20-%20lecture.htm. Philip Rieff, *The Triumph of the Therapeutic: Uses of Faith After Freud* (Chicago: University of Chicago Press, 1987), 3, 13; Bruce, *God Is Dead*, 25-26. For a sociologist's impressively detailed chart and discussion of the long-term factors that led to secularization in the West—with particular emphasis, following Max Weber, upon the Protestant Reformation—see Bruce, *God Is Dead*, 4-29.

32. Debunkers of the narrative of secularization take special delight in dismissing the connection between science and this alleged secularization; see Martin, "Does the Advance of Science Mean Secularization?" http://www.st-edmunds.cam.ac.uk/faraday/CIS/martin/ David%20Martin%20-%20lecture.htm. However, most seem, at least, to acknowledge that science has contributed to secularization by furthering a "rationalistic orientation to the world"; Bruce, *God Is Dead*, 117. Scientists do tend to be less religious, even in the United States: the percentage of U.S. scientists believing in "a personal God," according to one study, dropped from 28 percent in 1914 to only 7 percent in 1998; that would be a low number even for Europe. However, according to a 1969 study of the United States, those in the physical sciences were much more likely to regularly attend church, 43 percent, than social scientists, 31 percent; Bruce, *God Is Dead*, 109-10. Perhaps, as Bruce argues, physicists are more inclined to the certitudes of religion than, say, anthropologists (p. 117).

33. Norris and Inglehart, *Sacred and Secular*, 106-10.

34. Charles Taylor, *A Secular Age*, 17. Jacques Derrida writes of "sacrifice of self, of one's most precious interest" in *Acts of Religion*, 88.

35. Norris and Inglehart, *Sacred and Secular*, 74.

36. In America, as the sociologist José Casanova points out, progressive movements historically have tended to appeal to religious values rather than challenge them; "Rethinking Secularization."

37. Cited Le Beau, *The Atheist,* 148.
38. Ibid., 133.
39. Ibid., 261.
40. The statistics here are from Norris and Inglehart, *Sacred and Secular,* 90-91.
41. Charles Taylor admits to being somewhat flummoxed by the question of why America and Europe diverged—"the crucial question facing secularization theory" in *A Secular Age,* 529-30. Taylor is among those who suggest the tragic embarrassment of the First World War may have sped Europe toward secularization in the first sense (p. 522). The embarrassments of the United States—in Vietnam and later Iraq—were not, perhaps, on quite so large a scale.
42. Solomon, *Ellery's Protest,* 90.
43. The criticism here is from Casanova, "Rethinking Secularization"; Bruce, *God Is Dead,* 61-62, 71, 220-22. See also Norris and Inglehart, *Sacred and Secular,* 98-99.
44. Taylor has an explanation for this: "groups [that] feel suppressed or threatened . . . will look to some religious marker to gather round"; *A Secular Age,* 515.
45. The "supply-side" version of this theory, as proposed by Rodney Stark with Robert Finke and Laurence Iannaccone, argues that there is always "demand" for what religion offers: consolations, the promise of immortality. Hence, as the supply of religions increases, as it has in the American free-market, the populous will become more religious; see Casanova, "Rethinking Secularization"; Bruce, *God Is Dead,* 61-62, 71, 220-22. However, this theory has difficulty explaining the continual decline of religion in a place like Britain, despite the growth in the available religions in recent centuries. Stark is reduced to denying that decline; Stark, "Secularization, R. I. P.". We might instead question the constancy of that demand.
46. James Hudnut-Beumler, *In Pursuit Of the Almighty's Dollar: A History Of Money And American* Protestantism (Chapel Hill: University of North Carolina Press, 2007), 211.
47. Bruce, *God Is Dead,* 223-24. The Regent University School of Law was founded by the religious broadcaster Pat Robertson; Liberty University, founded by the late televangelist Jerry Falwell, also now has a law school. Religious involvement in higher education is not, of course, new, as discussed in chapter 4.
48. Casanova, "Rethinking Secularization"; Bruce, *God Is Dead,* 219-20. Taylor criticizes this theory but also includes some support for it; Charles Taylor, *A Secular Age,* 522-24.
49. Norris and Inglehard, *Sacred and Secular,* 106-10.
50. Ibid., 108.
51. The account here is based on that in Le Beau, *The Atheist,* 307-21; Seaman, *America's Most Hated Woman,* 262-333; also Murray, *My Life Without God,* 318-35.
52. Cited Le Beau, *The Atheist,* 365n.
53. John MacCormack of the *San Antonio Express-News.* William Murray also reported having asked his Republican acquaintants, including then Texas governor George W. Bush, for help on the case. "My good friend House Majority Leader Dick Armey," Murray writes, called in the FBI; Murray, *My Life Without God,* 322-33.
54. The legal resolution of this case was not entirely satisfactory. Waters was first convicted of violating parole and then, in a plea bargain on the kidnapping and murder, was allowed to plead guilty to one count of conspiracy to interfere with commerce by robbery and extortion, for which he was sentenced to an additional 20 years in prison; John MacCormack, "Details Aired in O'Hair Plea," *San Antonio Express-News,* January 30, 2001. Waters died in prison of lung cancer on January 27, 2003; Seaman, *America's Most Hated Woman,* 325. His friend, Gary Karr, was found innocent of conspiracy to kidnap O'Hair, her son and granddaughter, but "guilty of extortion, money laundering and two other charges" connected with their disappearance; John MacCormack, "O'Hair Defendant Found Guilty; Jury Acquits Karr on 1 of 5 Counts," *San Antonio Express-News,* June 3, 2000.
55. Cited Le Beau, *The Atheist,* 320-21. See also Murray, *My Life Without God,* 330.

CHAPTER 14: THIS BREACH OF NAÏVETÉ

1. Matthew Arnold, "Dover Beach," *The Victorian Web,* http://www.victorianweb.org/authors/arnold/writings/doverbeach.html.
2. Cited Grace Davie, *Religion in Britain Since 1945: Believing Without Belonging* (New York: Wiley, 1994), 1, 79.
3. Ibid., 38. Bruce presents this theory of "indifference," *God Is Dead,* 41-43. See Strauss, *Spinoza's Critique of Religion,* 274n.
4. I owe this notion to Charles Taylor, as I will note later in this chapter; see *God Is Dead,* 12-13. I employ, however, a somewhat broader definition of this third kind of secularism that Taylor introduces.

5. Norman Vincent Peale, *The Power of Positive Thinking* (New York: Prentice-Hall, 1952), viii, 177-78; see Bruce, *God Is Dead*, 209.

6. Matthew 19:29.

7. Peale, *The Power of Positive Thinking*, 15.

8. Ibid., x.

9. Bruce, *God Is Dead*, 204, 209.

10. Ibid., 210-11.

11. For a discussion of the phenomenon in Britain, see Davies, *The Strange Death of Moral Britain.*

12. These statistics are from Andrew M. Greeley, *Religious Change in America* (Cambridge, MA: Harvard University Press, 1989), 13-20.

13. Bruce, *God Is Dead*, 208. Greeley argues that this drop is mostly attributable to Catholics in *Religious Change in America*, 17-19.

14. Clarence Darrow, *The Story of My Life* (New York: Da Capo Press, 1996), 384-85.

15. Martin Buber: "The prophets of Israel have never announced a God upon whom their hearers' striving for security reckoned. They have always aimed to shatter all security and to proclaim in the opened abyss of the final insecurity the unwished for God . . ."; cited Strauss, *Spinoza's Critique of Religion*, 10. The God now proclaimed in many American synagogues has often been more amenable to the congregations' "striving for security."

16. This analysis is based on that in Bruce, *God Is Dead*, 205-7. See also Taylor, *A Secular Age*, 525.

17. *Joan of Arcadia* was broadcast on CBS in the United States from September 2003 to April 2005.

18. Salman Rushdie, *Imaginary Homelands: Essays and Criticism* (New York: Penguin, 1992), 377.

19. George Packer, "Not Wise," *New Yorker*, May 8, 2006. http://www.newyorker.com/archive /2006/05/08/060508ta_talk_packer.

20. David L. Schindler, "The Religious Sense and American Culture," in *Generative Thought: An Introduction to the Works of Luigi Giussani*, ed. Elisa Buzzi (Montreal: McGill-Queen's University Press, 2003), 86.

21. Pew Research, "Religion and Public Life Survey: Religious Landscape Survey, 2007," http:// religions.pewforum.org/reports#.

22. This 2008 survey is based on new interviews with a selection of participants in the 2007 survey; Pew Research, "Religion and Public Life Survey: Faith in Flux," http://www.pewforum .org/2009/04/27/faith-in-flux/.

23. Taylor, *A Secular Age*, 3.

24. Bruce, *God Is Dead*, 18.

25. Taylor, *A Secular Age*, 13, 21.

26. Ibid., 12-13.

27. Peter Gay brings up the classic example: those "who, witnessing the illness of a spouse or a child, would pray and send for the doctor in the same breath"; *A Godless Jew*, 12-13. The sociologist Andrew M. Greeley provides another, if less classic, example of how such internal conflicts manifest themselves, "One could easily (and honestly) say, 'Well, I believed with absolute confidence yesterday, for most of the day, and I think by this afternoon I will again, but this morning I have very strong doubts'"; *Religion in Europe at the End of the Second Millennium: A Sociological Profile* (New Brunswick, NJ: Transaction Publishers, 2004), 1.

28. Albert Goldman, *John Lennon* (New York: A Cappella, 1998), 77-78.

29. Ibid., 364-69, 548-49.

30. Ibid., 404.

31. "God," by John Lennon.

32. "Imagine" by John Lennon.

33. Bill Harry, *The John Lennon Encyclopedia* (London: Virgin, 2000), 8-9, 753.

34. "Penny Lane," by John Lennon and Paul McCartney. As this verse slyly notes, this modern feeling of being in a play has itself become a kind of play. For John Lennon's involvement in the third verse of this Paul McCartney song, see Barry Miles, *Paul McCartney: Many Years from Now* (New York: Owl Books, 1998), 308.

35. Cited James Risen, "A Nation Challenged: The New Tape," *New York Times*, December 28, 2001, http://www.nytimes.com/2001/12/28/world/nation-challenged-new-tape-its-express -delivery-its-details-bin-laden-s-latest.html; Cited Marc Aronson, "Unholy Wars," *School Library Journal*, November 1, 2001.

36. "Growing Disbelief," *The Economist*, August 22, 2012, http://www.economist.com/blogs /democracyinamerica/2012/08/atheism; WIN-Gallup International, Global Index of Religiosity and Atheism, 2012, http://www.wingia.com/web/files/news/14/file/14.pdf.

37. This is based on results from the General Social Survey of the social science research orga-
     nization NORC at the University of Chicago. See William Harms, "Belief in God Rises with
     Age, Even in Atheist Nations," April 18, 2012, http://news.uchicago.edu/article/2012/04/18
     /belief-god-rises-age-even-atheist-nations#sthash.7vh0VZRo.pdf. This is also supported by
     the WIN-Gallup poll; Global Index of Reliogiosity and Atheism, 2012, http://www.wingia
     .com/web/files/news/14/file/14.pdf.
38. Andrew Higgins, "A More Secular Europe, Divided by the Cross," *New York Times*, June 17,
     2013, http://www.nytimes.com/2013/06/18/world/europe/a-more-secular-europe-divided
     -by-the-cross.html?ref=world&_r=0.
39. Thirty percent instead answered that they are "not a religious person," 5 percent described
     themselves as a "convinced atheist" and 5 percent didn't respond or said that they "don't
     know"; Global Index of Religiosity and Atheism, 2012, http://www.wingia.com/web/files
     /news/14/file/14.pdf.
40. Eighty-two percent of Americans "say it is at least somewhat important"; Pew Research,
     "Religion and Public Life Survey: Religious Landscape Survey, 2007, http://religions.pew
     forum.org/pdf/report2religious-landscape-study-chapter-1.pdf.
41. Charles Bradlaugh, "Humanity's Gain from Unbelief."

EPILOGUE: ABOVE US ONLY SKY

1. "A Plea for Atheism," in Bradlaugh, *Theological Essays*, 8.
2. Andrew S. Curran, "Diderot, an American Exemplar? Bien Sûr!" *New York Times*, January
    24, 2013.
3. Blom, *A Wicked Company*, xii.
4. Laurie Goodstein, "Judge Rejects Teaching Intelligent Design," *New York Times*," December
    21, 2005.
5. Leviticus 20:13.
6. Salman Rushdie, "Imagine No Heaven," *The Guardian*, October 15, 1999, http://www
    .guardian.co.uk/books/1999/oct/16/salmanrushdie.
7. Salman Rushdie, "Religion, As Ever, Is the Poison in India's Blood," *The Guardian*, March 8,
    2002, http://www.guardian.co.uk/books/2002/mar/09/society.salmanrushdie.
8. Rushdie, "Imagine No Heaven."

INDEX

ACKNOWLEDGMENTS

I BEGIN, AS ALWAYS, BY EXPRESSING MY GRATITUDE TO THE TWO people who started me on some of the paths I have followed in writing this book, Bernard Stephens and Lillian Sklaire Stephens.

My progress on those paths was aided considerably by the work of two writers and historians who traveled many of them before me: Jennifer Michael Hecht, author of the wonderfully rich and engaging *Doubt: A History, The Great Doubters and Their Legacy of Innovation from Socrates and Jesus to Thomas Jefferson and Emily Dickinson* (San Francisco: Harper San Francisco, 2003); and John Mackinnon Robertson, who wrote a number of volumes on freethinking a century ago. They introduced me to a number of the sources I have made use of here.

Ben Stein and Ben Vershbow at the Institute of the Future of the Book set me up with a blog, WithoutGods.com, as I was working on this project. The idea was to test and hone some of these ideas in an online conversation—at a point when it was still possible to improve the book. Two of those who joined in that conversation were particularly helpful in the testing and honing: Jeanette McVicker and Jay Saul.

Thanks, too, to the Center for Religion and Media at New York University for inviting me to participate in their Working Group on Secularism and to the Center for Inquiry at the University of Buffalo for inviting me to teach in their "Beyond Belief" program.

These pages have been strengthened by the work of many very capable researchers, most at New York University. Any list of them must begin with an extraordinary young woman Kaylan Connally, an undergraduate at the time. Kaylan's curiosity, intelligence and thoroughness bolstered my research and significantly broadened its reach at many turns; she later played a role in bringing the book to Palgrave Macmillan. Special thanks, too, to John Sillings who has expanded my thinking on these matters and others. Kaylan and John were originally students in an Advanced Honors Seminar on the History of Disbelief I have taught for many years at NYU, as was a dedicated and talented researcher I worked with more recently, Jordan McFadden. This book has benefited greatly from the comments and insights of the dozens of fine students who have participated in that course. Quite a few other first-rate researchers also worked on the book—tracking down information and supplying new perspectives; they have included in the final stages, when references needed to be secured and deadlines pressed, three exceptionally capable and insightful journalists, Katie Ryder, Meredith Bennett-Smith and Ben Brody.

The manuscript was read and improved in various incarnations by Daniel Lazare, Arthur Engoron, Jim Hauser, Thomas Studwell, Jerry Lanson, Noah Stephens-Davidowitz, Seth Stephens-Davidowitz, Lauren Stephens-Davidowitz and Walter Wild. A rabbi, Reuben Modek, gave me an important insight into this history.

I have had the benefit of two fine editors at Palgrave Macmillan. Laura Lancaster sharpened the book's focus; Elisabeth Dyssegaard sharpened its prose. My agent John Wright nudged me in productive directions at many stages in what has been a decade-long process; I am grateful for his support and dedication.

The individuals mentioned here, of course, do not necessarily agree with all my arguments, and any errors remain my own.

My largest debt, as always, is to my wife, Esther Davidowitz. Though no one would accuse her of lacking a mind of her own, she does agree with most of my arguments in this book. One early clue that we were compatible was that we had the same favorite Beatle. *Imagine* was the song I sang when our first child was first placed in my arms.